THE POLITICS OF RACE

African Americans and the Political System

Theodore Rueter

M.E. Sharpe
Armonk, New York
London, England

Library of Congress Cataloging-in-Publication Data

The politics of race : African Americans and the
political system / Theodore Rueter (editor).
p.   cm.
Includes bibliographical references (p.   ) and index.
ISBN 1-56324-564-7 (cloth : acid-free paper).
ISBN 1-56324-565-5 (pbk. : acid-free paper).
1. Afro-Americans—Politics and government.
I. Rueter, Theodore.
E185.615.P549   1995
323.1′196073—dc20   95-5901
CIP

Printed in the United States of America

The paper used in this publication meets the minimum requirements of
American National Standard for Information Sciences—
Permanence of Paper for Printed Library Materials,
ANSI Z 39.48-1984.

EB (c)   10   9   8   7   6   5   4   3   2   1
EB (p)   10   9   8   7   6   5   4   3   2   1

Contents

About the Contributors   ix

Preface   xi

I.   Overview   1

1.   The Politics of Race
      Theodore Rueter   5

2.   Rejection and Protest: An Historical Sketch
      *Report of the National Advisory Commission
         on Civil Disorders*   27

3.   Race and the Crisis of the American Spirit
      Bill Clinton   46

II.   Cultural Politics and Political Ideology   53

4.   Postmodern Racial Politics in the United States:
      Difference and Inequality
      Howard Winant   55

5.   Malcolm X and the Revival of Black Nationalism
      Michael Eric Dyson   71

6.   False Prophet: The Rise of Louis Farrakhan
      Adolph Reed Jr.   77

7.   The New Black Conservatives
      Theodore Rueter   85

III. **Interest Groups and Political Parties** **113**

8. The Dual Agenda of African American Organizations since
   the New Deal: Social Welfare Policies and Civil Rights
   Dona Cooper Hamilton and Charles V. Hamilton   115

9. The Democrats and Liberal Guilt
   Peter Brown   134

10. The 1992 Republican "Tent": No Blacks Walked In
    Louis Bolce, Gerald De Maio, and Douglas Muzzio   152

IV. **Gender** **165**

11. In Quest of African American Political Woman
    Jewel L. Prestage   169

12. Gender, Race, and the State Legislature: A Research Note
    on the Double Disadvantage Hypothesis
    Gary Moncrief, Joel Thompson, and Robert Schuhmann   185

V. **Congress** **193**

13. The Congressional Black Caucus Revolution
    William Clay   199

14. Strategies for Increasing Black Representation in Congress
    Carol Swain   212

15. What Color Is Your Gerrymander? The Constitution and
    White Minority Districts
    Lani Guinier   226

VI. **The Presidency** **231**

16. The Politics of Race: From Kennedy to Reagan
    Edward Carmines and James Stimson   233

17. The Reagan Attack on Race Liberalism
    Thomas Byrne Edsall with Mary D. Edsall   253

VII. **The Judicial System** **267**

18. The Constitution, the Supreme Court, and Racism:
    Compromises on the Way to Democracy
    William J. Daniels   271

19. The New Supreme Court and the Politics of Racial Equality
Christopher E. Smith   278

20. Beyond the Rodney King Story: Police Conduct and
     Community Relations
NAACP   292

VIII. State and Urban Politics   **301**

21. Can Black Candidates Win Statewide Elections?
Raphael J. Sonenshein   307

22. The End of the Rainbow: America's Changing Urban Politics
Jim Sleeper   325

23. Race and the American City
Bill Bradley   334

24. How the Rioters Won
Midge Decter   343

IX. Public Policy   **353**

25. The Urban Underclass and the Poverty Paradox
Paul E. Peterson   359

26. How the Great Society "destroyed the American family"
Daniel Patrick Moynihan   375

27. The Clinton Administration and African-Americans
Monte Piliawsky   385

About the Editor   **399**

About the Contributors

Louis Bolce is associate professor of political science at Baruch College, City University of New York.

Bill Bradley is the senior United States senator from New Jersey.

Peter Brown is a political correspondent for Scripps-Howard News Service.

Edward Carmines is professor of political science at Indiana University.

Bill Clinton is the forty-second president of the United States.

William Clay is a Democratic congressman from Missouri.

William J. Daniels is professor of political science at the Rochester Institute of Technology.

Gerald De Maio is associate professor of political science at Baruch College, City University of New York.

Midge Decter is a Distinguished Fellow of the Institute for Religion and Public Life.

Michael Eric Dyson is professor of American civilization and Afro-American studies at Brown University.

Mary D. Edsall is a Washington, D.C., writer.

Thomas Byrne Edsall is a reporter for the *Washington Post*.

Lani Guinier is a professor at the University of Pennsylvania Law School.

Charles V. Hamilton is the Wallace S. Sayre Professor of Government at Columbia University.

Dona Cooper Hamilton is associate professor of social work at Lehman College, City University of New York.

Gary Moncrief is professor of political science at Boise State University.

Daniel Patrick Moynihan is the senior United States senator from New York.

Douglas Muzzio is professor of political science at Baruch College, City University of New York.

Paul E. Peterson is Henry Shattuck Professor of Government at Harvard University.

Monte Piliawsky is professor of political science at Penn Valley Community in Kansas City.

Jewel L. Prestage is honors professor of political science at Prairie View A & M University.

Adolph Reed Jr. is professor of political science at Northwestern University.

Theodore Rueter has taught political science at Middlebury College, Georgetown University, and Smith College.

Robert Schuhmann is a research assistant at the Institute of Policy Studies, College of Charleston.

Jim Sleeper is a columnist for the *New York Daily News*.

Christopher E. Smith is associate professor of political science at the University of Akron.

Raphael J. Sonenshein is associate professor of political science at California State University, Fullerton.

James Stimson is Arleen Carlson Professor of Political Science at the University of Minnesota.

Carol Swain is assistant professor of politics and public affairs at the Woodrow Wilson School of Public Affairs at Princeton University.

Joel Thompson is professor of political science at Appalachian State University.

Howard Winant is associate professor of sociology at Temple University.

Preface

The readings in *The Politics of Race: African Americans and the Political System* examine the major issues involving race and American politics. This book can be used in courses on American government, racial politics, urban politics, black studies, American studies, public policy, and political ideology. The purpose of this volume is to add a racial element to the study of American politics.

This book features readings from some of the most noteworthy students of American politics, including Midge Decter, Charles V. Hamilton, Daniel Patrick Moynihan, Paul E. Peterson, Adolph Reed Jr., Lani Guinier, Bill Clinton, Bill Bradley, and Thomas Byrne Edsall. There are also reports from the Kerner Commission and the NAACP. I have selected readings from political scientists, sociologists, historians, journalists, legal scholars, and public officials. The authors represent a broad range of ideological, methodological, and theoretical perspectives.

The readings examine a variety of topics: blacks in American history, the role of the black vote in recent presidential elections, race-related Supreme Court rulings, blacks and the Democratic Party, blacks and the Republican Party, black conservatism, Afrocentrism, multiculturalism, black interest groups, African American women, the role of race in postwar presidential administrations, black mayors, black state legislators, the urban underclass, and the Los Angeles riots. The readings also highlight a number of prominent individuals, including Malcolm X, Louis Farrakhan, Thomas Sowell, Doug Wilder, Tom Bradley, Rodney King, and black members of Congress.

Organization

The readings are organized according to the standard topics of a course on American government. Part I covers American racial politics, black history, and social problems. Parts II, III, and IV concern inputs to the American political system, including cultural politics, political ideology, interest groups, political parties, and gender. Parts V through VIII examine the role of race in decision-making institutions and locales: Congress, the presidency, the judicial system, and state and urban politics. Finally, Part IX involves the relationship between race and public policy—the outputs of the American political system.

Theme

The theme of this book is that race is a critical element in American politics and government, if not *the* critical element. Race has played a central role in consti-tutional development and Supreme Court rulings. Race is a fundamental dividing line in political ideology and public opinion. Race is at the heart of the debate over "who gets what, when, and how."

This theme pervades the readings. The Kerner Commission report on urban riots chronicles the prominent role of blacks in American history. William Daniels documents the salience of race in decisions by the Supreme Court. Jewel L. Prestage argues that race is a more defining characteristic than gender for most African American women. Peter Brown, Edward Carmines and James Stimson, and Thomas Byrne Edsall and Mary Edsall argue that race is at the forefront of American party politics and public policy. Carol Swain contends that debates over congressional redistricting are largely about race. Raphael J. Sonenshein notes the obstacles facing blacks in winning statewide elections.

Acknowledgments

I am grateful to Michael Weber of M.E. Sharpe for his assistance and encourage-ment in the preparation of this text. Thanks also go to Clyde Wilcox of George-town University for suggesting that I contact Michael.

Theodore Rueter

Part I
Overview

This part provides an introduction to American racial politics. The first reading, "The Politics of Race" by Theodore Rueter, explores approaches to the study of race and American politics (including the role of race in political science theory and sociological theory), the role of race in American society (focusing on the condition of the underclass and the role of race in popular culture), American racial attitudes (centering on public opinion, Louis Farrakhan, Khallid Abdul Muhammad, and black separatism), and the significance of the black vote in presidential elections. The reading's central argument is that race is a defining characteristic in American politics and society.

The second selection is from the Kerner Commission report on the urban riots of the 1960s. The commission was appointed by President Lyndon Johnson and headed by Otto Kerner, the governor of Illinois. The Kerner Commission report warned that "our nation is moving toward two societies, one black, one white, separate and unequal."

The portion of the Kerner Commission report reprinted here chronicles the history of blacks in America. It begins with the Civil War, which was fought over whether Southern states had the right to maintain slavery and secede from the Union. It then discusses Reconstruction, when the nation ratified the Thirteenth Amendment to the Constitution, which banned slavery; the Fourteenth Amendment, which provided for equal protection of the laws; and the Fifteenth Amendment, which guaranteed the right to vote regardless of race.

Following Reconstruction, the Supreme Court upheld the doctrine of "separate but equal" in the 1896 case *Plessy v Ferguson.* Similarly, the nation witnessed the growth of the Ku Klux Klan, a white supremacist organization that lynched blacks and burned crosses on the lawns of blacks.

The Kerner Commission report also reviews the debate within the black community at the beginning of the twentieth century. The principal black leaders

1

were Booker T. Washington, who favored accommodation toward whites and black self-help; W. E. B. Du Bois, founder of the Niagara Movement, devoted to the immediate implementation of social and economic progress; and Marcus Garvey, founder of the United Negro Improvement Association, which favored the return of blacks to Africa.

The election of Franklin Roosevelt and America's entry into World War II brought further changes for blacks in America. Roosevelt instituted the New Deal, a series of federal programs that helped blacks by pulling the economy out of the Great Depression. World War II saw the desegregation of the armed forces, by order of President Harry Truman.

The Kerner Commission report also discusses the civil rights movement, starting with the Montgomery bus boycott, fomented by the refusal of Rosa Parks, on December 1, 1955, to sit in the "back of the bus." It also describes the NAACP, the nation's oldest and largest civil rights organization, and the Southern Christian Leadership Conference, a civil rights group headed by Martin Luther King Jr. More radical groups included the Black Muslims, once headed by Malcolm X (who was assassinated in Harlem in 1965 by religious opponents, possibly aided by the FBI); the Freedom Rides, a series of bus trips across the South in 1961, organized by the Congress of Racial Equality; and the Black Power movement, which emphasized black consciousness and militancy. The reading also reviews the Civil Rights Act of 1964, which prohibited discrimination in public accommodations.

The Kerner Commission report draws on extensive studies of the history of blacks in America. One such study is *The Philadelphia Negro: A Social Study* (1899) by W. E. B. Du Bois. Du Bois, a Harvard-trained historian, marshaled massive amounts of empirical data on black life, documenting the realities of racism. He conducted an innovative door-to-door survey of the occupations, values, political life, social interactions, and family life of the 45,000 blacks in the Seventh Ward of Philadelphia. Du Bois rejected the theory of social Darwinism (the survival of the fittest). He argued that the slum was a symptom of the deficiencies of society and that public discussion of "black criminality" was racist mythology. Du Bois demanded to know, "How long can a city teach its black children that the road to success is to have a white face?"

The seminal study of blacks in America is *From Slavery to Freedom: A History of the Negro People in the United States* by John Hope Franklin, professor of history and law at Duke University, and the nation's most distinguished black historian. Franklin analyzes the African way of life, the slave trade, the Civil War, Reconstruction, the New Deal, and the civil rights movement.

The final reading in this part is a speech by Bill Clinton, the forty-second president of the United States. Clinton spoke on November 13, 1993, at the church where Martin Luther King gave his last sermon. Clinton has often spoken in black churches, and his speech was extremely emotional.

In this speech, Clinton emphasized his common ground with the black community. He outlined his administration's domestic accomplishments: the appointment of significant numbers of African Americans to major positions; the "motor voter" bill, allowing individuals to register to vote where they register their car; the family-leave bill, allowing parents twelve weeks of time off without pay; reform of the college loan program to expand availability and reduce cost; the national service program to allow students to earn money for college by working in a public service job; and the earned income tax credit, which reduced taxes on low-income families. Clinton also took credit for improving the national economy.

What is notable about Clinton's speech is its candid discussion of the problems afflicting the black community. Speaking in the voice of Martin Luther King Jr., he said, "I did not live and die to see the American family destroyed. I did not live and die to see 13-year-old boys get automatic weapons and gun down 9-year-olds just for the kick of it. I did not live and die to see young people destroy their own lives with drugs and then build fortunes destroying the lives of others." Clinton deplored the fact that "more than 37,000 people die from gunshot wounds in this country every year. Gunfire is the leading cause of death in young men."

Clinton then pushed his own legislative agenda to deal with these issues. The first item was his crime bill, which called for more police officers, boot camps for young offenders, a ban on assault weapons, and a five-day waiting period for the purchase of a handgun. (Clinton's crime bill passed Congress in the summer of 1994.) President Clinton also urged Congress to pass a health care bill "that will make drug treatment available for everyone."

Clinton ended on an emotional note. He called on the country to "deal with the ravages of crime and drugs and violence" and deal with the breakdown of the family and the community and the disappearance of jobs. Taking action, he said, will require reaching "deep inside to the values, the spirit, the soul, and the truth of human nature. . . ."

1

The Politics of Race

Theodore Rueter

In this introduction to the study of race and American government, I will examine approaches to the study of black politics, the role of race in American society, American racial attitudes, and the significance of the black vote in American presidential elections. My argument is that the matter of race is at the core of American politics and American society.

Race and the Study of American Politics

The field of black politics is growing in size and theoretical sophistication. There are several academic journals concerned largely with black politics, including *National Political Science Review* (published by the National Association of Black Political Scientists), *The Black Scholar, The Black Politician, Black World, Journal of Black Politics, Journal of Black Studies, Western Journal of Black Studies, National Minority Politics, Review of Black Political Economy, Transitions, The Crisis: A Record of the Darker Races, Journal of Ethnic Studies,* and *Phylon: The Atlanta University Review of Race and Culture.* There is an increasing demand for political scientists who study African American politics.

The field of black studies was advanced greatly by the 1989 publication of *Blacks and American Society: A Common Destiny,* edited by Gerald David Jaynes and Robin M. Williams Jr. This massive report was prepared by the Committee on the Status of Black Americans of the National Research Council. It includes exhaustive reviews of the literature on racial segregation, racial attitudes and behavior, black social institutions, black political participation, black economic performance, black public health, and black educational achievement. Other extremely useful volumes are *The Negro Almanac: A Reference Work on the African-American* and the *Encyclopedia of Black America.*

Theoretical Assumptions

Students of race and politics in America make a number of assumptions. One is that the study of black politics enriches the study of American politics. Analysts can better understand white voting behavior by studying black voting behavior, just as examining the role of the Congressional Black Caucus deepens our understanding of Congress as a whole.

Another assumption is that race is a central variable in American politics. Students of American political behavior typically consider such factors as gender, income, class, geography, and family background as predictors of voting patterns. Students of race and American politics maintain that race and ethnicity have not received sufficient attention.

A further supposition is that blacks are unlike other ethnic groups in American society. Blacks came to the United States involuntarily, have not assimilated as easily as European immigrants, and have suffered much greater degrees of discrimination.

Finally, scholars of black politics assume that mass political behavior must be disaggregated, by gender, age, income, and religion. While African American political behavior may be more uniform than that of whites, there are still deep cleavages.

Of these factors, perhaps the most significant is gender. Unlike whites, African Americans have not experienced a gender gap. Politically, black women tend to identify more with their *race* than with their *gender.*

Women have long played an important reformist role in American politics. Progressive reformers throughout American history, including Charlotte Perkins Gilman and Jane Hull, have argued that electing women to public office would reduce corruption and improve the condition of the poor. Indeed, the ten black women elected to Congress in 1992 have focused their efforts on child immunization, Medicaid funding for abortion, and passage of the Family Preservation Act (intended to prevent family breakup and the need for foster care).

Religion also plays a major role in black political life. Clyde Wilcox and Sue Thomas, political scientists at Georgetown University, recently examined religion and feminist attitudes among African American women. They found that religious activism is an important determinant of the political attitudes of black women. While most religious black women oppose abortion, they also favor gender equality. Wilcox and Thomas conclude that African American women who attend church regularly but do not watch television evangelists "interpret their orthodox doctrine as promoting feminism."

Black ministers and the black church play a vital role in community political organization. Much of the black civil rights movement has been led by ministers, including Martin Luther King Jr., Jesse Jackson, Andrew Young, Benjamin Hooks, and Benjamin Chavis. Black political candidates often raise money in black churches, and white candidates commonly court the black vote by preaching in black churches. In 1993, Ed Rollins, a consultant to Christine Todd Whitman, the Republican candidate for governor of New Jersey, caused a storm by claiming that he had passed out "street money" to black ministers to ask them *not* to get out the vote for Jim Florio, the incumbent Democratic governor. Rollins later admitted that he had made the entire story up; black New Jersey ministers threatened to sue for defamation of character.

Sociological Approaches

Students of race and politics in America often employ a multidisciplinary approach. For example, racial considerations have played a major role in sociological theory. Some sociological theories emphasize order; others emphasize power, conflict, exploitation, stratification, and subordination.

Perhaps the most celebrated order-focused theory is Robert E. Park's concept of cyclical race relations. Park, a sociologist at the University of Chicago, argued in *Race and Culture* (1950) that there is an evolving pattern in the interaction between racial groups: (1) contact; (2) conflict; (3) accommodation; and (4) assimilation. Park's optimistic theory sees the improvement of race relations as consistent with the general progress of society and humanity.

Park's approach has been subject to intense criticism. The major objection is that assimilation is hardly the only possible outcome of inter-ethnic contact. Other possible consequences include exclusion and annihilation, symbiosis (a stable relation of more or less equally beneficial exchange between members of distinct groups), ethnic stratification (involving subordination within a single political system), and pluralism (the egalitarian integration of distinct ethnic groups with a common political and economic system).

Another theory of race relations is the ethnic group model. This model views blacks in terms of the experience of other immigrant groups in the United States. It holds that while society is divided into separate groups, the most powerful social force is assimilation. If white Europeans can enter the American mainstream, then African Americans can too. In this paradigm, social equilibrium is maintained by consensus, and the likelihood of large-scale conflict is minimal.

Several prominent books on black studies have employed the ethnic group model. In 1944, Swedish sociologist Gunnar Myrdal published *An American Dilemma,* in which he argued that the separate institutions of the black community represent a form of social pathology, because they are deviations from the American standard of assimilation. Myrdal assembled an enormous amount of data, and demonstrated the tension between American ideals and the reality of racial subordination.

Similarly, in 1939 E. Franklin Frazier wrote *The Negro Family in the United*

States. Frazier, a student of Robert Park, analyzed the impact of slavery, emancipation, and urbanization on the black family. Frazier contended that American blacks comprise a distinct minority group that has faced nearly insurmountable obstacles to assimilation. He maintained that the black family places inordinate responsibility on the female, attaches great significance to variations in skin color, and exhibits excessive levels of social disorganization and illegitimacy. He also argued that the American black middle class lacks the strong entrepreneurial tradition that has been a core value of middle classes worldwide.

Another sociological theory, the colonial model, takes the subordination process of American ethnic and racial relations as the central factor. In this view, black people form "internal colonies" which are subject to exploitation. Blacks are an oppressed minority, which breeds resistance. The colonial model views underdevelopment, imperialism, and racism in an international context.

Race and Political Science Theory

Another way to study race and politics in America is to employ traditional theories of political science. One theory is *pluralism,* which holds that political conflict is organized around group interests. Pressure groups may be defined as individuals who share interests and interact for the purpose of affecting public policy. Each interest group has access to power resources, such as time, money, prestige, contacts, media access, the right to vote, and the right to petition elected representatives. Pluralist theory sees the political process as relatively open, and sees government as a relatively unbiased arbiter of competing interest groups. For pluralists, elections are a means of determining the "collective wish." Political equilibrium is maintained by compromise, and competition among groups ensures that no single powerful group can dominate public policy. The classic statements of pluralist theory are David Truman's *The Governmental Process* (1951) and Robert Dahl's *Polyarchy, Participation, and Opposition* (1956).

There are several criticisms of pluralist theory. One is that some groups are inherently more influential than others; groups that represent business interests are generally more powerful than those with mass memberships. Further, there is little evidence that groups determine policy by negotiating among themselves or forming coalitions. Rather, a lobbying group typically seeks to carve out a policy niche for itself in which it can be dominant, safe from conflict with competitors. Finally, most people do not belong to interest groups and thus are underrepresented by the interest-group structure. There is a strong class basis to the patterns of interest-group membership. Well-educated people with higher incomes are much more represented than the less educated and the less affluent. As E. E. Schattschneider wrote in *The Semisovereign People* (1960), "The flaw in the pluralist heaven is that the heavenly chorus sings with a strong upper-class accent."

In one sense, the experience of blacks in American politics is consistent with pluralist theory. Throughout American history, there have been numerous black interest groups, including the National American Political League (organized in 1908), the National Association for the Advancement of Colored People (organized in 1910), the National Independent Political League (organized in 1912), the National Labor Congress (organized in 1924), and the National Negro Congress (organized in 1936). More recent black interest groups include the Southern Christian Leadership Conference (SCLC), the Congress on Racial Equality (CORE), and the Student Non-Violent Coordinating Committee (SNCC).

Indeed, the heads of the leading predominantly black organizations meet on a periodic basis to exchange information, discuss mutual concerns, and plan joint strategies. Members of the Black Leadership Forum include the NAACP, the NAACP Legal Defense and Education Fund, the National Urban League, the National Business League, the National Council of Negro Women, the National Urban Coalition, Operation PUSH, the Martin Luther King Jr. Center for Social Change, the Congressional Black Caucus, the National Black Caucus of Local Elected Officials, the A. Philip Randolph Institute, the Opportunities Industrialization Centers, and the Joint Center for Political and Economic Studies.

In other ways, however, pluralist theory is inapplicable to black America. Blacks have undoubtedly faced greater obstacles than other interest groups, due to white antagonism. Further, the success of black pressure groups may depend less on their leadership, social status, or cohesion than on the attitude of white America.

One prominent book on American racial politics offers an important modification of pluralist theory. In *Southern Politics in State and Nation* (1949), V. O. Key wrote that "politics usually comes down, over the long run, to a conflict between those who have and those who have less." Key, then a professor of government at Harvard University (and one of the pioneering analysts of voting behavior), submitted a theory of "modified class politics." In this model, people are divided along liberal and conservative lines rather than sectional or factional interests. In Key's view, the struggle between classes overshadows the battle between racial, religious, and sectional interests. "Modified class conflict," therefore, meant that the debate over economic issues would not result in violence.

Several African American scholars have criticized pluralist theory. The radical viewpoint is represented by *Black Power: The Politics of Liberation in America* (1967), written by Stokely Carmichael, a Black Panther, and Charles V. Hamilton, a professor of political science at Columbia University. This book analyzed racial issues in terms of "institutionalized racism." Carmichael and Hamilton maintain that American blacks can ill afford to believe that their liberation will be achieved through traditional political processes, since American racism makes existing political structures irrelevant. They conclude that "we must begin to think of the black community as a base of organization to control institutions in that community."

Another perspective rejects pluralism because of its overemphasis on politics as a means of economic advancement. In *Markets and Minorities* (1981),

Thomas Sowell, a senior fellow at the Hoover Institution on War, Revolution, and Peace, criticizes blacks for pursuing a *political* strategy for material progress, rather than an *economic* strategy. Sowell, the nation's most prominent black conservative, argues that many ethnic immigrant groups have flourished under a system of laissez-faire economics. He argues against affirmative action, minimum wage legislation, and occupational safety regulations. Sowell reiterates these arguments in *Race and Economics* (1975); *The Economics and Politics of Race: An International Perspective* (1983); *Civil Rights: Rhetoric or Reality?* (1984); *Preferential Policies: An International Perspective* (1990); and *Race and Culture: A World View* (1994).

A second theory of American politics is *elitism*. Elitist theory rejects the pluralist claim that power is widely dispersed among interest groups. Instead, elite theorists maintain that power is concentrated among a handful of elites. Elite networks are dominated by upper-income people who lead powerful institutions, such as business corporations and key federal agencies.

Sociologist C. Wright Mills, in *The Power Elite* (1959), argued that power in America is held by a small number of corporate executives, top-ranking military leaders, and the highest civilian political leaders (including the president and a few Cabinet members). In elitist theory, the masses have little power. Instead, they "pursue meaningless lives, manipulated by the power elite through the use of mass media communications." In Mills's view, average citizens are apathetic, cynical toward politics, concerned only with popular culture, and unable to influence national policy. Further, even the associations intended to provide power to the masses (such as labor unions) are controlled by an internal elite; this concept, popularized by Robert Michels, is known as the "Iron Law of Oligarchy."

Similarly, Peter Bachrach and Morton Baratz advance an elitist theory of "non-decisions," or "the two faces of power." In their view, elites have the power not only to affect the outcome of policy disputes but also to keep certain matters off the policy agenda. Elites do not necessarily have the power to tell the masses what to think; rather, they have the power to tell the masses what to think *about.*

In the 1992 presidential election, the condition of the ghetto underclass was clearly a non-issue. Neither George Bush nor Ross Perot actively courted the black vote. Bill Clinton not only seemed to take the black vote for granted; he also seemed to fear that placing too much emphasis on the needs of African Americans would offend white suburban voters. All three candidates apparently believed that the election would be won or lost in the (predominantly white) suburbs.

One book on racial politics that employs an elitist perspective is *Negro Politics: The Search for Leadership,* written in 1960 by James Q. Wilson. Wilson was previously professor of government at Harvard University; he now teaches in the School of Business at UCLA. *Negro Politics* concerns black politics in Chicago, particularly the relationship between blacks and the Chicago Democratic political machine. Wilson argued that the extent of black political organization in Chicago was dependent upon the extent of *white* political organization, and that the fortunes of the former were wedded to those of the latter. In his view, urban political machines helped to facilitate black political accommodation.

However, Wilson noted that the rewards of the machine for blacks were usually low, except for those in machine leadership positions. Indeed, the white political machine often did not even have to appoint a black boss. In many cases, especially around the turn of the century, the machine simply absorbed the black Republican leaders of the city and their defunct political clubs.

The theory of elitism has clear relevance for black politics. Black Americans are underrepresented among corporate, military, and political elites. Also, the NAACP certainly lacks the political power of business groups such as the National Association of Manufacturers or the United States Chamber of Commerce. In addition, some black politicians owe their political advancement to white patrons.

A third traditional theory of politics is *Marxism,* which focuses on the distribution and concentration of property ownership, and contends that workers are increasingly marginalized and immiserated, due to exploitation. Production changes such as automation create an ever-growing mass of unemployed workers. This "reserve pool of the unemployed" drives down wage rates for those who are employed. According to Marxist theory, the essence of politics is class struggle. Marxists believe that the essential goal of capitalists is control of the means of production.

One of the modern classics of Marxist theory is Paul Sweezy's *The Theory of Capitalist Development* (1942). Sweezy argues that modern capitalism has produced racism, militarism, and imperialism. In his view, the economic underdevelopment of black America is the direct result of slavery, sharecropping, peonage, and low-wage industrial labor. The model of "conduit colonialism" holds that America's liberal governmental policies within a capitalist economy have come to reinforce the subordinate economic position of blacks.

Another race-related book that employs a Marxist perspective is William K. Tabb's *The Political Economy of the Black Ghetto* (1970). Tabb contends that the economic relationship between the ghetto in America and the national economy closely parallels the relationship between the Third World and the advanced industrial countries. Just as in less developed countries, American ghettos have high birth rates, low per-capita incomes, and unskilled residents. Savings rates are low, goods and services tend to be imported, and only the most labor-intensive goods are produced locally. The ghetto has one basic export: unskilled labor.

Manning Marble presents similar arguments in *How Capitalism Underdeveloped Black America* (1983). Writing in the tradition of Walter Rodney's *How Europe Underdeveloped Africa* (1972), Marble maintains that "the most striking fact about American economic history and politics is the brutal and systematic underdevelopment of Black people." In his view, each advance in white freedom was purchased by black enslavement, and the white state and corporate power were made possible by black powerlessness. Marble reviews the history of slavery, peonage, and low wages in black America. The creativity of Marble's analysis is consistent with the flourishing intellectual tenor of black studies and black politics.

To summarize, analysts assume that the study of black politics enhances the study of American politics, that race is a critical factor in American politics, and that African Americans are unlike other ethnic groups in American society. Analysts of American racial politics employ sociological theories (the cyclical race relations model, the ethnic group model, and the colonial model), as well as standard theories of political science (pluralism, elitism, and Marxism).

Race and American Society

The matter of race is central to American social relations and political attitudes. Perhaps the most significant race-related problem in American society is the condition of the underclass. The statistics are shocking. The infant-mortality rate among blacks is more than double the average for whites. Black children are three times more likely than whites to live in a single-parent household. More than 40 percent of all black children live in poverty. Blacks, about 12 percent of the American population, account for almost 30 percent of all AIDS cases in the United States. Homicide is now the leading cause of death for African American males between the ages of fifteen and thirty-four. Nearly half of all murder victims in the United States are black. Almost one-quarter of all blacks between the ages of eighteen and twenty-nine are in prison, on probation, or on parole.

Many recent books have been published on the underclass. Leon Dash, in *When Children Want Children: The Urban Crisis of Teenage Childbearing*, reports on his conversations with sexually active teenagers who live in a Washington public housing project. Alex Kotlowitz, in *There Are No Children Here: Two Boys Grow Up in the Other America*, reports on life in a Chicago public housing project. Christopher Jencks recently wrote *Rethinking Social Policy: Race, Poverty, and the Underclass*, in which he argues that discussions of social policy need to place less emphasis on political principles and more attention on specific programs. Finally, Jencks and Paul Peterson co-edited *The Urban Underclass*, a comprehensive overview of American social conditions and policy.

Many recent movies have addressed the matter of race. In the last several years, Spike Lee has produced "She's Gotta Have It" (about the sexual exploits of a black woman), "Mo' Better Blues" (about black jazz musicians), "Do the Right Thing" (about racial tensions in Brooklyn), "Jungle Fever" (about interracial dating), and "Malcolm X" (about the slain black leader). Other recent black-oriented films include "Boyz N the Hood" (about gangs in South Central Los Angeles), "Colors" (about the police and gangs in Los Angeles), "A Rage in Harlem" (about black anger), "Straight Out of Brooklyn" (about a black teenager's attempt to escape the ghettos of Brooklyn), "South Central" (about a father's efforts to save his son from a life of gang violence), "Menace II Society" (about black gangs), "Poetic Justice" (about a love relationship in South Central Los Angeles), and "Fresh" (about a twelve-year-old drug runner).

Indeed, several of these films became political issues in their own right. Spike Lee urged black teenagers to skip school on the opening day of "Malcolm X," and was criticized for his stereotypical portrayal of Jews in "Mo' Better Blues." The opening of "Boyz N the Hood" was greeted with gang-related violence in many cities. Also, the phrase "jungle fever" has entered the popular language.

Black rappers such as Ice Tea, Sister Souljah, Public Enemy, and N. W. A. (Niggers with Attitude) have also become increasingly prominent—and controversial. Black rap lyrics have discussed cop killing, rioting, and "wilding." In a 1992 interview with *The Washington Post*, Sister Souljah said, "I mean, if black people kill black people every day, why not have a week and kill white people?"

Black writers are also gaining new eminence. Recent best-selling novels by black writers include Alice Walker's *The Color Purple*, about a girl growing up in the post-Reconstruction South; Toni Morrison's *Beloved*, about a black woman who escaped from slavery; John Edgar Wideman's *Philadelphia Fire*, about urban decay; and Terry McMillan's *Waiting to Exhale*, about four black women in Phoenix. Other prominent black writers include Paule Marshall, Alex Haley, and Zora Neale Hurston. Terry McMillan recently edited *Breaking Ice*, the first anthology of black fiction published in twenty years. Maya Angelou delivered an original poem at President Clinton's inauguration.

There is other evidence of the increasing importance of race in American society. The Ku Klux Klan has reemerged in several Northern cities, including Janesville, Wisconsin. Efforts by city officials in Dubuque, Iowa, to increase the number of blacks in their community by guaranteeing jobs and housing were met with bitter resistance. "Speech codes" designed to limit racially inflammatory rhetoric have been instituted at major American universities. New York City has suffered through racial incidents at Howard Beach in Queens, where four white youths attacked four black men on December 19, 1986; Bensonhurst, where a black youth, Yusuf Hawkins, was shot to death in August 1989 after being chased by a gang of white teens; Central Park, where, in April 1989, a young white woman jogger was beaten by a group of black youths who described their activities as "wilding"); and Crown Heights, where a Hasidic Jew, Yankel Rosenbaum, was murdered by a mob of young blacks as they yelled, "Kill the Jew." Finally, Los Angeles experienced five days of rioting in the spring of 1992 after the acquittal of four white police officers for the brutal beating of black motorist Rodney King. The riots were the worst in the nation's history, with forty-seven deaths and an estimated $1 billion in property damage.

My argument in this part has been that race is a dominant issue in American society. The condition of the American urban underclass has attracted significant attention, and public interest in race is reflected in books, movies, and music. Finally, American society has been recently plagued by numerous hate crimes and racial incidents.

American Racial Attitudes

Racial attitudes have been explored in many best-selling books. Studs Terkel uncovers the depths of racial angst in *Race: How Blacks and Whites Think and Feel about the American Obsession.* Cornel West, in *Race Matters,* attempts to fuse the love ethic of the black church "with the political insights of the Black Panthers." Shelby Steele's *The Content of Our Character: A New Vision of Race in America* argues that blacks should abandon their sense of victimization and instead adopt a strategy of self-reliance. Patricia Williams, in *The Alchemy of Race and Rights,* explores the depths of black pain, rage, cynicism, and distrust. Derrick Bell, in *And We Are Not Saved: The Elusive Quest for Racial Justice* (1987) and *Faces at the Bottom of the Well: The Permanence of Racism in America* (1992), uses dramatic fables, dialogues, allegorical stories, and legal precedents to examine the nature of racism in American society. In *Reflections of an Affirmative Action Baby,* Yale law professor Stephen Carter reviews the debate over affirmative action in intensely personal terms.

One trend in racial attitudes is the rise of black rejectionism. In Milwaukee, Michael McGee, a Black Panther (and former city councilman), has threatened to "recruit blacks around the country to cut phone lines, burn tires on freeways, and attack other institutions unless the government creates jobs, improves education and housing, and takes over steps against urban poverty by January 1, 1995." McGee wears military fatigues and carries a rifle.

Louis Farrakhan, leader of the Nation of Islam, is another leader of black rejectionism. He has called whites "devils" and Judaism a "gutter religion," and once called Hitler "wickedly great."

One of the most powerful new voices for black rejectionism is Khallid Abdul Muhammad, formerly the chief spokesman for the Nation of Islam (before Louis Farrakhan suspended him). In November 1993, Khalid gave a three-hour speech at Kean College in Union, New Jersey, in which he justified the Holocaust, called for the murder of South African whites, and ridiculed homosexuals. Speaking of black conservatives, Khallid said, "When white folks can't defeat you, they'll always find some bootlicking, buttlicking, bamboozled, half-baked, half-fried, sissified, punkified, pasteurized, homogenized nigger that they can trot out in front of you." On South African whites, he bellowed, "We kill the women. We kill the babies. We kill the blind. We kill the cripples. We kill them all. We kill the faggot. We kill the lesbian. When you get through killing them, go to the goddamn graveyard and dig up the grave and kill them again because they didn't die hard enough."

In May 1994, Khallid gave a speech at the University of California-Riverside, attended by about two thousand people, all but about ten of whom were black.

Khallid warned the white people in the audience (whom he referred to as "Suzy, Bill, Bob, Jill, and Heather") to "buckle your seat belts, because it's gonna be a rough ride." He said that he "came to tell the truth, whether you like it or not," and that he was a "truth terrorist" and a "knowledge gangster." He announced gleefully that "I didn't come to pin the tail on the *donkey;* I came to pin the tail on the *honkey."* Several times, Khallid asked for "a black round of applause." He opened by welcoming "my brothers and sisters—and others." Pointing to the cameras, he screamed, "I don't give a *damn* what you say about me!"

Much of Khallid's speech consisted of racist rantings. He referred to white people as "no-good bastards" and "butt-licking fuckers." He stated that "the white man isn't *a* devil; the white man is *the* devil." He informed white people that "your time is up!" and that he "intends to give the white man hell from the cradle to the grave." He claimed that whites think of blacks as "buck-naked, swinging from trees eating bananas and coconuts." He called Jesse Jackson "a handkerchief head," referred to "an old, white, no-good, so-called Jew," and asserted that the black holocaust "is one hundred times worse than the Jewish Holocaust. Theirs was six years; ours is *five hundred* years and counting."

Many of Khallid's remarks were blatantly sexual. He bragged that black erections are much bigger than white erections. He referred to Elizabeth Taylor as "some whore in Hollywood screwing everything that's not screwed down." He asserted that while the goal of basketball "is to keep black players from putting the big ball in the hole," black guys "are scoring from three-point range." He noted that white fathers pass out "long, strong black (or brown) cigars, rather than scrawny little white cigarettes." He averred that little white golf balls "represent what the white man thinks of himself."

Some of Khallid's remarks about racism in everyday life rang true. He observed that angel food cake is white, while devil's food cake is black; that to "blackball" someone is to do them harm; that a black cat represents bad luck; and that wearing white is appropriate for a wedding, while black is suitable for a funeral.

Some of Khallid's rhetoric was even worthy of praise. The crowd applauded a group of ex-gang members who had turned their lives around. Khallid urged black students to take "physics, math, agronomy, animal husbandry, and engineering" instead of "underwater bubblebath or watercoloring." He encouraged black men and black women to respect each other and to develop a sense of black pride. He excoriated the black race for having "gone from pyramids to projects."

Khallid compared himself to Malcolm X. He noted that Malcolm had been suspended from the Nation of Islam by Elijah Muhammad, just as *he* had been suspended by Louis Farrakhan. However, he assured the crowd that "there will be no Farrakhan-Khallid split" (in part, perhaps, because his own nine-year-old son is named "Farrakhan").

Another trend, besides black rejectionism, is racial separatism. School districts in New York, Detroit, and Minneapolis have established separate schools for black males; many other school districts are introducing curricula based on Afrocentrism. Malcolm X, an advocate of racial solidarity, has become a cultural icon for many young black males.

Further, there is increasing black support for reparations—cash payments from the federal government to the children of slaves. Decades ago, this idea was trumpeted by Marcus Garvey, then by Malcolm X. It currently has the support of National Coalition of Blacks for Reparations in America (N'COBRA), Jesse Jackson, Coretta Scott King, and nineteen members of the Congressional Black Caucus, as well as the city councils of Detroit, Cleveland, and Washington, D.C.

In the view of reparationists, the problems plaguing the modern black community—family disintegration, crime, welfare dependency, and poverty—are the legacy of the capture of Africans and their bondage in America. Also, if Japanese-Americans were paid reparations for their internment during World War II, surely African-Americans are far more deserving.

Walter Williams, a conservative economist at George Mason University in Virginia, is an ardent opponent of reparations, on moral grounds. Noting that he is in the top 1 or 2 percent of income earners in the country, he argues that it is "perverse to suggest that some poor white kid who's the son of a coal miner in West Virginia" owes him money.

The rise of black rejectionism and black separatism reflects the fact that many blacks are deeply suspicious of whites. A poll of New York City blacks in 1990 indicated that 10 percent believe that "AIDS was deliberately created in a laboratory in order to infect black people," and that 25 percent believe "the government makes sure that drugs are easily available in poor black neighborhoods to harm black people." Blacks in Washington, D.C., speak openly of "the plan" of the white power structure to drive up real estate prices in order to drive blacks out. Many black politicians have alleged that Marion Barry, Mike Tyson, Michael Jackson, Gus Savage, and Clarence Thomas have all been singled out for prosecution or harassment because of their race.

Kimberly Crenshaw, a law professor at UCLA, argues that these feelings are perfectly understandable, because of the ill will that has been "directed toward us in employment, in health care institutions, in housing, and especially in the criminal justice system." Therefore, she says, when black people see a black man "standing in handcuffs or being hauled before a court, they are ready to believe that brother is innocent without even hearing the charges against him."

Clearly, there are vast differences between the way white and black Americans view reality. A 1992 *Washington Post* poll indicated that 71 percent of blacks surveyed nationwide believed they were not achieving equality as quickly as they could because whites did not want them to advance, while only 35 percent of whites agreed that racism holds blacks behind. The racial divide is also very evident in the O. J. Simpson case. A July 1994 *Los Angeles Times* poll found that 70 percent of blacks were "very" or "somewhat" sympathetic toward Simpson, compared to 38 percent of whites.

There is also the potential for a white backlash against blacks. A 1994 survey by the Times Mirror Center for the People and the Press showed that 51 percent of whites agreed with the statement that "equal rights have been pushed too far in this country." In California in 1994, the passage of Proposition 187, which is intended to restrict the access of illegal immigrants to governmental services, may signify rising feelings of racism and nativism among whites.

Race and Presidential Elections

The matter of race is not only central to the problems of American society; it has also been a key issue in American presidential elections.

According to Hanes Walton, a political scientist at the University of Michigan, the black presidential vote "assumes a fourfold significance." First, many analysts consider it a measure of black political participation and influence. Second, a largely cohesive black vote may be pivotal in close presidential elections. Third, the black vote in presidential elections constitutes a "symbolic and substantive expression of black values and preferences through interest-group articulation and preferences." Finally, the black presidential vote is an instrument of political brokering and bargaining by black leaders, seeking to serve black interests through influencing the presidency.

Blacks first played a major role in American presidential politics in 1904, when the black National Liberty Party was organized. George Edwin Taylor was the party's candidate for president.

The racial issue was critical to the presidential election of 1948. At the Democratic National Convention in Philadelphia, Hubert Humphrey, then mayor of Minneapolis, encouraged the party to "leave the dark light of states' rights and enter the bright light of civil rights." As Humphrey was speaking, Senator Strom Thurmond of South Carolina led a convention walkout. Thurmond formed his own party, and ran for president under the "Dixiecrat" label.

The presidential election of 1960 reinforced the "pivotal black vote" thesis. Black votes contributed significantly to John Kennedy's 110,000-vote margin over Richard Nixon. The Gallup Poll estimated that 70 percent of black voters supported Kennedy. Black support may have been the margin of victory for Kennedy in eleven states (Illinois, New Jersey, Michigan, South Carolina, Texas, Delaware, Maryland, Missouri, North Carolina, Pennsylvania, and Nevada).

The 1960 election also witnessed the formation of the Afro-American party. Organized in Alabama, the party ran two blacks, the Rev. Clennon King and Reginald Carter, for president and vice president. The ticket received 1,485 votes, all from Alabama.

In 1964, race was central to George Wallace's presidential campaign. Throughout the 1960s, Wallace, the Democratic governor of Alabama, proclaimed "segregation today, segregation tomorrow, segregation forever!" In 1962, he opposed the efforts of federal marshals to integrate the University of

Alabama. Wallace opposed mandatory school busing and neighborhood integration. He proclaimed that "there's not a dime's worth of difference between the two parties," and that federal bureaucrats were "pointy-headed intellectuals who can't park a bicycle straight."

Wallace challenged President Lyndon Johnson for the 1964 Democratic presidential nomination. Wallace received 30 percent of the vote in the Indiana primary and 43 percent of the vote in the Maryland primary, demonstrating strong support among Northern blue-collar workers—those most susceptible to appeals based on racism and resentment.

The 1964 general election was significant in several respects. One is that it was the last time that a Democratic presidential candidate won a majority of the white vote. However, the 1964 election also argues against the pivotal black vote thesis. President Johnson won in a landslide, carrying forty-four states; he could have been elected without a single black vote. Johnson defeated Arizona Senator Barry Goldwater, an opponent of federal civil rights legislation. Goldwater's most famous line during the campaign was, "Extremism in the defense of liberty is no vice; moderation in the pursuit of justice is no virtue."

Despite the less-than-critical role of black votes in his election, Johnson made racial issues a priority in his administration. Johnson launched the Great Society and the War on Poverty, intended to rebuild urban America, reduce malnutrition, provide housing, and improve education. He signed the Civil Rights Act of 1964, the 1965 Voting Rights Act, and the Open Housing Act of 1968.

The presidential election of 1968 was notable for several reasons. One was that there were several black candidates for the presidency. Eldridge Cleaver, minister of information for the Black Panther Party, was the candidate of the Peace and Freedom Party. His campaign slogan was "Let a nigger have control of the nuclear button." Also, actor/activist Dick Gregory ran for president as an independent. At the Democratic convention in Chicago, the District of Columbia delegation nominated Reverend Channing Phillips as a favorite son.

Race played a central role in the general election campaign of 1968. The Republican nominee, former vice president Richard Nixon, employed a "Southern strategy" in his race for the White House, based on winning the votes of Southern, white, conservative, blue-collar Democrats). Nixon also railed against crime and lawlessness, repeatedly using the slogan "law and order." Many critics charge that this phrase was racially coded.

In 1968, George Wallace again ran for president, this time as the candidate of the American Independent Party. In November, Wallace won five states: Alabama, Arkansas, Georgia, Louisiana, and Mississippi.

Race also played a vital role in the 1972 presidential campaign. George Wallace ran again, this time in the Democratic primaries. He won primaries in Florida, Michigan, Maryland, and Tennessee, and finished second in Wisconsin, Pennsylvania, Oregon, West Virginia, and Indiana. Wallace focused on white resentment over affirmative action and school busing. He dropped out of the race after being shot in Laurel, Maryland, on May 15, 1972, by Arthur Bremer.

The 1972 election also witnessed the first "serious" black presidential candidacy. Representative Shirley Chisholm, a Harlem Democrat, sought the Democratic nomination. She entered ten primaries, averaging thirty-five thousand votes in each state (about 3 percent of the total). She ran relatively well in California, Florida, Michigan, and North Carolina. She gathered thirty-five convention delegates—7 percent of the total black delegates.

The issue of race was also a key to the 1976 presidential election. Once again, George Wallace was a candidate for the Democratic nomination. Wallace lost the Florida Democratic primary to Jimmy Carter, the former governor of Georgia. Carter's victory earned him the gratitude of Democratic Party officials, who were nervous about Wallace's popularity.

During the Pennsylvania primary, Carter appealed to white urban ethnics. He spoke of the legitimate right of white neighborhoods to maintain "ethnic purity." This phrase struck many as a racist slur. Carter was bailed out from this gaffe by the strong support of Georgia Congressman Andrew Young (whom Carter later named United States ambassador to the United Nations).

Carter could not have won the general election without the support of black voters. In 1976, almost two-thirds of registered black voters went to the polls. Over 90 percent of them voted for Carter (compared to 48 percent of white voters).

After defeating Massachusetts Senator Edward Kennedy and California Governor Jerry Brown for the Democratic presidential nomination, Carter lost the 1980 general election to Ronald Reagan, the former governor of California. Throughout his public career, Reagan complained of high government spending and taxation; he assailed "welfare queens" who supposedly purchase orange juice with food stamps and then "use the change to purchase vodka." Reagan opened his fall campaign with a rally in Philadelphia, Mississippi, previously a hotbed of the Ku Klux Klan.

The Reagan administration proved troublesome to civil rights advocates. Reagan opposed affirmative action and extension of the Voting Rights Act. His administration reduced the growth of federal domestic spending, granted tax-exempt status to racially segregated schools (including Bob Jones University in Greenville, South Carolina), and convinced Congress to reduce taxes on the wealthy.

The 1984 presidential election was a watershed for black politics. Jesse Jackson, president of Operation PUSH (People United to Serve Humanity) and a former aide to Martin Luther King Jr., made a strong bid for the Democratic presidential nomination. Undeniably charismatic and eloquent, Jackson received almost 19 percent of the total primary vote. Many black leaders, however, supported former vice president Walter Mondale for the nomination, because of his long record of backing black causes.

In 1988, Jackson again sought the Democratic presidential nomination. This time, he became more than a symbolic candidate, receiving seven million votes. He won primaries in five states (Alabama, Georgia, Louisiana, Mississippi, and Virginia) and the District of Columbia, and finished second in twenty-four others. Out of thirty-six primaries, he finished first or second in thirty.

Jackson lost the presidential nomination to Massachusetts Governor Michael Dukakis. Throughout the campaign, relations between the two men were tense. Prior to the Democratic National Convention, Jackson campaigned openly for the vice presidential nomination. Dukakis went through the motions of considering Jackson, but then picked Texas Senator Lloyd Bentsen. Jackson complained that he learned of the Bentsen selection from the news media, rather than Dukakis. At the convention, Dukakis was overshadowed by Jackson. On the Fourth of July (after the convention), the Dukakis and Jackson families met at the Dukakis home in Brookline, Massachusetts. Jackson let it be known that he didn't care for the food that had been prepared.

In 1988, Lenora Fulani ran for president as the candidate of the New Alliance party, a quasi-Marxist group that advocates a "progressive agenda" and believes that racism is endemic to American society. Fulani's name was on the ballot in all fifty states. Fulani, a New York City psychologist, is author of *The Psychopathology of Everyday Racism and Sexism* (1988) and *The Politics of Race and Gender in Therapy* (1988).

In 1988, the Republican nominee was George Bush, the incumbent vice president. Many blacks were suspicious of Bush because of his vote as a United States congressman against the 1964 Civil Rights Act. In 1988, Lee Atwater, Bush's campaign chairman, advised Bush to run on divisive, race-based "wedge" issues (such as crime, welfare, and affirmative action), in order to paint Dukakis as a liberal outside the political mainstream. Most notable among these issues was the matter of Willie Horton, a black convict. While on furlough from a Massachusetts prison, Horton raped a white woman and stabbed her fiancé in Maryland. Television advertisements prepared by the Bush campaign (and independent groups) showed Horton's menacing, black face. Another Bush commercial showed dozens of prisoners moving through a revolving door, as the narrator related stories of crime in Massachusetts. After the campaign, Atwater expressed the wish that Horton had not been black, so that the supposedly central issue of criminal justice would not have been obscured by the matter of race.

Bush was the easy winner in the fall election. Dukakis carried only ten states: Delaware, Hawaii, Iowa, Massachusetts, Minnesota, Oregon, Rhode Island, Washington, West Virginia, and Wisconsin. What is notable about these states is that they are disproportionately white. The possible inference is that racial and political liberalism may be more acceptable in areas where racial issues are less central.

President Bush's major contribution to the politics of race was his nomination of Clarence Thomas to be an associate justice on the United States Supreme

Court. In 1991, Thurgood Marshall, the first black to serve on the Court, re-signed his seat, citing his age. Marshall had been a pioneer in the civil rights movement, as the legal adviser to the NAACP as well as solicitor general in the Johnson Administration (responsible for arguing the president's positions before the Supreme Court). Marshall had been at the forefront of judicial efforts to protect the rights of the accused, guarantee the right to an attorney, and expand voting rights.

On July 1, 1991, Bush announced the Thomas nomination. Then a member of the Court of Appeals for the District of Columbia, Thomas had spoken out against affirmative action, the welfare state, and excessive federal regulation. Bush claimed that Thomas was the "best" available nominee, and that the color of Thomas's skin had "absolutely nothing" to do with the nomination.

The Thomas nomination divided the black community. On the one hand, some black interest groups favored Thomas, arguing that a black conservative is preferable to a white conservative. *Washington Post* columnist William Rasp-berry approvingly quoted a friend who said, "Given a choice between two con-servatives, I'll take the one who's been called 'nigger.' " Benjamin Hooks, head of the NAACP, was reluctant to oppose Thomas because Bush's subsequent nominee would be "a white Genghis Kahn."

Most black groups, though, opposed Thomas's nomination, on the grounds of his perceived insensitivity to the interests of the poor, as well as his conservative ideology. All but one member of the Congressional Black Cau-cus (Republican Gary Franks of Connecticut) signed a statement arguing that Thomas had a "rigidly harsh ideology," and that his legal vision "is at odds with the black experience." It called Thomas "the quota nominee" who would fail to protect blacks from "the tyranny of legalized racism and hostile major-ity rule."

Several months after the Thomas nomination, another source of opposition arose: Anita Hill's accusation that he had sexually harassed her. Hill, a professor at the University of Oklahoma Law School, had worked with Thomas at the Equal Employment Opportunity Commission and the federal Department of Education.

The Thomas/Hill hearings mesmerized the nation for a week. Some black leaders were aghast at Hill's accusations, arguing that blacks should not air their dirty laundry in public. Others feared that Hill's allegations would reinforce public perceptions of the black male as an uncontrollable sexual brute. Orlando Patterson, professor of sociology at Harvard University, suggested in a *New York Times* op-ed that Thomas may have knowingly lied about harassing Hill, but did so because he believed that the penalty for his transgression—denial of a seat on the Supreme Court—was inappropriate for the offense.

After the Senate Judiciary Committee hearings, the Senate voted to con-firm Thomas, 52–48. Thomas was forty-three when he joined the Court; he promises to serve on the Court for another forty-three years. He has be-come so sensitive to criticism that he refuses to read any newspaper other than the reliably conservative *Washington Times*. (He also listens to Rush Limbaugh's radio program.)

The 1992 presidential campaign was also infused with racial issues. Perhaps the most significant element of the campaign was Jesse Jackson's absence. Jackson decided not to run because of his fear of being tagged a three-time presidential loser. (He also decided against running for mayor of Washington, D.C., in 1990 and 1994, in spite of the fact that he probably could have won easily.) Instead, Jackson won election as a "shadow senator" from the District of Columbia. The sole function of this unpaid, non-voting position is to lobby for D.C. statehood.

During the 1992 campaign, Jackson attempted to serve as an elder statesman. He endorsed no candidate during the primaries. At the convention, he was relegated to a minor role. He was allowed to speak at the convention only after publicly endorsing the Clinton-Gore ticket (on his own CNN talk show). With no delegates, and with Clinton in complete control of the convention, Jackson was relatively powerless.

Jackson's absence from the presidential race cleared the way for the candidacy of L. Douglas Wilder. The grandson of slaves, Wilder was elected governor of Virginia in 1989 (largely on the basis of his pro-choice stand on abortion). Many observers were astounded that Virginia, the seat of the Confederacy, would elect a black governor.

Wilder's presidential bid never caught fire, even among blacks. He dropped out of the race prior to the New Hampshire primary. At the Democratic convention, in a bid for attention, Wilder flirted with the possibility of becoming Ross Perot's running mate. (Perot dropped out of the presidential race—temporarily—on the final day of the Democratic convention.)

Race was also a major issue in the 1992 Republican presidential primaries. The politics of racial resentment was represented by two candidates: Pat Buchanan, a journalist and former aide to Presidents Nixon and Reagan, and David Duke, a member of the Louisiana state legislature, and the former president of the National Association for the Advancement of White People. Both Buchanan and Duke spoke out strongly against affirmative action, welfare spending, gay rights, and mandatory school integration. Both spoke in favor of the superiority of European culture, and both favored limits on immigration.

Lenora Fulani, the New Alliance Party candidate for president in 1988, also sought the presidency in 1992. While the party was on all fifty state ballots in 1988, it was on only forty ballots in 1992.

The politics of race also played a role in the quixotic presidential campaign of Ross Perot, the Texas billionaire. On July 13, 1992, Perot spoke before a meeting of the NAACP, in Nashville. Referring to effects of economic decline, Perot declared, "And I don't have to tell you who gets hurt by this. You people—your people do." The flap over Perot's remark contributed to his short-lived withdrawal from the race four days later.

Racial politics played a central role in the Clinton campaign. One week before the general election, a poll by the Joint Center for Political and Economic Studies showed that 84 percent of blacks disapproved of President Bush's performance in office. Surveys indicated that Clinton carried 82 percent of the black vote, and that black turnout was relatively high. (Clinton carried 39 percent of the white vote, compared to 41 percent for Bush and 20 percent for Perot.) The only groups offering comparable levels of support to Clinton were Jews (78 percent) and Latinos (62 percent).

The black vote also proved critical in Clinton's Electoral College majority. Blacks voted overwhelmingly for Clinton in Louisiana, Georgia, New Jersey, and Ohio; he carried those states by no more than four percentage points.

In the 1992 campaign, Bill Clinton had a paradoxical relationship with the black community. On the one hand, Clinton, a Southern Baptist, has a special affinity with blacks. He was raised, in part, by his grandparents, who owned a grocery store in a black neighborhood of Hope, Arkansas. Clinton feels comfortable preaching in black churches, and he has always attracted black votes in Arkansas. In 1992, he succeeded in forming a truly biracial political coalition (something that Jesse Jackson, head of the "Rainbow Coalition," was never able to do).

On the other hand, Clinton made obvious moves to distance himself from certain elements of the black community. He made it clear to Jesse Jackson that he was not under consideration for the vice presidency. Clinton focused his rhetoric on suburban voters and the "middle class," which many blacks took as racial code words. Even after the Los Angeles riots, Clinton placed little emphasis on urban issues. As governor of Arkansas, he signed several death warrants.

Most significantly, Clinton went out of his way to criticize a black rap artist, Sister Souljah, in the presence of Jesse Jackson. Sister Souljah (Lisa Williamson) had received an award from the Rainbow Coalition for her work with black youth. Clinton criticized her statement that black gang members ought to devote a week to killing white people. Jackson sat expressionless as Clinton delivered his condemnation. While many blacks complained of Clinton's public show of disrespect toward Jackson, many white voters inferred that Bill Clinton (unlike Walter Mondale and Michael Dukakis) was not going to coddle Jesse Jackson.

Some analysts view black political behavior in 1992 as a sign of political sophistication. Black leaders may have realized that trumpeting their demands upon Clinton during the campaign would be counterproductive—that it could alienate white voters and cost Clinton the election. The preferable strategy, according to this reasoning, was to remain relatively quiet during the campaign, but then line up with a list of demands *after* the election. Ron Brown, chairman of the Democratic National Committee during the 1992 campaign (and a former associate of Jesse Jackson), agreed with this viewpoint. He stated that Clinton's treatment of Jesse Jackson had nothing to do with whether Clinton would address the needs of black Americans.

The election of Bill Clinton as president in 1992 may have a substantial impact on black politicians. Clinton named an unprecedented number of blacks to his Cabinet. Jesse Brown, formerly the head of the Disabled American Veterans, was appointed secretary of veterans affairs; Ron Brown, former chairman of the Democratic National Committee, was named commerce secretary; Mike Espy, a former congressman from Mississippi, served as secretary of agriculture for twenty months (before resigning over alleged ethical improprieties); Hazel O'Leary, a Minnesota power company executive, was selected as secretary of energy; and Lee Brown, former New York City police commissioner, was named drug czar (a cabinet-level position). Vernon Jordan, former chairman of the Urban League (and now a high-powered Washington lawyer-lobbyist) was co-director of Clinton's presidential transition.

With the increased prominence of these individuals, the power of Jesse Jackson may decline. Jackson's political future may depend upon passage of a Constitutional amendment granting statehood to the District of Columbia. While President Clinton has offered support for this amendment (which would make it possible for Jackson to become a full-fledged United States senator), it is most unlikely that Congress would pass it, or that 38 state legislatures would ratify it. Few white Democratic congressmen have made D.C. statehood a priority, and few Republican state legislators will support a measure almost guaranteed to add two black liberal Democrats to the United States Senate.

Clinton's election could prove highly significant for African Americans. On the one hand, Clinton is committed to many goals shared by most blacks. Clinton convinced Congress to pass the "motor voter" bill, whereby individuals can register to vote when they register their car. This measure could increase voter registration (particularly among blacks), which could improve the electoral fortunes of the Democratic Party. In addition, President Clinton's first budget created "empowerment zones" in inner-city neighborhoods (to stimulate business investment), expanded the earned income tax credit (to assist the working poor), and increased funding for child immunization and food stamps. Further, Clinton is a strong advocate of welfare reform. He proposes a "New Covenant," whereby the federal government would expand job training, day care, and health insurance for welfare recipients; in exchange, welfare recipients would be required to obtain employment after two years. Finally, President Clinton and Hillary Rodham Clinton have made health reform a major priority, especially the extension of health coverage to the uninsured (a disproportionate number of whom are black).

Clinton's record on race-related issues has earned him praise. Harvard University government professor Martin Kilson, writing in the Spring 1993 issue of *Dissent* (a radical journal), referred to Clinton as a "shrewd liberal Southern politician," a "proactive racial liberal," and an "innovative liberal president." Kilson had particular praise for Clinton's cabinet selections.

However, President Clinton's relations with the black community have sometimes been stormy. Perhaps the most notable controversy was the aborted nomination of Lani Guinier as assistant attorney general for civil rights. Guinier, a professor at the University of Pennsylvania Law School, and the former chief legal counsel to the NAACP Legal Defense and Education Fund, was a friend of Bill and Hillary Clinton from their days as students at Yale Law School.

Republican senators and conservative activists launched a strong campaign against Guinier's confirmation. They objected to her views on affirmative action and minority voting rights. In particular, they disliked her contention that blacks in legislative bodies should have some form of legislative veto over relevant legislation, and that black politicians who appeal to white voters are not "authentic" representatives of black interests. Conservative activists labeled Guinier the "quota queen" (reminiscent of President Reagan's frequent complaints about "welfare queens").

As public discussion intensified, President Clinton decided to read Guinier's controversial writings for himself (which he had not done prior to her nomination). In a teary-eyed announcement, Clinton withdrew the Guinier nomination, saying he could not fight for a nominee whose views he did not share.

After Clinton's action, Guinier held a defiant press conference at the Justice Department (courtesy of Attorney General Janet Reno) and went on the lecture circuit to denounce Clinton for political cowardice. The Congressional Black Caucus protested Clinton's action, and refused to suggest another candidate for the job.

There were other race-related controversies in the early days of the Clinton administration. The president eventually fired Surgeon General Jocelyn Elders (an African American), because of her polemical statements on abortion, teenage pregnancy, and masturbation. President Clinton broke his campaign promise to allow free entrance of Haitian refugees. Clinton's economic stimulus package, which contained funds for summer jobs in inner-city neighborhoods, was defeated by the Senate. The Congressional Black Caucus threatened to vote against President Clinton's budget if it did not include sufficient funds for social service programs. Some black members of Congress complained that the federal government seemed more interested in assisting victims of the Midwestern floods of 1993 than in helping the residents of South Central Los Angeles. Black congressmen also objected to the Clinton crime bill (because it expands the death penalty), the Clinton health care proposal (because he backed away from his commitment to universal health-care access), and the Clinton welfare reform proposal (because the two-year limitation on welfare benefits is "punitive").

Jesse Jackson may well challenge Bill Clinton for the presidency in 1996, either in the Democratic primaries and/or as an independent in the general election. Jackson complains that Clinton has offered inadequate support for D.C. statehood, economic revitalization, workers' rights, national health care, and social services. He also protests that the Clinton-supported crime bill passed in the summer of 1994 expanded the federal death penalty, and failed to include a provision whereby death-row inmates could challenge their executions on the basis of racial disparities in sentencing.

A Jackson presidential candidacy could doom Clinton's reelection in 1996. First, primary challenges to incumbents presidents are usually very damaging. Gerald Ford was challenged by Ronald Reagan in 1976, Jimmy Carter was challenged by Ted Kennedy and Jerry Brown in 1980, and George Bush was challenged by Pat Buchanan in 1992. In each case, the incumbent lost in the general election. Second, to maintain his support among black voters, Clinton would have to move to the ideological left—thus alienating independents and Republicans, and jeopardizing his claim to being a "New Democrat." Third, if Jackson ran as an independent in the general election, Clinton could lose his most reliable voting bloc. In the 1990s and beyond, there are few realistic scenarios for a Democratic presidential victory without overwhelming support from the black community.

President Clinton's reelection in 1996 could also be endangered by the possible candidacy of retired General Colin Powell, the former chairman of the Joint Chiefs of Staff and an African American. A CNN/*USA Today* poll in 1994 showed that Powell could defeat Clinton, 54 percent to 34 percent, in a one-on-one race.

There are major uncertainties concerning a Powell candidacy. One is where he stands on the issues. As chairman of the Joint Chiefs of Staff (and as President Reagan's national security adviser), Powell's primary role was advising the president *in private*. Powell has spoken on domestic policy in only the most general terms, calling for greater personal initiative and responsibility.

Similarly, it is not known whether Powell is a Democrat, a Republican, or an independent. While some analysts have assumed that Powell is a Republican (having served two Republican presidents), he also served in the Carter administration. It is perhaps noteworthy that, in 1964, while stationed in Alabama, Powell had an "All the Way with LBJ" bumper sticker on his car.

Conclusion

The thesis of this essay is that race is central to American society, social science theory, political ideology, mass opinion, popular culture, and social conflict. In addition, racial politics has played an important role in presidential elections and the conduct of the presidency. Increasingly, the politics of America is the politics of race.

2

Rejection and Protest: An Historical Sketch

Report of the National Advisory Commission on Civil Disorders

Introduction

The events of the summer of 1967 are in large part the culmination of 300 years of racial prejudice. Most Americans know little of the origins of the racial schism separating our white and Negro citizens. Few appreciate how central the problem of the Negro has been to our social policy. Fewer still understand that today's problems can be solved only if white Americans comprehend the rigid social, economic, and educational barriers that have prevented Negroes from participating in the mainstream of American life. Only a handful realize that Negro accommodation to the patterns of prejudice in American culture has been but one side of the coin—for as slaves and as free men, Negroes have protested against oppression and have persistently sought equality in American society.

What follows is neither a history of the Negro in the United States nor a full account of Negro protest movements. Rather, it is a brief narrative of a few historical events that illustrate the facts of rejection and the forms of protest.

We call on history not to justify, but to help explain, for black and white Americans, a state of mind. . . .

Civil War and "Emancipation"

Negroes volunteered for military service during the Civil War, the struggle, as they saw it, between the slave states and the free states. They were rejected.

Not until a shortage of troops plagued the Union Army late in 1862 were segregated units of "United States Colored Troops" formed. Not until 1864 did these men receive the same pay as white soldiers. A total of 186,000 Negroes served.

The Emancipation Proclamation of 1863 freed few slaves at first, but had immediate significance as a symbol. Negroes could hope again for equality.

But there were, at the same time, bitter signs of racial unrest. Violent rioting occurred in Cincinnati in 1862, when Negro and Irish hands competed for work on the riverboats. Lesser riots took place in Newark, New Jersey, and in Buffalo and Troy, New York, the result of combined hostility to the war and fear that Negroes would take white jobs.

The most violent of the troubles took place in New York City Draft Riots in July 1863, when white workers, mainly Irish-born, embarked on a three-day rampage.

> Desperately poor and lacking real roots in the community, they had the most to lose from the draft. Further, they were bitterly afraid that even cheaper Negro labor would flood the North if slavery ceased to exist.
>
> All the frustrations and prejudices the Irish had suffered were brought to a boiling point. . . . At pitiful wages, they had slaved on the railroads and canals, had been herded into the most menial jobs as carters and stevedores. . . . Their crumbling frame tenements . . . were the worst slums in the city.

Their first target was the office of the provost-marshal in charge of conscription, and 700 people quickly ransacked the building and set it on fire. The crowd refused to permit firemen into the area, and the whole block was gutted. Then the mob spilled into the Negro area, where many were slain and thousands forced to flee town. The police were helpless until federal troops arrived on the third day and restored control.

Union victory in the Civil War promised the Negroes freedom but hardly equality or immunity from white aggression. Scarcely was the war ended when racial violence erupted in New Orleans. Negroes proceeding to an assembly hall to discuss the franchise were charged by police and special troops, who routed the Negroes with guns, bricks, and stones, killed some at once, pursued and killed others who were trying to escape.

Federal troops restored order. But 34 Negroes and four whites were reported dead and over 200 people were injured. General Sheridan later said:

> At least nine-tenths of the casualties were perpetrated by the police and citizens by stabbing and smashing in the heads of many who had already been wounded or killed by policemen . . . it was not just a riot but "an absolute massacre by the police . . ." a murder which the mayor and police . . . perpetrated without the shadow of necessity.

Reconstruction

Reconstruction was a time of hope, the period when the 13th, 14th, and 15th Amendments were adopted, giving Negroes the vote and the promise of equality.

But campaigns of violence and intimidation accompanied these optimistic expressions of a new age, as the Ku Klux Klan and other secret organizations sought to suppress the emergence into society of the new Negro citizens. Major riots occurred in Memphis, Tennessee, where 46 Negroes were reported killed and 75 wounded, and in the Louisiana centers of Colfax and Coushatta, where more than 100 Negro and white Republicans were massacred.

Nevertheless, reconstruction reached a legislative climax in 1875 with passage of the first Civil Rights law. Negroes now had the right to equal accommodations, facilities, and advantages of public transportation, inns, theaters, and places of public amusement, but the law had no effective enforcement provisions and was, in fact, poorly enforced. Although bills to provide federal aid to education for Negroes were prepared, none passed, and educational opportunities remained meager.

But Negroes were elected to every Southern legislature, 20 served in the U.S. House of Representatives, two represented Mississippi in the U.S. Senate, and a prominent Negro politician was Governor of Louisiana for 40 days.

Opposition to Negroes in state and local government was always open and bitter. In the press and on the platform they were described as ignorant and depraved. Critics made no distinction between Negroes who had graduated from Dartmouth and those who had graduated from the cotton fields. Every available means was employed to drive Negroes from public life. Negroes who voted or held office were refused jobs or punished by the Ku Klux Klan. One group in Mississippi boasted of having killed 116 Negroes and of having thrown their bodies into the Tallahatchie River. In a single South Carolina county, six men were murdered and more than 300 whipped during the first six months of 1870.

The federal government seemed helpless. Having withdrawn the occupation troops as soon as the Southern states organized governments, the President was reluctant to send them back. In 1870 and 1871, after the 15th Amendment was ratified, Congress enacted several laws to protect the right of citizens to vote. They were seldom enforced, and the Supreme Court struck down most of the important provisions in 1875 and 1876.

The End of Reconstruction

As Southern white governments returned to power, beginning with Virginia in 1869 and ending with Louisiana in 1877, the program of relegating the Negro to a subordinate place in American life was accelerated. Disenfranchisement was the first step. Negroes who defied the Klan and tried to vote faced an array of deceptions and obstacles—polling places were changed at the last minute without notice to Negroes, severe time limitations were imposed on marking complicated ballots, votes cast incorrectly in a maze of ballot boxes were nullified. The suffrage provisions of state constitutions were rewritten to disenfranchise Negroes who could not read, understand, or interpret the Constitution. Some state constitutions permitted those who failed the tests to vote if their ancestors had been eligible to vote on January 1, 1860, when no Negro could vote anywhere in the South.

In 1896, Negroes registered in Louisiana totaled 130,344. In 1900, after the state rewrote the suffrage provisions of its constitution, Negroes on the registration books numbered only 5,320. Essentially the same thing happened in the other states of the former Confederacy.

Segregation by Law

When the Supreme Court, in 1883, declared the Civil Rights Act of 1875 unconstitutional, Southern states began to enact laws to segregate the races. In 1896, the Supreme Court in *Plessy v. Ferguson* approved "separate but equal" facilities; it was then that segregation became an established fact, by law and by custom. Negroes and whites were separated on public carriers and in all places of public accommodation, including hospitals and churches. In courthouses, whites and Negroes took oaths on separate Bibles. In most communities, whites were separated from Negroes in cemeteries.

Segregation invariably meant discrimination. On trains all Negroes, including those holding first-class tickets, were allotted a few seats in the baggage car. Negroes in public buildings had to use freight elevators and toilet facilities reserved for janitors. Schools for Negro children were at best a weak imitation of those for whites, as states spent 10 times more to educate white youngsters than Negroes. Discrimination in wages became the rule, whether between Negro and white teachers of similar training and experience or between common laborers on the same job.

Some Northern states enacted civil rights laws in the 1880s, but Negroes in fact were treated little differently in the North than in the South. As Negroes moved north in substantial numbers toward the end of the century, they discovered that equality of treatment was only a dream in Massachusetts, New York, or Illinois. They were crowded by local ordinances into one section of the city where housing and public services were generally substandard. Overt discrimination in employment was a general practice. Employment opportunities apart from menial tasks were few. Most labor unions excluded Negroes from membership—or granted membership in separate and powerless Jim Crow locals. Yet when Negroes secured employment during strikes, labor leaders castigated them for not understanding the principles of trade unionism. And when Negroes sought to move into the mainstream of community life by seeking membership in the organizations around them—educational, cultural, and religious—they were invariably rebuffed.

That northern whites would resort to violence was made clear in anti-Negro riots in New York, 1900; Springfield, Ohio, 1904; Greensburg, Indiana, 1906; Springfield, Illinois, 1908.

The latter was a three-day riot, initiated by a white woman's claim of violation by a Negro, inflamed by newspapers, intensified by crowds of whites gathered around the jail demanding that the Negro, arrested and imprisoned, be lynched. When the sheriff transferred the accused and another Negro to a jail in a nearby town, rioters headed for the Negro section and attacked homes and businesses owned by or catering to Negroes. White owners who showed handkerchiefs in their windows averted harm to their stores. One Negro was summarily lynched, others were dragged from houses and streetcars and beaten. By the time National Guardsmen could reach the scene, six persons were dead—four whites and two Negroes; property damage was extensive. Many Negroes left Springfield, hoping to find better conditions elsewhere, especially in Chicago.

By the 20th century, the Negro was at the bottom of American society. Disenfranchised, Negroes throughout the country were excluded by employers and labor unions from white collar jobs and skilled trades. Jim Crow laws and farm tenancy characterized Negro existence in the South. About 100 lynchings occurred every year in the 1880s and 1890s; there were 161 lynchings in 1892. As increasing numbers of Negroes migrated to Northern cities, race riots became commonplace. Northern whites, even many former abolitionists, began to accept the white South's views on race relations.

Booker T. Washington

Between his famous Atlanta Exposition Address in 1895 and his death in 1915, Booker T. Washington, principal of the Tuskegee Normal and Industrial Institute in Alabama and the most prominent Negro in America, secretly spent thousands of dollars fighting disfranchisement and segregation laws; publicly he advocated a policy of accommodation, conciliation, and gradualism. Largely blaming Negroes themselves for their condition, Washington believed that by helping themselves, by creating and supporting their own businesses, by proving their usefulness to society through the acquisition of education, wealth, and morality, Negroes would earn the respect of the white man and thus eventually gain their constitutional rights.

Self-help and self-respect appeared a practical and sure, if gradual, way of ultimately achieving racial equality. Washington's doctrines also gained support because they appealed to race pride—if Negroes believed in themselves, stood together, and supported each other, they would be able to shape their destinies.

The Niagara Movement

In the early years of the century, a small group of Negroes, led by W.E.B. Du Bois, formed the Niagara Movement to oppose Washington's program, which they claimed had failed. Washington had put economic progress before politics, had accepted the separate-but-equal theory, and opposed agitation and protest. Du Bois and his followers stressed political activity as the basis of the Negro's future, insisted on the inequity of Jim Crow laws, and advocated agitation and protest.

In sharp language, the Niagara group placed responsibility for the race problem squarely on the whites. The aims of the movement were voting rights and "the abolition of all caste distinctions based simply on race and color."

Although Booker T. Washington tried to crush his critics, Du Bois and the Negro "radicals," as they were called, enlisted the support of a small group of influential white liberals and socialists. Together, in 1909–1910, they formed the National Association for the Advancement of Colored People.

The NAACP

The NAACP hammered at the walls of prejudice by organizing Negroes and well-disposed whites, by aiming propaganda at the whole nation, by taking legal action in courts and legislatures. Almost at the outset of its career, the NAACP prevailed upon the Supreme Court to declare unconstitutional two discriminatory statutes. In 1915, the Court overruled the Oklahoma "grandfather clause," a provision in several Southern state constitutions that excluded from the vote those whose ancestors were ineligible to vote in 1860. Two years later, the Supreme Court outlawed municipal residential segregation ordinances. These NAACP victories were the first legal steps in a long fight against disfranchisement and segregation.

The Federal Government

During the first quarter of the 20th century, the federal government enacted no new legislation to ensure equal rights or opportunities for Negroes and made little attempt to enforce existing laws despite flagrant violations of Negro civil rights.

In 1913, members of Congress from the South introduced bills to federalize the Southern segregation policy. They wished to ban interracial marriages in the District of Columbia, segregate white and Negro federal employees, and introduce Jim Crow laws in the public carriers of the District. The bills did not pass, but segregation practices were extended in federal offices, shops, restrooms, and lunchrooms. The nation's capital became as segregated as any in the former Confederate states.

East St. Louis, 1917

Elsewhere there was violence. In East St. Louis, Illinois, a riot in July 1917 claimed the lives of 39 Negroes and nine whites, as a result of fear by white working men that Negro advances in economic, political and social status were threatening their own security and status.

When the labor force of an aluminum plant went on strike, the company hired Negro workers. A labor union delegation called on the mayor and asked that further migration of Negroes to East St. Louis be stopped. As the men were leaving City Hall, they heard that a Negro had accidentally shot a white man during a holdup. In a few minutes rumor had replaced fact: the shooting was intentional—a white woman had been insulted—two white girls were shot. By this time 3,000 people had congregated and were crying for vengeance. Mobs roamed the streets, beating Negroes. Policemen did little more than take the injured to hospitals and disarm Negroes.

The National Guard restored order. When the governor withdrew the troops, tensions were still high, and scattered episodes broke the peace. The press continued to emphasize the incidence of Negro crimes, white pickets and Negro workers at the aluminum company skirmished and, on July 1, some whites drove through the main Negro neighborhood firing into homes. Negro residents armed themselves. When a police car drove down the street Negroes riddled it with gunshot.

The next day a Negro was shot on the main street and a new riot was underway. The authority on the event records that the area became a "bloody half mile" for three or four hours; streetcars were stopped, and Negroes, without regard to age or sex, were pulled off and stoned, clubbed and kicked, and mob leaders calmly shot and killed Negroes who were lying in blood in the street. As the victims were placed in an ambulance, the crowds cheered and applauded.

Other rioters set fire to Negro homes, and by midnight the Negro section was in flames and Negroes were fleeing the city. There were 48 dead, hundreds injured, and more than 300 buildings destroyed.

World War I

When the United States entered World War I in 1917, the country again faced the question whether American citizens should have the right to serve, on an equal basis, in defense of their country. More than two million Negroes registered under the Selective Service Act, and some 360,000 were called into service.

The Navy rejected Negroes except as menials. The Marine Corps rejected them altogether. The Army formed them into separate units commanded, for the most part, by white officers. Only after enormous pressure did the Army permit Negro candidates to train as officers in a segregated camp. Mistreated at home and overseas, Negro combat units performed exceptionally well under French commanders, who refused to heed American warnings that Negroes were inferior people.

Mobbed for attempting to use facilities open to white soldiers, Negro soldiers returning home suffered indignities. Of the 70 Negroes lynched during the first year after the war, a substantial number were soldiers. Some were lynched in uniform.

Postwar Violence

Reorganized in 1915, the Ku Klux Klan was flourishing again by 1919. Its program "for uniting native-born white Christians for concerted action in the preservation of American institutions and the supremacy of the white race" was implemented by flogging, branding with acid, tarring and feathering, hanging and burning. It destroyed the elemental rights of many Negroes, and of some whites.

Violence took the form of lynchings and riots, and major riots by whites against Negroes took place in 1917 in Chester, Pennsylvania, and Philadelphia; in 1919 in Washington, D.C., Omaha, Charleston, Longview, Texas, Chicago, and Knoxville; in 1921 in Tulsa.

The Chicago riot of 1919 flared from the increase in Negro population, which had more than doubled in 10 years. Jobs were plentiful, but housing was not. Black neighborhoods expanded into white sections of the city, and trouble developed. Between July 1917 and March 1921, 58 Negro houses were bombed, and recreational areas were sites of racial conflict.

The riot itself started on Sunday, July 27, with stone throwing and sporadic fighting at adjoining white and Negro beaches. A Negro boy swimming off the Negro beach drifted into water reserved for whites and drowned. Young Negroes claimed he had been struck by stones and demanded the arrest of a white man. Instead, police arrested a Negro. When Negroes attacked policemen, a riot was in the making. News spread to the city, white and Negro groups clashed in the streets, two persons died, and 50 were wounded. On Monday, Negroes coming home from work were attacked; later, when whites drove cars through Negro neighborhoods and fired weapons, Negroes retaliated. Twenty more were killed and hundreds wounded. On Tuesday, a handful more were dead, 129 injured. On Wednesday, losses in life and property declined further. Rain began to fall; the mayor finally called in the state militia. After nearly a week of violence, the city quieted down.

The 1920s and the New Militancy

In the period between the two World Wars, the NAACP dominated the strategy of racial advancement. The NAACP drew its strength from large numbers of

Southern Negroes who had migrated to Northern cities; from a small but growing Negro group of professionals and businessmen who served them; from an
upsurge of confidence among the "New Negro," race-proud and self-reliant,
believing in racial cooperation and self-help and determined to fight for his
constitutional rights; from writers and artists known as the "Harlem Renaissance" who used their own cultural tradition and experience as materials for their
works. W. E. B. Du Bois, editor of *The Crisis,* the NAACP publication, symbolized the new mood and exerted great influence.

The NAACP did extraordinary service, giving legal defense to victims of race
riots and unjust judicial proceedings. It obtained the release of the soldiers who
had received life sentences on charges of rioting against intolerable conditions at
Houston in 1917. It successfully defended Negro sharecroppers in Elaine, Arkansas, who in 1919 had banded together to gain fairer treatment, who had
become the objects of a massive armed hunt by whites to put them "in their
place," and who were charged with insurrection when they resisted. It secured
the acquittal, with the help of Clarence Darrow, of Dr. Ossian Sweet and his
family who had moved into a white neighborhood in Detroit, shot at a mob
attacking their home, killed a man, and were eventually judged to have committed the act in self-defense.

The NAACP tried vainly to promote passage of an anti-lynching bill, but its
most important activity was its campaign to secure enforcement of the 14th and
15th Amendments. It conducted sustained litigation against disfranchisement and
segregation, and embarked upon a long fight against the white primaries in the
Southern states. The NAACP attacked one aspect of discrimination at a time,
hacking away at the structure of discrimination. Local branches in Northern and
border cities won a number of important victories, but full recognition of the
Negroes' constitutional rights was still a future prospect.

Less successful were attempts to prevent school segregation in Northern cities, which followed the migration of large numbers of rural black folk from the
South. Gerrymandering of school boundaries and other devices by boards of
education were fought with written petitions, verbal protests to school officials,
legal suits and, in several cities, school boycotts. All proved of no avail.

The thrust of the NAACP was primarily political and legal, but the National
Urban League, founded in 1911 by philanthropists and social workers, sought an
economic solution to the Negroes' problems. Sympathetic with Booker T.
Washington's point of view, believing in conciliation, gradualism, and moral
suasion, the Urban League searched out industrial opportunities for Negro migrants to the cities, using arguments that appealed to the white businessman's
sense of economic self-interest and also to his conscience.

Also espousing an economic program to ameliorate the Negroes' condition
was A. Philip Randolph, an editor of the *Messenger.* He regarded the NAACP as
a middle-class organization unconcerned about pressing economic problems.
Taking a Marxist position on the causes of prejudice and discrimination, Ran-

dolph called for a new and radical Negro unafraid to demand his rights as a member of the working class. He advocated physical resistance to white mobs, but he believed that only united action of black and white workers against capitalists would achieve social justice.

Although Randolph addressed himself to the urban working masses, few of them ever read the *Messenger*. The one man who reached the masses of frustrated and disillusioned migrants in the Northern ghettos was Marcus Garvey.

Separatism

Garvey, founder in 1914 of the Universal Negro Improvement Association (UNIA), aimed to liberate both Africans and American Negroes from their oppressors. His utopian method was the wholesale migration of American Negroes to Africa. Contending that whites would always be racist, he stressed racial pride and history, denounced integration, and insisted that the black man develop "a distinct racial type of civilization of his own and . . . work out his salvation in his motherland." On a more practical level he urged support of Negro businesses, and through the UNIA organized a chain of groceries, restaurants, laundries, a hotel, printing plant, and steamship line. When several prominent Negroes called the attention of the United States Government to irregularities in the management of the steamship line, Garvey was jailed, then deported for having used the mails to defraud.

But Garvey dramatized, as no one before, the bitterness and alienation of the Negro slum dwellers who, having come North with great expectations, found only overcrowded and deteriorated housing, mass unemployment, and race riots.

The Depression

Negro labor, relatively unorganized and the target of discrimination and hostility, was hardly prepared for the depression of the 1930s. To a disproportionate extent, Negroes lost their jobs in cities and worked for starvation wages in rural areas. Although organizations like the National Urban League tried to improve employment opportunities, 65 percent of Negro employables were in need of public assistance by 1935.

Public assistance was given on a discriminatory basis, especially in the South. For a time Dallas and Houston gave no relief at all to Negro families. In general, Negroes had more difficulty than whites in obtaining assistance, and the relief benefits were smaller. Some religious and charitable organizations excluded Negroes from their soup kitchens.

The New Deal

The New Deal marked a turning point in American race relations. Negroes found much in the New Deal to complain about: discrimination existed in many agencies; federal housing programs expanded urban ghettos; money from the Agricultural Adjustment Administration went in the South chiefly to white landowners, while crop restrictions forced many Negro sharecroppers off the land. Nevertheless, Negroes shared in relief, jobs, and public housing, and Negro leaders, who felt the open sympathy of many highly placed New Dealers, held more prominent political positions than at any time since President Taft's administration. The creation of the Congress of Industrial Organizations (CIO), with its avowed philosophy of non-discrimination, made the notion of an alliance of black and white workers something more than a visionary's dream.

The depression, the New Deal, and the CIO reoriented Negro protest to concern with economic problems. Negroes conducted "Don't Buy Where You Can't Work" campaigns in a number of cities, boycotted and picketed commercial establishments owned by whites, and sought equality in American society through an alliance with white labor.

The NAACP came under attack from Negroes. Du Bois resigned as editor of *The Crisis* in 1934 because, believing in the value of collective racial economic endeavor, he saw little point in protesting disfranchisement and segregation without pursuing economic goals. Younger critics also disagreed with NAACP's gradualism on economic issues.

Undeterred, the NAACP broadened the scope of its legal work, fought a vigorous though unsuccessful campaign to abolish the poll tax, and finally won its attack on the white primaries in 1944 through the Supreme Court. But the heart of its litigation was a long-range campaign against segregation and the most obvious inequities in the Southern school systems: the lack of professional and graduate schools and the low salaries received by Negro teachers. Not until about 1950 would the NAACP make a direct assault against school segregation on the legal ground that separate facilities were inherently unequal.

World War II

During World War II, Negroes learned again that fighting for their country brought them no nearer to full citizenship. Rejected when they tried to enlist, they were accepted into the Army according to the proportion of the Negro population to that of the country as a whole—but only in separate units—and those mostly noncombat. The United States thus fought racism in Europe with a segregated fighting force. In some instances at home, Negro soldiers were unable to secure food, even though German prisoners of war were being served. The Red Cross, with the government's approval, separated Negro and white blood in banks established for wounded servicemen—even though the blood banks were largely the work of a Negro physician, Charles Drew.

Not until 1949 would the Armed Forces begin to adopt a firm policy against segregation.

Negroes seeking employment in defense industries were embittered by policies like that of a West Coast aviation factory which declared openly that "the Negro will be considered only as janitors and in other similar capacities. . . . Regardless of their training as aircraft workers, we will not employ them."

Two new movements marked Negro protest: the March on Washington, and the Congress of Racial Equality (CORE). In 1941, consciously drawing on the power of the Negro vote and concerned with the economic problems of the urban slum-dweller, A. Philip Randolph threatened a mass Negro convergence on Washington unless President Roosevelt secured employment for Negroes in the defense industries. The President's Executive Order 8802 establishing a federal Fair Employment Practices Commission forestalled the demonstration. Even without enforcement powers, the FEPC set a precedent for treating fair employment practice as a civil right.

CORE, founded in 1942–43, grew out of the Fellowship of Reconciliation, a pacifist organization, when certain leaders became interested in the use of nonviolent direct action to fight racial discrimination. CORE combined Gandhi's techniques with the sit-in, derived from the sit-down strikes of the 1930s. Until about 1959, CORE's main activity was attacking discrimination in places of public accommodation in the cities of the Northern and Border states, and as late as 1961, two-thirds of its membership and most of its national officers were white. . . .

The Postwar Period

White opinion in some quarters of America had begun to shift to a more sympathetic regard for Negroes during the New Deal, and the war had accelerated that movement. Thoughtful whites had been painfully aware of the contradiction in opposing Nazi racial philosophy with racially segregated military units. In the postwar years, American racial attitudes became more liberal as new nonwhite nations emerged in Asia and Africa and took increasing responsibilities in international councils.

Against this background, the growing size of the Northern Negro vote made civil rights a major issue in national elections and, ultimately, in 1957, led to the federal Civil Rights Commission, which had the power to investigate discriminatory conditions throughout the country and to recommend corrective measures to the President. Northern and Western states outlawed discrimination in employment, housing, and public accommodations, while the NAACP, in successive court victories, ended racially restrictive covenants in housing, segregation in interstate transportation, and discrimination in publicly-owned recreational facilities. The NAACP helped register voters, and in 1954, *Brown v. Board of Education* became the triumphant climax to the NAACP's campaign against educational segregation in the public schools of the South.

CORE, demonstrating in the Border States, its major focus on public accommodations, began experimenting with direct-action techniques to open employment opportunities. In 1947, in conjunction with the Fellowship of Reconciliation, CORE conducted a "Journey of Reconciliation"—what would later be called a "Freedom Ride"—in the states of the Upper South to test compliance with the Supreme Court decision outlawing segregation on interstate buses. The resistance met by riders in some areas, the sentencing of two to 30 days on a North Carolina road gang, dramatized the gap between American democratic theory and practice.

But what captured the imagination of the nation and of the Negro community in particular, and what was chiefly responsible for the growing use of direct-action techniques, was the Montgomery, Alabama, bus boycott of 1955–1956, which catapulted into national prominence the Reverend Martin Luther King, Jr. Like the founders of CORE, King held to a Gandhian belief in the principles of pacifism.

Even before a court decision obtained by NAACP attorneys in November 1956 desegregated the Montgomery buses, a similar movement had started in Tallahassee, Florida. Afterward another one developed in Birmingham, Alabama. In 1957, the Tuskegee Negroes undertook a three-year boycott of local merchants after the state legislature gerrymandered nearly all of the Negro voters outside of the town's boundaries. In response to a lawsuit filed by the NAACP, the Supreme Court ruled the Tuskegee gerrymander illegal.

These events were widely heralded. A "new Negro" had emerged in the South—militant, no longer fearful of white hoodlums or mobs, and ready to use his collective weight to achieve his ends. In this mood, King established the Southern Christian Leadership Conference in 1957 to coordinate direct-action activities in Southern cities.

Negro protest had now moved in a vigorous fashion into the South, and like similar activities in the North, it was concentrated in the urban ghettos.

The Persistence of Discrimination

Nonviolent direct action attained popularity not only because of the effectiveness of King's leadership but because the older techniques of legal and legislative action had had limited success. Impressive as the advances in the 15 years after World War II were, in spite of state laws and Supreme Court decisions, something was still clearly wrong. Negroes were disfranchised in most of the South, though in the 12 years following the outlawing of the white primary in 1944, the number of Negroes registered in Southern states had risen from about 250,000 to nearly a million and a quarter. Supreme Court decisions desegregating transportation facilities were still being largely ignored in the South. Discrimination in employment and housing continued, not only in the South but also in Northern states with model civil rights laws. The Negro unemployment rate steadily moved upward after 1954. The South reacted to the Supreme Court's decision on school desegregation by outlawing the NAACP, intimidating civil rights leaders, bringing "massive resistance" to the Court's decision, curtailing Negro voter registration, and forming White Citizens' Councils. . . .

Student Involvement

The Negro protest movement would never be the same again. The Southern college students shook the power structure of the Negro community, made direct action temporarily pre-eminent as a civil rights tactic, speeded up the process of social change in race relations, and ultimately turned the Negro protest organizations toward a deep concern with the economic and social problems of the masses.

Involved in this was a gradual shift in both tactics and goals: from legal to direct action, from middle and upper class to mass action, from attempts to guarantee the Negro's constitutional rights to efforts to secure economic policies giving him equality of opportunity in a changing society, from appeals to the sense of fair play of white Americans to demands based upon power in the black ghetto.

The successes of the student movement threatened existing Negro leadership and precipitated a spirited rivalry among civil rights organizations. The NAACP and SCLC associated themselves with the student movement. The organizing meeting of the Student Nonviolent Coordinating Committee (SNCC) at Raleigh, North Carolina, in April 1960 was called by Martin Luther King, but within a year the youth considered King too cautious and broke with him.

The NAACP now decided to make direct action a major part of its strategy and organized and reactivated college and youth chapters in the Southern and Border states.

CORE, still unknown to the general public, installed James Farmer as national director in January 1961, and that spring joined the front rank of civil rights organizations with the famous Freedom Ride to Alabama and Mississippi that dramatized the persistence of segregated public transportation. A bus-burning resulted in Alabama, and hundreds of demonstrators spent a month or more in Mississippi prisons. Finally, a new order from the Interstate Commerce Commission desegregating all interstate transportation facilities received partial compliance. . . .

"Freedom Now!"

As the direct-action tactics took more dramatic form, as the civil rights groups began to articulate the needs of the masses and draw some of them to their demonstrations, the protest movement in 1963 assumed a new note of urgency, a demand for complete "Freedom Now!" Direct action returned to the Northern cities, taking the form of massive protests against economic, housing and educational inequities, and a fresh wave of demonstrations swept the South from

Cambridge, Maryland, to Birmingham, Alabama. Northern Negroes launched street demonstrations against discrimination in the building trade unions and, the following winter, school boycotts against de facto segregation.

In the North, 1963 and 1964 brought the beginning of the waves of civil disorders in Northern urban centers. In the South, incidents occurred of brutal white resistance to the civil rights movement, beginning with the murder of Mississippi Negro leader Medgar Evers and four Negro schoolgirls in a church in Birmingham. . . .

The March on Washington

The massive anti-Negro actions in Birmingham and numerous other Southern cities during the spring of 1963, compelled the nation to face the problem of race prejudice in the South. President Kennedy affirmed that racial discrimination was a moral issue and asked Congress for a major civil rights bill. But a major impetus for what was to be the Civil Rights Act of 1964 was the March on Washington in August 1963.

Early in the year, A. Philip Randolph issued a call for a March on Washington to dramatize the need for jobs and to press for a federal commitment to job action. At about the same time, Protestant, Jewish, and Catholic churches sought and obtained representation on the March committee. Although the AFL-CIO national council refused to endorse the March, a number of labor leaders and international unions participated.

Reversing an earlier stand, President Kennedy approved the March. A quarter of a million people, about 20 percent of them white, participated. It was more than a summation of the past years of struggle and aspiration. It symbolized certain new directions: a deeper concern for the economic problems of the masses; more involvement of white moderates; and new demands from the most militant, who implied that only a revolutionary change in American institutions would permit Negroes to achieve the dignity of citizens.

President Kennedy had set the stage for the Civil Rights Act of 1964. After his death President Johnson took forceful and effective action to secure its enactment. The law settled the public accommodations issue in the South's major cities. Its voting section, however, promised more than it could accomplish. Martin Luther King and SCLC dramatized the issue locally with demonstrations at Selma, Alabama, in the spring of 1965. Again the national government was forced to intervene, and a new and more effective voting law was passed.

Failures of Direct Action

Birmingham had made direct action respectable, but Selma, which drew thousands of white moderates from the North, made direct action fashionable. Yet as early as 1964, it was becoming evident that, like legal action, direct action was an instrument of limited usefulness. This was the result of two converging developments.

In deep South states like Mississippi and Alabama, direct action had failed to desegregate public accommodations in the sit-ins of 1960–1961. A major reason was that Negroes lacked the leverage of the vote. The demonstrations of the early 1960s had been successful principally in places like Atlanta, Nashville, Durham, Winston-Salem, Louisville, Savannah, New Orleans, Charleston, and Dallas—where Negroes voted and could swing elections. Beginning in 1961 Robert Moses of SNCC, with the cooperation of CORE and NAACP, established voter registration projects in the cities and county seats of Mississippi. He succeeded in registering only a handful of Negroes, but by 1964, he had generated enough support throughout the country to enable the Mississippi Freedom Democratic Party, which he had created, to challenge dramatically the seating of the official white delegates from the state at the Democratic National Convention.

In the black ghettos of the North direct action also largely failed. Street demonstrations did compel employers, from supermarkets to banks, to add many Negroes to their work force in Northern and Western cities, in some Southern cities, and even in some Southern towns where the Negroes had considerable buying power. However, separate and inferior schools, slum housing, and police hostility proved invulnerable to direct attack. . . .

"Black Power"

In this setting the rhetoric of "Black Power" developed. The precipitating occasion was the Meredith March from Memphis to Jackson in June 1966, but the slogan expressed tendencies that had been present for a long time and had been gaining strength in the Negro community.

Black Power first articulated a mood rather than a program—disillusionment and alienation from white America and independence, race pride, and self-respect, or "black consciousness." Having become a household phrase, the term generated intense discussion of its real meaning, and a broad spectrum of ideologies and programmatic proposals emerged.

In politics, Black Power meant independent action—Negro control of the political power of the black ghettos and its conscious use to better slum dwellers' conditions. It could take the form of organizing a black political party or controlling the political machinery within the ghetto without the guidance or support of white politicians. Where predominantly Negro areas lacked Negroes in elective office, whether in the rural Black Belt of the South or in the urban centers, Black Power advocates sought the election of Negroes by voter registration campaigns, by getting out the vote, and by working for redrawing electoral districts. The basic belief was that only a well-organized and cohesive bloc of Negro voters could provide for the needs of the black masses. Even some Negro politicians allied to the major political parties adopted the term "Black Power" to describe their interest in the Negro vote.

In economic terms, Black Power meant creating independent, self-sufficient Negro business enterprise, not only by encouraging Negro entrepreneurs but also by forming Negro cooperatives in the ghettos and in the predominantly black rural counties of the South. In the area of education, Black Power called for local community control of the public schools in the black ghettos.

Throughout, the emphasis was on self-help, racial unity, and, among the most militant, retaliatory violence, the latter ranging from the legal right of self-defense to attempts to justify looting and arson in ghetto riots, guerrilla warfare, and armed rebellion.

Phrases like "Black Power," "Black Consciousness," and "Black Is Beautiful" enjoyed an extensive currency in the Negro community, even within the NAACP and among relatively conservative politicians, but particularly among young intellectuals and Afro-American student groups on predominantly white college campuses. Expressed in its most extreme form by small, often local, fringe groups, the Black Power ideology became associated with SNCC and CORE.

Generally regarded as the most militant among the important Negro protest organizations, they have different interpretations of the Black Power doctrine. SNCC calls for totally independent political action outside the established political parties, as with the Black Panther Party in Lowndes County, Alabama; questions the value of political alliances with other groups until Negroes have themselves built a substantial base of independent political power; applauds the idea of guerrilla warfare; and regards riots as rebellions.

CORE has been more flexible. Approving the SNCC strategy, it also advocates working within the Democratic Party; forming alliances with other groups and, while seeking to justify riots as the natural explosion of an oppressed people against intolerable conditions, advocates violence only in self-defense. Both groups favor cooperatives, but CORE has seemed more inclined toward job-training programs and developing a Negro entrepreneurial class, based upon the market within the black ghettos.

Old Wine in New Bottles

What is new about "Black Power" is phraseology rather than substance. Black consciousness has roots in the organization of Negro churches and mutual benefit societies in the early days of the republic, the antebellum Negro convention movement, the Negro colonization schemes of the 19th century, Du Bois' concept of Pan-Africanism, Booker T. Washington's advocacy of race pride, self-help, and racial solidarity, the Harlem Renaissance, and the Garvey movement. The decade after World War I—which saw the militant, race-proud "new Negro," the relatively widespread theory of retaliatory violence, and the high tide of the Negro-support-of-Negro-business ideology—exhibits striking parallels with the 1960s.

Similarly, there are striking parallels between both of these periods and the late 1840s and 1850s when ideologies of self-help, racial solidarity, separatism and nationalism, and the advocacy of organized rebellion were widespread.

The theme of retaliatory violence is hardly new for American Negroes. Most racial disorders in American history until recent years were characterized by white attacks on Negroes. But Negroes retaliated violently during Reconstruction, just after World War I, and in the last four years.

Black Power rhetoric and ideology actually express a lack of power. The slogan emerged when the Negro protest movement was slowing down, when it was finding increasing resistance to its changing goals, when it discovered that nonviolent direct action was no more a panacea than legal action, when CORE and SNCC were declining in terms of activity, membership, and financial support. This combination of circumstances provoked anger deepened by impotence. Powerless to make any fundamental changes in the life of the masses—powerless, that is, to compel white America to make those changes—many advocates of Black Power have retreated into an unreal world, where they see an outnumbered and poverty-stricken minority organizing itself independently of whites and creating sufficient power to force white America to grant its demands. To date, the evidence suggests that the situation is much like that of the 1840s, when a small group of intellectuals advocated slave insurrections, but stopped short of organizing them.

The Black Power advocates of today consciously feel that they are the most militant group in the Negro protest movement. Yet they have retreated from a direct confrontation with American society on the issue of integration and, by preaching separatism, unconsciously function as an accommodation to white racism. Much of their economic program, as well as their interest in Negro history, self-help, racial solidarity and separation, is reminiscent of Booker T. Washington. The rhetoric is different, but the programs are remarkably similar.

The Meaning

By 1967, whites could point to the demise of slavery, the decline of illiteracy among Negroes, the legal protection provided by the constitutional amendments and civil rights legislation, and the growing size of the Negro middle class. Whites would call it Negro progress from slavery to freedom toward equality.

Negroes could point to the doctrine of white supremacy, its widespread acceptance, its persistence after emancipation, and its influence on the definition of the place of Negroes in American life. They could point to their long fight for full citizenship, when they had active opposition from most of the white population and little or no support from the government. They could see progress toward equality accompanied by bitter resistance. Perhaps most of all, they could feel the persistent, pervasive racism that kept them in inferior segregated schools, restricted them to ghettos, barred them from fair employment, provided double standards in courts of justice, inflicted bodily harm on their children, and blighted their lives with a sense of hopelessness and despair.

In all of this and in the context of professed ideals, Negroes would find more retrogression than progress, more rejection than acceptance.

Until the middle of the 20th century, the course of Negro protest movements in the United States except for slave revolts, was based in the cities of the North, where Negroes enjoyed sufficient freedom to mount a sustained protest. It was in the cities, North and South, that Negroes had their greatest independence and mobility. It was natural, therefore, for black protest movements to be urban-based—and, until the last dozen years or so, limited to the North. As Negroes migrated from the South, the mounting strength of their votes in Northern cities became a vital element in drawing the federal government into the defense of the civil rights of Southern Negroes. White rural Negroes today face great racial problems, the major unsolved questions that touch the core of Negro life stem from discrimination embedded in urban housing, employment, and education.

Over the years the character of Negro protest has changed. Originally it was a white liberal and Negro upper class movement aimed at securing the constitutional rights of Negroes through propaganda, lawsuits, and legislation. In recent years the emphasis in tactics shifted first to direct action and then—among the most militant—to the rhetoric of "Black Power." The role of white liberals declined as Negroes came to direct the struggle. At the same time the Negro protest movement became more of a mass movement, with increasing participation from the working classes. As these changes were occurring, and while substantial progress was being made to secure constitutional rights for the Negroes, the goals of the movement were broadened. Protest groups now demand special efforts to overcome the Negro's poverty and cultural deprivation—conditions that cannot be erased simply by ensuring constitutional rights.

The central thrust of Negro protest in the current period has aimed at the inclusion of Negroes in American society on a basis of full equality rather than at a fundamental transformation of American institutions. There have been elements calling for a revolutionary overthrow of the American social system or for a complete withdrawal of Negroes from American society. But these solutions have had little popular support. Negro protest, for the most part, has been firmly rooted in the basic values of American society, seeking not their destruction but their fulfillment.

3

Race and the Crisis of the American Spirit

Bill Clinton

The proverb says, "A happy heart doeth good like medicine, but a broken spirit dryeth the bone." This is a happy place, and I'm happy to be here. I thank you for your spirit.

By the grace of God and your help, last year I was elected President of this great country. I never dreamed that I would ever have a chance to come to this hallowed place where Martin Luther King gave his last sermon. I ask you to think today about the purpose for which I ran and the purpose for which so many of you worked to put me in this great office. I have worked hard to keep faith with our common efforts: to restore the economy; to reverse the politics of helping only those at the top of our totem pole and not the hard-working middle class or the poor; to bring our people together across racial and regional and political lines; to make a strength out of our diversity instead of letting it tear us apart; to reward work and family and community and try to move us forward into the 21st century. I have tried to keep faith.

Thirteen percent of all my Presidential appointments are African-Americans, and there are five African-Americans in the Cabinet of the United States, 2½ times as many as have ever served in the history of this great land. I have sought to advance the right to vote with the motor voter bill, supported so strongly by all the churches in our country. And next week it will be my great honor to sign the Restoration of Religious Freedoms Act, a bill supported widely by people across all religions and political philosophies to put back the real meaning of the Constitution, to give you and every other American the freedom to do what is most important in your life, to worship God as your spirit leads you.

I say to you, my fellow Americans, we have made a good beginning. Inflation is down. Interest rates are down. The deficit is down. Investment is up. Millions of Americans, including, I bet, some people in this room, have refinanced their homes or their business loans just in the last year. And in the last 10 months, this economy has produced more jobs in the private sector than in the previous 4 years.

We have passed a law called the family leave law, which says you can't be fired if you take a little time off when a baby is born or a parent is sick. We know that most Americans have to work, but you ought not to have to give up being a good parent just to take a job. If you can't succeed as a worker and a parent, this country can't make it.

We have radically reformed the college loan program, as I promised, to lower the cost of college loans and broaden the availability of it and make the repayment terms easier. And we have passed the national service law that will give in 3 years, 3 years from now, 100,000 young Americans a chance to serve their communities at home, to repair the frayed bonds of community, to build up the needs of people at the grassroots, and at the same time, earn some money to pay for a college education. It is a wonderful idea.

On April 15th, when people pay their taxes, somewhere between 15 million and 18 million working families on modest incomes, families with children and incomes of under $23,000, will get a tax cut, not a tax increase, in the most important effort to ensure that we reward work and family in the last 20 years. Fifty million American parents and their children will be advantaged by putting the Tax Code back on the side of working American parents for a change.

Under the leadership of the First Lady, we have produced a comprehensive plan to guarantee health care security to all Americans. How can we expect the American people to work and to live with all the changes in the global economy, where the average 18-year-old will change work seven times in a lifetime, unless we can simply say we have joined the ranks of all the other advanced countries in the world; you can have decent health care that's always there, that can never be taken away? It is time we did that, long past time. I ask you to help us achieve that.

But we have so much more to do. You and I know that most people are still working harder for the same or lower wages, that many people are afraid that their job will go away. We have to provide the education and training our people need, not just for our children but for our adults, too. If we cannot close this country up to the forces of change sweeping throughout the world, we have to at least guarantee people the security of being employable. They have to be able to get a new job if they're going to have to get a new job. We don't do that today, and we must, and we intend to proceed until that is done.

We have a guarantee that there will be some investment in those areas of our country, in the inner cities and in the destitute rural areas in the Mississippi Delta, of my home State and this State and Louisiana and Mississippi and other places like it throughout America. It's all very well to train people, but if they don't have a job, they can be trained for nothing. We must get investment to those places where the people are dying for work.

And finally, let me say, we must find people who will buy what we have to produce. We are the most productive people on Earth. That makes us proud. But what that means is that every year one person can produce more in the same amount of time. Now, if fewer and fewer people can produce more and more things, and yet you want to create more jobs and raise people's incomes, you have to have more customers for what it is you're making. And that is why I have worked so hard to sell more American products around the world, why I have asked that we be able to sell billions of dollars of computers we used, not to sell to foreign countries and foreign interests, to put our people to work.

Why? Next week I am going all the way to Washington State to meet with the President of China and the Prime Minister of Japan and the heads of 13 other Asian countries, the fastest growing part of the world, to say, "We want to be your partners. We will buy your goods, but we want you to buy ours, too, if you please." That is why.

That is why I have worked so hard for this North American trade agreement because we know that Americans can compete and win only if people will buy what it is we have to sell. There are 90 million people in Mexico. Seventy cents of every dollar they spend on foreign goods, they spend on American goods. People worry fairly about people shutting down plants in America and going not just to Mexico but to any place where the labor is cheap. It has happened.

What I want to say to you, my fellow Americans, is nothing in this agreement makes that more likely. That has happened already. It may happen again. What we need to do is keep the jobs here by finding customers there. That's what this agreement does. It gives us a chance to create opportunity for people. I have friends in this audience, people who are ministers from my State, fathers and sons, people—I've looked out all over this vast crowd and I see people I've known for years. They know. I spent my whole life working to create jobs. I would never knowingly do anything that would take a job away from the American people. This agreement will make more jobs. Now, we can also leave it if it doesn't work in 6 months. But if we don't take it, we'll lose it forever. We need to take it, because we have to do better.

But I guess what I really want to say to you today, my fellow Americans, is that we can do all of this and still fail unless we meet the great crisis of the spirit that is gripping America today.

When I leave you, Congressman Ford and I are going to a Baptist church near here to a town meeting he's having on health care and violence. I tell you, unless we do something about crime and violence and drugs that is ravaging the community, we will not be able to repair this country.

If Martin Luther King, who said, "Like Moses, I am on the mountaintop, and I can see the promised land, but I'm not going to be able to get there with you, but we will get there." If he were to reappear by my side today and give us a report card on the last 25 years, what would he say? You did a good job, he would say, voting and electing people who formerly were not electable because of the color of their skin. You have more political power, and that is good. You did a good job, he would say, letting people who have the ability to do so live wherever they want to live, go wherever they want to go in this great country. You did a good job, he would say, elevating people of color into the ranks of the United States Armed Forces to the very top or into the very top of our Government. You did a very good job, he would say. He would say, you did a good job creating a black middle class of people who really are doing well, and the middle class is growing more among African-Americans than among non-African-Americans. You did a good job. You did a good job in opening opportunity.

But he would say, I did not live and die to see the American family destroyed. I did not live and die to see 13-year-old boys get automatic weapons and gun down 9-year-olds just for the kick of it. I did not live and die to see young people destroy their own lives with drugs and then build fortunes destroying the lives of others. That is not what I came here to do. I fought for freedom, he would say, but not for the freedom of people to kill each other with reckless abandon, not for the freedom of children to have children and the fathers of the children walk away from them and abandon them as if they don't amount to anything. I fought for people to have the right to work but not to have whole communities and people abandoned. This is not what I lived and died for.

My fellow Americans, he would say, I fought to stop white people from being so filled with hate that they would wreak violence on black people. I did not fight for the right of black people to murder other black people with reckless abandon.

The other day the Mayor of Baltimore, a dear friend of mine, told me a story of visiting the family of a young man who had been killed—18 years old—on Halloween. He always went out with little bitty kids so they could trick-or-treat safely. And across the street from where they were walking on Halloween, a 14-year-old boy gave a 13-year-old boy a gun and dared him to shoot the 18-year-old boy, and he shot him dead. And the Mayor had to visit the family.

In Washington, DC, where I live, your Nation's Capital, the symbol of free-dom throughout the world, look how that freedom is being exercised. The other night a man came along the street and grabbed a 1-year-old child and put the child in his car. The child may have been the child of the man. And two people were after him, and they chased him in the car, and they just kept shooting with reckless abandon, knowing that baby was in the car. And they shot the man dead, and a bullet went through his body into the baby's body, and blew the little bootie off the child's foot.

The other day on the front page of our paper, the Nation's Capital, are we talking about world peace or world conflict? No, big article on the front page of the *Washington Post* about an 11-year-old child planning her funeral: "These are the hymns I want sung. This is the dress I want to wear. I know I'm not going to live very long." The freedom to die before you're a teenager is not what Martin Luther King lived and died for.

More than 37,000 people die from gunshot wounds in this country every year. Gunfire is the leading cause of death in young men. And now that we've all gotten so cool that everybody can get a semiautomatic weapon, a person shot now is 3 times more likely to die than 15 years ago, because they're likely to have three bullets in them. One hundred and sixty thousand children stay home from school every day because they are scared they will be hurt in their school.

The other day I was in California at a town meeting, and a handsome young man stood up and said, "Mr. President, my brother and I, we don't belong to gangs. We don't have guns. We don't do drugs. We want to go to school. We want to be professionals. We want to work hard. We want to do well. We want to have families. And we changed our school because the school we were in was so dangerous. So when we stowed up to the new school to register, my brother and I were standing in line and somebody ran into the school and started shooting a gun. My brother was shot down standing right in front of me at the safer school." The freedom to do that kind of thing is not what Martin Luther King lived and died for. It's not what people gathered in this hallowed church for the night before he was assassinated in April of 1968. If you had told anybody who was here in that church on that night that we would abuse our freedom in that way, they would have found it hard to believe. And I tell you it is our moral duty to turn it around.

And now I think finally we have a chance. Finally I think, we have a chance. We have a pastor here from New Haven, Connecticut. I was in his church with Reverend Jackson when I was running for President on a snowy day in Connecticut to mourn the death of children who had been killed in that city. And afterward we walked down the street for more than a mile in the snow. Then, the American people were not ready. People would say, "Oh, this is a terrible thing, but what can we do about it."

Now when we read that foreign visitors come to our shores and are killed at random in our fine State of Florida, when we see our children planning their funeral, when the American people are finally coming to grips with the accumulated wave of crime and violence and the breakdown of family and community and the increase in drugs and the decrease in jobs, I think finally we may be ready to do something about it. And there is something for each of us to do. There are changes we can make from the outside in, that's the job of the President and the Congress and the Governors and the Mayors and the social service agencies. Then there's some changes we're going to have to make from the inside out, or the others won't matter. That's what that magnificent song was about, wasn't it? Sometimes there are no answers from the outside in; sometimes all the answers have to come from the values and the stirrings and the voices that speak to us from within.

So we are beginning. We are trying to pass a bill to make our people safer, to put another 100,000 police officers on the street, to provide boot camps instead of prisons for young people who can still be rescued, to provide more safety in our schools, to restrict the availability of these awful assault weapons, to pass the Brady bill and at least require people to have their criminal background checked before they get a gun, and to say, if you're not old enough to vote and you're not old enough to go to war, you ought not to own a handgun, and you ought not to use one unless you're on a target range.

We want to pass a health care bill that will make drug treatment available for everyone. We have to have drug treatment and education available to everyone and especially those who are in prison who are coming out. We have a drug czar now in Lee Brown, who was the police chief of Atlanta, of Houston, of New York, who understands these things. And when the Congress comes back next year we will be moving forward on that.

We need this crime bill now. We ought to give it to the American people for Christmas. And we need to move forward on all these other fronts. But I say to you, my fellow Americans, we need some other things as well. I do not believe we can repair the basic fabric of society until people who are willing to work have work. Work organizes life. It gives structure and discipline to life. It gives meaning and self-esteem to people who are parents. It gives a role model to children.

The famous African-American sociologist William Julius Wilson has written a stunning book called *The Truly Disadvantaged,* in which he chronicles in breathtaking terms how the inner cities of our country have crumbled as work has disappeared. And we must find a way, through public and private sources, to enhance the attractiveness of the American people who live there to get investment there. We cannot, I submit to you, repair the American community and restore the American family until we provide the structure, the value, the discipline, and the reward that work gives.

I read a wonderful speech the other day given at Howard University in a lecture series funded by Bill and Camille Cosby, in which the speaker said, "I grew up in Anacostia years ago. Even then it was all black, and it was a very poor neighborhood. But you know, when I was a child in Anacostia, 100 percent African-American neighborhood, a very poor neighborhood, we had a crime rate that was lower than the average of the crime rate of our city. Why? Because we had coherent families. We had coherent communities. The people who filled the church on Sunday lived in the same place they went to church. The guy that owned the drugstore lived down the street. The person that owned the grocery store lived in our community. We were whole." And I say to you, we have to make our people whole again. This church has stood for that. Why do you think you have 5 million members in this country? Because people know you are filled with the spirit of God to do the right thing in this life by them.

So I say to you, we have to make a partnership, all the Government Agencies, all the business folks, but where there are no families, where there is no order, where there is no hope, where we are reducing the size of our armed services because we have won the cold war, who will be there to give structure, discipline, and love to these children? You must do that. And we must help you.

Scripture says, you are the salt of the Earth and the light of the world. That if your light shines before men they will give glory to the Father in heaven. That is what we must do. That is what we must do. How would we explain it to Martin Luther King if he showed up today and said, yes, we won the cold war. Yes, the biggest threat that all of us grew up under, communism and nuclear war, communism gone, nuclear war receding. Yes, we developed all these miraculous technologies. Yes, we all have got a VCR in our home. It's interesting. Yes, we get 50 channels on the cable. Yes, without regard to race, if you work hard and play by the rules, you can get into a service academy or a good college, you'll do just great. How would we explain to him all these kids getting killed and killing each other? How would we justify the things that we permit that no other country in the world would permit? How could we explain that we gave people the freedom to succeed, and we created conditions in which millions abuse that freedom to destroy the things that make life worth living and life itself? We cannot.

And so I say to you today, my fellow Americans, you gave me this job, and we're making progress on the things you hired me to do. But unless we deal with the ravages of crime and drugs and violence and unless we recognize that it's due to the breakdown of the family, the community, and the disappearance of jobs, and unless we say some of this cannot be done by Government, because we have to reach deep inside to the values, the spirit, the soul, and the truth of human nature, none of the other things we seek to do will ever take us where we need to go.

So in this pulpit, on this day, let me ask all of you in your heart to say we will honor the life and the work of Martin Luther King, we will honor the meaning of our church, we will somehow by God's grace, we will turn this around. We will give these children a future. We will take away their guns and give them books. We will take away their despair and give them hope. We will rebuild the families and the neighborhoods and the communities. We won't make all the work that has gone on here benefit just a few. We will do it together by the grace of God.

Part II

Cultural Politics and
Political Ideology

Many scholars and activists have argued that race is a critical element in the formation of political ideology.

The first reading, "Postmodern Racial Politics in the United States: Difference and Inequality," by Howard Winant, a sociologist at Temple University, was originally published in *Socialist Review,* a radical journal. Winant asserts that "the contemporary United States faces a pervasive crisis of race" and that American citizens are more conflicted over race than over "any other social or political issue." The American " 'race problem' " has generated "ferocious antagonisms" between slaves and masters, natives and settlers, new immigrants and established residents, low-wage workers and higher-wage workers.

Winant analyzes the racial discourse of four groups: the Far Right, the New Right, neoconservatives, and radical democrats. For each group, race is linked to a comprehensive political and cultural agenda.

The first group, the Far Right, is opposed to affirmative action and immigration. Some members of the Far Right openly advocate white supremacy. This perspective, represented by David Duke of Louisiana, a former candidate for the Republican presidential nomination, maintains that whites are victims of racial inequality.

Winant then analyzes the racial rhetoric of the New Right. This group, epitomized by Pat Buchanan, a candidate for the Republican presidential nomination in 1992 and 1996, asserts that minority rights are a threat to "traditional American values." The New Right uses such racial code words as busing, quotas, welfare, and "English only."

Winant also examines the racial views of the neoconservative movement. Neoconservatives believe in universalism, democracy, egalitarianism, individualism, and assimilation. They fear that the continuing efforts of minorities to stress racial differences threaten these values.

Finally, Winant discusses his own perspective, radical democracy. He states that "radical democratic discourse acknowledges the permanence of racial difference in U.S. society," and that "racial themes have marked and molded U.S. economic life, political processes, and cultural frameworks since colonial times." He is optimistic that political ideology and public policy will increasingly see poverty as a class-based issue, rather than a race-based issue, since racially inclusive policies are more likely to attract public support.

The next reading, "Malcolm X and the Revival of Black Nationalism," is by Michael Eric Dyson, professor of American civilization at Brown University. The article originally appeared in *Tikkun,* a bimonthly journal of liberal Jewish thought. Dyson is author of *Reflecting Black: African-American Cultural Criticism* (1993), which includes discussions of rap music, black preaching, Michael Jackson, Michael Jordan, novelist Toni Morrison, and black supremacist Leonard Jeffries.

In this selection, Dyson argues that the cultural renaissance of Malcolm X is the result of black America's "search for a secure and empowering racial identity." Dyson criticizes black nationalists for ignoring the importance of class and gender. He contends that an alternative strategy, "bourgeois liberal integrationism," has failed to bring the black masses "within striking distance of prosperity." Dyson proposes a third course, democratic socialism, which would promote the redistribution of power and income.

The next reading is entitled "False Prophet: The Rise of Louis Farrakhan." The author, Adolph Reed Jr., is professor of political science at Northwestern University. He examines the biography and philosophy of Louis Farrakhan, leader of the Nation of Islam, one of the nation's fastest-growing religious sects. Farrakhan favors economic self-reliance, separate schools, and the formation of an independent state. Reed has called Farrakhan "a talented demagogue" who "mingles banalities, half-truths, distortions, and falsehoods to buttress simplistic and wacky theories."

There is a strong similarity between the views of Louis Farrakhan and those of Leonard Jeffries, chairman of the Department of Black Studies at the City University of New York. Jeffries, a black supremacist, contends that Jews and Italians have conspired to denigrate blacks in films. He also maintains that African "sun people" are intellectually and morally superior to European "ice people."

The final reading in this part, "The New Black Conservatives" by Theodore Rueter, examines the backgrounds of eight prominent black conservatives: Clarence Thomas, Stephen Carter, Alan Keyes, Glenn Loury, Thomas Sowell, Shelby Steele, Walter Williams, and Robert Woodson. It also explores their views on affirmative action, education, housing, immigration, economic policy, welfare dependency, and "victimization." In addition, the reading discusses political attitudes within black America, the status of black conservative politicians, and various explanations for the rise of black conservatism.

4

Postmodern Racial Politics in the United States: Difference and Inequality

Howard Winant

Let me begin with a controversial claim: the contemporary United States faces a pervasive crisis of race, a crisis no less severe than those of the past. The origins of the crisis are not particularly obscure: the cultural and political meaning of race, its significance in shaping the social structure, and its experiential or existential dimensions all remain profoundly unresolved as the United States approaches the end of the twentieth century. As a result, the society as a whole and the population as individuals suffer from confusion and anxiety about the issue (or complex of issues) we call race.

This situation should not be surprising. We may be more afflicted with anxiety and uncertainty over race than we are over any other social or political issue. Racial conflict is the archetype of discord in North America, the primordial conflict which in many ways has structured all others. Time and time again what has been defined as "the race problem" has generated ferocious antagonisms: between slaves and masters, between natives and settlers, between new immigrants and established residents, and between workers divided by wage discrimination. Time and time again this "problem" has been thought resolved or supplanted by other supposedly more fundamental conflicts, only to blaze up anew. Tension and confusion in postwar racial politics and culture are merely the latest episode in this seemingly permanent drama.

Howard Winant, "Postmodern Racial Politics in the United States: Difference and Inequality." *Socialist Review,* January 1990, pp. 121–146. © Duke University Press, 1990. Reprinted with permission of the publisher.

In the years since World War II, however, United States society has undergone very rapid and dramatic racial transformations.* We first experienced a morally and politically compelling mobilization of racial minority movements, led by the black movement, in the 1950s and 1960s. This challenge, which some described as approaching revolutionary proportions, was followed immediately by an equally comprehensive wave of racial reaction in the 1970s and 1980s characterized by wholesale denial of the existence of racial inequality and injustice.

Nor were these trends confined to any narrow political or cultural terrain. They enveloped U.S. society. Indeed, these racial crosscurrents, as I have argued elsewhere,[1] were the chief determinants of the postwar political order. They generated both the New Left and the New Right, lent order and strategy to the antiwar movement which spelled the end of the Pax Americana, and thoroughly restructured U.S. political life. They politicized the social, such that the issue of difference became a potential axis of political and cultural mobilization (for example in the women's movement).

The racial minority movements of the postwar period recomposed U.S. political institutions, particularly the state and parties. They thus made possible not only the reforms of the 1960s, but also the resurgence of conservative and indeed reactionary movements, policies, and party realignments which took shape in the late 1970s and 1980s. In respect to movements, the appearance of a series of right-wing social movements in the 1970s owed their origins to the "backlash" which had confronted the racial minority movements from the mid-1960s onward. In respect to policies, the cheerful rehabilitation of regressive incomes policies (the "supply-side"), the assault on abortion rights, the evisceration of civil rights enforcement, even the defense buildup, can all be related to postwar racial conflicts. In respect to parties, the confused and divided condition of the Democrats certainly has major racial overtones; while the Republican's cynical "southern strategy" based on "coded" racial appeals and its consequent successors, including the Bush campaign's obsession with black rapist Willie Horton, are the underlying factors in the Republican resurgence and the triumph of Reaganism.

What happens now? By all accounts the political pendulum is swinging back from right to center. Yet ominous trends remind us that racial conflict has not been domesticated. There are rumblings from a modernized Klan and a racist far right; impoverished slum dwellers, disproportionately composed of racial minorities, signify a social order in decline; and an ongoing social policy of neglect, whether benign or malign, suggests that racism has not been banished from high places.

On the analytical level, the work of the new right and neoconservative ana-

---

*A note on terminology: much of the literature on race addresses issues in purely black–white terms. Such a framework is clearly inadequate unless dictated by the specific content of a given study (e.g., an analysis of slavery). My practice is to refer to race in general. If, however, discussion is focused upon a particular group or intergroup relationship, I indicate this in the text.

lysts,[2] which grounded the reactionary racial policy of the late 1970s and 1980s, is being challenged by a more liberal and activist policy approach.[3] But overall, there is a notable absence of radical perspectives on race. Even radicals have been confused by the racial crosscurrents of the postwar period. We are now at a crisis point, however, at which further confusion would be dangerous. We need to develop a new perspective on race, one that recognizes the postmodern character of contemporary and future racial politics. Only such a radical perspective will be adequate to conceptualize the present racial situation in the United States, much less to imagine the future. The purpose of this essay is to provide the beginnings of such an interpretation.

Basing my approach on racial-formation theory, I interpret contemporary U.S. racial dynamics as a combination of cultural and structural relationships, inherently unstable and contested politically throughout society. Thus the meaning of race, the categories available for racialization of social groups, and the configuration of racial identities, both group and individual, I suggest, exemplify (though they do not exhaust) the cultural dimensions of racial dynamics in the forthcoming period. Structural relationships, on the other hand, might include (but should not be limited to) racial inequality and stratification, as well as the political articulation of race in movements, parties, and state institutions.

I think the postmodern perspective is a valid one with which to characterize the present. What is postmodern about racial dynamics? How do contemporary patterns differ from those of the preceding "modern" epoch during which biologistic views of race were effectively challenged both theoretically and practically?*

Today there is no longer any single articulating principle or axial process with which to interpret the racial dimensions of all extant political/cultural projects. In the absence of a comprehensive challenge to the racial order as a whole, racial categories, meanings, and identities have become "decentered." This situation contrasts with the earlier postwar period, in which such axial projects did exist: the civil rights movement of the 1950s and 1960s and the racial reaction of the 1970s and 1980s. These currents provided a framework in which the whole range of racial politics and racial discourse could be interpreted.

Postmodern racial politics and culture can only exist in the structured absence of this sort of racial order. Indeed the decenteredness of the contemporary racial situation reflects an unprecedented level of societal ambivalence about race. A wide variety of initiatives of projects coexist and compete in the effort to con-

---

*For present purposes modernism in regard to race can be associated with the ethnicity paradigm, which for the first time systematically located racial meanings and identities on a social, rather than biological, terrain. The origins of this view can be located in the fusion of a variety of currents of thought and action in the early twentieth century: the founding of the NAACP and other groups, the emergence from progressivism of the "cultural pluralism" tendency, the beginning of the Chicago school of sociology, etc. The argument here is not that no "modernist" currents predated this period, but rather that they were marginal until this point.

struct a new racial hegemony, but they do not offer any real prospect of clarifying or resolving ambivalent racial meanings or identities.

Postmodern racial politics, then, consists of a proliferation of racial projects— a wide range of competing discourses and political initiatives which explain issues in terms of race and undertake political mobilization along racial lines, all operating in the absence of a clear logic of racial hegemony or opposition. These projects emanate from the most diverse sources: on the cultural side, religious, literary, social, psychological, and even popular-culture frameworks (such as film or rock) have become sites for the contestation of racial meanings. On the structural side, we have a racially defined underclass (the existence and significance of which is of course hotly debated), extensive racial conflict in both major political parties and in all branches of the state, and the reappearance (in suitably modernized form) of the Klan and its heirs in mainstream politics. In themselves, many of these phenomena are not new. What is new, I suggest, is the lack of any fundamental ordering principle or hegemonic racial logic.

Postmodern Racial Politics: Discourse and Structure

Because racial politics are now "decentered," alternative projects can no longer be placed along one supposedly objective continuum, either a political spectrum (for example, from "revolution" to "reaction") or an economic one (for example, from "progressive" to "regressive" redistribution). Because today the correspondence between racial difference and inequality is weaker than ever, everything depends on the process by which the social structure undergoes racial signification. (By racial signification I mean reference to race in all its forms.)

The referential framework involved in racial signification cannot be fully explored here, even if limited solely to the United States. The roots of racial signification lie very deep in U.S. culture and history.[4] Constantly modified, permanently unstable, the system of racial reference has undergone increasingly rapid change in the postwar period, spurred on first by racial minority movements and subsequently by reaction and "backlash."

From a racial formation perspective, these conflicts can be understood schematically as a series of cultural and political projects. Taking the system of racial signification (or discourse) and the social-structural dynamics of race in the United States, let us identify, in ideal-typical fashion, four basic projects of racial projects: the *far-right project,* the *New Right project,* the *neoconservative project,* and the *radical democratic project.* All four are attempts to articulate contemporary racial meanings and identities in new ways, to link race with more comprehensive political and cultural agendas, to interpret social structural phenomena (such as inequality or social policy) with regard to race. Each project involves a unique conception of racial difference, a theoretical approach— whether explicit or implicit—to the chief structural problem of racial inequality, a potential or actual political constituency, and a concrete political agenda.

The Far Right Project

Far right racial discourse has always represented race in terms of rights and privileges. Racial difference directly confers or denies access to rights and privileges. In the era preceding the movements of the 1950s and 1960s, racial privileges were enforced, particularly in the far right stronghold of the deep South, through terror. While violence against racial minorities—and Jews*—has by no means ceased, and sectors of the far right maintain the explicit neofascism of the past, significant modernizing currents have appeared over the last few years.† These tendencies actively seek to renovate the far right's traditions of white racial nationalism[5] and open advocacy of white supremacy without entirely breaking with the past. Rather, the traditional neofascism is muted and modernized, largely as a result of the challenges posed by the 1960s. What can white racial privilege mean in an era of supposed "equal opportunity"? The far right, no less than other U.S. political currents, has been forced to rearticulate racial meanings, to reinterpret the content of "whiteness" and the politics that flows from it.

For at least the "modernized" sector of the far right, the response has been political mobilization on racial grounds: if blacks have their organizations and movements, why shouldn't whites? The appearance of white student unions on college campuses, modeled on David Duke's National Association for the Advancement of White People, exemplifies the new trend. Far right groups recognize that open avowal of white supremacy, or explicit defense of white racial privilege, will be counterproductive in the present period. However, they differ from the many avowedly white supremacist groups in their willingness to engage in mainstream politics. They also diverge from the New Right model in their willingness to organize whites against nonwhites, to operate as a "self-help group":

> Many of their activities are geared to illustrate the ineffectuality of the state and the need for stronger action on the part of private citizens. In June, 1986, members of the Klan, in a school bus with the letters KKK on it, began to patrol the Texas Mexican border for "illegal aliens." Grand Dragon Charles Lee, who is campaigning for governor of Texas, said that the Klan was concerned that Mexicans and Central Americans take jobs away from white Americans. "If the federal government will not protect the people of Texas," Lee said, "the people themselves will do it."[6]

---

*Tom Metzger, one of the chief Klan leaders in the United States, met with Louis Farrakhan in 1985, presumably to discuss their common dislike of Jews among other matters. See Judith Cummins, "Klan Leader Met With Farrakhan," *The New York Times,* October 3, 1985.

†In this respect, Omi and I erred in presenting the far right as incapable of rearticulating its previous racial discourse of explicit white supremacy. The "modernizing" sectors, I am now suggesting, do precisely that. For our earlier view, see Omi and Winant, *Racial Formation,* pp. 114–18.

For the far right, it is now whites who are the victims of racial inequality. Indeed in some areas of the country (like California) and in some types of social space (like the big city), whites are threatened with losing their majority status and becoming a racial minority. In view of the far right, the new inequality resulting from government efforts threatens both "whiteness" and the traditional privileges granted to whites. Therefore the far right project invokes a traditional fascist theme, betrayal:

> The Klan in the 20s made a mistake thinking that evil resided in men who came home drunk or in Negroes who walked on the wrong side of the street. Today we see the evil is coming out of the government. To go out and shoot a Negro is foolish. It's not the Negro in the alley who's responsible for what's wrong with this country. It's the traitors in Washington.[7]

Although the far right retains many traditional (and thus, in my view, marginal) racist groups, its chief dynamism comes from its ability to present itself as the tribune of disenfranchised whites—in other words to create organizations and make demands that parallel those of the civil rights movement, but whose demands are reactionary in the literal sense: they seek a return to the earlier status quo. As a case study, consider the following leaflet distributed in the San Francisco area in 1987:

A CHALLENGE TO **WHITE PEOPLE**

Are you tired of . . .

—"Affirmative Action" quotas that discriminate against whites in hiring, promotion, and admission to colleges and graduate schools?

—A non-enforced immigration policy that allows millions of illegal immigrants each year to flood our country, taking away jobs, consuming vital natural resources, and taking over politically?

—Forced integration of our schools, causing White families to leave our largest cities, which are then taken over, one by one, by hordes of non-Whites?

—Immigrants who refuse to learn *our* language and demand that we pay for education and even ballots in *theirs?*

—Hundreds of non-White political organizations receiving foundation grants and tax exemptions, while our people are voiceless and disregarded by the politicians?

—Attempts by the media to conceal or downplay all these problems, while they foist a false sense of racial guilt on whites?

If so, why not join with thousands of your White kinsmen who are looking out for *WHITE* interests?[8]

Notice that the racial reforms of the 1960s are blamed for creating many of the supposed inequalities listed here: "discrimination" against whites, immigration of minorities,* school integration, bilingual education, etc. In the far right's view, the state has been captured by the "race mixers" and will have to be recaptured by white racial nationalists in order to end the betrayal of the United States' true interests.

Although it is deeply divided between modern and traditional currents, the far right is clearly undergoing a process of adaptation to the contemporary political climate and is regaining some of the influence lost in the earlier postwar period.[9] It continues to wield substantial influence and actively to rearticulate racial difference.

The New Right Project

In the discourse of the New Right, racial difference is persistent and invidious. The assertion of minority racial identities and rights in mainstream culture—for example in educational settings, popular culture, the established churches, the urban political process, and national-policy arenas—is perceived by the New Right as a comprehensive threat to "traditional American values." The fact that these identities and rights were demanded (and, from the New Right perspective, granted) in tandem with women's and anti-imperialist demands was particularly threatening, and evoked a species of reactionary and authoritarian populist response which has a venerable history in the United States.[10] As Walter Dean Burnham notes:

> Wherever and whatever the pressures of "modernization"—secularity, urbanization, the growing importance of science—have become unusually intense, episodes of revivalism and culture-issue politics have swept over the American social landscape. In all such cases at least since the end of the Civil War, such movements have been more or less explicitly reactionary, and have frequently linked with other kinds of reaction in explicitly political ways.[11]

It was the New Right that began the process of reactionary racial rearticulation in the 1960s with the Wallace campaign, and later delivered the White House to the Republican Party in 1968 through the so-called "southern strategy" developed by Kevin Phillips.[12] The New Right has substantially expanded and consolidated its position during the Reagan years, to no small extent due to this practice of "coding" racial meanings so as to appeal to white fears. Negative racial signification—the articulation of racial meaning and identities in conflictual, albeit somewhat masked terms—thus remains an important political strategy. The racial meaning of specific "code words," such as busing, quotas,

---

*Here the problem would be the 1965 Immigration Reform Act, which eliminated the racial quotas that had existed since the 1920s.

welfare, and "English only," is by now familiar. As Jesse Jackson used to say, "It's not the bus. It's us."[13] The increased use of "coding" was itself a reactionary response to the upsurge of minority movements of the 1960s, which discredited the use of overly racist appeals without obviating their effectiveness.[14] The 1988 Bush presidential campaign's incessant hammering on the theme of law and order and its scurrilous use of the image of a black rapist to mobilize white voters, exemplifies the ongoing efficacy of racial coding in the mainstream political process.

The New Right is distinguished from the far right by its commitment to state activity, to a policy agenda in which the state can be used to dismantle the social-structural gains of racial minorities, to enforce "traditional" values, and to discredit demands for a redistributive or egalitarian social policy. Where the far right sees betrayal—the state is in the hands of the "race mixers"—the New Right sees strategic opportunities.

The New Right project also resembles neoconservatism while remaining distinct from it. Like neoconservatism, the New Right attempts to rearticulate themes of racial equality in terms of civil privatism: equality is strictly a matter of individual actions, of striving, merit, and deserved achievement on the one hand; and of intentional discrimination against specific individuals on the other. All group distinctions are invidious. The New Right diverges from neoconservatism, however, in its willingness to practice racial politics subtextually, through coding and the manipulation of racial fears. In practice, it recognizes the persistence of racial difference in U.S. society. Precisely because of its willingness to exploit racial fears and employ racially manipulative practices, the New Right has been effective in achieving much of its agenda for political and cultural reaction and social structural recomposition. These achievements were crucial to the New Right's ability to provide a solid base of electoral and financial support for the Republican Party and the Reagan "revolution." The demagoguery employed in regard to Willie Horton shows this strategy is far from exhausted. Neoconservatism has not, and could not, deliver such tangible political benefits, and in fact lacks an equivalent mass political base. That is why the neoconservatives are seen as a bunch of "pointy-headed intellectuals" by many on the New Right.

The Neoconservative Project

Neoconservative discourse engages in denial of racial difference. This is a "negative" form of racial signification, which I label *hegemonic universalism.* For neoconservatism, racial difference is something to be overcome, a blight on the core U.S. political and cultural values, universalism and liberalism.

The structural consequence of the neoconservative stance is a basic anti-statism and laissez-faire attitude on the part of neoconservatives.[15] Neoconservatism involves a fundamental suspicion of racial difference, which it equates (or reduces) to ethnicity. The neoconservative project has cast doubt on the tractability of issues of racial equality, tending to argue that the state cannot ameliorate poverty through social policy, but in fact only exacerbates it.[16] Here the neoconservative project has distanced itself quite substantially from the liberal statism with which its chief spokespeople once identified.

The logic of this transformation is not hard to uncover. To be sure, the neoconservatives were once adherents of mainstream liberalism, and indeed identified themselves with the "moderate" wing of the civil rights movement. But once the anachronistic system of racial segregation had been eliminated, adherents of what was to become the neoconservative position expected the salience of racial categories to decline sharply.[17] The continuing focus on race in U.S. political and cultural discourse was surprising and threatening to them, and indeed in their view threatening to the fundamental tenets of U.S. liberalism. According to neoconservative analysts, established principles—the fundamentally integrative, if not assimilationist, character of the "American ethnic pattern" (Glazer), market rationality (Sowell, Gilder), antistatism (Murray), the merits of individualism, and respect for the "high culture" of the West[18]—were jeopardized by the continuing efforts of minority, radical, and countercultural currents of all sorts to stress racial difference.[19]

The appeal to universalism—for example in terms of educational or literary standards or social policy—is far more subtle than open or coded appeals to white racial fears, since it has greater capacity to represent race in terms that are apparently egalitarian and democratic. Indeed, the very hallmark of the neoconservative argument has been that, beyond the proscription of explicit racial discrimination, every invocation of racial significance manifests "race-thinking" and is thus suspect:

> In the phrase reiterated again and again in the Civil Rights Act of 1964, no distinction was to be made in the right to vote, in the provision of public services, the right to public education, on the ground of "race, color, religion, or national origin." Paradoxically, we then began an extensive effort to record the race, color and (some) national origins of just about every student and employee and recipient of government benefits or services in the nation. . . . This monumental restructuring of public policy . . . , it is argued by Federal administrators and courts, is required to enforce the laws against discrimination. . . . It is a transitional period, they say, to that condition called for in the Constitution and the laws, when no account at all is to be taken of race, color and national origin. But others see it as a direct contradiction of the Constitution and the laws, and of the consensus that emerged after long struggle in the middle 1960s.[20]

Glazer leaves little doubt that he agrees with the latter sentiment. Thus, for neoconservatism the reforms of the 1960s created the conditions for a diminution of racial difference and a trend toward equality (understood in a formal rather than substantive sense), but this very achievement was negated by unwarranted state activity and radical minority demands for "group rights."

This position has emerged as a consistent viewpoint that has more in common with neoclassical economics than it does with a commitment to the welfare state. Extended beyond the realm of state activity and structure—for after all, the chief preoccupation of neoconservatives is the defense of traditional "liberal" values— the neoconservative project is now coming into conflict even with the cultural pluralism that its proponents once strongly advocated.[21]

The implications of hegemonic universalism extend beyond strictly racial issues to a quasi-imperial defense of the political and cultural canons of Western culture. Thus, for example, university programs of African-American or other racial-minority studies (which right-wing zealots have sarcastically labeled "oppression studies")* are to be opposed as much as state-mandated policies of affirmative action.[22] It is this logic, which with a breathtaking sweep affirms the superiority of both laissez-faire social policies and European intellectual traditions, that underlies the neoconservative project. As Houston Baker has argued in regard to various academic "canons" and their neoconservative advocates,

> The scenario they seem to endorse reads as follows: when science apologizes and says there is no such thing, all talk of "race" must cease. Hence "race," as a recently emergent, unifying, and forceful sign of difference in the service of the "Other," is held up to scientific ridicule as, ironically, "unscientific." A proudly emergent sense of ethnic diversity in the service of the new world arrangements is disparaged by white male science as the most foolish sort of anachronism.[23]

Thus, the neoconservative perspective with its characteristic hegemonic universalism is not as inclusionary as it superficially appears. Indeed, neoconservatism suffers from bad faith. It may serve for some as a rationalizing formula, a lament about the complexities of a social world in which the traditional truths and the traditional speakers, writers, and political actors have come under challenge from a host of "others," but as soon as it advances beyond critique to proposals for action its professed universality and liberality are quickly replaced by formulas for repression.

What we can learn from neoconservatism is not that liberalism or "Western values" have ongoing value; nor that a tolerance for ethnic (not to mention racial) diversity is growing. Rather, what the neoconservative perspective offers is perhaps the most sophisticated ideological use of universalism and egalitarian-

---

*Throughout the land, efforts to "revise the canon" to include works of non-Western and female authors have been met by howls of protest, leading us to speculate that neoconservatism has made at least as many inroads in literary studies as it has in the social sciences. The extreme case is undoubtedly Allen Bloom's aptly titled *The Closing of the American Mind* (New York: Simon and Schuster, 1987), which squarely challenges any principle of relativism or egalitarianism in culture.

ism. The needs of "others," both political and cultural, cannot be addressed from this perspective, since the most basic need racial minorities have is that of recognition. Racial difference exists; it cannot be dismissed or declared anachronistic merely to satisfy a political or cultural formula such as a putative "American ethnic pattern," whose reality or permanence, needless to say, is far from proved.[24] Neoconservative appeals to universalism are political strategies that decontextualize race and thus obscure racial difference. Neoconservative suspicions about the state involve at least tacit acceptance of "objective" racial inequalities,* often masked by supposedly utilitarian arguments that state policies "don't work" in the realm of race. Therefore the neoconservative project, despite its protestations to the contrary, must be viewed as an attempt to maintain political and cultural arrangements that systematically place racial minorities (and women, though that is another story) at a disadvantage, both social-structurally and culturally. Neoconservatism involves a Eurocentric "standpoint epistemology"[25] no less than the explicitly racist and sexist discourses that triumphant liberalism and modernism replaced in the earlier part of the century.

The Radical Democratic Project[26]

Radical democratic discourse acknowledges the permanence of racial difference in U.S. society. When claims of universality are relaxed, the effect is to recognize the fluidity of racial themes in U.S. politics and culture and to accept both the continuity and the variability of race in sociopolitical arrangements and cultural life. Racial themes have marked and molded U.S. economic life, political processes, and cultural frameworks since colonial times. Racial signification has always been part of the framework of our culture, as well as a primary source of opposition and contestation.

Of the four ideal types suggested here, the radical democratic project has the greatest resonance with the postmodern politics of race. This is because radical

---

*Without entering too far into the question of what constitutes "objective" racial inequality it must be recognized that on such issues as levels of unemployment, returns to education, infant mortality, etc., the evidence is rather unambiguous. If anything the data minimize inequality. Take unemployment: here official statistics neglect the informal economy, which is a primary source of employment and locus of discrimination against racial minorities, particularly undocumented workers. Unemployment data measure only "active" job seekers, not those who have been without (formal) jobs for a long time or those who have become discouraged in their job search. These constructions of the data on unemployment have a political subtext: the reduction of the numerator on the monthly Bureau of Labor Statistics report obviously improves the image of those in power. (See David Gordon, "6% Unemployment Ain't Natural," in *Social Research* vol. 54, no. 2 (Summer, 1987).) There are also ample grounds on which to question the racial logic of unemployment figures, which rely on census categories. (See Omi and Winant, *Racial Formation*, pp. 3–4, 75–76.)

democratic discourse can acknowledge and affirm difference, both racial and otherwise, without simultaneously defending inequality; thus there is no necessity to view race in a unitary and therefore reductionist framework.* From this standpoint, I think, it is most possible to recognize both the necessary permanence and ongoing instability of racial meanings and identities in the contemporary United States.

I would like to include in the radical democratic category the various forms of racial politics that have survived from the minority upsurge of the 1960s. This category would encompass at least the range of political and intellectual currents which in earlier work Omi and I have labeled cultural radicalism, left/Marxist currents, and electoral/institutional initiatives.[27] What is particularly notable about these political tendencies today is their general disability: they seem largely unable to compete effectively on the contemporary terrain of racial politics. The weakness of leftist radicalism on issues of race is of course nothing new in the United States, but as ever it remains a dangerous opening to inequality, repression, and ultimately neofascism. Since one of my chief preoccupations here is to provide theoretical and analytical ammunition to the radical democratic project, and since space limitations preclude any serious treatment of the debilitated "surviving" currents, I prefer to concentrate my attention on two more promising radical democratic developments. One of these is the presidential campaign of Jesse Jackson; the other is the analysis of racial inequality developed by William J. Wilson. . . .

Moving from race to class, I would like to suggest, is at the heart of the radical democratic project. At the risk of seeming presumptuous, an even bolder assertion might be warranted: *in the postmodern political framework of the contemporary United States, hegemony is determined by the articulation of race and class.* The ability of the right to represent class issues in racial terms is central to the current pattern of conservative hegemony. All three rightist projects—those of the far right, the New Right, and the neoconservatives—partake of this logic. Conservative/reactionary politics today move from class to race—it articulates class issues in racial terms. In so doing, it builds on a thematic current in the United States that can be understood as "divide and conquer," dual/split labor markets, white skin privilege, immigrant exclusion, or internal colonialism. The name of this current is racism.

Conversely, any challenge to this current must move from race to class, or surely fall victim to the same hegemonic strategies that have doomed so many other progressive political initiatives. Traditional left politics (both social-

---

*Of the other three racial projects, only the far right unequivocally affirms racial difference, but it does this in a premodern fashion, asserting a reactionary racial essentialism. The New Right and neoconservative projects, conversely, fail to uphold the fluidity of racial categories and the necessary permanence of difference.

democratic and revolutionary), which have been steeped in class reductionism, provide innumerable examples of this fate. In the particular conditions of U.S. politics, the left has never been able to subordinate race to class; this strategy is less viable in the postmodern period than ever before.

What would a radical democratic articulation of race and class look like? A full answer to this question must await large-scale political and cultural experimentation, but a limited and schematic response is already possible. First, such an approach cannot be a mere inversion—whether innocent or cynical—of the New-Right strategy of racial coding. It must affirm diversity and the ongoing reality of racial difference in U.S. cultural and political life. Indeed it must go further and create (or recreate) a joyful appreciation of racial difference that goes well beyond mere tolerance. One of the striking features of the contemporary racial situation is that many examples of such an appreciation exist in civil society—in music and art, sexual relationships, educational and religious settings, or in the media . . . —without finding any political articulation at all. Where, with the possible exception of the Jackson campaign and its local spinoffs and supporters, is there any political acknowledgement of the pleasures of racial difference? Even Jackson's expressions are limited by a general focus on tolerance.

Additionally, a radical democratic articulation of race and class must acknowledge that racial minority status generally serves as a marker in class formation. Class position, whether understood in Weberian or Marxian categories, whether taken as indicating membership in the working-class/unemployed categories, or in the lower-class/underclass categories, is in many respects racially assigned in the United States. This should come as no surprise to those familiar with the literature on social stratification or on the dynamics of labor market segmentation, but the inordinate focus placed on the black middle class today sometimes obscures this point.[28]

It follows from this that radical democratic challengers should regard the question of discrimination as a racial process with class consequences. The reactionary redefinition of the nature of racial discrimination (in the "reverse discrimination" arguments of the 1970s and 1980s) is something that only happens to individuals, and thus has no history of preponderant collective logic in the present, conveniently suppressing the fact that discrimination drives all wages down.*

This recognition should lead us back to the point made by Martin Luther

---

. . .

*My point here is definitely not to endorse the segmentation view which sees racial discrimination as a class-based "divide and conquer" tactic. Rather it is something of the reverse: to challenge leftists and progressives who advance programs for "full employment" or for an "expanded welfare state" to take race seriously as a starting-point for these initiatives, rather than as a problem which will be resolved when the supposedly larger class issues have been addressed.

King, Jr., Orlando Patterson, and others, that struggles for racial equality are linked with both the expansion of democracy and large-scale economic welfare. In short, a greater attentiveness to racial politics is a precondition for the sorts of reforms we seek under the general heading of "social democracy.". . .

Notes

1. Michael Omi and Howard Winant, *Racial Formation in the United States: From the 1960s to the 1980s* (London and New York: Routledge, 1986).

2. Some key texts here are Nathan Glazer, *Affirmative Discrimination: Ethnic Inequality and Public Policy* (New York: Basic Books, 1978); Charles Murray, *Losing Ground: American Social Policy, 1950–1980* (New York: Basic Books, 1984); Thomas Sowell, *Markets and Minorities* (New York: Basic Books, 1981).

3. Probably the most important work to date from this perspective is William Julius Wilson, *The Truly Disadvantaged* (Chicago: University of Chicago Press, 1987). See also Sar M. Levitan and Charles M. Johnson, *Beyond the Safety Net: Reviving the Promise of Opportunity in America* (Cambridge, MA: Ballinger, 1984).

4. These roots involve most primarily the origins of the United States as a nation state, and therefore reflect its partially genocidal and partially revolutionary heritage. For a provocative account of the historical framework in which race came to "signify" in the Americas, see Orlando Patterson, "The Black Community: Is There a Future?" in Seymour Martin Lipset, ed., *The Third Century: America as a Post-Industrial Society* (Stanford, CA: The Hoover Institution Press, 1979), pp. 244–58.

5. See Ronald Walters, "White Racial Nationalism in the United States," *Without Prejudice,* vol. 1, no. 1 (Fall 1987).

6. Michael A. Omi, *We Shall Overturn: Race and the Contemporary American Right* (PhD dissertation, University of California, Santa Cruz, 1987), p. 113.

7. Klansman Thomas Robb, quoted in *Newsweek,* March 4, 1985, p. 25.

8. Leaflet distributed by the White Aryan Resistance (WAR); Concord, CA.

9. See Howard Schuman et al., *Racial Attitudes in America: Trends and Interpretations* (Cambridge, MA: Harvard University Press, 1985), p. 123.

10. For a somewhat similar argument focused on the feminist movement, see Rosalind Petchesky, *Abortion and Women's Choice* (Boston: Northeastern University Press, 1985), pp. 251–85.

11. Walter Dean Burnham, "Post-Conservative America," *Socialist Review* 72 (1983), p. 125.

12. Kevin Phillips, *The Emerging Republican Majority* (New York: Anchor Books, 1970). Phillips' book was based on analyses done for the Nixon campaign.

13. For a more extensive discussion of the racial codeword phenomenon, see Omi, *We Shall Overturn,* pp. 127–67. Another good source is David Edgar, "Reagan's Hidden Agenda: Racism and the New American Right," *Race and Class,* vol. 22, no. 3 (1981).

14. See Omi and Winant, *Racial Formation in the United States,* pp. 120–21.

15. The most relevant work here is Nathan Glazer, *Affirmative Discrimination;* Murray, *Losing Ground;* and Sowell, *Markets and Minorities.* Other important work is Daniel Bell, *The Cultural Contradictions of Capitalism* (New York: Basic Books, 1976); George Gilder, *Wealth and Poverty* (New York: Basic Books, 1981). Obvi-

ously there are differences among these writers, but on the core ideas there is general agreement.

16. This is particularly the position of Gilder and Murray, but see also Walter Williams, *The State Against Blacks* (New York: McGraw-Hill, 1982).

17. This was the very position that they criticized later as the "liberal expectancy." See Nathan Glazer and Daniel Moynihan, eds., *Ethnicity: Theory and Experience* (Cambridge, MA: Harvard University Press, 1975), p. 7. This phrase was originally coined by another key ethnicity theorist, Milton Gordon, whose *Assimilation in American Life* (New York: Oxford University Press, 1964) was an early statement of views which would evolve ten years later into neoconservatism. In fairness it should be noted that Glazer and Moynihan also criticize the "radical expectancy," that is, Marxism, which predicted the dissolution of racial and ethnic divisions in the "final conflict" of class struggle. To the extent that by 1975 these authors were recognizing the irreducibility of ethnicity, they can be applauded. However, Glazer in particular continued to argue that racial difference was but one form of ethnic difference. In other words, he still reduced race to ethnicity. On these points see Omi and Winant, *Racial Formation*, pp. 18–24.

18. Not surprisingly some of the most important work on the cultural logic of race has appeared in critical literary frameworks. For a useful survey of these approaches to the subject see the articles collected in Henry Louis Gates, Jr., ed., *"Race," Writing, and Difference* (Chicago: University of Chicago Press, 1986).

19. For a terse summary statement of this position, see Irving Kristol, "What Is a Neoconservative?" *Newsweek* (January 19, 1976), p. 87. Perhaps the most definitive rendering of this position is the one advanced by Murray:

> My proposal for dealing with the racial issue in social welfare is to repeal every bit of legislation and reverse every court decision that in any way requires, recommends, or awards differential treatment according to race, and thereby put us back onto the track that we left in 1965. We may argue about the appropriate limits of government intervention in trying to enforce the ideal, but at least it should be possible to identify the ideal; Race is not a morally admissible reason for treating one person differently from another. Period. (Charles Murray, *Losing Ground: American Social Policy, 1950–1980* (New York: Basic Books, 1984), p. 223.

20. Glazer, *Affirmative Discrimination*, p. 4.

21. Glazer and Moynihan were early advocates of ethnic pluralism as a route to political power and thus greater equality for blacks. See *Beyond the Melting Pot*. Even in the later *Affirmative Discrimination*, Glazer affirms as one of the three formative principles of "the American ethnic pattern" the idea that "no group . . . would be required to give up its group character and distinctiveness as the price of full entry into the American society and polity" (p. 5). Yet it is questionable how much this pluralism can be sustained without a recognition of racial difference, since race is at a minimum an important dimension of political mobilization.

22. Murray, *Losing Ground*; Glazer, *Affirmative Discrimination*; Thomas Sowell, *Ethnic America* (New York: Basic Books, 1981).

23. Houston A. Baker, Jr., "Caliban's Triple Play," in Gates, ed., *"Race," Writing, and Difference*, p. 385; emphasis original.

24. Ronald Takaki has re-read Glazer's three main theoretical sources—Hans Kohn, Yehoshua Arieli, and Seymour Martin Lipset—and argues that the first two commit egregious errors of historical fact in their treatment of racial minorities, while the third (Lipset) explicitly disclaims conclusions of the type that Glazer reaches. Ronald Takaki, "Reflections on Racial Patterns in America: An Historical Perspective," in W. A. Van

Horne and T. A. Tonneson, eds., *Ethnicity and Public Policy* (Madison: University of Wisconsin Press, 1982), pp. 10–16.

25. Sandra Harding, *The Science Question in Feminism* (Ithaca: Cornell University Press, 1986), chapter 7, makes a lucid case for racial and gender "differences" as contrasting worldviews, as "standpoint epistemologies" historically constructed by the experience of domination and resistance.

26. The whole notion offered here of radical democracy owes a great deal to the pathbreaking work by Chantal Mouffe and Ernesto Laclau, *Hegemony and Socialist Strategy* (London: Verso, 1985).

27. See Omi and Winant, "By the Rivers of Babylon: Race in the United States," Part II, *Socialist Review* 72 (1983), pp. 37–40.

28. Bart Landry, *The New Black Middle Class* (Berkeley: University of California Press, 1987).

5

Malcolm X and the Revival of Black Nationalism

Michael Eric Dyson

The cultural rebirth of Malcolm X is the remarkable result of complex forces converging to lift him from his violent death in 1964. Malcolm's championing of the common Black person, and his crusade against the vicious stereotypes that have for centuries crippled Black communities, have won him a new generation of admirers. Indeed, a large part of the cultural crisis that has precipitated Malcolm's mythic return is rooted in an ongoing quest in Black America: the search for a secure and empowering racial identity.

That quest is perennially frustrated by the demands of our culture to cleanse ethnic and racial particularity at the altar of a superior American identity, substituting the terms of one strain of nationalism for the priorities of another. By this common ritual of national identity, for instance, the Irish, Poles, Italians, and Jews have been absorbed into a universal image of common citizenship. But the transformation of Black cultural identity is often poorly served by this process, impeded as much by the external pressures of racism and class prejudice, as by internal racial resistance to an "inclusion" that would rob Blacks of whatever power and privilege they enjoy in their own domains.

Malcolm's reborn appeal is also linked to the resurgence of Black nationalism over the last two decades. Gusts of racial pride sweep across Black America as scholars retrieve the lost treasures of an unjustly degraded African past, continu-

Reprinted from TIKKUN MAGAZINE, A BI-MONTHLY JEWISH CRITIQUE OF POLITICS, CULTURE, AND SOCIETY. Subscriptions are $31.00 per year from TIKKUN, 251 West 100th Street, 5th floor, New York, NY 10025.

ing a project of racial reclamation begun in earnest in the 1960s but recast to fit the needs of end-of-the-century utopian nationalists, ranging from followers of Leonard Jeffries to what Huey Newton termed "pork-chop nationalists." The Afrocentric movement has quickened the debate about multicultural education and cast a searching light upon the intellectual blindnesses and racist claims of Eurocentric scholars, even as it avoids acknowledging the romantic features of its own household. Malcolm's unabashed love for Black history, his relentless pedagogy of racial redemption through cultural consciousness and racial self-awareness, mesh effortlessly with Black Americans' recovery of their African roots.

Malcolm's take-no-prisoners approach to racial crisis appeals to young blacks disaffected from white society and alienated from older Black generations whose contained style of revolt owes more to Martin Luther King, Jr.'s nonviolent philosophy than to X's advocacy of self-defense. Rap music has adopted Malcolm's militant posture, while exaggerating to shrill effect the already disturbing machismo and misogyny that laced his early rhetoric. Malcolm's articulation of Black rage—which, by his own confession, tapped a vulnerability even in Martin Luther King, Jr.—is the centerpiece of much of rap rhetoric, replacing a concrete politics aimed at renewing the conditions of social and moral decadence it graphically portrays. Ironically, the venting of anger, while cathartic and at moments even healthy, ultimately betrays the monumental task of supplying strategic alternatives to the unstinting suffering of aggrieved Blacks.

If the reemergence of Black nationalism and Malcolm's explosive popularity go hand in hand—are parallel responses to the continuing plague of an equally rejuvenated racism—then not only their strengths, but their limitations as well are mutually revealing. For example, Malcolm's brand of Black nationalism was not only a fierce attack on white Americans, but a sharp rebuke as well to Black women. A product of his times, Malcolm went to extremes in demonizing women, saying that the "closest thing to a woman is a devil."

Although he later amended his beliefs, confessing his regret at "spit[ting] acid at the sisters" and contending that they should be treated equally, Malcolm's Black nationalist heirs have failed to take his reformed position on gender seriously. Like the early Malcolm and other sixties nationalists, contemporary Black nationalists have cast the pursuit of racial liberation in terms of a quest for masculine self-realization. Such a strategy not only borrows ideological capital from the white patriarchy that has historically demeaned Black America, but it blunts awareness of how the practice of patriarchy by Black men has created another class of victims within Black communities.

Further, the strategy of viewing racial oppression exclusively through a male lens distorts the suffering of Black women at the hands of white society and loses focus on the especially difficult choices that befall Black women caught in a sometimes bewildering nexus of relationships based on race, class, and gender. Reducing Black suffering to its lowest common male denominator not only presumes a hierarchy of pain that removes priority from the Black female struggle; it also trivializes the analysis and actions of Black women in the realization of Black liberation. Malcolm's heirs ignored the virtues of his later, enlightened attitudes toward gender.

The cultural renaissance of Malcolm X also embodies the paradoxical nature of Black nationalist politics over the past two decades: Those most aided by its successes have rarely stuck around to witness the misery of those most hurt by its failures. The truth is that Black nationalist rhetoric has helped an expanding Black middle class gain increased material comfort, while Black nationalism's most desperate constituency—the working class and working poor—continue to toil in the aftermath of nationalism's unrealized political promise. Talk of Black cultural solidarity and racial loyalty has propelled the careers of intellectuals, artists, and politicians as they seek access to institutions of power and ranks of privilege as esteemed *vox populi*. Yet the irony is that the perks and rewards of success insulate them from the misery of their constituencies, cutting them off from the very people on whose behalf they claim to speak.

The greatest irony of contemporary Black nationalism may be its use by members of the Black middle class to consolidate their class interests at the expense of working and poor Blacks. By refusing to take class seriously—or only half-heartedly as they decry, without irony, the moves of a self-serving Black bourgeoisie!—many nationalists discard a crucial analytical tool for exploring the causes of Black racial and economic suffering.

This is not to say that nationalism's vaunted alternative, bourgeois liberal integrationism, has enjoyed wide success, either, in bringing the Black masses within striking distance of prosperity, or at least to parity with white middle and working classes. Commentators usually gloss over this fact when comparing the legacies of Malcolm X and Martin Luther King, Jr. For the most part, Malcolm and Martin have come to symbolize the parting of paths in Black America over the best answer to racial domination. While Malcolm's strident rhetoric is keyed in by nationalists at the appropriate moments of Black disgust with the pace and point of integration, King's conciliatory gestures are evoked by integrationists as the standard of striving for the promised land of racial harmony and economic equity.

In truth, however, King's admirers have also forsaken the bitter lessons of his mature career in deference to the soaring optimism of his dream years. King discerned as early as 1965 that the fundamental problems of Black America were economic in nature, and that a shift in strategies was necessary for the civil rights movement to become a movement for economic equality. After witnessing wasted human capital in the slums of Watts and Chicago, and after touring the rural wreckage of life in Mississippi's deep Delta, King became convinced that the only solution to Black suffering was to understand it in relation to a capitalist economy that hurt all poor people. He determined that nothing short of a wholesale criticism and overhaul of existing economic arrangements could effectively remedy the predicament of the Black poor and working class.

This is a far cry from contemporary Black capitalist and business strategies that attempt to address the economic plight of Black Americans by creating more Black millionaires. Highly paid entertainers and athletes participate in the lucrative culture of consumption by selling their talents to the highest bidder in the marketplace—a legacy, we are often reminded, of King's, and the civil rights movement's, vision of a just society where social goods are distributed according to merit, not color. King's willingness, toward the end of his life, to question the legitimacy of the present economic order and to challenge the logic of capital has been obscured by appeals to his early beliefs about the virtues of integration.

The relative failure of both Black nationalist and integrationist strategies to affect large numbers of Black Americans beyond the middle and upper class raises questions about how progressives can expand Malcolm's and Martin's legacies to address the present crises in Black America. Black progressive intellectuals and activists must view class, gender, and sex as crucial components of a complex and sophisticated explanation of the problems of Black America. There are at least two advantages to such an approach. First, it provides a larger range of social and cultural variables from which to choose in depicting the vast array of forces that constrain Black economic, political, and social progress. Second, it acknowledges the radical diversity of experiences within Black communities, offering a more realistic possibility of addressing the particular needs of a wide range of Blacks: the ghetto poor, gays and lesbians, single Black females, working mothers, underemployed Black men, and elderly Blacks, for instance.

Black progressives must also deepen Malcolm's and Martin's criticisms of capitalism and their leanings toward democratic socialism. The prevailing economic policies have contributed to the persistent poverty of the poorest Americans (including great numbers of Blacks), and the relative inability of most Americans to reap the real rewards of political democracy and economic empowerment. A democratic socialist perspective raises questions about the accountability of the disproportionately wealthy, providing a critical platform for criticizing Black capitalist and business strategies that merely replicate unjust economic practices.

A democratic socialist perspective—which criticizes capital accumulation and the maximization of profit for the few without regard to its effects on the many; which advocates an equitable redistribution of wealth through progressive taxation and the increased financial responsibility of the truly wealthy; and which promotes the restructuring of social opportunities for the neediest through public policy and direct political intervention—also encourages the adoption of political and social policies that benefit all Americans, while addressing the specific needs of Blacks, such as universal health care. Presently, Black Americans are overwhelmingly represented among the 37 million uninsured in our nation. A democratic socialist perspective asks why a nation that pays over $820 billion, or 13 percent of the G.N.P. for the well-insured cannot redistribute its wealth through a progressive tax of the wealthiest two percent (and a fair tax on the top

50 percent) of our country to help provide the $50 or $60 billion more needed to provide universal health coverage.

The quest for Black racial and economic justice has been heavily influenced by Black religious conceptions of justice, charity, equality, and freedom. During the civil rights movement, King articulated Black Christian conceptions of justice through the language of human rights and the political language of civil religion. Likewise, Malcolm X expressed his conceptions of divine retribution for racial injustice and the religious basis for healthy Black self-esteem through Black Islamic, and subsequently, orthodox Islamic belief that accorded with Black secular ideas about racial self-determination and cultural pride. A democratic socialist perspective encourages the broad expression of conceptions of justice, equality, and political freedom that are tempered by regard for the widest possible audience of intellectual interlocutors and political participants, including those trained in the rich traditions of Black social protest.

Finally, Black progressives must make sensible but forceful criticisms of narrow visions of Black racial identity, especially after the Clarence Thomas/ Anita Hill debacle. That wrenching drama provided a glimpse of the underdeveloped state of gender analysis in most Black communities and provoked a serious reconsideration of the politics of racial unity and loyalty. In reflecting on Clarence Thomas's nomination to the Supreme Court, Black Americans were torn between fidelity to principles of fairness and justice, on the one hand, whether Thomas was qualified for the nomination and devotion to race on the other, whether Blacks should support one of their own, despite his opposition to many of the legal principles cherished by Black communities.

The introduction of Anita Hill's perspective into this already complex calculus ripped open ancient antagonisms between Black women and men. In a public and painful manner, the hearings forced many Black Americans to a new awareness of the need to place principles of justice above automatic appeals to race loyalty premised exclusively on skin color. Many Americans, including many Blacks, came to a clearer understanding of the social construction of racial identity, recognizing that Black folk are by no means a homogeneous group. The differences that factors such as geography, sexual preference, gender, and class make in the lives of Black Americans are too complex to be captured in a monolithic model of racial unity. Progressive Blacks share more ideological and political ground with a white progressive such as Barbara Ehrenreich, for instance, than they do with conservatives of the ilk of Clarence Thomas, or even Anita Hill.

For Black leaders, the political and social significance of this fact should be the building of bridges across the chasm of color in the common embrace of ideals that transcend racial rooting. Progressive Blacks must join with progressive Latinas and Latinos, gays and lesbians, feminists, environmental activists, and all others who profess and practice personal and social equality and democracy.

The absence of sustained progressive Black political opposition, or even a radical political organization that expresses the views of the working class and working poor, signals a loss of political courage and nerve in the United States that characterized Malcolm and Martin at their best. The nature and history of the remembrance of these two figures is also instructive about the character of political leadership in our own times. That two dead leaders are the twin pillars of contemporary Black culture, and the continuing object of its most passionate declarations of admiration, trust, and hope—serving not as signs but substitutes for present Black leaders, who often lack (as do their white counterparts) integrity and a will to sacrifice—reveals the crisis of purpose and vision among contemporary Black leaders.

In the end, Malcolm and Martin are in varying degrees captives of their true believers, trapped by literal interpreters who refuse to let them, in Malcolm's words, "turn the corner." The bulk of each man's achievements lay in his willingness to place truth over habit in the quest for the best route to social reconstruction and racial redemption. Their legacy to us is the imagination and energy to pursue the goals of liberation upon as wide a scale as the complex nature of our contemporary crises demand and our talents allow.

6

False Prophet: The Rise of Louis Farrakhan

Adolph Reed Jr.

Louis Farrakhan is all over America. In the past year he has been the subject of widely publicized feature-length interviews in *The Washington Post* and *The Washington Times,* and in other nonblack publications as well. He tore up the campaign trail on behalf of local and Congressional candidates in the Nation of Islam's first direct foray into electoral politics. He was prominent at rallies and demonstrations in support of embattled former Washington Mayor Marion Barry, despite having denounced him only a few months earlier as a drug fiend and philanderer. Farrakhan has even been a featured solo guest on *Donahue.* He has kept up a torrid pace of speaking engagements and, of late, has begun to stake out a position critical of U.S. intervention in the Persian Gulf.

Recognition of Farrakhan as a public figure has been growing since his involvement in Jesse Jackson's first campaign for the Democratic presidential nomination in 1984. But understanding what his rise means in American life requires going back much further than that.

Louis Farrakhan, now 57, has been around a long time. Like Otis Redding, Aretha Franklin and hip-hop, he had considerable visibility among blacks before whites discovered him. For well over thirty years he has propagated a vision of political separatism and a program of moral rearmament, "self-help" business development and an idiosyncratic brand of Islamic religion. That vision and program, as well as his personal stature, grew from the soil of black nationalist

Reprinted from *The Nation,* January 21, 1991, pp. 51–56.

politics in the civil rights/black power era. To make sense of Farrakhan requires situating him within the organizational and ideological contexts from which he emerged. Doing so, moreover, indicates that his anti-Semitism and whatever he might think of whites in general are ephemeral in comparison with the truly dangerous tendencies he represents.

In the early 1960s, as Louis X, Farrakhan was minister of the Nation of Islam's important Boston mosque and a kind of understudy to Malcolm X. He sided conspicuously with Elijah Muhammad, founder and "Messenger" of the Nation, against Malcolm in the bitter 1963–65 conflict that ended with the latter's murder. Farrakhan replaced Malcolm as minister of the Harlem mosque and later became Muhammad's national representative.

The Messenger's core teachings include claims that blacks were the world's "original" race, from which all others derived; that black Americans are descended from an ancient, "lost" Asian tribe; that the white race originated from a demonic laboratory experiment and that Elijah Muhammad was divinely inspired. Following nationalist convention, the Muslims advocate the subordination of women, drawing on a rhetoric of domesticity, moral purity and male responsibility; predictably, they denounce feminism and gay rights as white decadence and as strategies to undermine black unity and moral fiber.

The Nation's secular program has always focused on "nation building," which in practice has meant business development and the creation of separate schools and other institutions. Those activities have been harnessed to the ultimate goal of political separation and the formation of an independent state. Under Muhammad that goal remained inchoate, appearing mainly as a millenarian dream, but for Farrakhan it figures more directly into programmatic rhetoric. Discussion of the proposed state's citizenry characteristically elides the distinction between the membership of the Nation of Islam and black Americans in general, but Farrakhan recently has indicated that one possible model entails putting the former in charge of the latter. The nation-building agenda also reinforces the organization's natalist ideology and long-standing opposition to abortion, which both Muhammad and Farrakhan have denounced as genocidal as well as immoral.

Farrakhan rose to prominence during the late 1960s and early 1970s, when Muhammad's Nation was trying to become more visible in public life and to establish a greater presence in the black activist arena. As Muhammad's representative, he participated in national black political forums, addressed the 1970 Pan-African Congress of nationalist activists (as did first-time black Mayors Richard Hatcher of Gary, Indiana, and Kenneth Gibson of Newark; Ralph Abernathy; National Urban League director Whitney Young Jr.; Jesse Jackson and others) and frequently spoke on black college campuses. During that period the Nation also expanded its business development agenda, which until then had centered mainly on mom-and-pop restaurants, takeout sandwich and baked goods shops, cut-and-sew operations catering to the organization's members (to satisfy the Muslim dress code) and the newspaper *Muhammad Speaks.* The Nation unveiled a set of ambitious goals, including establishment of agribusiness in the South, a medical complex in Chicago and large-scale international commerce anchored by fish imports from Peru. There was even talk that Muhammad would take advantage of Richard Nixon's definition of "black power" as "black capitalism" and apply for funds from minority economic development programs in the Office of Economic Opportunity or the Small Business Administration.

Two personal encounters I had with Farrakhan in late 1970 and early 1971 neatly reflect the discordant aspects of the Nation of Islam's thrust then and his place in it. One was a speech he gave at the predominantly black Fayetteville State University in North Carolina, where he scored mainstream civil rights spokespersons for their spinelessness and lack of vision. Of Ralph Abernathy's pledge to pursue King's "dream" as his successor at the Southern Christian Leadership Conference, Farrakhan quipped, "Talking about dreaming somebody else's dream! Don't you know that when you're dreaming, you're *asleep? Wake up,* black man!" And he chastised his mainly student audience for putative moral weakness. "Just as a bootmaker molds a boot, so the teacher molds the hearts and minds of the youth of our nation," he said, playing on the institution's history as a teachers' college. "And what are you going to teach them, *drunkard?* What are you going to teach them, *dope fiend?* What are you going to teach them, *foul, frivolous woman* who will lie down with a teacher to get a passing grade?" (Note that the woman, not the teacher, is his target.) With striking theatricality and stage presence, he punctuated each charge by pointing to a different section of the auditorium, as if exposing particular culprits.

The second encounter came soon thereafter. Along with other field-staff members of the North Carolina-based Foundation for Community Development, I was called in to Durham to attend a meeting with Farrakhan. He had come to the area as Muhammad's delegate, mainly to pursue contacts with officials of a well-established black bank and the North Carolina Mutual Life Insurance Company, then one of the largest black-owned businesses in the United States. He also wanted to examine the operations of the community development corporation that our agency had helped the local poor-people's organization create. At the meeting his demeanor was reserved, almost stilted, and he seemed (or tried to seem) in thrall to an image of black Durham as a center for business enterprise. (He had attended college in Winston-Salem during the early 1950s and quite likely imbibed that image then.) Although he made perfunctory gestures of appreciation for our reputation for grass-roots activism and black-power radicalism, he expressed only polite interest in the participatory and cooperative aspects of our community development approach. He was not much moved by the idea of organizing poor people to act on their own behalf.

While the Nation seemed to be growing and consolidating itself as a corporate enterprise, many of us in movement circles who watched from the outside wondered then how it would resolve the evident tension between its flamboyant rhetorical posture, so clear that night at Fayetteville State, and its very conventional business aspirations. Central in our minds was anticipation of the succession crisis likely to occur when Muhammad, who in 1970 was already a feeble septuagenarian, died or stepped down. For not only could Muslim operatives be seen hanging out with denizens of the underworld, but sectarian zealotry often condoned a strong-arm style.

The Uhuru Kitabu bookstore in Philadelphia, for example, was firebombed in 1970 when its proprietors—former Student Non-Violent Coordinating Committee workers—refused to remove a Malcolm X poster from the store's window after threats from local Muslims. In Atlanta in 1971 a dispute between Muslims and Black Panthers over turf rights for street-corner newspaper hawking erupted into a hundred-person brawl. In 1972 strife within New York's Temple Number 7 culminated in a three-hour fight and shootout that began in the mosque and spilled outside. A purge of remaining Malcolm X loyalists followed in New York and elsewhere, and factions within the Nation were implicated in assassinations of outspoken followers of Malcolm in Boston and in Newark, where the presiding minister of the mosque was gunned down.

Most chilling, in January 1973 a simmering theological dispute with members of the Hanafi Islamic sect in Washington ignited into an attack of which only zealots or hardened killers are capable. Seven Hanafis were murdered in their 16th Street residence, owned by Kareem Abdul-Jabbar; five of the victims were children, including babies who were drowned in the bathtub. (The Hanafis held the Nation responsible and four years later occupied a government building and B'nai B'rith center and took hostages to press their demands for retribution.)

In that climate it was reasonable to worry, upon Elijah Muhammad's death in 1975, that the friction might lead to open warfare among the organization's contending factions, particularly between those identified with Farrakhan, who stood for the primacy of ideology, and the Messenger's son Wallace (Warith) Deen Muhammad, who had been linked much more with the Nation's business operations than with its ideological mission. Consequences of that sort did not materialize, and W.D. succeeded his father without apparent conflict, or at least with no immediate, publicly noticeable disruption.

The tension between the two agendas inevitably came to a head, however. Since the early 1970s the Nation had sought explicitly to recruit a middle-class membership as part of its drive for economic development. College students and professionals who joined were likely to be rewarded with responsible positions in the administrative hierarchy, but the Nation had only limited success in gaining petit-bourgeois adherents. It was, after all, a bit much to expect a college-educated constituency to accept as religious principle that the pig is a hybrid of the dog, the cat and the rat or that whites derive from an evil wizard's botched experiment on subhuman creatures.

At the same time, instability grew in the Muslim business operations. For whatever reasons—probably among them was a reluctance to open records to outside scrutiny—the organization retreated from its ambivalent interest in pursuing federal economic-development support. Yet the projects on the board required both considerable specialized expertise and capitalization surpassing the Nation's liquidity. A $3 million "loan" from the Libyan government in 1972 was a stopgap. Despite its ideological boost as a statement of Islamic solidarity, however, the Libyan deal was also a signal that the Messenger Muhammad could not finance his bold schemes internally and was unwilling to do so through regular outside sources.

The desire to broaden the Nation's class base rested on more than a need for expertise. The early newspaper and the bean pie, restaurant and fish ventures relied on the super-exploitation of members' labor. The religio-racial ideology— much like family ideology in a mom-and-pop store—could impose on members, at least in the short run, jobs offering low wages, no benefits and sometimes even no wages. But while it might help keep a newspaper solvent or finance a new restaurant, that ideologically driven accumulation strategy could not begin to support hospital construction or complex international commerce. Tithes or direct investment by a more affluent membership might better help meet capital needs.

Thus, when W.D. Muhammad inherited the Nation of Islam, it was stymied by a fundamental contradiction: The motors of its success—the religio-racial ideology, hermetic separatism and primitive strategy of capital accumulation— had become impediments to realizing the objectives that success had spawned. Negotiating the contradiction was constrained, moreover, by Farrakhan, who constituted himself on the right flank as guardian of the Messenger's orthodoxy, ready to challenge deviations.

Those contrary tendencies coexisted no more than three years. Before the split became public knowledge Muhammad had introduced sweeping changes. He repudiated his father's idiosyncratic religious doctrines—no more Yacub, the evil wizard—in favor of conventional Islamic beliefs. He changed the sect's name to the World Community of Islam in the West to reflect a move toward traditional Islam. He rejected the Messenger's insistence on abstaining from secular politics; instead, he actively urged political participation. In 1976 Muhammad gave up on the goal of economic independence, dismantled the group's holdings and considered seeking Small Business Administration assistance for member-entrepreneurs. (Rumor has it that titles to all the Nation's assets were held not by the organization but by the Messenger himself, who died intestate. Supposedly, W.D. hastened to sell off everything and divided the proceeds equally among all his father's legitimate and illegitimate offspring.)

W.D. had been a very close ally of Malcolm X, reputedly even through the break with his own father, and within his first year as leader of the organization he renamed the Harlem mosque in Malcolm's honor. To Farrakhan's partisans, who often pointed to W.D.'s support for Malcolm as evidence of filial impiety, that gesture must have affirmed suspicions of his blasphemous inclinations. More strain must have developed from W.D.'s proclamation in 1975 that whites thenceforth would be welcome as members of the sect. In 1978 Farrakhan announced his departure and the formation of a new Nation of Islam on the basis of the Messenger's original teachings. In 1985 the World Community of Islam in the West officially disbanded, leaving Farrakhan's group as Elijah Muhammad's sole organizational legacy.

Through the early 1980s Farrakhan maintained a relatively low profile as he built his organization by replicating the old Nation's forms and cultivating a membership drawn from its main social base on the margins of black working-class life. He re-established the Fruit of Islam, the paramilitary security force, and he restored the old ideology, Yacub and all. He even concocted a version of the old bean pie-and-fish economic development formula via Power Products, a line of household and personal items. (To date, the line has not done well, and Farrakhan seems not to have given it much attention.) As if to underscore his loyalty to the elder Muhammad's vision, Farrakhan resumed his old title, national representative of the Honorable Eli ah Muhammad and the Nation of Islam. The chief public signal of the Nation of Islam's return was the appearance of young men on inner-city streets wearing the group's distinctive suit and bow tie and aggressively selling the *Final Call* newspaper, which, but for the different title, follows the format of the old *Muhammad Speaks*.

The original Nation of Islam had grown in prominence in the years after the Supreme Court's 1954 *Brown v. Board of Education* decision because the organization, primarily through Malcolm, chose to operate within the discursive realm created by the developing activist movement. Debate about politics and racial strategy—at widely varying levels of sophistication—was extensive, and the rising tide of activism lifted all ideological and organizational boats.

In the early 1980s, though, there was no hint of a popular movement, and black political discourse had withered to fit entirely within the frame of elite-centered agendas for race-relations engineering. The cutting edge of racial advocacy, for example, was what political scientist Earl Picard described astutely at the time as the "corporate intervention strategy," pioneered by Jesse Jackson at Operation PUSH and adopted with less rhetorical flair by the National Urban League and the N.A.A.C.P. This strategy consisted in using the threat of consumer boycott to induce corporations to enter into "covenants" binding them to hire black managers, contract with black vendors, deposit in black banks and recruit black franchisees. (For a while, the N.A.A.C.P. concentrated on Hollywood, identifying the fate of the race with its representation in the film industry.) At the same time Ronald Reagan was pressing ahead with a rhetoric and battle plan steeped in racial revanchism, and official black opposition ranged from feeble to incoherent. In that context, the Fruit of Islam selling newspapers outside the supermarket looked for all the world like living anachronisms.

In the race for the 1984 Democratic presidential nomination, however, Farrakhan demonstrated the new Nation of Islam's political departure from the old. Unlike Elijah Muhammad, Farrakhan did not remain publicly aloof from electoral politics. He openly supported Jackson's candidacy and even provided him with a Fruit of Islam security force. Because of Farrakhan's and the Nation's long association with anti-Semitic rhetoric, his closeness to Jackson was thrown into relief in the wake of the "Hymietown" controversy.)

Milton Coleman, the *Washington Post* reporter who disclosed Jackson's remarks, was condemned widely as a race traitor, but Farrakhan raised the ante: "We're going to make an example of Milton Coleman. One day soon, we will punish you by death, because you are interfering with the future of our babies— for white people and against the good of yourself and your own people. This is a fitting punishment for such dogs." (Farrakhan has always denied he made these remarks.)

That inflamed rhetoric, along with Farrakhan's reference to Judaism as a "gutter religion," prodded a temporizing Jackson to distance himself publicly from Farrakhan, and the incident made sensationalistic copy throughout the information industry. For those with longer memories Farrakhan's attack on Coleman was a chilling reminder of the thuggish currents of the past. Indeed, his theretofore most notoriously threatening pronouncement—against Malcolm X—had set a frightening precedent. In December 1964 he wrote in *Muhammad Speaks:*

> Only those who wish to be led to hell, or to their doom, will follow Malcolm. The die is set and Malcolm shall not escape, especially after such foolish talk about his benefactor in trying to rob him of the divine glory which Allah has bestowed upon him. Such a man as Malcolm is worthy of death—and would have met with death if it had not been for Muhammad's confidence in Allah for victory over the enemies.

Two months later Malcolm was assassinated.

In retrospect, the significance of the Milton Coleman incident lay in how it propelled Farrakhan into the new, mass-mediated space in Afro-American politics first carved out by Jesse Jackson. Jackson's 1984 campaign oscillated between simplistic racial appeals ("It's our turn now!") and claims to represent some larger "moral force." As I have argued in *The Jesse Jackson Phenomenon,* that oscillation was rooted in a contradiction between the campaign's public posture as the crest of a broadly based social movement and the reality that it could rely on black votes only. The pressure to increase the black vote justified a mobilization strategy that often approached pure demagogy. In an August 1984 interview with *Ebony,* Jackson described himself as the carrier of "the emotions and self-respect and inner security of the whole race." The messianism implicit in that perception of his racial role appeared more clearly in his insinuation in that same interview that a Virginia supporter's terminal cancer was cured by going to a Jackson rally. In the midst of the Reagan counterrevolution and black elites' typically uninspired and ineffectual responses, that sort of demagogic appeal found a popular audience. With no more promising agenda available, racial cheerleading at least offered a soothing catharsis. The promise of deliverance by proxy, of racial absorption into Jackson's persona, consoled some with simple explanations and apparently easy remedies ("If all black people could just get together behind Jesse . . .").

But between 1984 and 1988 Jackson moved to consolidate his position as a racial broker in mainstream national politics and to expand his domain to include putative representation of all the "locked out." That shift required soft-pedaling the race line, and instead of making sharp denunciations of the nasty grass-roots racism expressed in Howard Beach and Forsyth County, Georgia, he attempted to invoke the common interests of poor whites and poor blacks. Jackson's transition from the posture of militant insurgent to a more subdued insider's style left vacant the specific racial space that he had created and that had proved to be marketable. Louis Farrakhan's emergence as a national political figure is largely the story of his efforts to replace Jackson as central embodiment and broker of the black race-nationalist political persona. Those efforts began, at least symbolically, with Jackson's grudging acquiescence to white pressure to criticize Farrakhan after the "Hymietown" incident.

The notoriety acquired in that incident fueled Farrakhan's rise in two ways. First, it simply increased his name recognition, especially among a younger generation with no recollection of the old Nation of Islam and his role therein. Second, the heavy barrage of sensationalistic coverage and the sanctimonious white response to the affair afforded an image of Farrakhan and Jackson joined in racial martyrdom. Repudiation of Farrakhan has become a litmus test imposed by white opinion makers for black participation in mainstream politics, and many blacks perceive the test as a humiliating power play. Farrakhan's messianic pretensions, moreover, give him a style something like a counterpunching boxer, and he deftly turned the assault on him into evidence of his authenticity as a race leader. Whites and their agents, the argument goes, expend so much energy on discrediting him because he is a genuine advocate of black interests and thus a threat to white racial domination. In that view, the more he is attacked, the greater his authenticity and the more emphatically he must be defended.

Farrakhan hardly invented this style. Jackson and his black supporters have routinely dismissed criticism by accusing critics of either racism or race treason. Marion Barry, Gus Savage and legions of less prominent malefactors have wrapped themselves in red, black and green rhetoric to conceal abuses of public trust or other failings. Nor is the practice an "African survival." Jimmy Swaggart, Billy James Hargis, Richard Nixon and Oliver North all claim to have been beleaguered by a comparable conspiracy of liberal-communists. Farrakhan stands out because he has been cast in our public theater—like Qaddafi and Noriega, both of whom he has defended—as a figure of almost cartoonishly demonic proportions. He has become uniquely notorious because his inflammatory nationalist persona has helped to center public discussion of Afro-American politics on the only issue (except affirmative action, of course) about which most whites ever show much concern: What do blacks think of whites?

7

The New Black Conservatives

Theodore Rueter

Adam Myerson, editor of *Policy Review* and vice president for educational affairs at the Heritage Foundation, wrote recently that "an earthquake is about to rock American politics at its foundations. Sometime before the end of this century, a very substantial minority, if not a majority, of African Americans are going to begin identifying with political conservatism rather than political liberalism."[1]

Myerson maintains that this earthquake is about to hit because "liberalism is totally unprepared to take charge of the next stage of the civil rights revolution: The restoration of strong families and communities in America's poor and working-class neighborhoods." Equalizing opportunities for African American children is impossible, he says, "when 70 percent of them are growing up without fathers." The American dream cannot be shared "when mothers are afraid to let their children play outside, when businesses are afraid to open shop, and mailroom clerks are afraid to work overtime or go to night school lest they be shot or robbed on the way home." Myerson charges that "liberalism has no answers for these catastrophes."[2]

To address contemporary social problems, black conservatives favor equal opportunity instead of affirmative action, and personal initiative instead of the welfare state. Black conservatives favor free markets, individual responsibility, cultural conservatism, and a "color-blind" approach to public policy.

Black conservatives have been under attack for these views. They have been called "racial traitors"[3] and "right-wing racists."[4] They have been accused of self-hatred, of egoism, of being disrespectful toward the poor, of being "house niggers," and of being "willing to sell out an entire race for the sake of their own gratification."[5] Spike Lee claims that Malcolm X would call Clarence Thomas "a handkerchief head, a chicken- and biscuit-eating Uncle Tom."[6] Lee also said that

Michael Williams, undersecretary of education in the Bush administration, and an opponent of minority scholarships, "should be beat with a Louisville Slugger in an alley."[7]

For their part, black conservatives seem to view black liberals with equal disdain. Clarence Thomas has stated that all civil rights leaders ever do is "bitch, bitch, bitch, moan and moan and whine,"[8] and that they have "deep-seated animosity" toward black conservatives.[9] Political activist Alan Keyes accuses civil rights leaders of "intellectual totalitarianism."[10] Another black conservative urges blacks to abandon the "politically correct" positions of the "liberal paternalistic plantation."[11]

Black conservatives are becoming increasingly prominent. Martin Kilson, professor of government at Harvard University, states that "the emergence of conservative activists among black intellectuals during the past decade or so represents a new leadership stratum among black Americans. While their numbers are small, the impact of their political presence has been quite significant."[12]

This paper will profile the best-known black conservatives, then examine the battle for black America, in terms of public opinion, electoral behavior, and ideology. Finally, it will explore various political, economic, and social explanations for the growth of black conservatism.

Black Conservative Intellectuals

There have always been black conservatives in America. Perhaps the original black conservative was Booker T. Washington, founder of the Tuskegee Institute in Alabama, and an advocate of self-help and self-respect. In addition, George S. Schuyler, called "the preeminent black conservative in this century,"[13] published a column in *The Pittsburgh Courier* for decades. His book, *Black and Conservative,* is considered a minor classic.[14]

Certainly the best-known contemporary black conservative is Clarence Thomas, an associate justice on the United States Supreme Court. The grandson of Georgia sharecroppers, Thomas was abandoned by his father at age seven. He did not have a home with running water and indoor toilet until he was seven. He was educated by Catholic nuns, "all of whom were adamant that I grow up to make something of myself."[15] He graduated from Holy Cross College and Yale Law School.

Before joining the Supreme Court, Thomas served for 16 months as an associate justice on the United States Court of Appeals for the District of Columbia. From 1982 to 1990 he was chairman of the United States Equal Employment Opportunity Commission, where he was criticized for taking a narrow view of civil rights law and for being unsympathetic to age discrimination cases. In 1981, he was assistant secretary of education for civil rights. Prior to that, he was an aide to Missouri Republican Senator John Danforth, a corporate attorney, and an assistant attorney general of the state of Missouri.

President Bush nominated Thomas to the Supreme Court on July 1, 1991. He was confirmed by a vote of 52–48, after a bitter battle that developed when Anita Hill, a University of Oklahoma law professor, accused Thomas of sexual harassment. The Thomas/Hill hearings before the Senate Judiciary Committee captivated the nation for a week. The hearings heightened awareness of sexual harassment, damaged the reputation of the United States Senate, and damaged the reputation of Clarence Thomas.[16]

While not as well known as Clarence Thomas, several other black conservatives are gaining increasing attention:

Stephen Carter is William Nelson Cromwell Professor of Law at Yale University, where he specializes in Constitutional law.[17] Carter was a law clerk to Supreme Court Justice Thurgood Marshall. He has appeared on CNN and CSPAN, and has written for the *New York Times*.[18] His book, *Reflections of an Affirmative Action Baby,* received a front page, above-the-fold review in the *New York Times Book Review*.[19] His second book is *The Culture of Disbelief: How American Law and Politics Trivialize Religious Devotion,* which was read and endorsed by President Clinton.[20] He has also written *The Confirmation Mess: Cleaning Up the Federal Appointments Process,*[21] as well as numerous law review articles.

Carter states, "I got into law school because I am black."[22] He tells the story of being initially rejected by Harvard Law School, but then being admitted once the admissions committee discovered "additional information that should have been counted in your favor."[23] Carter was told by one Harvard official that they had initially rejected him because "we assumed from your record that you were white."[24]

Carter has deeply mixed feelings about affirmative action. He asserts that affirmative action reinforces racial stereotypes and benefits middle- and upper-class blacks rather than the underclass. He believes that affirmative action reinforces the assumption "that black people cannot compete intellectually with white people."[25] Similarly, he maintains that affirmative action creates the "Best Black Syndrome," wherein the achievements of blacks are compared to those of other blacks, rather than to professionals as a whole.

Alan Keyes is a Baltimore-based radio talk show host, columnist, and lecturer, as well as a candidate for the 1996 Republican presidential nomination.

Keyes has held a variety of posts. He was interim president of Alabama A & M University, director of Citizens Against Government Waste (a lobby group with four hundred thousand members), a resident scholar at the American Enterprise Institute, and assistant secretary of state for international organization affairs and ambassador to the United Nations Economic and Social Council (both in the Reagan administration, where he was a protégé of Jeane Kirkpatrick). He was the Republican nominee for the United States Senate from Maryland in 1988 and 1992. He holds a Ph.D. in government from Harvard University and is the author of *Masters of the Dream: The Strength and Betrayal of Black America.*[26]

A fiery public speaker, Keyes based his political campaigns on the need for moral revival. "The debate over abortion epitomizes how we define freedom," he said. "Abortion is a moral wrong. We have the opportunity, the duty to stand up and say, 'Nay!'" Keyes also speaks against homosexuality, teen-age pregnancy, "godless" schooling, and the loss of "those values that made this country what it is."

Glenn Loury is professor of economics at Boston University. He formerly taught political economy at the Kennedy School of Government at Harvard University. He earned a Ph.D. in economics from MIT, and has taught at the University of Michigan. He grew up on the south side of Chicago. He is co-editor (with James Q. Wilson) of *Families, Schools, and Delinquency Prevention*[27] and author of *One by One From the Inside Out: Race and Responsibility in America.*[28] His articles have appeared in major national publications.[29] He is a consulting economist for the Rockefeller Foundation, AT&T, the Federal Trade Commission, and the Congressional Joint Economic Committee.

On the issue of tenant management of public housing, Loury has called it "a good idea," since it would create more effective, socially responsible management. However, he also contended that "it is not a complete housing program," since it would "not change the fact that people are poor," and since it would do nothing to create additional housing.

Loury is also ambivalent about the idea of all-black public schools, which have been created in Milwaukee, New York, and Minneapolis. He comments, "There is no compelling evidence that segregation will help influence black male behavior positively—but you can't assume that it *won't* work." While Loury concludes that it makes sense to experiment with all-black education, due to the failings of urban public schools, he also found it "deeply troubling" that so many blacks favor withdrawal from mainstream white society. He warns that "all of the answers are not in and of blacks."[30]

Thomas Sowell is a Senior Fellow at the Hoover Institution on War, Peace, and Revolution at Stanford University. A native of Harlem, he holds a Ph.D. in economics from the University of Chicago. He has taught at Amherst, Cornell, Brandeis, Howard, and UCLA, and has written twenty books.[31] He writes a nationally syndicated newspaper column.

The majority of Sowell's writings focus on the economics of race and ethnicity. His central argument is that blacks should imitate the success of other immigrant groups, such as Koreans and Jews. He is a strong opponent of affirmative action, because it proposes to remedy economic problems through political means.

Shelby Steele is professor of English at San Jose State University. He came to prominence with the publication of *The Content of Our Character: A New Vision of Race in America,* which argues that blacks' own sense of "victimization" is a far stronger barrier to progress than racism.[32] His articles have appeared in major national publications,[33] and he has appeared on "Nightline." On the December 21, 1990, edition of "The McLaughlin Group," *New Republic* contributing editor

Morton Kondracke called Steele the "thinker of the year." Columnist Ellen Goodman calls *The Content of Our Character* "part of the national debate about racial policies."[34]

Steele takes a psychological approach to the problem of race in America. He contends that whites should rid themselves of a sense of guilt, and that blacks should rid themselves of a sense of victimization. He states, "The message to blacks must be: America hurt you badly and that is wrong, but entitlements only prolong the guilt, while development overcomes it." He asserts that "selfish white guilt is really self-importance" and a form of "moral colonialism."[35] He contends that blacks face barriers to development because "the memory of oppression has such power, magnitude, depth, and nuance that it constantly drains our best resources into more defense than is strictly necessary."[36] Steele believes that many blacks have an obsessive "enemy-memory," which leads to psycho-emotional irrationality.

Walter Williams is John M. Olin Professor of Economics at George Mason University. He writes a nationally syndicated newspaper column, is on the board of contributors of *Reason* magazine (a libertarian publication), and is a regular commentator on "The Nightly Business Report" on PBS. He has appeared on "Face the Nation," "Nightline," "Firing Line," and "Crossfire," and has been the guest host of the Rush Limbaugh radio program. He grew up in a Philadelphia ghetto, was court-martialed by the Army for racial activism, and was a militant Black Panther sympathizer.[37]

In *The State Against Blacks*, Williams argues that black poverty is better explained by economic and social rules than by racial discrimination. He contends that such regulations as minimum wage laws, occupational licensing, and labor unions restrict the ability of low-skilled blacks to advance economically.[38]

Robert Woodson is the founder and president of the National Center for Neighborhood Enterprise. He was formerly associated with the American Enterprise Institute. He attended graduate school in social work, and was president of a local NAACP chapter. He was offered the position of chief deputy to Jack Kemp, housing and urban development secretary in the Bush administration, but declined. He is the editor of *On the Road to Economic Freedom: An Agenda for Black Progress.*[39]

Woodson describes himself not as a "conservative," but as "a populist who believes that poor people should control the institutions that control their lives."[40] His primary mission is to promote the economic "empowerment" of the poor, through tenant management (or ownership) of public housing, school choice, and drug-free zones. He blames white liberal social workers for helping to make blacks dependent on government aid.

Other significant black conservatives include:

John Shipley Butler, professor of sociology and management at the University of Texas at Austin, and author of *Entrepreneurship and Self-Help Among Black Americans: A Reconsideration of Race and Economics*[41]

Stanley Crouch, the recipient of a 1993 MacArthur Foundation "genius" fellowship, and author of *Notes of a Hanging Judge: Essays and Review, 1979–1989*[42]

Eileen Gardner, a psychologist who is a Senior Fellow at the Heritage Foundation, and editor of *A New Agenda for Education*[43]

Ken Hamblin, a nationally syndicated radio talk show host who is based in Denver

Jay Parker, former chairman of Young Americans for Freedom

Armstrong Williams, a Washington, D.C., public relations executive, a radio talk show host, a frequent contributor to the op-ed page of *USA Today,* a former associate of Clarence Thomas at the Equal Employment Opportunity Commission, and a former aide to Senator Strom Thurmond. He is the author of *The Conscience of a Black Conservative: Letters to a Young Black Man*[44]

Anne Wortham, a sociology professor at the University of Missouri, and author of *The Other Side of Racism: A Philosophical Study of Black Race Consciousness*[45]

The Battle for Black America

The debate over the Clarence Thomas nomination demonstrated the political and intellectual turbulence within black America. While liberalism has been and continues to be the dominant political tradition within black America, black conservatism is making strides.

Black Public Opinion and Electoral Behavior

There is much evidence of black support for liberalism. Black support for Democratic presidential candidates stood at 74 percent in 1976, 73 percent in 1980, 80 percent in 1984, 77 percent in 1988, and 82 percent in 1992.[46] In 24 presidential primary exit polls conducted in 1988, Jesse Jackson received 92 percent of the black vote.[47]

Public opinion polls also reveal the strength of liberal attitudes among blacks. A nationwide survey by the Joint Center for Political and Economic Studies and the Gallup organization sampled 1,067 blacks and 1,414 whites on a variety of social issues. The data indicate that the black middle class is more conservative than the black lower class, especially on the issue of affirmative action. However, at each income level, blacks have substantially more liberal attitudes than whites on social welfare spending, affirmative action, defense spending, and moral values.[48]

There is much evidence that the views of black conservatives are out of step with the views of mainstream black America. According to surveys by ABC/*Washington Post* and Gallup/*Newsweek,* "only about 5 percent of blacks currently identify with the GOP."[49] In addition, "only about 20 percent of blacks are willing to classify themselves as conservatives."[50]

There is a strong consensus among African Americans on several issues. A 1991 Gallup/*Newsweek* poll indicated that "almost 80 percent of blacks accept the civil rights leadership's view that the federal government is doing too little to help blacks."[51] Also, the same survey showed that 70 percent of blacks "consider quotas necessary to achieve fairness in education, hiring, and promotion; only about three in ten think fairness can be achieved without quotas."[52] Similarly, numerous polls have shown that black support for school integration is "virtually universal."[53]

Black public opinion is not always one-sided. According to surveys by ABC/*Washington Post,* black opinion is divided "between those who accept and those who reject the proposition that blacks have helped to cause many of the problems they face."[54] African Americans are similarly divided on the question of affirmative action. One poll showed that 50 percent of blacks agreed that "because of past discrimination against black people, qualified blacks should receive preference over equally qualified whites in such matters as getting into college or getting jobs," while 50 percent disagreed.[55]

A 1992 poll sponsored by the Joint Center for Political and Economic Studies had several interesting results. Nearly one-third of the poll respondents identified themselves as "conservative." In addition, 88 to 91 percent of black respondents said they favor school choice, letting tenants buy public housing, and evicting tenants from public housing if they are convicted of using or selling drugs. Fifty-seven percent of black respondents opposed "additional benefits for single welfare mothers who have additional children."[56]

However, this same poll revealed some strikingly nonconservative views as well. Seventy-nine percent of black respondents "favor affirmative action, 76 percent want to cut defense dramatically and use the money for urban programs, 81 percent think too little money is being spent on education, 83 percent favor Afrocentric education, 80 percent favor new government initiatives to help young black men, two-thirds are Democrats, and 75 percent rate Jesse Jackson favorably."[57]

Liberal attitudes are also prevalent among the nation's black political establishment. All but two members of the Congressional Black Caucus are liberal Democrats. Much of the black political leadership (including the Congressional Black Caucus, the Leadership Conference on Civil Rights, and the NAACP) opposed the Clarence Thomas nomination.

One reason for the dominance of liberalism within black America is the Republican Party's image problem. The party of Jesse Helms, Barry Goldwater, Ronald Reagan, David Duke, and Pat Buchanan is unlikely to command anything approaching majority black support.[58] Northwestern University political scientist Adolph Reed argues that black allegiance to the Republican Party is "unthinkable," because of their "pandering to demagoguery" about "crime," "welfare fraud," and "traditional values." He contends that such rhetoric is a "scarcely veiled assault on black-identified legislation and programs."[59]

Many black political analysts are confident that liberalism will remain the dominant black ideology. San Francisco State University political scientist Robert C. Smith offers several reasons. One is that black conservatism "ignores the continuing significance of racism on the psychic and material well-being of blacks." Another is that "the objective economic interests of low income and occupational status groups" is best served by the low-unemployment/high-inflation policy of the Democratic Party. Further, a disproportionate number of middle-class blacks are government employees, and thus are not likely to support conservative calls for reductions in government spending.[60] Paraphrasing Frederick Douglass, Smith concludes that "with respect to the complex set of economic and social problems confronting the Afro-American community, liberalism is the deck, all else the sea."[61]

While black support for liberalism is strong, there is also evidence of a growth of conservatism in the black community. A *USA Today* poll indicates that 54 percent of blacks supported the Clarence Thomas nomination (even though 52 percent said that Thomas does not reflect the views of most blacks).[62] An ABC/*Washington Post* poll in 1989 indicated that 60 percent of blacks agreed with the statement "If blacks would try harder, they could be just as well off as whites."[63] A survey by Northwestern University's Survey Laboratory indicated that 94 percent of blacks (as opposed to 90 percent of whites) agreed that "hard work" is "essential/very important for getting ahead in life."[64]

Black conservatives are also beginning to seek elective office. In 1986, William Lucas ran unsuccessfully for governor of Michigan.[65] In 1988, Alan Keyes received 37 percent of the vote against Maryland Senator Paul Sarbanes,[66] and Maurice Dawkins received 29 percent of the vote against Virginia Senator Charles S. Robb.[67] In 1992, Alan Keyes received 29 percent of the vote against Maryland Senator Barbara Mikulski.[68]

The 1990 election was something of a breakthrough for black conservatives. Gary Franks was elected to the House of Representatives from Connecticut's nearly all-white Fifth District, becoming the first black Republican congressman since Chicago's Oscar de Priest left office in 1935. He has attracted a great deal of press attention.[69]

Also in 1990, Kenneth Blackwell received 49 percent of the vote in Ohio's First Congressional District[70] and Al Brown received 39 percent of the vote in Kentucky's Third Congressional District.[71] Finally, a 1990 exit poll conducted by Voter Research and Surveys found that 22 percent of blacks had voted for Republican congressional candidates.[72]

The 1994 mid-term elections were significant in several ways. First, exit polls indicated that several Republican candidates received a surprising percentage of the black vote. California Governor Pete Wilson and Michigan Governor John Engler each got 16 percent of the black vote; incoming Pennsylvania Governor Tom Ridge received 13 percent. Also, Bernadette Castro, who challenged Daniel Patrick Moynihan for a Senate seat from New York, received 20 percent of the black vote.[73]

The 1994 elections also witnessed the election of two black Republican congressmen (both from largely white districts). In Connecticut, Gary Franks was elected to a third term with 52 percent of the vote. Even more notably, J. C. Watts defeated his opponent, 52 percent to 43 percent, in Oklahoma's Fourth District. Watts was a star quarterback for the University of Oklahoma Sooners, and then played in the Canadian Football League for six years. He is an active member of the Fellowship of Christian Athletes. During the campaign, he called his opponent "a liberal lawyer who's all over the map on the issues."[74]

Finally, in 1994, twenty-four black Republicans ran for the U.S. House of Representatives.[75] Eight of these candidates won at least 40 percent of the vote.[76] Most notably, Marc Little, a Florida television personality and entrepreneur, captured 42 percent of the vote against black liberal Representative Corinne Brown. In Missouri, Ron Freeman received 43 percent of the vote in the Fifth District.[77]

One of the most interesting candidates in 1994 was Guy Wilson, a black Libertarian, who ran for Congress in California's Thirty-seventh district. Wilson supports school vouchers, abolition of the Food and Drug Administration, and repeal of the Sixteenth Amendment. He opposes gun control and "three strikes" laws. He is fond of the motto "Live free or die!"[78] Wilson received 22 percent of the vote.

The Black Intellectual Debate

The increasing prominence of black conservatives has created an intense debate within the black community.[79] One criticism of black conservatives is that they are tools of the white establishment. Martin Kilson maintains that black conservatives "essentially defend the plutocratic power boundaries that make up the American power establishment."[80] The behavior of black conservatives, according to Kilson, is explained by the fact that "newcomers to national elite roles in American society seem impelled toward conservatism by anxieties about self-worth that antedated their class mobility."[81] Conservatism offers newcomers "a sense of substantive status-identity, contrasted to the mercurial or tenuous status-identity connected with their original ethnic or religious background."[82]

While black conservative "newcomers" are seeking an identity, according to Kilson, they are alienated from every possible affiliation. One potential role is that of "dissenters." Stephen Carter compares black conservatives to such historical giants as W. E. B. Du Bois, Paul Robeson, and Martin Luther King Jr.[83]

Kilson rejects this comparison. He writes, "Carter is confusing two different genres of Afro-American dissenters: activist dissenters and ritualistic dissenters." While activist dissenters seek to assist the weak and the excluded against "greed, privileges, and oppression," ritualistic dissenters seek, "above all, obfuscation, manipulating the dissident tradition" to "support established patterns of power."[84]

Black conservatives may also be alienated from the African American community. Cornel West, professor of Afro-American Studies at Harvard University, contends that "the overriding aim of the new black conservatives is to undermine the position of the black liberals."[85] He claims that black conservatives have spent limited effort developing and promoting a policy agenda, because they are "obsessed" with criticizing the liberal perspective.[86]

Another reason that black conservatives are alienated from the black community, according to Martin Kilson, is that the legacy of conservatism is racism. American conservatives "typically ignored the authoritarian and violent racial-caste practices and values arrayed against black Americans in southern states where the vast majority of blacks lived."[87] He states that American conservatism has exhibited a "crass indifference" to "problem-solving responses to our race-caste legacy, claiming a nearly zero track record in constructive programs, whether in the private or the public sector."[88]

Cornel West maintains that black conservatives place excessive faith in market capitalism. He states that the market is no substitute for the welfare state, since the private sector "is simply uninterested" in creating jobs for the poor.[89] Whereas black conservatives believe that transfer payments to the black needy create dependency and destroy self-reliance, West maintains that cutting welfare "will not promote self-reliance or strong black families but will only produce even more black cultural disorientation and more devastated black households." Without income and without jobs, the black poor "become even more prone toward criminality, drugs, and alcoholism."[90]

Several critics have also offered a sexual- and gender-based analysis of black conservatism. Cornel West chides black conservatives for failing to examine "the pervasiveness of sexual and military images used by the mass media and deployed by the advertising industry in order to entice and titillate consumers." In West's view, black conservatives are guilty of overlooking "the degree to which market forces of advanced capitalist processes thrive on sexual and military images."[91]

Similarly, Julianne Malveaux, an economist and syndicated columnist, asserts that black conservatism is a masculine ideology which reinforces capitalist patriarchy.[92] The very language of black conservatism is based on sports metaphors such as "rules of the game," level playing field," "success," and "winners."[93] Black male conservatives "are exercising their masculinist game" by opposing affirmative action and "placing a higher priority on rules and appearances than on outcomes and equity."[94] According to Malveaux, "women don't see the world in such combative terms. Life is not so clear cut for those well acquainted with the double shift, with dashed hopes and broken promises."[95]

Black conservatives have also been criticized for their views on affirmative action. Julianne Malveaux states that "some of the black men who are affirmative action-bashing are really trying to affirm that their status is the result of a fair fight."[96] Martin Kilson suggests that the "status devaluation associated with the best black syndrome is clearly the primary motivation surrounding the emergence of many new black conservatives."[97]

Kilson also maintains that black conservatives "fail to recognize that the best black syndrome issue would exist whether or not affirmative-action policies prevailed." This is because most white Americans "still cling to a deep psychocultural investment in neoracist interactions with black Americans, one such interaction being an emotional incapacity to view black achievers through the same prisms through which they view white achievers."

This argument seems spurious. Black achievement without affirmative action would create *greater* cognitive dissonance to white racists than black achievement under affirmative action. Carter's thesis is that affirmative action *reinforces* the very tendency Kilson identifies—the emotional inability of some whites to view black achievement in the same manner as white achievement.

Finally, Kilson argues against Shelby Steele's concept of the "enemy-memory." Kilson criticizes Steele for failing to compare "black Americans' victimization under white supremacy" with the experience of Jews under anti-Semitism. Kilson states that "the Jewish-American 'enemy-memory' movement and its activism have scarcely harmed Jewish social mobility, although, for Steele, 'enemy-memory' is supposed to extract a grave price in social mobility."[98] Kilson believes that if Jewish Americans have "pragmatically disciplined 'enemy-memory' behavior," then "the vast majority of black Americans are capable of doing the same."[99]

This argument may be misguided. The fact that Jews have advanced economically in spite of their "enemy-memory" does not deny the impact of "victimization" psychology and the memory of oppression upon black Americans. In addition, Jewish Americans did not come to the United States involuntarily, and have faced far less discrimination than blacks.

While critics have raised many objections to black conservatism, Cornel West offers some praise. He states that "the new black conservatives have had their most salutary effect on the public discourse by highlighting the breakdown of the moral fabric in the country and especially in black working poor and very poor communities."[100]

Explaining the Rise of Black Conservatism

The increasing prominence of black conservatives is the result of several political and economic factors: the salience of the racial issue in American politics, the efforts of the Republican Party and the conservative movement, the rightward shift in American politics, the growth of the black middle class, and the nature of the contemporary American political economy.

Race and American Politics

The first explanation for the increasing significance of black conservatives is that the mind of America is clearly on race. *Washington Post* reporter Thomas Byrne Edsall argues that race is the most important issue facing American society, and that "black" has become a code word for crime, poverty, welfare, and drugs.[101]

There is much evidence of racial tension in America. A recent poll showed that 25 percent of blacks agreed with the statement that the government "deliberately makes sure that drugs are easily available in poor neighborhoods in order to harm black people." Thirty-two percent of blacks agreed that the government singles out black elected officials for prosecution, and 10 percent of blacks agreed that AIDS "was deliberately created in a laboratory in order to infect black people."[102]

Many whites have similarly negative attitudes toward blacks. The National Opinion Research Center's General Social Survey for 1990 found that 74 percent of whites thought that blacks are more likely to prefer living on welfare. Sixty-two percent of whites regarded blacks as less likely to be hard-working, 53 percent thought blacks less intelligent, and 51 percent thought blacks less patriotic.[103]

Racial tensions have been aggravated by a series of recent incidents. In New York City, whites attacked blacks in Howard Beach and in Bensonhurst; a group of blacks attacked a white woman jogging in Central Park; in Crown Heights, a mob of young blacks killed a Hasidic Jew, Yankel Rosenbaum; and Tawana Brawley, supported by race-baiter Al Sharpton, charged (falsely) that she had been beaten by a white man and deposited in a garbage can.[104] In Washington, D.C., black leaders charged that the 1990 arrest of Mayor Marion Barry for cocaine possession was motivated by racial considerations. In Milwaukee, former alderman Michael McGee, a rifle-toting member of the Black Panthers, threatens terrorist actions if conditions for blacks do not improve.[105]

There is little doubt that race plays a strong role in American politics. For example, the black vote was the margin of victory for Jimmy Carter in 1976 in Alabama, Florida, Louisiana, Maryland, Mississippi, Missouri, New York, North Carolina, Ohio, Pennsylvania, South Carolina, Texas, and Wisconsin.

The issue of race was particularly evident in the 1988 presidential campaign. George Bush made Willie Horton, a black murderer and rapist, a symbol for lawlessness, terror, and liberalism. Eight of the ten states that voted for Michael Dukakis (Hawaii, Iowa, Massachusetts, Minnesota, Oregon, Vermont, Washington, and Wisconsin) have disproportionately small black populations.

Recently, the Republican Party has made racial quotas a major campaign issue. In 1990, North Carolina Senator Jesse Helms won reelection (against a black candidate, former Charlotte mayor Harvey Gantt) with the help of a television commercial showing the hands of a white man crumbling a rejection letter as a stern voice stated, "You needed that job, and you were the best qualified. But it had to go to a minority because of racial quotas." Some political strategists urged President Bush to emphasize the "KKK" issues: Kuwait, quotas, and crime.[106]

Reagan, Republicans, and Conservatives

Black conservatism has also grown because of the efforts of the Reagan administration, the conservative movement, and the Republican Party.[107] Indeed, Mack

Jones argues that "the prominence of black political thinkers is directly proportionate to the power and prestige of their white patrons."[108]

On December 12 and 13, 1980, the Institute for Contemporary Studies, a conservative think tank, sponsored a Conference on Black Alternatives at the Fairmont Hotel in San Francisco, which attracted a great deal of attention.[109] Clarence Thomas, then an aide to Missouri Senator John Danforth, attended the conference, where he met Hoover Institution Fellow Thomas Sowell, George Mason University Economics Professor Walter Williams, San Diego Urban League President Clarence Pendleton, and broadcaster Tony Brown.[110] Harvard University Government Professor Martin Kilson, Columbia University Political Science Professor Charles Hamilton, and University of Chicago Economics Professor Milton Friedman also attended the Fairmont conference.

The incoming Reagan administration was represented at the conference by Edwin Meese, counsel to the president. The president of the Institute for Contemporary Studies noted that Meese's presence revealed "the depth of the new administration's interest in exploring new policy alternatives."[111]

In September 1982, the New Coalition for Economic and Social Change hosted a conference on "Rethinking the Black Agenda," co-sponsored by the Heritage Foundation, a conservative think tank.[112] Speakers included Heritage President Edwin Feulner, Sequoia Institute President (and former Reagan adviser) Robert Hawkins, and Charles Murray, author of the controversial *Losing Ground: American Social Policy, 1950–1980.*[113]

President Reagan was at odds with the traditional civil rights establishment throughout his first term. Black leaders were distressed by Reagan's talk of "welfare queens," by his granting of tax-exempt status to segregated Bob Jones University, by his opposition to extension of the Voting Rights Act, by his opposition to the Martin Luther King holiday, and by his support for the white South African government.

Five days before his second inaugural, Reagan further distanced himself from established civil rights leaders by meeting with about twenty black conservatives in the White House. The group was headed by Robert Woodson (president of the National Center for Neighborhood Enterprise), and called itself the Council for a Black Economic Agenda.

The meeting was the brainchild of James Cicconi, a White House political aide. In a series of memos, Cicconi advised President Reagan to give attention to potentially friendly blacks and to disregard his black antagonists. "For the immediate future," wrote Cicconi, "we must avoid the 'established' black leadership. Such leaders are unremittingly hostile to this President and cannot be expected to take a constructive approach." Cicconi also maintained that the established black leadership was more interested in personal power and publicity than in "new approaches to black problems." He asserted that civil rights leaders are "personally and rhetorically committed to a philosophy which cannot be reconciled with our own."[114]

Reagan also furthered the black conservative movement with his appointments. Clarence Thomas served for one year as undersecretary of education for civil rights, and then chaired the Equal Employment Opportunity Commission for eight years. In 1981, Thomas Sowell had his choice of being secretary of housing and urban development or a member of the Council of Economic Advisers.[115] In 1987, Glenn Loury was offered the position of undersecretary of education.[116] Alan Keyes served in prominent foreign policy positions at the State Department and the United Nations. Clarence Pendleton chaired the United States Civil Rights Commission, and Samuel Pierce headed the Department of Housing and Urban Development.

Several black conservatives were appointed by President Reagan to sub-Cabinet positions. Jake Simmons served as undersecretary of the interior. Harold Daly was director of the Mineral Management Service in the Department of the Interior. Melvin Bradley was named a consultant on Urban Affairs in the White House Office of Policy Development. Richard Douglas served as deputy assistant secretary of agriculture. Arthur Teele was named head of the Urban Mass Transportation Administration.[117]

President Bush also named black conservatives to key positions. He appointed Clarence Thomas to the Court of Appeals of the District of Columbia in 1990, and then nominated him for the Supreme Court in 1991. Bush's secretary of health and human services, Louis Sullivan, took conservative positions on abortion and health care. Bush's assistant secretary of education for civil rights, Michael Williams, announced the administration's short-lived ban on minority scholarships. Kenneth Blackwell, an unsuccessful 1990 Congressional candidate from Ohio, became deputy undersecretary of housing and urban development for intergovernmental relations. Kay James, formerly with the National Right to Life Committee, became an assistant secretary of health and human services. Finally, Bush nominated William Lucas, a former Wayne County commissioner, to be assistant attorney general for civil rights; the nomination was rejected by the Senate.

Bush also appointed a number of black conservatives to the White House staff. Joseph Perkins, formerly an assistant to Vice President Quayle and formerly an editorial writer for the *Wall Street Journal,* is now an editorial writer for the *San Diego Union.* Bush's congressional liaison, Frederick McClure, helped to prepare Clarence Thomas for his Supreme Court confirmation hearings. Claudia Butts, formerly of the Heritage Foundation, was Bush's liaison with blacks.

A number of organizations are actively promoting the ideas and careers of black conservatives. The Institute for Contemporary Studies, located in San Francisco, sponsored the 1980 Fairmont Conference on black alternatives. The Heritage Foundation sponsors a "New Majority Project," and has published two editions of *A Conservative Agenda for Black Americans.*[118] Robert Woodson's National Center for Neighborhood Enterprise has produced a number of books and videotapes on school choice, economic opportunity, drugs, and tenant management of public housing. It sponsored a national conference on black self-reliance in August 1991. Further, the Lincoln Institute for Research and Education, founded in 1978 by Jay Parker (a former state chairman of Young Americans for Freedom), publishes a quarterly journal, the *Lincoln Review,* and distributes a number of books by black conservatives.

Perhaps the most significant organization promoting black conservatism is the National Center for Public Policy Research. This group worked with sixteen black conservatives to produce *Black America 1994: Changing Directions,* intended to compete with the National Urban League's annual *State of Black America* report.[119] It also sponsors Project 21, formed in 1992, which is aimed at creating alternative black leadership for the 21st century. Project 21 presents seminars and maintains a speakers bureau. Its purpose is to "promote the views of those African-Americans whose entrepreneurial spirit, sense of family and commitment to individual responsibility has been forgotten by many in Washington."

In addition, black conservatives have formed their own political organization, the Black America Political Action Committee. The group held a press conference at the National Press Club on November 10, 1994, which was broadcast live by CSPAN. Horace Cooper (legislative assistant to Republican Congressman Dick Armey), Teresa Doggett (unsuccessful Republican candidate for controller of Texas), Raynard Jackson (Washington, D.C., bureau chief for *National Minority Politics*), Phyllis Berry Myers (co-chair of the Committee),[120] Gwen Daye Richardson (editor of *National Minority Politics*), Willie Richardson (publisher of *National Minority Politics*), Alvin Williams (executive director of the committee), and Armstrong Williams (talk show host and newspaper columnist) all spoke at the press conference.

The Black America Political Action Committee was formed in September 1994. It has three components. The first is campaign contributions to (primarily federal) candidates. In 1994, the committee gave a total of $9,500 to eleven candidates; it hopes to distribute a million dollars in 1996.[121]

The second aspect is the Committee for Local Self-Government, which charters state and local political action committees. At the end of 1994, the committee had chartered fifteen state PACs; their goal is to charter thirty by the end of 1995.

Finally, the committee has created the Center for Effective Community Leadership, a 501(c)(3) organization which provides training in public speaking, campaign management, volunteer coordination and media appearances.

Several Christian organizations are assisting the cause of black conservatism. Focus on the Family, headed by James Dobson (which sponsors a daily 30-minute radio program), is organizing a ministry program dedicated to restoring the black family. The Christian Coalition, founded by Pat Robertson, is attempting to register black and Hispanic members. Also, the Traditional Values Coalition is attempting to unite white and black pastors in opposition to the governmental legitimation of homosexuality.

Syndicated columnist Cal Thomas believes that white conservatives should be even more active in promoting black conservatism. He calls on conservative political groups to establish a scholarship program for young black conservatives, to "break the hold liberals have had on the 'black' vote for the last half-century."[122]

The cause of black conservatism is increasingly well represented in the media. There are at least four black conservatives who host radio talk shows: Armstrong Williams of Washington, D.C.; Bill Thomas of Norfolk, Virginia; Alan Keyes of Baltimore; and Ken Hamblin of Denver (and a national network).[123] At minimum, there are five black conservative periodicals: *Destiny,* published by Emanuel McLittle in Lansing, Michigan; *National Minority Politics,* published in Houston by Willie Richardson; *Urban Family,* published by John Perkins in Pasadena, California; *Issues and Views,* a compilation of newspaper columns, published by Elizabeth Wright in New York; and the aforementioned *Lincoln Review.*

Black conservatives are also present on television. Tony Brown regularly presents a conservative viewpoint on "Tony Brown's Journal" on PBS. Black conservatives were profiled on ABC's "20/20" on May 13, 1994. Gwen Daye Richardson, editor of *National Minority Politics,* appeared on CSPAN's "Journalists Roundtable" on November 11, 1994 (and received great praise from many callers). Congressman Gary Franks was profiled on "Eye to Eye" on CBS on November 10, 1994; incoming Congressman J. C. Watts was profiled on the ABC Sunday Night News on November 6, 1994, and appeared on the "MacNeil-Lehrer NewsHour" on November 10, 1994.

There was even a television program with a black conservative character. "704 Houser," produced by Norman Lear, appeared briefly on CBS. The main character was a black Archie Bunker (704 Houser Street was the address occupied by the Bunkers on "All in the Family"). Rush Limbaugh had Norman Lear on his radio program to discuss the show.

The cause of black conservatism has also been aided by the Republican Party. The National Black Republican Council, headed by Fred Brown, has 25,000 members. The Council of 100, a national organization of black Republicans, was founded in 1974 by civil rights activist Samuel C. Jackson to facilitate the inclusion of blacks in the party. In 1989, Republican National Committee chairman Lee Atwater, deeply involved in the 1988 Willie Horton commercials, proclaimed his goal of welcoming more blacks into the GOP. Atwater created an "Outreach Division" of the RNC, which has now been subsumed within a newly created Office of Political Coalitions. The central purpose of the outreach program is to recruit black Republican candidates to run for office.[124]

There are various motivations for white Republicans and white conservatives to support black conservatives. One is that black conservatives make opposition to affirmative action and liberal social welfare programs more politically acceptable. Indeed, what alarmed black liberals about the Clarence Thomas appointment was that it provided "intellectual comfort and political cover to ideological forces which have consistently opposed all progressive causes."[125] Similarly, *Wall Street Journal* columnist Paul Gigot claims that the Clarence Thomas appointment "immediately makes legitimate a competing, which is to say non-liberal, view of the black American experience."[126]

Another reason for white Republicans to support black conservatives is to appeal to white moderate suburban voters (the central Republican constituency). Supporting constructive approaches to the problems of racial minorities and the poor helps to reassure suburban Republicans of their own opposition to racism and discrimination.

Finally, the current Republican position on race puts the Democratic Party in a number of dilemmas. The Republican Party is cooperating with black and Hispanic groups on the issue of legislative redistricting. Republicans have proclaimed their concern for the underrepresentation of racial and ethnic minorities in legislative bodies, and support efforts to create more districts with greater minority populations. Of course, what Republicans are attempting to do is to *dilute* minority voting strength by packing minorities into a smaller number of districts. The dilemma for Democrats is that they are being put in the position of opposing additional minority districts.[127]

In addition, having a solid core of black supporters is a mixed blessing for the Democrats. Political reporter Peter Brown contends that the Democratic Party will not be able to capture the presidency as long as it is perceived as the party of racial minorities.[128] National Democratic candidates who appear to be excessively compliant with black interests—or with Jesse Jackson—will drive away many white voters. Also, numerous surveys indicate that white voters are reluctant to vote for black candidates.[129]

On the other hand, a decision by the national Democratic Party to greatly distance itself from black issues and candidates could also cause problems. A black third party, or an independent presidential candidacy by Jesse Jackson, would make a Democratic presidential victory virtually impossible.

While the national Republican Party is making efforts to attract black voters, a skeptic might conclude that Republicans do not want *too many* blacks in the GOP, given that this would make it difficult for them to exploit the racial issue in American politics.

The Rightward Shift in American Politics

Another, complementary, explanation for the increased prominence of black conservatives is the fact that American politics has moved rightward over the past 20 years. Kevin Phillips argues that the America of the late 1960s—"of urban riots, the Woodstock Nation, and Charles Reich's *The Greening of America*," has given way to a nation of "Sun Belt ascendancy, supply-side economics, the computerized New Right, electronic revivalism, neoconservatism, resurgent campus ROTC and even Grand Ole Opry performances on public television." Phillips calls this "an extraordinary political and ideological metamorphosis."[130]

The phenomenal changes in American society since the Johnson presidency produced dramatic changes in American politics. Alan Crawford argues that the striking growth of the "New Right" was the result of the movement's ability to feed on the status anxiety and resentment of the working and middle class.[131] Kevin Phillips asserts the American conservatism of the 1980s was the result of the forces of cultural anomie, religious fundamentalism, economic apprehension, nationalism, and frustration.[132]

Conservatism in the 1980s was an intellectual response to the turmoil of the 1960s.[133] Gillian Peele contends that "the most immediate key to understanding the political positions and style of neoconservatism is . . . the decade of the sixties."[134] Similarly, the autobiographical musings of Norman Podhoretz, editor of *Commentary,* convey the disturbances of the 1960s as a pivotal period in American history.[135]

Peter Steinfels argues that such post-war neoconservatives as Daniel Bell, Seymour Martin Lipset, Richard Hofstader, Nathan Glazer, and Daniel Patrick Moynihan emphasized a number of key words and concepts, such as mass politics, mass culture, mass society, consensus, and the end of ideology. Neoconservatives feared excessive moralism in politics, and instead prescribed compromise.[136]

Much of the neoconservative movement was a response to the perceived failures and excesses of liberalism. Lyndon Johnson's Great Society and War on Poverty created Head Start, VISTA, the Community Action Program, the Elementary and Secondary Education Act, the Job Corps, public housing, and Medicaid. In keeping with liberal analysis, the National Advisory Commission on Civil Disorders (the "Kerner Commission") blamed the urban riots of the 1960s on a mixture of poverty, slum housing, and inadequate schools. It recommended a broader role for the state, including a comprehensive attack on de facto segregation, the creation of two million new jobs for ghetto residents, the construction of six million new units of public housing, and the institution of a national system of income supports.[137]

Neoconservatives argue that the Great Society fostered welfare dependency and sapped personal initiative. They maintain that increased levels of illegitimate teenage pregnancy are consistent with an ethic of irresponsibility, made possible by the welfare state.[138]

Neoconservatives also believe that the welfare state creates an unjustified sense of entitlement among certain sectors of the population, especially the poor and racial minorities. Clarence Thomas complained in a 1987 interview that his sister, then a welfare recipient, "gets mad when the mailman is late with her welfare check. That's how dependent she is. What's worse is that now her kids feel entitled to the check, too. They have no motivation for doing better or getting out of that situation."[139]

Further, conservative analysts such as Milton Friedman and George Gilder blame the state for obstructing the economy's "natural" tendencies toward recovery. Conservative economists maintain that the growth of the welfare state and the public sector has a negative impact on incentive and productivity.[140]

Neoconservatives also stress the limits to government action. Daniel Patrick Moynihan is particularly emphatic on this point. His *Maximum Feasible Misunderstanding* was an analysis of the failures of the Community Action Program.[141] He declared in 1968 that "somehow liberals have been unable to acquire from life what conservatives seem to be endowed with at birth, namely, a healthy skepticism of the powers of government agencies to do good."[142]

In 1969, Richard Nixon summarized the conservative critique of the Great Society. "For the past five years," he said, "we have been deluged by government programs for the unemployed, programs for cities, programs for the poor, and we have reaped from these programs an ugly harvest of frustration, violence, and failure across the land."[143]

Besides the perceived failure of anti-poverty programs, the growth of conservatism is also a response to the ostensible breakdown in social behavior. Issues such as abortion, school prayer, busing, and the Equal Rights Amendment aroused popular fear of family disintegration, secularization, and promiscuity. Kristin Luker has demonstrated that disagreement on abortion is symptomatic of conflict over much larger issues, including sex roles, sexual behavior, the importance of the individual, and family life.[144]

Ronald Reagan attempted to appeal to this apparent yearning for greater social stability. Throughout his presidency, he stressed the themes of "family," "work," "neighborhood," "faith," "peace," and "freedom." John Kenneth White asserts that Reagan had success in transforming "that great barometer of American culture, prime-time television," as evidenced by the popularity of "The Cosby Show" and "Leave it to Beaver."[145]

Washington Post reporter E.J. Dionne notes that American conservatives in the 1970s and 1980s "took advantage of the public's uneasy sense that the sexual revolution, looser laws on drugs and pornography, even feminism itself, were the values of a self-centered individualism."[146] He notes the paradox that the Religious Right "became an important factor in American politics because of liberal victories."[147]

The Rise of the Black Middle Class

Another possible explanation for the rise of black conservatism is the increasing economic polarization of black America.[148] On the one hand, the problems of the urban black underclass are worsening dramatically and average black family income rose less than average white family income during the last twenty years.[149] However, at the same time, there are increasing numbers of middle class and affluent blacks.[150]

In 1989, for example, nearly one in seven black households had an annual income of $50,000 or more. The similar figure for 1967 was one in seventeen.[151] By 1989, there were almost twice as many affluent black families as there had been ten years before.[152] The increasing numbers of affluent blacks (many of whom are the children of affirmative action) may be receptive to a philosophy stressing individual economic advancement.[153]

The American Political Economy

A final explanation for the rise of black conservatism is the changing American political economy. The recent intellectual and fiscal attack on the Great Society was facilitated, in part, by the relative decline of the American economy. In an era of dwindling resources, the American public has not been willing to finance an ever-expanding welfare state. Given these circumstances, it is receptive to "conservative" approaches to social problems, especially when they are articulated by blacks.

In 1941, Henry Luce proclaimed that the post-war period would be "the American century."[154] His prediction proved to be short-lived. By the 1990s, many Americans awoke to the reality that the dream was over. Once able to project a prosperous and secure future, the United States now confronts tremendous economic uncertainty, with a mounting federal debt, large-scale corporate layoffs, and the tremendous growth of part-time jobs with low wages.[155] During the 1960s, overall real U.S. growth averaged 4.1 percent a year. In the 1970s, the GNP grew by only 2.9 percent a year.[156]

Internationally, the United States slipped from its premier position in the world economy. America's share of world manufacturing exports has fallen significantly.[157] Once the world's largest creditor, the United States is now the world's largest debtor. By 1971, the United States could no longer afford to redeem foreign-held dollars at thirty-five dollars an ounce. On August 15, 1971, President Nixon closed the "gold window," which precipitated the collapse of the Bretton Woods agreement, the American-centered system that had dominated post-war international finance.[158]

In addition, the institutional/economic basis of black liberalism may be crumbling. Up until recently, government employment has been the most significant route for black economic advancement. The public sector employs nearly 30 percent of the black labor force (and nearly half of college-educated blacks), as bus drivers, mail carriers, schoolteachers, police officers, and hospital receptionists. The problem for black America, in the words of Adam Myerson, is that "the growth of government employment is now over. Taxpayers simply won't permit it to continue." President Clinton "is promising to cut the federal work force by 12 percent," and the new mayors of Los Angeles, New York, and Philadelphia, facing near-bankruptcy, "are scaling back the number of new jobs. The liberal black leadership can fight a rearguard battle to protect existing public sector jobs.

But it will be unable to provide economic opportunity for younger generations of blacks."[159]

Similarly, industrial labor unions—another bulwark of black economic advancement—are also experiencing hard times. The civil rights movement paved the way for many blacks to obtain high-wage, high-benefits jobs in the auto and steel industries in the Midwest and Northeast. However, American manufacturing is under stiff competition from around the world, meaning that the days of "high pay for semiskilled labor are over."[160] Therefore, the political power of labor unions—advocates of such liberal nostrums as an increased minimum wage and national health insurance—will probably continue to decline.

Conclusion

Each of these factors—the role of race in American politics, the activities of white conservatives, the general rightward turn in American politics, the rise of the black middle class, and the changing nature of the American political economy—is in some measure responsible for the increasing prominence of black conservatives. Black conservatism threatens the political and intellectual hegemony of liberalism in black America, and offers a challenging set of ideas to improve American society.

Notes

1. Adam Myerson, "Manna 2 Society: The Growing Conservatism of Black America," *Policy Review* (spring 1994): p. 4.

2. Ibid., pp. 5–6.

3. Benjamin Hooks, quoted in "Defying the Stereotypes: The New Clout of 'Black Conservatives,'" *Newsweek*, July 15, 1991, p. 19.

4. Congressman Charles Rangel, quoted in Marilyn Rauber, "NAACP Takes Slap at Thomas," *New York Post*, July 9, 1991, p. 2.

5. Syl Jones, "Black Conservatives Willing to Sell Out Race," *Minneapolis Star-Tribune*, July 18, 1991, p. A19.

6. Quoted in *US News and World Report*, July 22, 1991, p. 16.

7. "Playboy Interview: Spike Lee," *Playboy*, June 1991, p. 68.

8. Quoted in Juan Williams, "A Question of Fairness," *Atlantic Monthly*, October 1987, p. 80.

9. Clarence Thomas, "Why Black Americans Should Look to Conservative Policies," *The Heritage Lectures: No. 119* (Washington, D.C.: The Heritage Foundation, 1987), p. 6.

10. Quoted in Perry Lang, "Black Conservatives in Spotlight," *San Francisco Chronicle*, July 6, 1991, p. 1.

11. Peter Bell, "Clarence Thomas: Nation Needs More Like Him," *Minneapolis Star-Tribune*, July 9, 1991, p. 9A.

12. Martin Kilson, "Anatomy of Black Conservatism," *Transitions* 59 (n.d.): p. 4.

13. Cornel West, *Race Matters* (Boston: Beacon Press, 1993), p. 49.

14. George S. Schuyler, *Black and Conservative: The Autobiography of George S. Schuyler* (New Rochelle, N.Y.: Arlington House, 1966).

15. "Excerpts From News Conference Announcing Court Nominee," *New York Times*, July 2, 1991, p. A10.

16. At least eight books have been written on the Thomas-Hill hearings: David Brock, *The Real Anita Hill: The Untold Story* (New York: The Free Press, 1993); John Danforth, *Resurrection: The Confirmation of Clarence Thomas* (New York: Viking Penguin, 1994); Toni Morrison, editor, *Race-ing Justice, En-gendering Power: Essays on Anita Hill, Clarence Thomas, and the Construction of Social Reality* (New York: Pantheon, 1992); Jane Mayer and Jill Abramson, *Strange Justice: The Selling of Clarence Thomas* (New York: Houghton Mifflin, 1994); Timothy M. Phelps, *Capitol Games: Clarence Thomas, Anita Hill, and the Story of a Supreme Court Nomination* (New York: Hyperion, 1992); Clarence Thomas, *Confronting the Future: Selections From the Senate Confirmation Hearings and Prior Speeches* (Washington, D.C.: Regnery Gateway, 1992); Ronald S. Roberts, *Clarence Thomas and the Tough Love Crowd: Counterfeit Heroes and Unhappy Truths* (New York: New York University Press, 1994); and Robert Chrisman and Robert Allen, editors, *Court of Appeal: The Black Community Speaks Out on the Racial and Sexual Politics of Thomas vs. Hill* (New York: Ballantine, 1992).

17. While Carter is very ambivalent about affirmative action, he rejects the label "black conservative," since it is often used to stifle intellectual dissent. See Carter, "Why 'Black Conservative' Is Pejorative," chap. 7 in *Reflections of an Affirmative Action Baby* (New York: Basic Books, 1991), pp. 143–168. In addition, Carter's "conservative" credentials are cast into doubt by his support of Lani Guinier's nomination as assistant attorney general for civil rights. Guinier contends that America is a racist society, that black politicians who appeal to white voters are not "authentic" blacks, and that black legislators should have some form of veto over relevant legislation.

18. Stephen L. Carter, "I Am an Affirmative Action Baby," *New York Times*, August 5, 1991, p. A13.

19. David J. Garrow, "Is There a Correct Way to be Black?" *New York Times Book Review*, September 1, 1990, pp. 1, 16. Garrow states that Carter's argument "is likely to be extremely influential" (p. 16).

20. (New York: Basic Books, 1993).

21. (New York: Basic Books, 1994).

22. Carter, *Reflections of an Affirmative Action Baby*, p. 11.

23. Ibid., p. 16.

24. Ibid., p. 15.

25. Ibid., p. 47.

26. (New York: William Morrow, 1995).

27. (New York: Springer-Verlag, 1987).

28. (New York: The Free Press, 1995).

29. See, for example, "A New American Dilemma," *New Republic*, December 31, 1984, pp. 14–18; "The Moral Quandary of the Black Community," *The Public Interest* 79 (spring 1985), pp. 9–22; and the symposium on "Moving Up at Last?" *Harper's*, February 1987, pp. 35–39, 42–46.

30. Lecture, Minneapolis, Minnesota, November 12, 1990.

31. See *Race and Economics* (New York: David McKay, 1975); *Ethnic America* (New York: Basic Books, 1981); *Markets and Minorities* (New York: Basic Books, 1981); *The Economics and Politics of Race: An International Perspective* (New York: Quill, 1983); *Civil Rights: Rhetoric or Reality?* (New York: Quill, 1984); *Preferential Policies: An International Perspective* (New York: St. Martin's Press, 1990); and *Race and Culture: A World View* (New York: Basic Books, 1994).

32. (New York: St. Martin's Press, 1990).

33. See, for example, "Ghettoized by Black Unity," *Harper's*, May 1990, pp. 20–23;

"On Being Black and Middle Class," *Commentary,* January 1988, pp. 42–47; and "A Negative Vote on Affirmative Action," *New York Times Magazine,* May 13, 1990, pp. 46–49, 73, 75. Steele was profiled in Sylvester Monroe, "Up From Obscurity," *Time,* August 13, 1990, p. 45; and in Wil Haygood, "Shelby Steele," *Boston Globe,* June 6, 1991, pp. 77, 80–81.

34. "Delicious Books for Summer," *Minneapolis Star-Tribune,* July 9, 1991, p. 8A.

35. Shelby Steele, "White Guilt," *The American Scholar* 59, no. 4 (autumn 1990), p. 506.

36. Steele, *The Content of Our Character: A New Vision of Race in America* (New York: St. Martin's Press, 1990), p. 151.

37. Thomas Sowell, "Dissenting Views Are Common in Every Group," *Conservative Chronicle* (September 18, 1991): p. 15.

38. (New York: McGraw-Hill, 1982).

39. (Chicago: Regnery-Gateway, 1987).

40. Press conference, National Press Club, July 18, 1991.

41. (Binghamton: State University of New York Press, 1993).

42. (New York: Oxford University Press, 1990).

43. (Washington, D.C.: The Heritage Foundation, 1985).

44. (New York: Simon and Schuster, 1995).

45. (Columbus: Ohio State University Press, 1981).

46. Reported in "A Portrait in Black and White," *The American Enterprise* (January/February 1990): p. 101; and Martin Kilson, "Clinton and the 'Race Issue,'" *Dissent* (spring 1993): p. 151.

47. Reported in Martin Plissner and Warren Witofsky, "The Changing Jackson Voter," *Public Opinion* (July 1988): p. 56.

48. Susan Welch and Lorn Foster, "Class and Conservatism in the Black Community," *American Politics Quarterly* 15, no. 4 (October 1987): pp. 445–470. Similar results are reported in Charles V. Hamilton, "Measuring Black Conservatism," in *The State of Black America, 1982* (Washington, D.C.: National Urban League, 1982), pp. 113–140; and in Richard Seltzer and Robert C. Smith, "Race and Ideology: A Research Note Measuring Liberalism and Conservatism in Black America," *Phylon,* 46, no. 2 (June 1985): pp. 98–105.

49. Reported in Lee Sigelman and James S. Todd, "Clarence Thomas, Black Pluralism, and Civil Rights Policy," *Political Science Quarterly* (summer 1992): p. 238.

50. Ibid., p. 239.

51. Ibid., p. 241.

52. Ibid., p. 245.

53. Ibid., p. 245. See also Lee Sigelman and Susan Welch, *Black Americans' Views of Racial Inequality: The Dream Deferred* (New York: Cambridge University Press, 1991), p. 121.

54. Sigelman and Todd, "Clarence Thomas," p. 241.

55. Ibid., p. 243.

56. Reported in *Policy Review* (spring 1994): p. 5.

57. David A. Bositis, "Myerson Confused," *Policy Review* (summer 1994): p. 88.

58. The history of black support for the Republican Party is reviewed in Matthew Rees, *From the Deck to the Sea: Blacks and the Republican Party* (Dover, N.H.: Longwood Press, 1991).

59. Adolph L. Reed, *The Jesse Jackson Phenomenon and the Crisis of Purpose in Afro-American Politics* (New Haven: Yale University Press, 1986), pp. 131–132.

60. Robert S. Smith, "The Place of Liberalism in Afro-American Thought," paper presented at the 1984 annual meeting of the American Political Science Association, pp. 28–29.

61. Ibid., p. 1.

62. Tom Squitieri, "Poll: Blacks Split on Thomas," *USA Today*, July 5–7, 1991, p. 1A.

63. Reported in *The American Enterprise* (January/February 1990): p. 100. The similar figure for whites was also 60 percent.

64. Reported in Howard Schuman, Charlotte Steeh, and Lawrence Bobo, *Racial Attitudes in America: Trends and Interpretations* (Cambridge: Harvard University Press, 1985), p. 159.

65. "The Races for Governor," *New York Times*, November 6, 1988, p. A32. Lucas received 31 percent of the vote. However, black support for Lucas was only slightly higher than customary black support for Republican candidates. See Richard Scammon, "Voting Patterns," *Public Opinion* (January/February 1988): p. 51.

66. "The 1988 Elections: Northeast," *New York Times*, November 9, 1988, p. A28. See also Alan Keyes, "My Race for the Senate: Can a Black Conservative Receive a Fair Trial from the American Media?" *Policy Review* (spring 1989): pp. 2–8.

67. "The 1990 Elections: South," *New York Times*, November 9, 1988, p. A27.

68. "The New Senate: Who Arrives, Who Runs," *New York Times*, November 5, 1992, p. B6.

69. See Nick Bravo, "New Star for G.O.P. is Conservative and Black," *New York Times*, November 25, 1990, pp. 1, 10; Jacqueline Trescott, "Rep. Gary Franks, Unexpected Republican," *Washington Post*, July 31, 1991, pp. B1, B2; and Gary Franks, "The Role of Black Conservative Leaders in the 1990s," *The Heritage Lectures: No. 303* (Washington, D.C.: The Heritage Foundation, 1991).

70. *New York Times*, November 8, 1990, p. A16. Blackwell was appointed treasurer of Ohio by Governor Vovonovich. He won the position in his own right in November 1994.

71. *New York Times*, November 8, 1990, p. A17.

72. E. J. Dionne Jr. and Richard Morin, "Good News for the GOP—If It's True," *Washington Post National Weekly Edition*, December 17–23, 1990, p. 37. However, this survey may have over-sampled affluent black suburbanites to the exclusion of blacks in the inner city. Also, in the sixteen gubernatorial and Senate races where the black vote was significant enough to be measured by exit polls, the Republican portion of the black vote averaged 14 percent.

73. David S. Broder, "The Long Road Back: Clinton and the Democrats Face a Difficult and Uncertain Journey," *Washington Post National Weekly Edition*, November 21–27, 1994, p. 6.

74. Kevin Merida, "Black Stars Rising in GOP: Candidates Challenge Party Stereotypes," *Washington Post*, October 30, 1994, p. A1.

75. David A. Bositis, "African-Americans and the 1994 Mid-Terms," Joint Center for Political and Economic Studies, 1994, pp. 18–20.

76. Sam Fulwood III, "Black Interests Try to Get a Political Grip," *Los Angeles Times*, November 11, 1994, p. A20.

77. "Who Won Where: Results in the 435 Races for the House," *New York Times*, November 10, 1994, pp. B14–15.

78. Ted Johnson, "Foe's Indictment Spurs Libertarian," *Los Angeles Times*, October 18, 1994, pp. B3, B8.

79. This summary of the debate is taken from Martin Kilson, "Anatomy of Black Conservatism"; Julianne Malveaux, "Why Are the Black Conservatives All Men?" *Ms.*, March/April 1991, pp. 60–61; and Cornel West, *Race Matters*, pp. 47–59.

80. Kilson, "Anatomy of Black Conservatism," p. 19.

81. Ibid., p. 13.

82. Ibid. Kilson bases this analysis on Thorstein Veblen, *Theory of the Leisure Class* (New York: B. W. Huebsch, 1924).

83. Carter, *Reflections of an Affirmative Action Baby*, pp. 99–123.
84. Kilson, "Anatomy of Black Conservatism," p. 15.
85. West, *Race Matters*, p. 55.
86. Ibid., p. 59.
87. Kilson, "Anatomy of Black Conservatism," p. 7.
88. Ibid., p. 6.
89. West, *Race Matters*, pp. 57–58.
90. Ibid., p. 57.
91. Ibid., p. 56.
92. The title of Malveaux's article ("Why Are the Black Conservatives All Men?") is not completely accurate. It is true that the most prominent black conservatives (Thomas, Carter, Keyes, Loury, Sowell, Steele, Williams, and Woodson) are men. However, as indicated elsewhere, there are several noteworthy black conservative women, including Claudia Butts, Eileen Gardner, Kay James, Phyllis Berry Myers, Gwen Daye Richardson, and Anne Wortham.
93. Malveaux, "Why Are the Black Conservatives All Men?" p. 60.
94. Ibid., p. 61.
95. Ibid.
96. Ibid.
97. Kilson, "Anatomy of Black Conservatism," p. 14.
98. Ibid., p. 9.
99. Ibid., p. 10.
100. West, *Race Matters*, p. 55.
101. Thomas Byrne Edsall with Mary Edsall, *Chain Reaction: The Impact of Race, Rights, and Taxes on American Politics* (New York: W. W. Norton, 1991).
102. Jason DeParle, "Talk of Government Being Out to Get Blacks Falls on More Attentive Ears," *New York Times*, October 29, 1990, p. B7.
103. "Whites Retain Negative View of Minorities, a Survey Finds," *New York Times*, January 10, 1991, p. C19.
104. The racial situation in New York City is reviewed in Jim Sleeper, *The Closest of Strangers: Liberalism and the Politics of Race in New York* (New York: W. W. Norton, 1990).
105. David Mariniss, "Trouble Brewing in Milwaukee," *Washington Post National Weekly Edition*, July 30–August 5, 1990, pp. 9–10.
106. *Newsweek*, July 15, 1991, p. 6.
107. See "With a Friend in the White House, Black Conservatives are Speaking Out," *National Journal*, March 14, 1981, pp. 435–439; and "Black America Under the Reagan Administration: A Symposium of Black Conservatives," *Policy Review* (fall 1985): pp. 27–41.
108. Mack Jones, "The Political Thought of the New Black Conservatives: An Analysis, Explanation, and Interpretation," in Franklin D. Jones and Michael O. Adams, editors, *Readings in American Political Issues* (Dubuque, Iowa: Kendall/Hunt, 1987), p. 27. For a critical and detailed examination of the conservatives' sprawling intellectual empire, see Sidney Blumenthal, *The Rise of the Counter-Establishment: From Conservative Ideology to Political Power* (New York: Perennial Library, 1988), especially pp. 147–160.
109. See "Blacks and Mr. Reagan," *Washington Post*, December 15, 1980, p. 20; and Juan Williams, "Black Conservatives, Center Stage," *Washington Post*, December 16, 1980, p. 21.
110. Brown, the host of his own public affairs program on PBS, has converted to "the party that was organized in 1854 to oppose the expansion of slavery." Brown wrote that the Democratic Party's "something-for-nothing entitlement dogma" could not be relied upon to lift blacks from poverty, and that the Republican strategy of "self-help" is a "time-tested economic solution." "On Becoming a Republican," *Wall Street Journal*, August 5, 1991, p. A12.

111. H. Monroe Browne, preface to *The Fairmont Papers: Black Alternatives Conference* (San Francisco: Institute for Contemporary Studies, 1981), p. xii.

112. Mack Jones, "The Political Thought of the New Black Conservatives," p. 28.

113. (New York: Basic Books, 1984).

114. Cited in Fred Barnes, "Inventanegro, Inc.," *New Republic,* April 15, 1985, p. 9.

115. Lee Daniels, "The New Black Conservatives," *New York Times Magazine,* October 4, 1981, p. 23; and Herbert H. Denton, "Meese Pledges Cabinet, Top Jobs for Blacks," *Washington Post,* December 15, 1980, pp. A1, A6.

116. Loury's nomination was withdrawn after he was charged with assault. "Arrested: Glenn Loury," *Time,* December 14, 1987, p. 84. Loury had previously been arrested for cocaine and marijuana possession.

117. *The Negro Almanac: A Reference Work on the African-American,* 5th ed. (Detroit: Gale Research, Inc., 1989), p. 256.

118. Joseph Perkins, editor, *A Conservative Agenda for Black Americans,* 2d ed. (Washington, D.C.: The Heritage Foundation, January 1990).

119. National Center for Public Policy Research, *Black America 1994: Changing Directions.* Contributors to the volume include Horace Cooper (legislative director to Congressman Dick Armey), Glenn Loury (professor of economics at Boston University), and Kevin Pritchett (deputy staff director for Senator Trent Lott, and editor emeritus of the *Dartmouth Review*).

120. Phyllis Berry Myers was a staff assistant for Democratic Congressman Charlie Rose of North Carolina, a campaign staffer for President Ford in 1976, the director of the Republican National Committee's minority outreach program under Chairman Bill Brock, an aide to Secretary of Education Terrell Bell in the Reagan administration, and the director of congressional affairs at the Equal Employment Opportunity Commission under Clarence Thomas. She testified on behalf of Clarence Thomas at his Senate Judiciary Committee confirmation hearings. Telephone interview, Phyllis Berry Myers, November 29, 1994.

121. Alvin Williams, executive director, Black America Political Action Committee, telephone interview with the author, November 28, 1994. The eleven candidates were Gary Franks (reelected to Congress from Connecticut), J. C. Watts (elected to Congress from Oklahoma), Ken Blackwell (elected treasurer of Ohio), Vikki Buckley (elected secretary of State in Colorado), Ron Freeman (unsuccessful congressional candidate in Missouri), Jo Baylor (unsuccessful congressional candidate in Texas), Michelle Dyson (unsuccessful congressional candidate in Maryland), Marvin Scott (unsuccessful congressional candidate in Indiana), Marc Little (unsuccessful congressional candidate in Florida), Debra Cruel (unsuccessful candidate for state representative in Pennsylvania), and Jim Paul (unsuccessful congressional candidate in Florida—who is white).

122. Cal Thomas, "Conservatives Could Bridge the Racial Divide," *The Conservative Chronicle,* September 25, 1991, p. 16.

123. Jim Kennelly, "Radio's Rising Black Conservatives," *USA Weekend,* April 1–3, 1994, p. 16.

124. Matthew Rees, "Black and Right," *The New Republic,* September 30, 1991, p. 21.

125. Mack Jones, "The Political Thought of the New Black Conservatives," p. 46.

126. Paul Gigot, "The Real Reason the Black Caucus Opposes Thomas," *Wall Street Journal,* July 12, 1991, p. A12.

127. Richard L. Berke, "GOP Tries a Gambit With Voting Rights," *New York Times,* April 14, 1991, p. 5.

128. Peter Brown, *Minority Party: Why Democrats Face Defeat in 1992 and Beyond* (Washington, D.C.: Regnery Gateway, 1991).

129. See, for example, Jack Citrin, Donald Philip Green, and David O. Sears, "White

Reactions to Black Candidates: When Does Race Matter?" *Public Opinion Quarterly* 54, no. 1 (spring 1990): pp. 74–96.

130. Kevin P. Phillips, *Post-Conservative America: People, Politics, and Ideology in a Time of Crisis* (New York: Vintage, 1983), p. xvii.

131. Alan Crawford, *Thunder on the Right: The 'New Right' and the Politics of Resentment* (New York: Random House, 1980).

132. Phillips, *Post-Conservative America,* pp. xix–xx.

133. This is the central argument of Peter Steinfels, *The Neoconservatives: The Men Who Are Changing America's Politics* (New York: Simon and Schuster, 1979).

134. Gillian Peele, *Revival and Reaction: The Right in Contemporary America* (Oxford: Oxford University Press, 1984), p. 21.

135. Norman Podhoretz, *Making It* (New York: Random House, 1967); and *Breaking Ranks: A Political Memoir* (New York: Harper and Row, 1979).

136. Steinfels, *The Neoconservatives,* pp. 32–40.

137. *Report of the National Advisory Commission on Civil Disorders* (Washington, D.C.: United States Government Printing Office, March 1, 1968).

138. Leon Dash provides evidence for this interpretation in *When Children Want Children: The Urban Crisis of Teenage Childbearing* (New York: William Morrow, 1989).

139. Williams, "A Question of Fairness," p. 75. See, however, Michael Ybarra, "For Judge Thomas' Sister, Getting Off Welfare is Point of Personal Pride," *Wall Street Journal,* July 17, 1991, p. A7.

140. Milton Friedman, *Capitalism and Freedom* (Chicago: University of Chicago Press, 1962); and George Gilder, *Wealth and Poverty* (New York: Basic Books, 1981).

141. Daniel Patrick Moynihan, *Maximum Feasible Misunderstanding: Community Action in the War Against Poverty* (New York: The Free Press, 1969).

142. Daniel Patrick Moynihan, "Where Liberals Went Wrong," in Melvin Laird, editor, *Republican Papers* (New York: Doubleday Anchor Books, 1968), p. 138.

143. Cited in Sar Levitan and Robert Taggart, *The Promise of Greatness* (Cambridge, Massachusetts: Harvard University Press, 1976), pp. 3–4.

144. Kristin Luker, *Abortion and the Politics of Motherhood* (Berkeley: University of California Press, 1984).

145. John Kenneth White, *The New Politics of Old Values* (Hanover, New Hampshire: University Press of New England, 2d ed., 1990), p. 121.

146. E. J. Dionne, *Why Americans Hate Politics* (New York: Simon and Schuster, 1991), p. 110.

147. Dionne, *Why Americans Hate Politics,* p. 224.

148. Franklin D. Gilliam Jr., in "Black America: Divided By Class?" *Public Opinion* (February/March 1986): pp. 53–57, argues against the "economic polarization thesis" regarding black attitudes. However, his data is from surveys taken in 1982, 1984, and 1986—before the current prominence of black conservatives, and before the dramatic increase in the number of affluent blacks.

149. United States Bureau of the Census, "Money Income and Poverty Status in the United States: 1989," *Current Population Reports* P–60, no. 168 (Washington, D.C.: United States Government Printing Office, 1990), table 8.

150. See Bart Landry, *The New Black Middle Class* (Berkeley: University of California Press, 1987); and William P. O'Hare, "In the Black," *American Demographics* 11 (November 1989): pp. 25–29.

151. Bureau of the Census, table 8.

152. William P. O'Hare, Kelvin M. Pollard, Taynia L. Mann, and Mary M. Kent, "African-Americans in the 1990s," *Population Bulletin* 46, no. 1 (Washington, D.C.: Population Reference Bureau Inc., July 1991), p. 29.

153. See Isabel Wilkerson, "A Remedy for Old Racism Has New Kind of Shackles; Children of Affirmative Action are Ambivalent," *New York Times,* September 15, 1991, sec. 1, pp. 1, 17.

154. Henry R. Luce, *The American Century* (New York: Farrar and Rinehart, 1941).

155. James O'Connor, among others, believes that federal budget deficits are a structural result of the American political system: "Every economic and social class and group wants government to spend more and more money on more and more things. But no one wants to pay new taxes or higher taxes on old things. Farmers want subsidies, organized labor wants more social insurance, and business wants the government to underwrite investments, and yet no one wants to assume higher costs in the form of taxes." *The Fiscal Crisis of the State* (New York: St. Martin's Press, 1973), p. 1.

156. Leonard Silk, "The Ailing Economy: Diagnoses and Prescriptions," *New York Times,* April 4, 1982, p. E4.

157. Barry Bluestone and Bennett Harrison argue that an essential cause of the decline of American manufacturing is the way massive financial resources and real plants and equipment have been "diverted from productive speculation, mergers and acquisitions, and foreign investment. Left behind are shuttered factories, displaced workers, and a newly emerging group of ghost towns." Bennett and Harrison estimate that "runaways," plant shutdowns, and permanent physical cutbacks cost the United States as many as thirty-eight million jobs in the 1970s. *The Deindustrialization of America* (New York: Basic Books, 1982), p. 6.

158. See Fred Block, *The Origins of International Economic Disorder* (Berkeley: University of California Press, 1977); and Joanna Gowa, *Closing the Gold Window: Domestic Politics and the End of Bretton Woods* (Ithaca: Cornell University Press, 1983).

159. *Policy Review* (spring 1994): p. 5.

160. Ibid.

Part III

Interest Groups and Political Parties

The following readings examine the significance of interest groups and political parties in black political life. The first reading, "The Dual Agenda of African American Organizations since the New Deal: Social Welfare Policies and Civil Rights" is by Dona Cooper Hamilton and Charles V. Hamilton, who are professors at the City University of New York and Columbia University, respectively. The Hamiltons consider the agenda of the National Association for the Advancement of Colored People (NAACP) and the National Urban League, the nation's two oldest and largest civil rights organizations. Since the New Deal, both groups have followed a dual agenda: the promotion of social welfare policies as well as the expansion of civil rights. Some prominent analysts have called on civil rights organizations to focus exclusively on race-neutral economic advancement, since race-specific policies such as affirmative action threaten the cohesion of the liberal/progressive alliance.

However, the Hamiltons note, "There have always been political realities complicating the relationship between the two agendas." They endorse the decision by the NAACP and the National Urban League to pursue both objectives.

The next two selections consider the relationship between blacks and political parties. Ever since the late 1800s, the great majority of black voters have identified with the Democratic Party. Some activists have accused the Democratic Party of taking the black vote for granted; others criticize the Democrats for "pandering" to black interests. On the other hand, black allegiance to the Democrats creates strategic opportunities for the Republican Party, since only a fairly small black vote for Republican presidential candidates could provide the margin of victory.

The second reading is by Peter Brown, a political reporter for Scripps-Howard News Service. It is taken from his book, *Minority Party: Why the Democrats*

Face Defeat in 1992 and Beyond. Brown criticizes the Democratic Party for aligning itself too closely with blacks, thereby alienating white suburbanites. Brown discusses "liberal guilt," the belief that "those who have prospered in American society have done so at the expense of those who have not, regardless of whether or not the successful person acted wrongly." This viewpoint holds that the only explanation for minority failure is racial discrimination. According to Brown, liberal guilt is the reason why many Democrats support affirmative action, are fearful of denouncing crime and welfare dependency, and are afraid to criticize Jesse Jackson.

The final selection is entitled "The 1992 Republican 'Tent': No Blacks Walked In." This reading, by three political scientists at Baruch College, analyzes data on black political attitudes and voting behavior. They contend that only cataclysmic social and political forces can displace the allegiance of blacks to the Democratic Party.

In 1988, George Bush received 10 percent of the black vote. During his term in office, he received relatively high approval ratings from black voters. However, this did not translate into black support at the polls in 1992, as he again received only 10 percent of black votes.

The authors note that it was the decline of *white* support for Bush that caused his defeat in 1992. In 1988, Bush received 58 percent of the white vote (compared to 41 percent for Dukakis). In 1992, Bush received 41 percent of the white vote (compared to 38 percent for Clinton).

In a previous article, these authors argued that if the Republican Party obtained 20 percent of the black vote, it could command near-permanent control of the White House. In this selection, they note that the GOP seems unwilling to adopt this strategy.

8

The Dual Agenda of African American Organizations since the New Deal: Social Welfare Policies and Civil Rights

Dona Cooper Hamilton and Charles V. Hamilton

There are several extant discussions of public policy, race, and politics in professional journals, books, popular media, and on the political stump. These discussions involve debates about the "underclass," about the most appropriate approaches to dealing with long-standing problems of racial discrimination, as well as the impact of racial issues on the major political parties, especially the Democratic party. The Supreme Court nomination of Clarence Thomas focused more attention on a group of African American conservatives who have challenged what they call the outmoded policies of the traditional civil rights movement. One of the discussions, which this article joins, has centered on concerns about the most effective ways to deal with the persisting socioeconomic problems of a vast number of African Americans. Some argue that these economic problems should take precedence over specifically defined "civil rights, race-specific" issues, and the civil rights groups should opt for more "universal" policies, ones that deal not only with race, but with the class dimension. In this way, the argument goes, the political coalitional base will be broadened, and blacks will benefit along with many others similarly situated. This is referred to as the "hidden agenda" of race politics. Others have pointed out that the explicit

Reprinted with permission from *Political Science Quarterly* 107, no. 3 (fall 1992): 435–452.

emphasis on race has over the last twenty years sent many former Democrats and supporters of civil rights into the Republican party ranks, thus diminishing the earlier coalition that brought to fruition the political achievements of the liberal and civil rights movements in the 1960s. The current admonition is that the civil rights forces need to focus much more on social welfare, less on civil rights. Unlike the conservative vs. liberal debate, this discussion is mainly one between left-of-center forces, ones who see themselves as progressive in both economic and racial matters. The suggestion is also made that the civil rights organizations have failed to recognize the central importance of socioeconomic structural consequences for poverty on not only blacks but other poor people as well. The charge is that the emphasis on civil rights per se has been too narrow, too race-focused, not only in the 1990s and 1960s, but even earlier. The argument is made that the social welfare agenda, one addressing the needs of *all* poor, black and white, has not received nearly the attention from civil rights groups that has been given the civil rights agenda. This emphasis, it is asserted, has been to the political and economic detriment of masses of black Americans. And the obvious conclusion is that this oversight needs to be remedied as liberals move into the 1990s and think about the kinds of politics necessary to mount viable political coalitions and fashion relevant policy demands.[1]

This article joins this particular discussion and examines the historical position taken by the major civil rights groups as far back as the New Deal. We focus on the two oldest and largest, the National Association for the Advancement of Colored People (NAACP) and the National Urban League (NUL). We contend that these civil rights groups have always understood the existence of *two* agendas: social welfare *and* civil rights, and they have attempted to deal with both. The struggle to achieve the goals of the civil rights agenda is well known. Much less is known about what those groups attempted to achieve regarding the social welfare agenda and how they responded to the political realities facing them over the decades. Indeed, many of the arguments made today about subordinating the race concern to the larger societal concern were made decades ago. Many of the warnings about political backlash made today were made decades before. In other words, harsh political realities faced in the 1990s are not new to the civil rights groups, who have always had to balance legitimate concerns for *both* agendas on a delicate scale of political calculation and pragmatic politics. Greater understanding of this history ought to improve discussion of the politics of race and social welfare today.

Concern about Other Matters

On 2 July 1939, Eleanor Roosevelt gave a speech before the 30th Annual Conference of the NAACP in Richmond, Virginia. She stated:

> It is a great pleasure to me to be here today, but I think I should say at the start that while I think you have been considering subjects which are of primary

importance to you as a group in this nation, I feel that I must talk to you as citizens of the United States on things which are not only of interest to you but which are of interest to every citizen in this country.[2]

Her point was that civil rights groups ought to be concerned with broader socioeconomic issues beyond the more narrow interests of their constituents in civil rights. In her speech she specifically mentioned education and health care, and she made reference to the "plight of *all* young people."

This was an often heard admonition to civil rights groups then. As far as we can tell, there were likely few, if any, in that audience that evening who disagreed with her. Certainly, the NAACP's leadership did not disagree. But the leaders must have had a sense of frustration, because they knew that they *had* been devoting a fair amount of attention over the decade precisely to such universal economic issues. Walter White, executive secretary of the NAACP, probably was turning over in his mind the correspondence two years earlier in 1937 between himself and Congressman Dow W. Harter (Ohio). Mr. White had received acknowledgment of a letter he had sent to several members of Congress. Harter's 25 October 1937 response read:

Dear Mr. White:

This will acknowledge receipt of your letter of October 21st. The Record will disclose that I have always been in favor of anti-lynching legislation. I am hopeful that a satisfactory bill may be passed at the coming session.

Very truly yours.

The next day, Walter White responded:

My dear Mr. Harter:

Thank you for your good letter of October 25. However, my letter to you of October 21 was not about the anti-lynching bill but regarding the passage of a nondiscriminatory wages and hours bill at the next session of Congress. I am not surprised that you assumed that my communication had reference to the anti-lynching bill since that has been the subject of our correspondence for so long a time. *But you can see from my letter of the 21st that after all I can write about other matters.*

Ever sincerely[3]

There *has* been over the past sixty years a social welfare agenda that has attempted to do what Eleanor Roosevelt advocated and many current-day analysts suggest. We know, understandably, a lot about the civil rights agenda. We know about the struggle to overturn *de jure* segregation, but very little is known about the struggle to achieve viable social welfare goals. Even in the 1930s complaints and criticisms were heard from blacks and whites urging the civil rights groups to pay more attention to socioeconomic problems. No less a sensitive activist-scholar than Ralph Bunche severely charged:

> It is typical of Negro organizations that they concern themselves not with the broad social and political implications of such policies as government relief, housing, socialized medicine, unemployment and old-age insurance, wages and hours laws, etc., but only with the purely racial aspects of such policies. They are content to let the white citizen determine the expediency of major policies, and the form and direction they will assume, while they set themselves up as watch dogs over relatively petty issues, as whether the Negro will get his proper share of the benefits and whether the laws, once made, will be fairly administered. They thus demark for the Negro a residual function in the society.[4]

Research in the archives of these organizations reveals a quite different story, that the organizations, in fact, had a dual agenda.

We focus on the following questions: What did these civil rights groups say and do about such other matters as social security, the various New Deal programs, health care, and employment? To what extent did they have a dual agenda that attempted to address not only civil rights issues but the broader socioeconomic issues as well? And equally important: how has that dual agenda evolved over the last sixty years? That is, what were the reactions to the civil rights groups as they pursued the dual agenda, and how did these reactions affect subsequent strategy choices?

We identify three distinct stages in the evolution of the dual agenda. *The Consensual Stage, the years of the New Deal into post-World War II.* The organizations attempted to reconcile their social welfare policy agenda with their civil rights agenda. Sometimes they even agreed to subordinate the latter to the former, when the political realities of the time indicated that civil rights issues were not popular and would only hinder the possible achievement of liberal social policies.

The Conflictual Stage, the 1950s into the early 1960s. During the conversion to a peace-time economy and the heightened mobilization of the civil rights movement we find continued agreement with the basic principles of the liberal-progressive forces pushing for particular kinds of social welfare policies. But now we see a new development, no longer a willingness to subordinate the civil rights agenda to the social welfare agenda. This development precipitated an intense debate within liberal circles, coming close at times to mutual questioning not only of strategy and tactics, but of veracity.

The Complementary Stage, beginning with the mid-1960s. On the heels of victories over *de jure* segregation and discrimination and with the rising concern about issues of poverty, still another shift occurred. The organizations, as before, supported liberal social welfare policies (for example, full employment, expanded health care, increased governmental attention to the poor). But now they began to say that more was needed. Socioeconomic conditions had become so severe among some groups (especially blacks and Latinos) that more would be needed in the way of governmental assistance for these groups if the conditions were to be overcome. The legacy of decades of neglect, of failure to deal adequately earlier, now required more than mere attention to the problems of everyone. A vast left-out group had formed, and additional, targeted social policies would be needed. Thus, the dual agenda took on a complementary dimension, which spoke of something in addition, of filling out or completing. At the same time, the civil rights groups would continue to push for the end to discrimination and to overcome the effects of past discrimination.

Each stage, of course, was influenced by its own peculiar brand of national politics and the economic environment. But an important point to emphasize is that throughout this sixty-year period, there has always been, in political terms at least, a distinction between social welfare issues and civil rights issues. This distinction became blurred in the euphoria of the mid-1960s with the passage of both civil rights laws and antipoverty legislation when official and activist rhetoric began to equate racial conditions with poverty (almost exclusively economic conditions).

The Consensual Stage

The New Deal is the proper beginning for this discussion, because then this country launched its modern-day version of the American welfare-state. With the Social Security Act of 1935, the country established a two-tier social welfare system.

The first tier (social insurance) was contributory, funded from payroll taxes levied on employers and employees. Covering retirement pension and unemployment compensation, it has expanded over the years to include dependents, survivors, disability, and health insurance. This was indeed landmark legislation coming out of the crisis of the Great Depression. In many ways, it laid a sound foundation for the future economic protection of a working-class America. It was based in the labor market. One was able to participate in this new, important social insurance system *if* one had a job that was covered by its benefits.

The second tier (public assistance) was for those unable and generally not expected to work. This included dependent children (Aid to Dependent Children, later expanded to Aid to Families with Dependent Children) and the elderly poor who had not contributed to the social security fund. It has expanded to include disability and health care assistance. This category of assistance was means-tested, meaning that one had to prove that one was poor and in need. But it was also perceived to provide help on a temporary basis, because the able-bodied recipients were expected eventually to enter the labor market and become self-supporting. The elderly and to some extent the disabled, of course, were considered deserving of help for the remainder of their lives.

The NUL and the NAACP certainly agreed with the ideological premises of the legislation. They also agreed that government should develop mechanisms for social security and that the labor market should be the basis for receiving benefits in the first tier. But they did not support the bill, because it did not coincide with their social welfare agenda, that is, universal coverage under the first tier. The initial legislation did not cover agricultural and domestic workers, and this meant that initially a good two-thirds of the black labor force was not covered. Of 5.5 million black workers in the country, 2 million worked at that time in agriculture, and 1.5 million in domestic service. These occupations were left out, not, ostensibly because of their race but because of their unfortunate position in the labor market. Thus what was perceived by some as a universal program was not that at all.

Testifying before the Senate Finance Committee on 9 February 1935, Attorney Charles H. Houston of the NAACP stated:

> The NAACP regrets that it cannot support the Wagner Economic Security Bill (S.1130). It approached the Bill with every inclination to support it, but the more it studied, the more holes appeared, until from a Negro's point of view it looks like a sieve with the holes just big enough for the majority of Negroes to fall through.[5]

He noted that provisions for old people (in the second tier) depended on the separate states adopting a program of assistance, and this was problematic in southern states where most elderly blacks lived. The NAACP thought it was likely that the black elderly would either be excluded from benefits or provided with very low levels of public assistance.

The NAACP favored a strictly federal old-age assistance program. The two tiers should be merged into one, under one national governmental program. Thus, the NAACP was not arguing for special treatment for blacks. The goal was to include blacks, to give them the same chance to be covered, to make it possible for them to contribute to the retirement funds, and therefore to be eligible for benefits. This meant, of course, being employed in occupations that were covered by the act. In this sense, the NAACP saw the social welfare agenda as consensual with the civil rights agenda. Both agendas sought no special treatment for blacks politically or economically. The appeal was economic, not race-specific.

Houston testified: "As to the agricultural worker, the situation is galling. First, throw him out of employment under the cotton reduction program, and then set up a program which excludes him from unemployment insurance! Frustration on top of frustration."[6]

The National Urban League was also critical of the proposed social security legislation. Its representative, T. Arnold Hill, testified in favor of the much more comprehensive and radical Lundeen Bill, which indexed benefits to the cost of living and were to be financed with inheritance and gift taxes. In addition, "it provided protection to all workers who refused to work as strike breakers or at less than the average local or trade union wage." Hill was of the opinion that the poorest groups should have "first call" on the benefits of the act.[7]

When the civil rights organizations sought help from liberal-progressive groups, they were sadly disappointed. In a 26 February 1935 memo to his NAACP colleagues, Roy Wilkins described a meeting he had with Abraham Epstein, executive secretary of the American Association for Old Age Security, a liberal organization strongly pushing for the Wagner Social Security Act. The memo revealed the rejection the civil rights groups faced in their attempt to form coalitions with their liberal friends. Wilkins wrote:

> Mr. Epstein, who has known of the work of the Association [NAACP] for many years and who is familiar with most of the problems of Negroes stated that colored people were in a tight place as far as this legislation was concerned, but he did not see that there was anything that could be done about it. *He said frankly that he was interested, first, in social insurance and that he did not see how we can solve the Negro problem through social insurance; in other words, there are realities existing with respect to Negroes and whites in this country which no program of social insurance can undertake to correct.* He suggested (1) that the Association not concern itself about the *contributory* old age assistance or the exclusion of farmers, domestics, and casuals from this contributory system. *The exclusion of these people means that they will not be required to contribute toward an old age pension fund and will not, therefore, draw any benefits from it.* The chief reason for such exclusion is the difficulty of collecting and administering these contributions. (2) That the exclusion of farmers, domestics, and casuals from the contributory old age assistance does not exclude them from the *non-contributory* old age pensions, to which they are entitled regardless of contributions to the Fund.[8]

But this was precisely what the NUL and the NAACP did *not* want. The Urban League's motto was "Jobs, not alms." There was serious concern that people left out of the first-tier social insurance system would be precariously on the margins of the economy and would run the risk of becoming perennial dependents and wards of the state. The civil rights groups foresaw the long-term danger in this, so much so that they were decidedly less interested in public assistance legislation. A 22 October 1947 NAACP memo on the need to amend the Social Security Act noted:

> The relief rolls are no substitute. Relief is a dole which robs a person of self-respect and initiative. Unemployment compensation is more like an insurance against hard times, and as insurance may be accepted with self-respect and self-assurance.[9]

As the civil rights groups saw matters, the dual agenda was really but one. Their concern for social welfare went hand in hand with their concern for civil rights. They advocated a social welfare agenda that extended first-tier coverage to lower paying jobs. (This was an effective response to some critics, then and later, who criticized the two organizations for being inattentive to the lower, working class and more concerned with helping middle class, white collar blacks.) And they advocated a civil rights agenda that would make jobs in the first tier available on a nondiscriminatory basis.

To the two civil rights groups, these were consensual goals. They consistently supported the more progressive measures, such as the comprehensive Wagner-Murray-Dingell Social Security Bill in 1943–1944. They certainly favored national government efforts in the areas of more federal aid to education, health care, and public housing. And they were consistently and actively on the side of organized labor in fighting the anti-union Taft-Hartley Law.

In pursuing this consensual approach the organizations even agreed at times to subordinate the civil rights agenda to the social policy agenda. This was the case with their support for the Wagner-Murray-Dingell Bill. Although the NAACP endorsed the bill, it questioned the lack of "safeguards for minority groups." NAACP officials had discussed this with Senator Robert Wagner, who had no objection to amending the bill to include an antidiscriminatory clause. But in anticipation of a "spirited fight over the Bill," the NAACP decided to give the bill its "unqualified support even though it [did] not contain anti-discriminatory clauses." The legislation was too important to jeopardize, and including such a clause might "endanger the measure."[10] The same position was evident in the NAACP's support in 1945 for the proposed Full Employment Bill. The question arose: should the NAACP insist that the bill contain a provision against racial discrimination in hiring, a practice which was quite prevalent? For political reasons, the organization opted to go along with its liberal allies who counseled not to raise the civil rights issue. In a 1945 memo, Leslie Perry, the NAACP's Washington lobbyist, wrote to Walter White:

> I had a long talk on Friday, July 6, with Bertram Gross, a member of Senator Murray's staff who helped draft the Full Employment Bill. He stated that Senator Murray greatly appreciated the resolution of the [NAACP] Board endorsing the Full Employment Bill. We discussed at some length the rationale of the bill. Gross called particular attention to the fact that the preamble states that it is the right of "all Americans" to be gainfully employed. *In those circumstances, he felt that no particular reference to racial groups as say, "without discrimination on account of race" was necessary. I heartily agree with him inasmuch as the bill will probably have tough going at best. If we put in it any provision which can be construed as a little FEPC [Fair Employment Practices Committee] its chances of enactment will be greatly lessened.* Frankly, in my judgment any such provision in the enactment clause would be completely meaningless in so far as it confers any positive benefits on minority

races. I think that the establishment of a national budget with respect to total employment would be an important and far reaching step and that the bill, therefore, merits our all-out support.[11]

And the NAACP did support the bill, although the final version fell far short of obtaining full employment guarantees.[12] This was an effort on the part of the civil rights groups to accommodate the two agendas, even though accommodation might mean at times subordination of civil rights to social welfare policy.

The two organizations wrestled with the problem of how to reconcile the two agendas. In congressional testimony in 1946 in support of a national health bill (S.1606), the health policy adviser to the NAACP, Montague Cobb, stated:

This Association [NAACP] is most acutely aware of the need for such legislation in respect to that segment of the population which it primarily represents (i.e., Negroes). It cannot be overemphasized, however, that health is not a racial problem, that the health conditions of Negroes are largely a reflection of their socio-economic circumstances, and that poor health in any segment of the population is a hazard to the nation as a whole.[13]

Cobb proceeded: ". . . The NAACP has a natural and vital interest in any measures which make for the improvement of the *general* health, particularly that of the economically poorly circumstanced." In his testimony, he constantly linked the health needs "of Negroes as well as of millions of whites in poor economic circumstances."[14]

Even though health care facilities in the local and state agencies would remain segregated, the NAACP, while expressing strong opposition and "concern" about that situation, opted not to push the issue, but to ask for fair, equitable treatment. In other words, it was prepared to support the liberal social policy, even though this meant maintaining the "separate but equal" racial practice. The same issue was faced on the subject of federal support for education in 1945. A proposed measure, S. 181, Educational Finance Act of 1945, clearly would not deal with the problem of segregated schools. Nonetheless, the NAACP felt compelled to support the bill. Testifying before a Senate committee, Leslie Perry stated:

While this legislation will not wipe out existing differentials obtaining in State expenditures for Negro and white schools, current estimates of the funds Negro schools will receive under it indicate that in practically every one of these States per capita expenditures for Negro pupils and teachers will increase by more than 100 percent. . . .

As much as we deplore the discriminatory action of many States . . . I want to make it clear that we do not regard this legislation as a proper vehicle or means of correcting this type of inequality.[15]

No one misunderstood the political bind the civil rights groups were in; they had to make hard strategic decisions given the political realities facing them. In fact, Perry testified that the organization would continue its fight through the courts challenging the segregated school systems. The organization was reconciling the two agendas by dealing with them in separate political decision-making arenas.

The Conflictural Stage

The benefits from social welfare, however, did not keep pace with the changes in the private sector economy and with the negative consequences of continued segregation and discrimination in the society. Structural economic developments—automation, urban renewal, factories moving out of the inner cities, suburban growth, continued racial segregation and discrimination—combined to limit participation of black Americans in the mainstream economy. In 1949 the NAACP began to pursue a strategy that put the liberals' social welfare agenda in open conflict with the civil rights agenda. The organization even drafted amendments to liberal social legislation that called for no federal funds to be allocated to any local district or state that would use such funds in a racially segregated or discriminatory manner. The vehicle for this was the controversial Powell Amendment, named after its congressional sponsor, Representative Adam Clayton Powell, Jr., from Harlem in New York. The catalyst, in fact, for this major shift in strategy was President Harry Truman's Committee on Civil Rights. The committee's 1947 Report, *To Secure These Rights,* went far beyond anything to date that spoke to forceful implementation of civil rights by the national government. Composed of a panel of independent-minded private citizens, the committee recommended:

> The conditioning by Congress of all federal grants-in-aid and other forms of federal assistance to public or private agencies for any purpose on the absence of discrimination and segregation based on race, color, creed, or national origin.[16]

Charles H. Houston of the NAACP urged the committee not to issue such a recommendation. In testimony before the committee, he felt that such action very likely would result in rejecting the aid funds ". . . and you would fail to give aid to people who need it most."[17]

But after the report's strong stand, the NAACP pursued the strategy in collaboration with Powell.[18] Clearly, the position of such a prestigious presidential committee would carry enormous weight with public opinion, or so it was hoped. At any rate, the main civil rights group could hardly be caught lagging in this matter. Its role was to lead, not follow. Perhaps this was the shift in political climate they could seize to make a major new thrust in the struggle for civil rights.

The point was that the organization decided not to continue the subordination strategy, and to argue that unless the civil rights agenda was included, then the social welfare agenda should not be enacted. Evidence was mounting even then that a rising tide did not necessarily lift all boats. Even with economic growth and universal programs, some people could and would be left behind.

The civil rights groups still favored the basic socioeconomic goals of the liberal agenda, but they were no longer sanguine that subordination of the civil rights agenda would yield the ultimate benefits sought. This strategy of denying funds to segregated facilities created an intense debate within liberal civil rights circles. Even some NAACP board members objected, as did Walter Reuther of the United Auto Workers, Eleanor Roosevelt, and liberal senators and representatives such as Paul Douglas of Illinois and Stewart Udall of Arizona. They argued that to continue to insist on the Powell Amendment would mean the defeat of otherwise very good and badly needed progressive social legislation. Not enough votes could be obtained in Congress, and this would give the southerners and conservatives cause to rejoice. Such a strategy, they concluded, would get neither the social legislation nor the civil rights protections.[19]

Congressman Udall pleaded in a letter to Clarence Mitchell of the NAACP's Washington Bureau and a staunch proponent of the Powell Amendment not to mix civil rights with aid to education:

> Of course, there is room for honest disagreement on this whole question. Perhaps our main differences arise from the fact that by habit we are schooled in the art of the possible, while *principle* is the central thing in your work— and rightly so. Sometimes in our desire to get half-a-loaf, our principles hang on the brink (and sometimes go over), but generally speaking we have found that a modest program is better than none.[20]

Senator Paul Douglas stated in a letter to the NAACP:

> I have joined in sponsoring 11 specific civil rights bills, and I will fight for them. But I wonder if our best chance for such gains is not in narrowing the issue so that our real supporters may all stand up and be counted on a single, clear civil rights issue, rather than being divided by a combination proposal which some proponents of all welfare legislation, joined with opponents of civil rights, will help to defeat.[21]

These were arguments the civil rights organizations had heard before and understood. But their political patience had run out. They had seen too often that otherwise good social legislation did not necessarily lead to sufficient advancement for blacks. And all the while some blacks were falling farther and farther behind. Roy Wilkins expressed the impatience and wariness in a letter to a group of liberals in New York who wanted the NAACP to back off:

> Our Association is committed to federal aid to education, but with assurances in the legislation that funds will not be used to further segregation. It would

seem that the friends of federal aid might well expend some of their persuasive powers on those who want to have their cake (segregation) and eat it, too (federal aid).[22]

The NAACP officials were keenly aware of the clash between the two agendas. Clarence Mitchell broached the issue directly when he stated that the NAACP "supported the great programs that improve the lot of the common man." But there were other equally important concerns, namely, civil rights. Mitchell's biographer quotes Mitchell as saying:

But blacks also wanted "an FEPC law to guarantee that we can get jobs in those plants where the minimum wage is a dollar or more. Blacks wanted to walk in the front door of hospitals that receive Federal grants instead of having to sneak in through the back door and ride up on the freight elevator to the wards or clinics. . . . We want enough civil rights bills passed to make it possible for us to enjoy the great benefits of social welfare laws without the threat of being shot down or bombed just because we also want to vote and enjoy the full rights of American citizenship in Atlanta, Georgia, as well as Atlantic City, New Jersey."[23]

This overtly conflicting stage of the dual agenda effectively ended with the passage of Title VI of the Civil Rights Law of 1964. That provision prohibited the use of federal funds in segregated facilities, exactly what the NAACP and the Powell Amendment sought. Now, for all official purposes racial segregation and discrimination were ended. De jure segregation was no longer sanctioned in those areas under the purview of federal protection. But this did not address an array of issues left in its wake. There was still discrimination in the private housing market; there were still problems of discrimination in voting regulations and laws; there were still educational systems that were segregated and not rapidly implementing the school desegregation decision of a decade before. Above all, there remained a class of citizens on the economic fringes of society. They were never effectively brought into the first-tier social insurance system; and when they were, they came in at the lower rungs of the labor market. Years of refusal to deal with a viable social welfare agenda advocated by the civil rights groups left a legacy as the society moved into the late-1960s and beyond.

The victories of the civil rights agenda—Supreme Court decisions, Civil Rights Act of 1964, Voting Rights Act of 1965, executive decrees of the early 1960s, Housing Law of 1968—set the stage for more concentrated attention to the social problems still persisting.

The Complementary Stage

Thus far we have emphasized the basic purposes and content of some of the social welfare policies of the civil rights groups. In the consensual stage the goal was to be included, to make the various New Deal programs truly universal, not restricted by race or other economic conditions. While the political realities made this goal unattainable, the groups persisted. At times, in the face of certain political realities, they reluctantly agreed to subordinate their civil rights agenda to the social welfare agenda in the hope that even within a racially segregated society there would be benefits of a substantial nature to blacks.

In the conflictual stage, the deliberate purpose was to challenge the political realities of the time, to put the two agendas into direct conflict. This was the experiential recognition that while the political realities were essentially the same as before, there was another reality: that unless the civil rights agenda was dealt with, blacks would likely end up permanently behind and, in fact, not be accorded sufficient benefits from the new and expanding social welfare policies. Structural socioeconomic changes were occurring that led to the conclusion that economic growth could occur for many and still leave others outside the orbit of a steadily advancing prosperity.

In each of the two stages, the civil rights groups understood that blacks shared common needs with other disadvantaged groups in the society. They never denied this relationship, but they also wanted the other recognition that race per se was also a factor that had to be dealt with. It was, indeed, during the conflictual stage that the mounting civil rights movement began to achieve its greatest victories in the courts and Congress over segregation and discrimination. Ironically, these victories created tension among some civil rights allies. The argument was made that it was not necessary to put the two agendas into conflict inasmuch as racial equality was being achieved. In time, it was hoped, separate civil rights laws would settle the racial issue. Thus, liberal social welfare policies should be pursued on their own merits, unhampered by appeals to race-specific remedies.

This argument was not entirely persuasive among some civil rights advocates. In April 1963, Clarence Mitchell testified before a House subcommittee about the discriminatory practices in administering the Manpower Development and Training Act:

> In its report on vocational training and apprenticeship, the Civil Rights Commission pointed out that there was a wide difference between the types of training offered at so-called Negro vocational schools and the training offered at schools predominantly white.
>
> Electronics, tool and die design, and machine shop training are vital areas for today's job training. These are made available to white young people, but even in many of the school systems that are supposed to be desegregated, the colored children are still jammed into such things as shoe repairing, dry cleaning, and auto mechanics. Very often even these courses use inferior equipment and those who take them come out unsuited for employment. . . . It is just amazing to see the difference between the type of training that is given in one school and in the other.[24]

The National Urban League was also sensitive to certain proposed aspects of the New Frontier's Vocational Education Act of 1963. Otis E. Finley testified that the NUL was wary of a provision that based allocation of funds on a needs-assessment by the states: "The experience of the Urban League indicates that this basis of need has always posed a problem with Negro youth." Suggesting that the basis for receiving educational funds should be a national needs test, he stated:

> . . . I would suggest that any consideration of the adoption of the Vocational Education Act would take a long hard look at this requirement of allotting funds on the basis of needs as determined by States and sections. . . . Expand vocational and technical training programs consistent with employment possibilities and *national* needs.
>
> The present needs of vocational education require massive financial support. Unless immediate steps are taken to provide these funds, the cost to the Nation will be even greater. *We face a clear alternative of providing our children with the best in education and training or paying for increased welfare costs, higher crime rates, and human demoralization. Either way money will be spent.*
>
> The Urban League believes that the problems confronting education today transcend State and local concerns, and thus now become an urgent national concern.[25]

Without question, there was a new, more liberal political environment in Washington and throughout most of the country in the 1960s. But the civil rights groups were aware that with the increase in social welfare legislation, there still had to be attention paid to the problems of continuing racial discrimination.

What developed in the early 1960s was the view that special efforts had to be made to help those, especially blacks, who had been left out for so long. Whitney M. Young, Jr., of the NUL proposed a domestic Marshall plan. Essentially a proposal to provide compensatory assistance on a massive scale, the NUL was going on record in favor of preferential treatment. In a speech at the National Conference of Churches in New York City on 30 January 1965, he told the audience:

> I say that for a century Negroes have borne a disproportionate burden of unemployment, and now it is of disaster proportions, and that emergency aid is needed. Not tomorrow, but now. Not when "full employment" is achieved, for there is no evidence that we will have full employment in the foreseeable future unless extraordinary emergency action is taken—but now.
>
> That is why the Urban League has called for special effort in employment, as well as in education, housing, health, and welfare. These are the crucial areas of concern in making equality a meaningful reality for Negroes. . . . A special effort in the area of employment for Negroes must be made.[26]

Years of failure to reconcile the two agendas during the consensual and conflictual stages had created a class of people with these special needs. This new complementary stage of the dual agenda would emphasize support as before for the universal social welfare programs, and it would also call for additional help for the most needy, especially blacks.

There was also a new dimension to the civil rights struggle at that point. In addition to the two older organizations, other organizations and leaders were emerging: Martin Luther King, Jr., and the Southern Christian Leadership Conference [SCLC]; James Farmer and the Congress of Racial Equality [CORE], (although founded in the early 1940s, its ranks now were growing with the Freedom Rides of 1961); the Student Nonviolent Coordinating Committee [SNCC]; Bayard Rustin (by no means new on the scene, but given greater prominence from his role as coordinator of the 1963 March on Washington) and in the late 1960s, George Wiley and the National Welfare Rights Organization [NWRO]. There were also numerous local protest and community activist groups around the country of varying sizes and duration, many developed out of the antipoverty programs of the Great Society.

In 1966, a major proposal, the Freedom Budget, was made by the A. Philip Randolph Institute under the direction of the venerable labor leader, A. Philip Randolph, and Bayard Rustin, calling for a $180 billion ten-year commitment to deal with the country's major socioeconomic problems. Drawn up by liberal black and white economists and policy analysts, the document was signed by many civil rights, liberal, labor, and religious leaders. This was distinctly not a racially-specific proposal, but everyone recognized the benefits to blacks if it were taken seriously. A central feature was the creation of jobs and the attainment of full employment. It was clearly an attempt to combine the class and race components of what had become a complex set of interrelated problems. But its price tag, apparently, was too high.

At one Senate subcommittee hearing, a witness suggested "that a careful reading of volumes like the Freedom Budget would be of very great value in terms of thinking on the part of our legislators toward really the eradication of poverty."[27] Senator Joseph Clark (D-PA) was blunt and candid in his response:

> . . . I have had a look at the [Freedom] budget and I think in the best of all possible worlds, it would be a wonderful thing but as a matter of pragmatic politics, it seems to me utterly unrealistic . . . and I don't think our constituents are anywhere near ready for that budget.[28]

The Poor People's Campaign, initially under King's leadership before his assassination, and the Wiley-led welfare rights movement gave further indication of the move toward greater attention to economic needs of poor people. Both movements were deliberately aimed at crossing racial lines and carving out a social welfare agenda of a decidedly liberal-progressive orientation. At his death in 1973, George Wiley was beginning to form a new organization, the Movement for Economic Justice, that would attempt to address in a comprehensive way the economic needs of a "majority" of Americans, namely those concerned about equitable redistribution of income, adequate jobs, and tax reform.

When the Nixon administration introduced the Family Assistance Plan [FAP], calling for a form of negative income tax and a guaranteed annual income, along with a "workfare" provision, most civil rights groups followed the lead of George Wiley of the NWRO and opposed the plan. Essentially, in their view, the amount to be received per poor family was too low. The new head of the National Urban League, Vernon E. Jordan, Jr., was clear in his deference to Wiley on this issue:

> George did the best organizing job of anybody after the sixties had reached their peak. When it came to welfare legislation, I was very impressed with his detailed knowledge. He could quote from page four of the bill and he knew what section A meant, and that was very important. He commanded support.[29]

Throughout the 1970s one of the main items on the social welfare agenda of the various civil rights groups was full employment. The specific legislative proposal was the Humphrey-Hawkins Full Employment Bill, which was the catalyst for the creation of an umbrella organization, the Full employment Action Council, a coalition of civil rights, labor, business, religious, academic, and liberal interest groups. Appropriately, it was cochaired by Murray H. Finley, president of the Amalgamated Clothing Workers of America, AFL-CIO, and Coretta Scott King, president of the Martin Luther King, Jr., Center for Nonviolent Social Change. Again, as with the Freedom Budget, the full employment bill was by no means a race-specific proposal. As its proponents viewed it, it addressed the needs of all persons "willing and able to work." The 1974 annual conference of the National Urban League devoted its four-day meeting to the theme: "Full Employment as a National Goal." The initial bill introduced by Congressman Augustus Hawkins (D-CA) and one of the featured speakers at the NUL conference, was race neutral, but it called for a commitment of expenditures the decision makers were not prepared to make. In 1978, a relatively weak Full Employment and Balanced Growth Act was passed.

Given the new civil rights laws against discrimination and segregation, some civil rights groups thought that the passage of a strong Full Employment Bill in the 1970s would have been a fitting (albeit, not final) achievement of their dual agenda. There would still need to be diligent enforcement of laws against racial discrimination. There would be no need to subordinate concern for civil rights to that for social welfare, as was often the case in the consensual stage. As a result of the end to de jure segregation, there would be no need to place the two agendas in conflict with each other.

Conclusion

Unlike earlier years, in the 1980s and 1990s there were no legal institutional barriers separating the two agendas. Passage of viable social welfare legislation would have to be done without restrictions based on race. The civil rights groups had always wanted that, and they were consistently in the ranks of the liberal-progressive forces. As the history recounted in this article indicates, except during the approximately fifteen-year period of the conflictual stage, the civil rights groups have been willing allies for a progressive alliance. When the legal barriers based on race that precipitated the disagreement in the 1950s over the Powell amendment were removed, the path for viable potential coalitions opened. But more often than not, sufficient allies were not available. The country moved to the right; the civil rights groups stayed left of center on social welfare issues.

In the late 1970s and into the 1980s, as the conservative mood accelerated, civil rights groups began to suspect that even the gains made in civil rights might be jeopardized. Thus, on the civil rights agenda, there came to be policy remedies such as affirmative action, goals, timetables, quotas, minority set-asides, and the like. These remedies are properly seen as part of the civil rights agenda. They are race-specific (and, of course, gender-specific in some cases). They aim to address needs created in the minds of the proponents by past and present discrimination. The important point, however, is that this civil rights agenda is not necessarily at odds with a liberal social welfare agenda.

The political coalitions conceivably available for pursuing a liberal social welfare agenda might well not be available for achievement of a race/gender-specific agenda. This is not unusual. As the three-stage evolutionary account reveals, over the last sixty years there have always been political problems between those supporting the respective agendas. There have always been political realities complicating the relationship between the two agendas. Civil rights groups struggling to achieve the goals of both agendas have known this all too well. In the 1990s, critics on the left and right raise questions long recognized by the civil rights groups. It was the civil rights groups that warned of a growing dependent class, not the conservative right. It was the civil rights groups that decades before called for real race-neutral social welfare policies. The current discussion over universal versus race-specific policies is not new. Neither is the concern for what is politically feasible or realistic. What is also clear is that past capitulation to conservative forces, leading to failure to enact truly universal programs, has created even more social and racial problems to be resolved. The civil rights leadership has not been unmindful of this fact. Rather than presenting new insights, present-day liberal and conservative policy analysts are finally beginning to acknowledge the truths understood and articulated all along by the civil rights groups as they dealt with both aspects of their dual agenda.

Notes

1. William Julius Wilson, *The Truly Disadvantaged* (Chicago: University of Chicago Press, 1987); William Julius Wilson, "Race-Neutral Policies and the Democratic Coali-

tion," *The American Prospect* 1 (Spring 1990): 74–81; Jim Sleeper, *The Closest of Strangers: Liberalism and the Politics of Race in New York* (New York: Norton, 1990); Thomas B. Edsall with Mary D. Edsall, *Chain Reaction: The Impact of Race, Rights, and Taxes on American Politics* (New York: Norton, 1992); Theda Skocpol, "Sustainable Social Policy: Fighting Poverty Without Poverty Programs," *The American Prospect* 1 (Summer 1990): 58–70.

2. Address by Eleanor Roosevelt before the National Association for the Advancement of Colored People (NAACP) Annual Conference, 2 July 1939, Richmond, Virginia, NAACP Papers, Manuscript Division, Library of Congress, Group 1, Box B-17.

3. Correspondence between Congressman Dow W. Harter and Walter White, 25 October 1937, 26 October 1937, NAACP Papers, Group 1, C-256. (Emphasis added.)

4. Ralph J. Bunche, "The Progress of Organizations Devoted to the Improvement of the Status of the American Negro," *The Journal of Negro Education* 8 (July 1939): 539–550.

5. Testimony of Charles Hamilton Houston, U.S. Senate Finance Committee, 74th Congress, 1st sess. 9 February 1935, NAACP Papers, Group I, C-257.

6. Ibid.

7. T. Arnold Hill, "A Statement of Opinion on H.R. 2822," 8 February 1935, National Urban League (NUL) Papers, National Urban League Library, New York, NY.

8. Memo from Roy Wilkins to the Board of Directors, NAACP, 26 February 1935, NAACP Papers, Group 1, C-257. (Emphasis added.)

9. Memo from Charles Hamilton Houston to Walter White, 22 October 1937, "Memorandum on Discrimination under the Federal Social Security Act," NAACP Papers, Group 1, C-406.

10. Letter from Leslie Perry to Roy Wilkins, 11 February 1944, NAACP Files, NAACP Papers, Group II, A-521.

11. Memo to Walter White from Leslie Perry, 10 July 1945, NAACP Papers, Group II, A-111. (Emphasis added.)

12. Stephen Kemp Bailey, *Congress Makes a Law, The Story Behind the Employment Act of 1946* (New York: Columbia University Press, 1950).

13. Statement, "Support of National Health Bill, S. 1606, on Behalf of the National Association for the Advancement of Colored People," *Journal of the National Medical Association* 38 (July 1946): 133–137.

14. Ibid., 134. (Emphasis added.)

15. Testimony of Leslie Perry, administrative assistant, Washington Bureau of the NAACP before the Senate Education and Labor Committee on S. 181, Educational Finance Act of 1945, 31 January 1945, NAACP Papers, Group II, A-663.

16. *To Secure These Rights, The Report of the President's Committee on Civil Rights* (New York: Simon & Schuster, 1947), 166.

17. William E. Juhnke, "President Truman's Committee on Civil Rights: The Interaction of Politics, Protest, and Presidential Advisory Commission," *Presidential Studies Quarterly* 14 (Summer 1989): 593–610, cited at 601.

18. See Charles V. Hamilton, *Adam Clayton Powell, Jr., The Political Biography of an American Dilemma* (New York: Atheneum, 1991), esp. chap. 10.

19. Ibid., 224.

20. Letter from Stewart Udall to Clarence Mitchell, 1 July 1955, NAACP Washington Bureau Papers, Box 71, Manuscript Division, Library of Congress.

21. Letter from Senator Paul Douglas to Clarence Mitchell, 11 March 1955, NAACP Washington Bureau Papers, Box 71, Manuscript Division, Library of Congress.

22. Letter from Roy Wilkins to Frederick F. Greenman, New York State Committee for the White House Conference on Education, 15 November 1955, NAACP Washington Bureau Papers, Box 71, Manuscript Division, Library of Congress.

23. Cited in Denton L. Watson, *Lion In the Lobby, Clarence Mitchell, Jr.'s Struggle for the Passage of Civil Rights Laws* (New York: William Morrow, 1990), 333.

24. Testimony of Clarence Mitchell before the House General Subcommittee on Education and Labor, 26 April 1963, Hearings, 88th Congress, 1st sess., 604–605.

25. Testimony of Otis E. Finley, assistant director in charge of Education and Youth Incentive, National Urban League, before the House General Subcommittee on Education and Labor, 88th Congress, 1st sess., 9 April 1963, 529–534. (Emphasis added.)

26. Remarks by Whitney M. Young, Jr., before the State of the Race Conference held at the National Council of Churches, 475 Riverside Drive, New York City, 30 January 1965, A. Philip Randolph Papers, Library of Congress. Several histories of this period have linked Young's thoughts to the speech by President Lyndon B. Johnson at Howard University on 4 June 1965. In that commencement address, Johnson talked of the "next, more profound stage of the battle for civil rights," namely, providing special efforts for those denied for so many years. ". . . equal opportunity is essential, but not enough." See Lee Rainwater and William L. Yancey, eds., *The Moynihan Report and the Politics of Controversy* (Cambridge, MA: M.I.T. Press, 1967).

27. Testimony by Arthur C. Logan, chairman, Antipoverty Committee, United Neighborhood Houses, New York City, before U.S. Senate Subcommittee on Employment, Manpower, and Poverty, Hearings held in New York City, 8 May 1967, 90th Congress, 1st sess.

28. Ibid.

29. Quoted in Nick Kotz and Mary Lynn Kotz, *A Passion for Equality, George Wiley and the Movement* (New York: Norton, 1977), 276.

9

The Democrats and Liberal Guilt

Peter Brown

As the 1990s dawned it was easy to see how differently Democrats and Republicans viewed America. Their national chairmen, in their politics and personas, told the tale.

Republican Lee Atwater, a prototypical baby-boomer whose taste ran to barbecues and blues music, could have easily sold insurance in any Sun Belt suburb. Atwater was a bantam rooster with a South Carolina twang whose hawkishness, both in personality and appearance, was honed when Southern Republicans needed every edge they could find. Atwater's aggressiveness made enemies who often charged he not only played rough, but also played dirty. Patricia Schroeder, a Democrat and liberal Colorado congresswoman, spoke for many inside her party when she labeled him "probably the most evil man in America" for his campaign tactics. Yet even his opponents acknowledged that Atwater probably had the sharpest political mind of his generation.

What Atwater understood was that reaching white middle-class voters required identifying with their everyday lives. To that end, he would watch MTV, the rock music video channel, in order to grasp what moved young people, or would literally disappear into suburban and rural America to visit with "Joe Six-pack."

The insights he garnered led him to harp constantly on Reagan's 1980 question that defeated Jimmy Carter, "Are *you* better off today than you were four years ago?"

From Peter Brown, *Minority Party: Why the Democrats Face Defeat in 1992 and Beyond,* 1991, pp. 127–150. Reprinted by permission of Regnery Gateway.

Democratic Chairman Ron Brown, a black New Yorker by birth, was, in contrast, as smooth as Atwater was jagged. It wasn't his color that made Brown less in tune with average voters. Ironically, given his Harlem—albeit middle-class—upbringing, it was his lifestyle. He skied in Aspen, vacationed in Europe, and ran among Washington's Democratic power brokers. Always impeccably groomed and coiffed, Brown had a smooth-as-silk appearance—monogrammed shirts, opal cuff links, and stylish suspenders—that reflected his years as a high-priced Washington lobbyist-lawyer.

Brown's climb up the ladder of the liberal establishment was aided by mentors ranging from Mario Cuomo to Ted Kennedy. They, more than his identification as Jesse Jackson's 1988 convention manager, won him the chairmanship of the Democratic National Committee.

The differences between Atwater and Brown were paradoxically symbolized by their common admiration of Lyndon Johnson. Atwater, a disciple of Machiavelli, respected LBJ's use of raw political power to get what he wanted. Brown, on the other hand, fixed on LBJ's burning desire to be remembered as the president who stamped out poverty.

"Republicans ask, 'Are *you* better off today?' Very selfish, very self-serving, a very nasty kind of question, although it gives an indication of their perspective," Brown states. "The questions Democrats ask, and the questions that ought to be asked are, 'Are *we* better off? Is our country better off?' And I think that series of questions, juxtaposed against theirs, really does give a clear distinction between the two parties."

Brown is right. There is no better explanation. Although Brown is more mainstream than Kennedy, Jackson, or Cuomo, he shares with them the political disease that has crippled the Democratic party for a quarter century: Liberal guilt.

This guilt is the belief that those who have prospered in American society have somehow done so at the expense of those who have not, regardless of whether or not the successful person acted wrongly. In racial terms, it is known as white guilt—the belief by some whites that the mere fact of being white gives them an unfair edge over blacks, an edge that can only be made right by atonement.

Black officials are much more open than whites in admitting that liberal guilt or white guilt has disappeared from most of America. In Atlanta, which has one of the nation's largest black middle-class populations and better race relations than most black cities encircled by white suburbs, it is an article of faith that both guilts are a thing of the past.

"Within the leadership of the Democratic party and within white liberals there's a feeling we have not done enough," says John Lewis, the black congressman from Atlanta. "You may want to call that white guilt, that people have been sensitized to the point that if we fail to make certain moves then the problem is going to get worse rather than better. But that is not shared by most white voters."

Andy Young, Atlanta's mayor for eight years, is even blunter: "It doesn't exist in most people's minds and it shouldn't. The liberal guilt syndrome is probably a Cambridge-Minneapolis-San Francisco syndrome. But most Democrats who run the national party have grown up with this liberal guilt. It's not even personal guilt, but a collective guilt of previous generations, a feeling you have to feel a conscience through guilt. It's one of the reasons the Democrats whom we have nominated for president do poorly. But it is totally irrelevant everywhere else. Most people don't feel guilt themselves and there is no reason why they should."

But Democratic leaders cannot discard that crucial piece of ideological baggage. It is there whenever they fail to focus on creating more wealth for society rather than redistributing what exists, mock the middle-class' obsession with its own woes, or blame their own failures on racial problems.

The Democrats are out of sync with voters because they are lost in time, thinking that the idealism that moved America in the 1960s is still flourishing today.

"What we are a victim of is not having the wrong attitude, but keeping that attitude too long. In the 1950s and 1960s that was the appropriate attitude. There is a liberal orthodoxy that has not changed," says former Colorado Governor Lamm. "The Democratic party is peopled by people out of the sixties who have not realized the dreams of the sixties can't be financed by the economy of the nineties. The social dreams of the sixties with their pat solutions have become unworkable. No one believes them anymore. We have a great variance between the orthodoxy of the people who run the Democratic party and the average voter, especially over race issues."

The Democrats put themselves in the same box as blacks in their social outlook—always viewing those who were unable to be part of the economic mainstream as victims. After all, this guilt-driven belief argued, if America truly is an egalitarian society, then everyone should be able to succeed. If, however, a pattern of nonsuccess exists, then look for a sinister force. Simple failure is not acceptable.

"The Democratic party has been locked into the victims theology: Even criminals are victims; minorities are total victims," Lamm believes. "The only explanation for minority failure is they are being discriminated against. The public realizes that is an inadequate explanation, while there is truth in it. We still tragically live in a society with racism. But you see throughout America people coming from Vietnam and Korea, people from Cuba, Pakistan, and succeeding beyond all measure. The idea that the Democratic party is out there still pushing busing and affirmative action and, to a degree, quotas" falls on deaf ears in middle-class America.

"The Democratic party always fights the last war, and it's very difficult for it not to," Lamm adds. "Most of our generals were trained in that war—the labor movement, the idealism of the sixties, the antiwar movement. That became the biggest thing in their lives. The biggest challenge of public policy is to understand when the world has changed and why."

This in many ways is reminiscent of the militarism that dominated the Soviet Union for forty-five years after World War II. The Soviet leadership was so mindful of Hitler's near victory that it emphasized defense concerns over the domestic population's economic needs. Domestic dissatisfaction, not an invading army, led to the ruptures within the Soviet Empire.

So too with the Democrats. Economics is a perfect example of the liberal guilt syndrome at work in American politics. Democrats are so tied to their habit of blaming the greedy rich for society's problems, they fail to see that the middle class no longer agrees.

Senator Gramm of Texas is largely correct in saying that Democrats "try to create this guilt feeling with the fairness issue" by arguing that because some groups do better than others the system is unfair.

But even Democrats finally began to realize they could no longer sell a national guilt trip and be nothing but the party of redistribution. Having spent millions of dollars on polls and focus groups telling them just that, the message by the early nineties finally began to sink in. Economic growth was the key issue. But for some, that meant advocating something they had always despised.

"It's embarrassing for a lot of Democrats to talk about creating wealth. It's an example of liberal guilt," states Lamm. "The liberal orthodoxy coming out of the 1930s–1960s was that the major role of public policy is to create a just society. Reagan and the Republicans realized that, whatever the validity of that, the new equation is you can't distribute what you don't earn. That a just society has to be rooted in an economically successful society. The idea that the Democratic party would be talking about wealth creation just goes against the last forty years of history. They will talk about jobs, but not the larger question of creating a competitive economy. Wealth isn't a dirty word, but they are schizophrenic. They have spent so much time talking about dividing wealth and the extremes of excessive wealth, that the idea of how you create wealth is very difficult for them."

It was never clearer that Democrats were out of step than during the 1988 presidential campaign when George Bush used the case of Willie Horton to charge Michael Dukakis with being soft on crime.

Horton, convicted of first-degree murder in 1974 for brutally killing a young gas station attendant, was sentenced to life in prison. Under the Massachusetts furlough program—set up by a Republican governor but supported by Dukakis—Horton was given ten furloughs. On his last one in June 1986, Horton fled to Maryland, where he raped a white woman and knifed her fiancé. Dukakis refused to apologize or to meet with Horton's Maryland victims, and brushed aside objections by averring that such incidents were part of the acceptable risk that came with furlough programs.

Bush used the issue on the stump and in TV commercials. He did not use

Horton's picture in his ads, but a Republican group, operating independently of his campaign, did. Willie Horton was black.

The issue was a major factor in moving Bush from a seventeen-point deficit in the summer of 1988 to an eight-point victory in November.

Bill Lacy, former Reagan White House political director, was sent by Atwater to run the California campaign in June of 1988 when Bush was eighteen points behind in the state. "I have seen hundreds of polls during my career, and I have never seen an issue cut against a candidate like that," Lacy said after testing the Horton issue.

But it wasn't only in California, where crime is big, that it worked so well. It melted Dukakis' support nationally because for years Democrats seemed to be the ones who worried more about due process for criminal defendants than the victim's well-being. They were the ones who cried police brutality and thought prisons should reform criminals rather than keep them off the streets.

But most of all, it worked because many Democratic officials—including Dukakis—opposed the death penalty, a punishment favored by four out of five voters in certain cases.

Liberals worried that the jury might make an irreversible mistake, agreeing with the Founding Fathers that better a thousand murderers go free than an innocent man be punished. But Main Street America in the 1990s thought otherwise. Not that most Americans wanted to punish the innocent. It was, rather, that they believed the criminal justice system had become slanted in favor of defendants.

"A claim that was based on thin air would not have been persuasive," sighed Virginia's Senator Robb. "You can't convince the American people that the Democratic party or a Democratic candidate is soft on any of those issues without some tangible evidence to support your accusation. But if you have a party and a candidate who has clearly taken some visible stands, then you can ridicule the party and the candidate . . . then it's very easy to create doubt, and that's what the Republican campaign did very effectively."

At first Dukakis ignored the Horton issue, accurately claiming that a president has little to do with state furlough programs. But soon even his own people saw the political weakness of their case.

Two weeks after the 1988 Democratic convention most of the party's top political minds were summoned to the Lafayette Hotel on the edge of Boston's Chinatown to allow the Dukakis high command to pick their brains concerning the fall campaign. It was early August, and although Bush had been using the Horton case on the campaign trail, the TV commercials had not yet begun to inundate the air. During the give-and-take, someone asked campaign manager Estrich how Dukakis planned to defend a program that gave a weekend pass to a cold-blooded killer who had no incentive to return to prison.

"Estrich admitted they had no real answer," recalled pollster Stan Greenberg, a participant. "What they looked for was a political answer. But what they didn't understand was how serious the charge was and their need to calm people's anxieties."

With no substantive answer to an issue that was increasingly damaging the campaign, Dukakis' Harvard Law School graduates followed the legal profession's time-honored adage: "When the law is on your side, argue the law. When the facts are on your side, argue the facts. When neither is on your side, argue emotional issues that change the subject."

And so the Dukakis brain trust unleashed their secret weapon. They brought Jesse Jackson before television cameras to denounce the Horton issue as "clearly a racist ploy." Vice presidential candidate Sen. Lloyd Bentsen and Dukakis pushed the same line—that the Horton issue was racist since it played on white Americans' stereotype of black crime.

Their rationale, as articulated by Geraldine Ferraro after the election, was: "I think most people seeing that ad would feel that they were in more danger because Willie Horton was black. I don't think people will articulate that or admit it. I don't think there would have been the same reaction if Willie Horton were white. And the reason is Willie Horton stared down at you and Willie Horton became the guy at the corner you are afraid of. Willie Horton became every single black anybody was afraid of when you walk down a street at night."

Because, to Democrats, leaders being called a racist was the moral equivalent of being charged with child abuse, they figured it would shame average voters into feeling Bush had played dirty. For a brief period the Republicans held their breath while in millions of living rooms across the country the white middle class considered the Democratic charge of racism.

It didn't take. The average voters just didn't go for the Democratic, liberal-guilt mindset. They just plain didn't feel guilty for being scared of black criminals and of perceiving them as a serious problem.

"Most white Americans did not think they were racist," said former New Jersey Governor Kean. But voters saw the Democratic charge of racism "as a product of liberal guilt and the average guy in the suburbs looked at the Willie Horton ad and said, 'It's true. There isn't anything here that's not true. And if it's true, what's wrong with it? I don't react that way to it.' I think the Democratic criticism of the ads did as much to publicize the ads and get people thinking about them as the ads themselves.

"I think the natural reaction [of] the liberal leadership of the Democratic party . . . was very different from the reaction of the American people," Kean felt. "They said the problem with the ad was the picture of Willie Horton. Why was it wrong? 'Well [they said], he was black and therefore that made the ad racist.' I don't think the average American reacted that way."

The Democratic counterattack failed. In fact, it just reinforced the white middle-class perception that Dukakis wasn't their type of guy, because they didn't understand why it was racist to talk about reality, and they saw black crime as a chilling reality.

"It's not that Democratic liberals dismiss it [the black crime rate] but they feel they are able to justify it as an outgrowth of conditions, poverty, and deprivation," explained Mike Espy, the black Mississippi congressman. "They see that as a valid excuse," but most "white Americans don't. . . ."

During the 1988 campaign, it was almost impossible to find prominent Democrats who would buck the party line that called the ad racist. But as the story faded, some of the more courageous Democrats began to air their opinions.

Invariably, they were moderates like Sen. Joe Lieberman of Connecticut, Gov. Jim Blanchard of Michigan, or former San Antonio Mayor Henry Cisneros. Quietly, some of these Democrats disagreed with the party line calling it racist for voters to act on stereotypes if those stereotypes, such as black criminals or welfare recipients, were validated by statistics.

Back in 1986 Blanchard, aware of the Democrats' ongoing problem with the crime issue, had wanted to distance himself from them. During his first term, he ended an early release program for prisoners, and in his reelection campaign he used a TV commercial that showed him slamming the prison door shut.

"To this day I think [Bush pollster Bob] Teeter [who lives in Michigan] saw it and borrowed it," says Blanchard.

When Blanchard first saw the Bush campaign's use of Horton he knew Dukakis was in deep trouble; the key issue was not race, but softness on crime.

"Being tough on crime is not a racist message," Blanchard stated in an interview months before he was defeated for reelection. Was the Horton ad racist? "I don't think the viewers looked at it that way. I don't think the people in Macomb County viewed it that way. People saw it, saw Dukakis let this guy out. They said, 'I don't like this kind of a guy. He's soft on crime. He's a soft-headed liberal. He doesn't think like me. It's the same soft-headed Democratic baloney.' I don't think anyone came up to me and said it was a racist commercial."

Cisneros was even blunter. "What they were saying was that Dukakis was not sufficiently strong on crime. It would have worked almost as well, and maybe better, if Horton had been white, and therefore it had nothing to do with race. I think the ad was fair politics at the margins. It was a legitimate public policy question. It basically described a true situation."

Lieberman, whose suburban-dominated state is much more moderate than the liberal bastions of neighboring New York and Massachusetts, feels that middle-class voters "resent the charge" that they are racist. "They have a right to resent it," Lieberman claims. "Most of these people consider themselves decent law-abiding people who are not racist. They don't like to be demeaned by a bunch of fancy-pants, self-righteous politicians who think they understand what motivates people.

"I don't think it is racist" for voters to respond to images that conform to their experiences and reality as they understand it, Lieberman continues. Liberals argue that "more people on welfare are white, but there are more white people. The same is true when it comes to crime. All you have to do is go to a jail. Clearly something has happened. You can give reasons—poverty and all—but the average man and woman . . . don't want those excuses. They just see the facts. They don't want a social sciences dissertation. I don't think there is racism in that sense."

But party leaders clung to their belief like members of the Flat Earth Society. Even after the election, most Democrats continued the argument. It spurred Republicans like South Carolina Gov. Carroll Campbell to mutter about "the new McCarthyism. What was so bad about McCarthy? He said that 'anyone who disagrees with me is a communist.' Now what happens? If anyone takes on anything the Democrats disagree with, they are a racist. Now who wants to be called a racist? It is the new defense. It is the same way McCarthy went up the ladder."

At a seminar held at Harvard's John F. Kennedy School of Government a few weeks after the 1988 election, the Bush and Dukakis brain trusts literally got into a shouting match over Horton. In the modern conference room Atwater and Roger Ailes, Bush's ad man, kept asking the Democrats: Would the Horton ads have been acceptable if Horton had been white? Were they unacceptable because he was black?

Estrich, fittingly seated almost directly across from Atwater, ducked that question, claiming the entire issue had not been fair play, as if a referee in a striped shirt should have thrown a penalty flag against the GOP.

But that really *was* the question. And there really *was* a referee. The voters. And they didn't see a violation. If they had, Bush wouldn't have won.

"Most white voters said, 'This is true, this is fact. It's not a matter of race,' " agrees a much calmer John Lewis, the black Georgia congressman. "None of us, no Democrat, no decent human being, would support what Willie Horton did. But to defend him, or identify with Horton by arguing that it was racist, was a loser politically."

When it comes to political losers, liberal guilt on the Willie Horton issue pales in comparison to liberal guilt on another matter. That is, do past wrongs against blacks and other minorities still demand remedial action? Should minorities receive preferences in jobs and education?

The idea grew out of LBJ's Civil Rights Act, which was passed with the understanding that the equal opportunity it guaranteed would not mean racial preferences. But, in fact, the act set up a federal Equal Employment Opportunity Commission (EEOC) to investigate complaints of discrimination in the workplace. Federal courts were authorized to order employers to take steps to overcome the effects of past discrimination, and told businesses and schools to take affirmative steps to seek out qualified minority applicants. It became known by its proponents, mostly Democrats, as affirmative action. Thus, despite the guarantees given by the authors of the civil rights laws, the EEOC broadened its mission. From enforcing antidiscrimination laws, it began to promote social engineering.

There were many statistical successes.

"The great equalizer in America is entrepreneurship," Peter Kelly, the former

DNC treasurer, opined. "In the construction field, which is my special area, it's been very difficult to get minorities involved because it requires capital, bonding, technical know-how. If we didn't have an affirmative action program in the cities, there would be no black subcontractors. We have been working hard at it for twenty years. When we first started, we could find no subcontractors qualified to do the jobs, zero. Now, twenty years later, in Hartford, Conn. [Kelly's hometown], we've got about fifty that do quite a good job. That would never have happened were it not for affirmative action. That's largely because minorities entered late into the economic scene and that's the only way we can get them in. Now, does that disadvantage majority [white] contractors? To some degree it does. But they have more than their share of opportunities."

Until the economy began to sour in the mid-1970s, polling showed public support for the programs. But, inevitably, the time came when there weren't enough good jobs or places in prestigious colleges to go around and the resentment that had been bubbling below the surface broke through into the open.

The issue of minority preference soon came to the fore and white cries of "reverse discrimination" changed the political landscape. Those who opposed the programs called them "quotas." They especially seethed at systems that created different standards—one for blacks and other minorities, the other for whites—in order to guarantee jobs and college admission for minorities. Most whites, rightly or wrongly, believed times had changed and blacks could compete equally. Racial preferences were now unfair. After all, they argued, they hadn't personally discriminated against blacks nor profited from past discrimination. Why should they be made to suffer?

The final straw, as far as the white middle class was concerned, came during the Carter years when the Democrats controlled the government. A Democratic administration, with the approval of the courts, created guidelines that effectively changed the rules: Employers and educators no longer had to provide equal opportunity as originally intended by the social planners of the Great Society, but equal results. In practical terms, if blacks constituted 20 percent of the employees in an organization, and if they did not get 20 percent of the promotions, the courts would start looking for discrimination.

Fittingly, the resentment in white America was highlighted in a situation at the University of California at Berkeley, the crown jewel of America's public education system. Located on Telegraph Hill across the bay from San Francisco, Berkeley led the student uprisings against American society during the 1960s and symbolized, in the eyes of middle-class America, student excesses of that time. A quarter-century later, burnt-out hippies still hung out on the periphery of the campus, and more natural food stores dotted the landscape than anywhere else in America.

While the current crop of students was more conservative than the sixties generation and business courses were the rage, the university faculty and administrators still lived in the past. Their mindset illustrated what twenty years of Democratic programs had wrought and why white America was seething.

In June 1989, although 61 percent of the state's high school graduates was white, only 33 percent of the entering freshmen at Berkeley was white. The reason: in an effort to give minorities a fair shake, the school had undertaken a two-tiered admissions system. All blacks and Hispanics in the top eighth of the state's public high school graduates were admitted, while much tougher standards were applied to whites and Asian-Americans.

The result? In 1989, more than 2,500 white and Asian-American applicants who were straight-A students in high school—records far superior to the minority requirement—were denied admission. In 1991, Berkeley officials began to change the admissions process, but by then serious alienation had already taken place among California students and parents. And the federal government was investigating whether the university was discriminating against whites and Asian-Americans.

Other colleges mirrored the Berkeley situation.

At the University of Virginia's stately Charlottesville campus that same fall of 1989, more than one out of two blacks with an average SAT score of 1023 was admitted, while only one in three whites with an average SAT of 1253 got in.

Admissions wasn't the only area with two sets of standards.

Many whites were especially enraged by the well-intentioned efforts of administrators to improve black graduation rates. At Penn State, a black student—regardless of need—who maintained a grade average in the C to C plus range received $550 in financial aid. If he or she did better the prize was $1,100. White kids might have better grades and greater financial need, but their race automatically disqualified them for these awards. Poor white students with good grades could often find financial aid elsewhere, but that didn't erase the anger. At Florida Atlantic University, which is state-funded, black students who qualified for admission were given free tuition, regardless of their economic situation. Whites, Hispanics, or Asian-Americans from poorer families weren't so lucky. When, despite preferential admissions, black graduation rates nationally remained far below whites, white resentment deepened.

An internal report that Berkeley won't release to the public showed that roughly only one in five admitted in 1982 under that program—those who would not otherwise have qualified for admission—had graduated five years later. And the Berkeley figures were no aberration. U.S. Department of Education figures showed that blacks and Hispanics were twice as likely as whites and Asian-Americans to drop out of college for academic reasons.[1]

And it wasn't just in education that a system of different standards for different races flourished. Perhaps the most glaring example of racial preferences was a program run by the federal government. Since the early 1970s the U.S. Department of Labor's Public Employment Service had used the General Aptitude Test Battery to rate candidates for jobs in private industry and in some state governments. The test is multiple choice and measures reading, math, vocabulary, spatial, perceptual, and dexterity skills.

But the social engineers in the Carter administration were dissatisfied with the results, because blacks did not score well. They decided the way to overcome the reluctance of employers to hire blacks was, in effect, to lie to them about how blacks did on the exam. And so, under the bureaucratic rubric of "within group score conversation," they changed the way scores were reported. Each test-taker was graded on how many questions he or she answered correctly, and then the score was compared to the nationwide pool of applicants—*of his or her race.*

In short, if a black person, an Hispanic, and a white person took the same test and got the same number of correct answers, they got widely different scores. For instance, if they were applying for what the government called "family four" jobs—those for auto mechanics or bookkeepers—and scored 300 points on the exam, black candidates would be listed as in the 83rd percentile, Hispanics, the 67th, and whites, the 44th. When the applicants' scores were sent to a potential employer, there was no indication of the person's race, only the percentile rank.

Because of bureaucratic sluggishness, this process, called "race-norming," didn't actually take effect until 1981, when the Reagan administration was in power. In 1986, the Justice Department threatened to bring suit against the program on the grounds that it discriminated against whites.

Roughly 16 million people had their GATB scores "race-normed" during the 1980s. In addition, an even larger number met a similar fate in private industry which "race-normed" the results of tests that companies designed themselves to evaluate job-seekers. If Democrats thought no one knew what was going on, they were right in part. It was so complicated that few understood its intricacies, but the public down deep knew that something was askew. And it brought out a sentiment Democrats should have been familiar with—aversion to special privileges.

Larry Holman, forty-seven, typified that resentment. In the fall of 1989, the lanky, gray-haired six-footer was in his fifth year as a shipping supervisor at Preis Enterprises in Waterloo, Iowa. He could see the state's economy was deteriorating and figured his job was likely to be the next casualty. So he moved in with his sister in Richmond, Virginia, and began looking for work. He soon found an opening at the James River Co., where he was told they could use his years of experience. But, they said, there was this technicality. He had to take an exam (the GATB) required of all applicants.

Holman, a high school graduate with some college credits, wasn't worried. In short order he received his score and a letter from the company saying they were putting his letter in the "inactive file" because of his low score. He threw it in the trash, so it's not known exactly how he did since those scores are confidential. But his sister, Maxine Ford, was there when he opened the letter.

"I'm nothing but a dummy," she remembers him saying when he opened the letter. "It was one of the hardest things I can ever remember in my life," is all Holman, a Vietnam veteran, will say of the experience. It never occurred to him that the score was anything but an accurate rate of how he did versus all test-takers.

Of course, since the results were "race-normed," that isn't what the score represented. Whether he would have gotten the job or not without the racial curve will never be known, nor is it known who got the job and whether that person was black, white, or Hispanic. What is clear, however, is that Holman—who subsequently found out about the scoring system—is bitter: "It's as if I only get two points for every touchdown I score and someone else gets twenty-four."

The political effect on Holman, a self-described independent, is predictable. "I blame the Democrats for these kinds of programs," he says.

This sort of resentment should not have surprised the Democrats. After all, Democrats have championed the fight against special privilege for decades. Historically, they have fought against special treatment for the rich, such as tax breaks for capital gains income, which they perceived as disproportionately helping the wealthy. But now, in the eyes of white, middle-class America, these same Democrats have become the advocates of special rules, first for blacks, later for women, or Hispanics, or whatever group might claim it needed help to compete equally in the marketplace.

White middle-class voters insisted they weren't being racist in opposing preferential treatment and, in fact, the majority weren't. The best evidence was the overwhelming opposition among them to Reagan's ill-conceived effort to give tax-exempt status to private segregated schools. White Americans did not want to go back to government-sanctioned discrimination against blacks; they just didn't like government-sanctioned policies they perceived as discriminatory against them. They felt that although those policies might once have been justified, times had changed.

Nita Lowey, a rare Democrat elected to represent the middle-class suburbs of New York's Westchester County, explained that people simply wanted to take care of themselves and their families first: "In middle-class America, where people feel they are struggling to make it on $30,000 a year, $40,000 a year, you don't want to be generous with the next job up the ladder and say, 'Give it to a black, I can wait.'"

Perhaps nowhere in the United States were the tensions created by such policies felt more strongly than in a two-story, Spanish-style building on the south side of Birmingham, Alabama. The changes in Fire Station #10 illustrate the split that decades of affirmative action/quotas have created in America.

The once prosperous all-white Avondale section of town has been declining for some time. Like Birmingham itself, the area has become increasingly black. And its fire station is not aging gracefully. The sleeping quarters are upstairs, as is the living area, where cactus plants grow in the large window planter in the firefighters' day room. On cold nights a fire blazes in the brick fireplace, and on rainy nights, the roof in the sixty-five-year-old building leaks.

The fire captain is Jackie E. Barton, the son of a railroad worker and clerical worker who grew up in an all-black neighborhood in Birmingham and graduated in 1967 from a segregated high school. The civil rights confrontations in Birmingham—some of the most tense of that decade—left an indelible mark on Barton, whose memories of childhood are filled with physical and economic injustices heaped on blacks, himself included. In 1969 he moved to Los Angeles because "I wanted to get away from Birmingham. There wasn't any opportunity here."

Soon afterwards, Barton, tall and solidly built with salt-and-pepper hair, a mustache, and silver wire-rim glasses, joined the air force. He spent six years as a military firefighter in Vietnam, Thailand, Korea, and the Philippines, and returned to Birmingham as a civilian in 1975. He began working as a firefighter for a military contractor and pursued that career in the Air National Guard.

He never thought much about working for the city when he got out of high school—blacks just didn't get those jobs then. The first black fireman was hired in 1968, the next in 1974. There were no black supervisors until 1982.

But by the early eighties things had begun to change. A consent decree was signed in 1981 settling a discrimination suit brought by blacks, and a system of racial hiring and promotion preferences was set up aimed at giving the fire department a work force and leadership that mirrored the local population—in other words, 28 percent black.

Barton, of course, took and passed the Birmingham Fire Department exam in 1976 well before the consent decree and was hired as a fireman in August of 1977. In 1985, when the directives of the consent decree were in effect, he was promoted to lieutenant, and in 1988 he made captain.

Assigned to the same firehouse are Robert Wilks, eleven other whites, and three other blacks. A year older than Barton, Wilks—who is white—has been a Birmingham fireman since 1967. With a decade more experience and much higher test scores than Barton, Wilks was passed over several times for lieutenant. One year he ranked third in the department on the exam while Barton ranked eighty-sixth. Wilks finally made lieutenant and worked under Barton, but he also scored higher than Barton in the captain's exam. (Charles Brush, also white, is the other lieutenant at Station #10 and has held that rank since 1977. Brush is president of the local firefighters union which has challenged the preferential hiring system.)

Wilks would like to be a captain and earn the $4,000 or so increase in salary, but he knows the city's policy obstructs his promotion. For a while city officials were promoting two blacks for every white, regularly passing over many top-scoring white candidates in favor of blacks with lower scores.

Barton and Wilks don't talk much. They work different shifts and often replace each other as the officer in charge, but Barton is the boss. There is no overt hostility. But there is lots of tension.

"If they want to be equal that's fine," Wilks states. "But the one who takes the test and comes out on top should win. I don't have any problems having a black lieutenant or captain providing he does as well as I did. Then he deserves it. We just carry on our regular business. I don't mention it to him and he doesn't either. There's always some tension," Wilks admits. "I am being penalized for what happened in the past. If you are going to be compensated, be compensated one time. He got the job because of affirmative action, then he got promoted because of it twice. That's three times he's been compensated. I didn't have anything to do with it. The middle-class white male is taking the brunt of affirmative action. It doesn't affect the lower class and the rich. It's the middle-class working man who has carried the brunt and that's not right. When they passed those civil rights laws, it's like saying everyone else has civil rights but the white male."

Barton, who was one of ten blacks in the six-hundred-member Fire Department in the predominantly black city when he was hired, figures it's only fair: "When I was growing up in Birmingham, I was discriminated against because I was black.

"It's hard for me to put myself in their shoes," Barton says of people like Wilks. "I'm trying to advance and never had a fair shake. It's hard to put yourself in their case. If it's not his fault, it was the fault of other whites who put the system in like that." Barton thinks there "was more resentment in 1985 [when he became a lieutenant] than when I made captain in 1988 or now. They have had time to see my performance. I'm sure there is still some resentment, but I can't let that stop me."

Besides, Barton believes that if the city hadn't formerly discriminated against blacks, he would have joined right out of high school like Wilks did. He has been a firefighter for just as long as Wilks, but the city's previous hiring policies prevented him from working there. As for the exam score, Barton doesn't say much. Some argue the exam is racially discriminatory, which brings howls from Wilks and white firefighters.

Bill Gray, a white who looks like the stereotype of the "good ol' boy" and is the size of an NFL linebacker, was once head of the local firefighters union. Gray is now a Republican state lawmaker representing an aging, heavily white section of Birmingham. He left the department—and, not coincidentally, the Democratic party also—because he felt he was "beating my head against the wall" looking for a promotion. He was fifteen years older than Wilks and he knew the dual system meant he'd probably never make captain.

"I know my daddy didn't, and I don't think my granddaddy owned any slaves [and] I don't think I [have] discriminated against blacks in my life," said Gray. "And if my granddaddy did, I'll tell 'em where he's buried and they can go out and stomp on his grave all they want. But don't take it out on my son. The black may be a superior athlete, not always, but he may be, and that's good. And my son may beat him on the fire department exam. But whatever exam, if he beats him on ability, my son ought to have it."

Most white Americans agreed with Gray.

"It's almost a nonissue in that it comes out regularly in focus groups we do with middle-class voters" throughout the country, Democratic pollster Greenberg stated. "There is no debate on affirmative action. Everybody's against it. There is a very small share of the [white] electorate—zero—that believes they have personal responsibility for this. That they ought to be paying for the injustice. They will acknowledge there was injustice. But people do not feel they are personally responsible and that they ought to be paying for it. They can't even begin to understand the logic on it. It does not even reach the level of common sense for the majority of Americans. They think they are being asked to pay a bill that is not theirs. There is no convincing them, particularly if they have not lived through the civil rights movement, why they should have to pay this bill. There are not two sides" to white public opinion. "It's odd that the Democratic party takes it as an accepted principle, whereas the base which we need to reach in order to win elections takes it as a conventional wisdom that it's an injustice to the middle class. It's a political problem of historic proportions."

The middle class went so far as to adopt the Republican description of the Democratic programs—"racial quotas." By the early 1990s, the huge majority of white voters agreed with Republicans like former New Jersey Governor Kean, who argued: "The Democratic party often starts with results and thinks they can guarantee them by changes in the law. You cannot do that; you cannot guarantee success. You cannot guarantee results, nor should you. Everyone ought to be brought up to the starting level, and then after that it's a race. Some people are going to fall behind, some move ahead. That's what capitalism is all about. I think Democrats reject that. If people are losing they try to find ways that fix the race. They want to take the guy who is winning and bring him back."

Seemingly aware of this, the centrist Democratic Leadership Council (DLC), headed by Senators Nunn and Robb and Governors Clinton and Blanchard, sought to give the party a facelift on the issue. It took on squarely the question of equal opportunity versus equal results and came out for the former. Yet at the very 1990 meeting in New Orleans where the position was announced, the DLC invited Jesse Jackson to speak, and he had a different message.

"Lyndon Johnson said we must fight for equal results. To me there must be a commitment not just to try, but to make it happen," Jackson told reporters. "If there is not a commitment to equal results, you will have the opportunity to enter school, but no real commitment to graduate children. It's not enough to demand equal opportunity for those who have been disadvantaged at the point the game is restarted. For those who have been the victims of negative action, there must be affirmative action. For those who are deprived at birth, there must be a head start to bring some equality to the situation. I tend to subscribe to Lyndon Johnson's position of a commitment to equal results, not just equal opportunities. To say you stand for equal opportunity, but not for equal results, is either a non sequitur, or a statement based on racist or sexist assumptions."

Any attempt to change the party's image on the issue became hopelessly muddled—a casualty of Jackson's ability to dominate the media.

In city after city, state after state, the Birmingham pattern existed—blacks were getting jobs over whites who scored better on the qualifying exam. Those who backed such programs felt that the instances in which better qualified whites were passed over were limited, but as time passed, it became a more pervasive practice. Blacks felt that they needed such programs because they didn't trust whites who made most of the hiring and promotion decisions to be fair unless forced to meet numerical targets.

As a party, Democrats were slow to understand. They believed they held the moral high ground, and thought that continued racism explained black misfortune and justified special treatment. They just saw a different 1990s America, one whose continued racism explained black misfortune and justified special treatment. "I think that if people conclude that they don't want to pay any longer for the misdeeds of their parents and grandparents, and therefore affirmative action and set-asides and those programs aren't appropriate, I can understand their thinking," DNC Chairman Brown remarked. "But I think their thinking is wrong. But I argue you still need those programs because there is at present racism and sexism that is not related to their parents and grandparents, but is related to an existing, recurring problem."

But Democrats like Brown focused too heavily on the big picture and not enough on the individual voter. New Jersey Gov. Jim Florio, when asked about Birmingham's Fire Station #10, refused even to discuss the issue from the perspective of those like Wilks. "I'm inclined to not want to deal with it on a micro-level because it's a trap," he said.

Actually, Jesse Jackson, when asked about Barton, Brush, and Wilks, said what white Democrats who supported such preferential programs believed, but were afraid to vocalize: "Those two white guys inherited the prerogative of a racial default."

Simply put, the Democrats viewed the Wilkses and the Brushes, who had benefited from being white most of their lives, as casualties of war, an unfortunate but necessary sacrifice to the altar of black progress.

It might be good philosophy, but it's lousy politics.

And that's why Florio was correct in saying the issue was a trap, and Democrats were the ones being caught. Because they blindly stuck to their position that the almost lock-step white opposition resulted from a misperception: "If affirmative action was interpreted properly," Brown explained, "there would be much greater support from people. The assumption now is that affirmative action means that unqualified people are now getting jobs or admitted to colleges."

In many ways it was like busing. Democrats believed the overall goal of having all children grow up in an integrated society justified forcing kids to pay the price—in terms of busing—for wrongs done by previous generations.

Supporters of the concept clung to Jackson's explanation that "affirmative action doesn't negate whites. It is designed to expand and make room for those who have been locked out historically."

But he was wrong, at least in the eyes of white America. Whites didn't necessarily think that unqualified blacks were getting jobs ahead of qualified whites. White America thought *less* qualified blacks were being preferred over *more* qualified whites as, for example, those who sought jobs through the Labor Department's Public Employment Service. Brown, Jackson, and the Democratic establishment never recognized that distinction, though it was critical.

The problem was that in an economy that wasn't growing dramatically, such as in the late 1980s, there just weren't enough good jobs to go around. The early battles had been over entry-level positions. But as the baby-boom hit middle age, the competition was for promotions, and it boiled down to blacks like Barton and whites like Wilks.

Yet even those like Peter Kelly, as politically in tune with Middle America as any recent Democratic national official, felt that the issue, whether called affirmative action or quotas, was worth the price the party was paying politically: "It may or may not be death for the party, but it's got to be done. In some regards it's being abused to death, in some it's working well. It's just one of those things you are going to have your fingers broken on."

What it boiled down to was the almost unanimous sense in the upper echelons of the Democratic party that government could dictate what initiative, hard work, and talent could produce. In their view, it was perfectly just for whites to suffer to help blacks because blacks at one time had been victims of legal discrimination. It truly was liberal guilt.

Nowhere was this double standard more apparent than on the 1988 campaign trail in which Jesse Jackson was the symbol for the aspirations of 30 million black Americans. Jackson's politics were well to the left of the political mainstream—his willingness to cut defense and embrace some of America's most contentious foes, as well as his wish to raise taxes and spend for social programs as if the Great Society were still in bloom.

Yet virtually none of the other six Democratic candidates for the presidential nomination dared criticize him, although they regularly chopped up one another.

"The handling of Jesse Jackson during the campaign debates was the most striking example. Liberal guilt played a big role," Bruce Babbitt, one of the six white candidates, recalled. "If you go back and look at those debates, Jackson was never challenged by any of us. It was a microcosm of the whole problem. I was really struck by the reality of being in a presidential debate in which a black American was a major candidate.

"It seemed nearly impossible that it could occur in my lifetime and that I could be on stage where there was such an extraordinary symbol of the progress that we had made. I was with him in the streets of Selma [Alabama] as a young man [marching for civil rights], and it never crossed my mind that the day would come in my lifetime, twenty-five years later, in which he would be a candidate for president of the United States with a large amount of white support.

"He's entitled to the benefit of a double standard. Although [at the time] my thought wasn't that explicit. There has been so much racism in this society and so much willingness to belittle blacks, that I am saying I am not willing to take that risk . . .

"All of the other candidates shared my sense of pride that this was a piece of history and he was entitled to have the fullness of the moment without being subjected to the sort of nit-picking standard we were all applying to each other."

Note

1. Dinesh D'Souza, "Sins of Admission," *The New Republic*, February 18, 1991, p. 33.

10

The 1992 Republican "Tent": No Blacks Walked In

Louis Bolce, Gerald De Maio,
and Douglas Muzzio

During the spring of 1990 there was considerable speculation among journalists and political commentators that George Bush might attract unprecedented numbers of black voters to his Republican presidential candidacy in the 1992 election. Bush's approval rating of 56 percent among blacks in March 1990—the highest for a Republican since Dwight Eisenhower—led Republican pollster (and later Bush-Quayle campaign chairman) Robert Teeter to suggest that Republicans might double their share of the African-American vote to about 20 percent.[1]

Twenty percent was the threshold that GOP strategists, including the then National Chairman Lee Atwater, believed would establish Republican dominance in American politics—not only in presidential elections but at the congressional level as well. To become a majority party, Atwater argued, Republicans had to attract just a fifth of black voters—the most loyal component of the Democratic coalition—into what he called the Republican "big tent" and the "G.O.P. Rainbow."[2]

In 1988 George Bush had won 10 percent of the black vote—the same level of support that Republican presidential candidates had averaged over the six presidential elections since 1964. Republican candidates averaged 58 percent of the white vote since Johnson-Goldwater, ranging from 47 to 68 percent; whites gave Bush 58 percent of their votes in 1988. While Republicans made signifi-

---

Reprinted with permission from *Political Science Quarterly* 107 (spring 1992): 63–79.

cant inroads into core Democratic constituencies such as white Catholics, blue collar workers, and white southerners, black voters had become more loyal to the Democrats.

The possibility of a Republican 20 percent solution led us to analyze the extensive exit poll sample of black voters surveyed by ABC News in the 1988 presidential election to assess its prospects.[3] The study focused on those segments of the black electorate that conventional wisdom suggested might be open to a Republican message—higher socioeconomic status blacks, those who were politically and culturally conservative, and entrepreneurs.

There was precious little in the 1988 election data that pointed to "any segment of the black community that could be successfully mined for Republican votes."[4] Bush did garner majorities among some black groups—the tiny fraction (6 percent) who were either self-identified Republicans, among whom he beat Michael Dukakis 74 to 24 percent, or those who were both politically conservative and wealthy or elderly (both less than 2 percent of all blacks). Bush beat Dukakis 66 to 34 percent among black conservatives making $50,000 or more a year and 56 to 44 percent among black conservatives over age 60. Bush did take 29 percent of blacks who called themselves conservative (18 percent of blacks), but no other meaningful social category of blacks gave Bush 20 percent of its vote. Particularly telling was the invariantly low levels of Republican party identification among blacks—6 percent in the 1988 and 1984 elections.[5]

The ABC News exit poll data graphically demonstrated that for blacks race was *the* variable explaining their vote, with demographics, socioeconomic status, and attitudes on issues and candidate qualities having at best marginal effects. With a handful of minor exceptions, African Americans overwhelmingly voted Democratic both for president and for Congress.

Bush's relatively high approval ratings among blacks eighteen months (and nearly three years) into his administration did not appear likely to translate into higher levels of black support in the 1992 election, since approval ratings a year before a presidential election had been unreliable predictors of voting behavior in the past; there was no reason to believe that George Bush represented a departure.

Nonetheless, some Republican optimism regarding inroads among African Americans seemed justified as the 1992 primary election approached; in late October 1991, 43 percent of blacks nationally approved Bush's job performance. Though down 34 points from the height of Bush's black popularity in the aftermath of the Gulf War in March 1991, Bush's approval among blacks was more than double the highest levels attained by Ronald Reagan.[6] The nomination of Clarence Thomas to the Supreme Court as well as Bush's signing the 1992 Civil Rights Act can be viewed as attempts to secure a larger share of the black vote (or as attempts to reassure his followers that he and they were not racists).

In the 1992 presidential and congressional elections was there an erosion of the black Democratic monolith? Did the existence of a substantial and highly visible third party candidate siphon off potential black support from George Bush (or Bill Clinton)? Did the absence of Perot candidates in House and Senate races affect the distribution of black and white voters at the congressional level? What impact did socioeconomic status, ideology, partisanship, economic perceptions, issues, and candidate qualities have in the voting decisions of blacks and whites? Which whites walked out of the Republican tent in 1992?

The Data

On 3 November 1992, George Bush received 10 percent of the black vote—exactly what he had received four years earlier—according to exit polls conducted by Voter Research and Surveys (VRS), the consortium established by ABC, CBS, CNN, and NBC after the 1988 presidential elections. VRS conducted a national exit poll of 15,490 voters leaving 300 polling places around the nation on election day; it also conducted 50 individual state polls with samples ranging from 459 in South Dakota to 2,268 in California. The national black sample was 1,539; the national white sample, 13,031. The sample sizes for the different attitudinal, demographic, and socioeconomic indicators vary, because respondents could omit answers on any individual question.

Exit polls have several qualities that make them valuable. One is their large sample size. The 1992 VRS exit polls, like those by ABC in 1988, permit extensive subgroup analysis about segments of the black community that standard data sets and pooled samples do not allow—for example, upper middle income (with annual incomes between $50,000 and $75,000) black conservatives. VRS's 1992 black sample is as large as the National Opinion Research Center's and Center for Political Studies' entire national samples.

Another advantage of exit polls is the immediacy of the survey to actual voting. Exit polls query real voters, thus eliminating response bias, particularly the recall problem, in which respondents polled at some remove from election day report their electoral behavior with some inaccuracy. For instance, 70 percent of respondents in the 1988 Center for Political Studies (CPS) National Election Study said that they had voted in the presidential election that year, when in fact the turnout had been 51.4 percent.[7] Still another benefit of VRS data is that the network consortium surveys representative state samples,[8] thus permitting state level analysis, such as the distribution of white and black Perot voters in the New York U.S. Senate race.

**1992: Blacks Remain in Democratic Camp
and Whites Pull Up Republican Stakes**

The 1992 story was much the same as 1988; the 1992 black presidential vote was almost entirely Democratic. Demographic, socioeconomic, residential, attitudinal, and behavioral factors were only loosely related to black partisanship and voting behavior. And this was true not only at the presidential level but was also reflected in the black vote for U.S. senators and representatives and governors. Blacks gave 87 percent of their votes to Democratic Senate candidates, 89 percent to Democratic House candidates, and 92 percent to Democratic gubernatorial candidates. In 1992, race was once again *the* predictor of the black vote. Whites were far more discriminating, giving a 54 to 46 percent margin to Democrats running for governor, a 51 to 49 edge to Democratic Senate candidates, and evenly splitting their House vote.

The presidential vote of whites is structured by ideology, partisanship, socioeconomic status, and issues, but this is rarely the case for blacks. Republican party affiliation is the only characteristic that translates into substantial black support for Bush and other Republican candidates. But even here the association is far weaker than for white voters. While the percentage of black self-described Republicans increased slightly from 6 percent in 1988 to 8 percent four years later, black Republicans gave Bush only 55 percent of their vote—13 percent less than their vote for Republican House candidates and 19 points less than they gave Bush in 1988. By contrast, 73 percent of white Republicans went for Bush in 1992, 17 percent voted for Ross Perot, and 10 percent for Bill Clinton. Nevertheless, Bush's white support tumbled even farther from four years earlier—19 points—and with profound consequences, since whites cast 87 percent of all votes for president.

Even among self-described conservative blacks Bush fared poorly. From this group, which constituted 18 percent of all black voters in both the 1988 and 1992 elections, Bush received only 29 percent of the vote in 1988 and 26 percent in 1992. Bush did not retain his 1988 black base; among blacks who said that they had voted for Bush in 1988 (20 percent of 1992 black voters), nearly half (49 percent) voted for Clinton in 1992. Another 13 percent voted for Perot. Only 38 percent remained with the president. By contrast, three in five whites who said that they had voted for Bush in 1988 (57 percent of 1992 white voters) stuck with the president; the rest split their votes between Clinton and Perot.

Economic well-being clearly influenced the white vote choice; it was far less salient for blacks. Bush received increasing pluralities of whites, as income rose from $30,000 a year; Clinton got pluralities of those making less than $15,000 and between $15,000 and $30,000 annually, doing best among the least well off.

If there is any segment of the black electorate with whom a Republican strategy might have had a chance of success, conventional wisdom suggests that it was with higher socioeconomic status blacks. High status blacks should have been substantially more likely than lower status blacks to have identified as conservative and Republican and to support Republican candidates, because the GOP is widely seen as favoring economic and social policies more consistent with the class interests of more affluent and conservative voters. The reality appears to be otherwise in 1992 as it was in 1988. More than four-fifths of black voters in all income categories, except those earning in excess of $75,000 a year, voted for Clinton. And among the highest income blacks, Clinton got two-thirds of their vote, with Bush nearly a quarter. Perot did not receive double digit support among any black income group.

High income (those making over $75,000 a year) black Republicans (only one percent of blacks surveyed) went for Bush 53 to 21 percent over Clinton, with Perot getting 26 percent of that vote. Meanwhile, black conservatives (8 percent of blacks), while giving Bush 32 percent of their vote, gave Clinton nearly twice as much—58 percent. Like 1988, no other meaningful subgroups of the black electorate gave Bush 20 percent of their vote. Upper middle class ($50,000 to $75,000) black conservatives were more than four times more likely to vote for Clinton than Bush—74 to 17 percent. By contrast, upper middle income white conservatives went for Bush with a 60 to 25 percent margin over his Democratic opponent. In sum, upscale blacks overwhelmingly supported Clinton, while their white counterparts similarly backed George Bush.

Education and employment status influence white voting patterns but, again, appear almost inconsequential for blacks. Clinton won pluralities of the less and most educated whites, while Bush garnered pluralities of college attendees and graduates. At least four in five blacks at all education levels voted for Clinton. Bush won pluralities of white full-time workers and homemakers, while Clinton captured pluralities among white part-time workers, retirees, and the unemployed. Blacks gave Clinton a minimum of four-fifths of their votes irrespective of employment status. Indeed, Bush captured nearly three times the percentage of unemployed white voters than black voters who worked full time.

The Democratic bias of African-American voters and their differences with white voters are further demonstrated by examining retrospective voting patterns on economic matters. Voters cast their ballots retrospectively when they base their vote choice on their evaluation of past performance of the party/candidate controlling/occupying the White House. Retrospective voting occurs when those who have benefited economically vote for the incumbent party/president, while those who have suffered vote for the challenger. It is the most common form of issue voting.[9] As in 1988, this expectation is borne out by white voters in 1992 but only marginally by blacks. VRS asked those leaving the polls whether they were better off financially than four years earlier, worse off, or about as well off. A third of whites said that they were worse off; 57 percent of those went for Clinton, 28 percent for Perot, and only 16 percent for Bush. Among the quarter of whites who said that they were better off, Bush won 64 percent of their vote, Clinton 21 percent, and Perot 15 percent. Whites whose financial situation was unchanged marginally went for Bush (44 percent compared to 37 percent for Clinton and 19 percent for Perot). For whites, at least, the guiding motto of the Clinton campaign—"It's the economy, stupid"—proved in harmony with retrospective voting.

Blacks, no matter what their financial situation compared to 1988, cast more than two-thirds of their votes for Clinton. Those whose financial situation deteriorated did give Clinton his highest share (89 percent) and Bush his lowest (5 percent). But the 14 percent who were financially better off gave Clinton 69 percent, Bush just 26 percent, and Perot 5 percent. The 37 percent who saw no change in their financial situation went 79 percent for Clinton, 13 percent for Bush, and 8 percent for Perot.

Voter perception of the state of the economy as being in poor shape worked in Clinton's favor among white and black voters, but, again, whites displayed far more variability. The nearly one-third (32 percent) of whites who thought that the state of the economy was poor gave Clinton 60 percent of their vote, while the near majority (48 percent) of blacks who held that view gave Clinton an overwhelming 91 percent. Whites who saw the economy as "not good" (48 percent) gave Clinton and Bush equal percentages of their vote (39 percent with Perot getting 22 percent). African Americans again overwhelmingly supported Clinton. Four-in-five (81 percent) of whites who saw the economy as "good"/"excellent" (20 percent of all white voters) went for Bush while the 8 percent of blacks who evaluated the economy positively still gave Clinton 53 percent of their votes.

Issues were far less meaningful as determinants of voting for blacks than for whites. VRS gave respondents nine choices of issues that "mattered most in deciding how you voted." Among white voters, issues made a difference in their presidential choice. Whites choosing economy/jobs, health care, the environment, and education gave majorities or pluralities to Clinton; those citing the deficit gave Perot a plurality; and those naming taxes, foreign policy, and family values gave Bush majorities. Blacks, on the other hand, gave Bill Clinton a majority, irrespective of what issue was important in deciding their vote. The lone exception was foreign policy where the 2 percent citing it gave him a near majority.

Abortion, though not a central concern of most voters, provides further evidence that stands on issues make little difference on black presidential voting but clearly structure white vote choice. Blacks, irrespective of their position on VRS's 4-point abortion scale, voted overwhelmingly for Bill Clinton: 85 percent who thought abortion should always be illegal voted for the Democratic candidate; 86 percent of blacks who believed that abortion should always be legal voted for Clinton. White voters were far more sensitive to the candidates' abortion stands as it related to their own positions on abortion. They divided along the "hard"/"easy" lines defined by social scientists.[10] Pro-choice voters (who want abortions "always" or "mostly" legal) went for Clinton (49 percent, with Bush at 29 and Perot at 22 percent). Those who wished to outlaw or at least substantially restrict abortion (making abortion "mostly" or "always" illegal) supported Bush (61 percent with 21 percent for Clinton, and 18 percent for Perot).

As with issues, the qualities of the candidates were far more influential with white voters than among the black electorate. Blacks gave majorities of their votes to Clinton irrespective of the candidate qualities that "mattered most" in deciding their vote. The only qualities that did not produce majorities that were overwhelming for Clinton were among the small proportions for whom "hav[ing] the right experience," "would have good judgment in a crisis," and, to a lesser degree, being "honest and trustworthy" mattered. White voters were again far more discriminating. Bush got overwhelming majorities among those who felt that experience, crisis judgment, and honesty were important, as well as a large plurality among those who believe that "ha[ving] strong convictions" was important. Clinton garnered majority support from whites who valued "car[ing] about people like me," "bring[ing] about needed change," "hav[ing] the best plan for the country," and "choice of vice president."

Blacks voted as they had since 1964—overwhelmingly Democratic. There was no 20 percent solution in 1992. But not getting the votes of one-in-five African Americans did not cost George Bush the presidency; what did was the defection of white voters from the president.

Many whites walked out of the Republican tent in 1992. George Bush's share of the white vote declined from 58 percent in 1988 to 41 percent four years later. These defectors included members of groups that had become mainstays of the Republican presidential coalition for the last quarter century. Perhaps most striking, especially after the Houston nominating convention, which was widely seen as inordinately influenced by religious conservatives, was the erosion of white born-again Christian support for President Bush. In 1988, white born-again Christians comprised 14 percent of the white electorate, and George Bush won 81 percent of their vote. White born-agains made up an even larger percentage of the vote in 1992 (19 percent) and although they were still among Bush's most supportive groups at 62 percent, nearly one in four abandoned the president. Bill Clinton did slightly better than Dukakis by winning 23 percent, with Ross Perot capturing 15 percent.

In the 1980s, the movement of born-again Christians to the Republican party was widely discussed in both the popular and scholarly press. A number of academic studies examining the relationship between conservative Protestant denominationalism and partisanship cautioned against identifying evangelicals and fundamentalists with the Republican party.[11] The 1992 election results underscore the need to qualify the identification of religious conservatism with support for Republican candidates.

Protestants, generally, defected from Bush's electoral coalition. In 1988, ABC found that "non-Catholic Christians" made up 56 percent of the white electorate, and Bush won 68 percent of them. In 1992, VRS categorized non-Catholic Christians into "Protestants" and "Other Christians," who comprised 44 and 13 percent, respectively, of the white vote. Bush won pluralities of 47 and 45 percent of these groups. Clinton was not the beneficiary of these non-Catholic Christian defectors, winning 34 percent of Protestants and 29 percent of other Christians, compared to Dukakis's 34 percent share of non-Catholic Christians in

1988. Perot captured 19 percent of white Protestants and 26 percent of the "other Christians." Perot's presence in the race gave these non-Catholic Christians a place to go and they went.

Catholics also moved away from Bush and the Republicans. In 1988 Bush and Dukakis split the white Catholic vote; in 1992 Clinton got 42 percent, while Bush got 37 percent, and Perot 22 percent. There has been debate among students of American electoral behavior over the drift of white Catholics in presidential contests. John Petrocik has argued that a decline in the Catholic contribution to the Democratic coalition can be traced to 1968, while Robert Axelrod sees the 1972 election as a turning point, as do Harold Stanley and Richard Niemi view the 1980 contest. Other scholars, such as Andrew Greeley and Henry Kenski, still view Catholics as disposed toward Democrats.[12] In 1992 white Catholics appear to have retained a loyalty to Democratic candidates, though not in the same proportions as elections of a generation ago.

President Bush's difficulties among the white electorate are underscored by several other groups that had been crucial to Republican electoral victories in the past: white independents, moderates, and conservatives. The pivotal independent vote—one-fourth of the white electorate in 1992—went to Clinton by a narrow margin (36 percent to 33 for Bush and 31 for Perot). In 1988 Bush won a clear majority (54 percent) of the independent white vote. Bush suffered among ideological moderates and conservatives as well. In 1988 Bush nearly split the white moderate vote with Dukakis winning 47 percent. In the three-candidate race in 1992, Clinton won a plurality with 44 percent to Bush's 34 percent. Ross Perot garnered more than a fifth of the white moderate vote. While white conservatives were among Bush's best groups (67 percent), he received more than four-fifths four years earlier. Here again, Ross Perot was a factor, capturing one-fifth of the white conservative vote.

A major problem for Bush and the Republicans in the 1992 elections was the substantial decline in the proportion of whites who described themselves as conservatives. In 1988, the modal ideological group was conservative (46 percent); in 1992 most whites called themselves moderate (41 percent). White conservatives, a core of the Republican electoral base, declined by more than a third from 1988 (from 46 to 31 percent). The drop among self-identified conservatives is particularly noticeable among whites in various SES and partisan categories. In 1992, unlike four years earlier, ideology was not related to income, education, or employment status. In 1988, more than half of whites earning in excess of $50,000 annually called themselves conservative; four years later, only 30 percent did. There was also a precipitous (40 percent) decline among white college graduates adopting the conservative label. Since conservatives are more likely to vote Republican than moderates or liberals, the 14 percentage point drop (64 to 50 percent) of white Republicans who identified as conservative in 1992 added to the erosion of the white conservative base and meant that Bush had a smaller pool to attract supporters from than he had in 1988. This sharp decline among self-described white conservatives in 1992 may be partly attributed to the connotations the label "conservative" took on with the rhetoric heard at the Republican convention in Houston.[13]

First-time voters are clearly essential to any future alignment of the parties. One in ten voters was casting a first ballot in 1992. Ross Perot made an impact among white first-timers, capturing one quarter of their vote. Clinton managed a plurality, winning 41 percent to Bush's 34 percent. Black first-time voters (17 percent) reflected vote choices virtually identical to those who had voted before (82 versus 84 percent for Clinton). Among whites who had previously cast ballots, Bush and Clinton were virtually tied (40 versus 39 percent). . . .

No 20 Percent Solution (The Republicans Never Really Tried)

In our earlier study of blacks and the Republican party, we predicted that it was most "unlikely that the outcome of the 1992 election will turn on the number of black votes George Bush receives." We added that even "should Bush win one in five black voters, there is no reason to believe that such support will be extended to Republican Senate and House candidates and into state executive and legislative races."[14]

The 1992 election did not turn on the number of black votes George Bush received. It was decided by the huge defection of white voters to independent Ross Perot. In 1988, George Bush had garnered 58 percent of the white vote (87 percent of all voters) compared to 41 percent for Mike Dukakis. This was enough to give Bush a 7.5 million vote margin over Dukakis despite Dukakis's winning 88 percent of the black vote (8 percent of all voters). In 1992, George Bush's share of the white vote (again 87 percent of all voters) had plummeted to 41 percent with 38 percent for Bill Clinton. Indeed, Bush would have needed to win over 70 percent of all black voters in order to compensate for his loss of whites to achieve a national popular vote plurality. Tellingly, Bush needed to have increased his share of the total white vote by 6 percent (conservatively assuming that all of the gain came from Perot's white voters) to have beaten Clinton in the popular vote. Blacks (again 8 percent of voters) can be seen to have made the difference for Clinton in the popular vote; his 82 to 11 percent margin over Bush provided Clinton with a nearly six percentage point total edge over Bush. Clinton won the popular vote by five percentage points.

Since the president is not elected by the popular vote but by an electoral vote majority, what might have been the outcome had Bush attracted 20 percent of the black vote in key electoral vote states? Of the ten largest electoral vote states in 1992—California (54), New York (33), Texas (32), Florida (25), Pennsylvania (23), Illinois (22), Ohio (21), Michigan (18), New Jersey (15), and North Carolina (14)—Bush won Texas, Florida, and North Carolina with only 10 percent or less of the black vote.[15] Of the Clinton states, two—Ohio and New Jersey—

would have moved into the Bush column had African Americans given as much as a fifth of their vote to the president. Had Bush received 17 percent of the black vote, rather than the 7 percent he actually garnered in Ohio, and had he gotten a 21 percent share of the black vote in New Jersey, instead of the 11 percent of black ballots that were actually cast for him, he would have captured those states' thirty-six electoral votes. In the remaining Clinton top ten states, Bush would have had to have won extraordinary shares of the black vote—45 percent in Michigan (he actually got 7 percent), 55 percent in Illinois (actually 5 percent), 92 percent in New York (actually 8 percent), an impossible 107 percent in Pennsylvania (actually 10 percent), and 133 percent in California (actually 9 percent).[16]

Two other Clinton states with large black electorates would have gone to Bush—Georgia (thirteen electoral votes, 20 percent black) and Louisiana (nine electoral votes, 27 percent black)—if Bush had gotten 11 percent rather than 9 percent in Georgia and 16 percent instead of 7 percent in Louisiana, for a total of 58 electoral votes. Had all four of these switches occurred, Bill Clinton would still have been elected president, albeit with a smaller, though still fairly comfortable, 312–226 (as opposed to a 370–168) majority.

Bush did worse, sometimes far worse, among black voters in 1992 than 1988 in eight of the ten largest electoral vote states. (In 1988 Bush won nine of these states, New York being the lone deviation.) The two exceptions were in Texas where he upped his share of the black vote from 6 to 10 percent and in Ohio where he went from 5 to 7 percent of the black vote. His decline in the other states ranged from a 23 to 10 percent drop in Florida and a 19 to 9 percent slide in California to one percentage point decreases in New York (9 to 8 percent) and in Michigan (8 to 7 percent).

But, again, Bush lost key electoral states in 1992 that he won four years earlier because whites deserted the Republican party; the voting behavior of the black electorate had nothing to do with Bush's change of fortune. In the six large states that Bush carried in 1988 but lost in 1992, Clinton's share of the white vote was virtually identical to Dukakis's four years earlier, deviating by only four percentage points in New Jersey, three in Ohio, and one point in the others. Bush's white support dropped substantially from 1988—20 points in California and Ohio, 19 points in Illinois and Michigan, 18 in New Jersey and 17 in Pennsylvania.

The 20 percent solution did not happen, in part because it was never tried and would not have worked since Bush's white base had so extensively eroded. The only serious Republican attempt to woo black voters was the nomination of Clarence Thomas to the Supreme Court. Such lack of effort is quite understandable; it didn't require political seers to argue that "It is almost inconceivable that the Republican party would attempt to outbid the Democrats for the support of blacks since the G.O.P.'s central electoral strategy since 1964 has been to win over racially conservative Independents and Democrats."[17] Indeed, the central message of the 1992 Republican convention, particularly in the speech by Pat Buchanan, was that the Republican tent was an exclusive one. Milton Bins and Faye Anderson, the chairman and executive director of the Council of 100, National Organization of Black Republicans, contend that black Republicans and independents who were receptive to Bush's message before the convention subsequently tuned out the president and his message because they "were offended by the racism and bigotry personified by Pat Buchanan." They find hope in the fact that the president was able to hold 10 percent of the black vote despite a "stalled economy, the divisive and alienating rhetoric of the party's right wing and single issue groups and the electorate's overwhelming desire for change." They also see positive signs in the strong showing of black Republican challengers in a number of congressional races and the fact that black voters were in part responsible for Republican Senators Alphonse D'Amato of New York and Arlen Specter of Pennsylvania narrowly retaining their seats. The fact that Clinton received a smaller percentage of the black vote (82 percent) than did Dukakis in 1988 (86 percent), Mondale in 1984 (90 percent), Carter in 1980 (85 percent) and Carter in 1976 (83 percent) offers them some small hope. Nonetheless, it is not at all clear whether the Republican party is ready to abandon its strategy of "add[ing] to the base by subtracting," which Bins and Anderson decry.[18] It is equally unclear whether the Republican candidates "need" black voters at the presidential and congressional levels.*

Notes

1. Fred Barnes, "Black Backing," *New Republic,* 28 May 1990, 11–13; Tom Wicker, "Bush and the Blacks," *New York Times,* 16 April 1990; Jessica Lee, "GOP Under Bush Attracts New Look from Black Voters," *USA Today,* 18 June 1990.

2. Alan Hertzke, "Populist Mobilization and Strategic Party Assimilation: The Lessons of Jackson and Robertson" (Unpublished ms., University of Oklahoma, Spring 1989); Fred Barnes, "Party of Lincoln," *New Republic,* 20 March 1989, 10–12; Barnes, "Black Backing"; Lee Atwater, "Toward a G.O.P. Rainbow," *New York Times,* 26 March 1989.

3. Louis Bolce, Gerald De Maio, and Douglas Muzzio, "Blacks and the Republican Party: The 20 Percent Solution," *Political Science Quarterly* 107 (Spring 1992): 63–79.

4. Ibid., 77.

5. In July 1991, 10 percent of blacks called themselves Republican. *New York Times,* 14 July 1991.

6. ABC News/*Washington Post* poll, 24–29 October 1991, Jeffrey Alderman, ABC director of polling, personal communication; Everett Carll Ladd, *The Ladd Report,* 4th ed., vol. 1 (New York: Norton, 1991), 13.

7. Michael M. Gant and Norman Luttbeg, *American Electoral Behavior* (Itasca, IL: F.E. Peacock Publishers, 1991), 84–86; Brian Silver, Barbara A. Anderson, and Paul Abramson, "Who Overreports Voting," *American Political Science Review* 80 (June

*The data used in this analysis are from the 1992 Voter Research and Surveys exit polls and the 1988 ABC News exit polls.

1986): 613–624; Stanley Presser, "Can Changes in Context Reduce Vote Overreporting in Surveys?" *Public Opinion Quarterly* 54 (Winter 1990): 586–593.

8. Herber Asher, *Polling and the Public* (Washington, DC: Congressional Quarterly Press, 1988), 99.

9. Morris P. Fiorina, *Retrospective Voting in American National Elections* (New Haven: Yale University Press, 1981).

10. Donald Granberg, "Pro-life or Reflection of Conservative Ideology? Analysis of Opposition to Legalized Abortion," *Sociology and Social Research* 52 (April 1978): 414–425; Louis Bolce, "Abortion and Presidential Elections: The Impact of Public Perceptions of Party and Candidate Positions," *Presidential Studies Quarterly* 28 (Fall 1988): 815–829.

11. Corwin Smidt, "Born-Again Politics: The Political Behavior of Evangelical Christians in the South and Non-South" in Tod A. Baker, Robert Steed, and Lawrence W. Moreland, eds., *Religion and Politics in the South* (New York: Praeger, 1983); Stuart Rothenberg and Frank Newport, *The Evangelical Voter* (Washington, DC: Free Congress Research & Education Foundation, 1984); Harold W. Stanley and Richard G. Niemi, "Partisanship and Group Support Over Time," in Richard G. Niemi and Herbert W. Weisberg, eds., *Controversies in Voting Behavior,* 3rd ed. (Washington, DC: Congressional Quarterly Press, 1993).

12. Robert Axelrod, "Where the Votes Come From: An Analysis of Electoral Coalitions, 1952–1968," *American Political Science Review* 66 (March 1972): 11–20; John R. Petrocik, *Party Coalitions* (Chicago: University of Chicago Press, 1981), 90–97; Andrew M. Greeley, *The American Catholic: A Social Portrait* (New York: Basic Books, 1977); Andrew M. Greeley, "Catholics and Coalitions: Where Should They Go?" in S. M. Lipset, ed., *Emerging Coalitions in American Politics* (San Francisco: Institute for Contemporary Studies, 1978); Henry C. Kenski and William Lockwood, "The Catholic Vote from 1980–1986: Continuity or Change?" in Ted G. Jelen, ed., *Religion and Political Behavior in the United States* (New York: Praeger, 1989); Stanley and Niemi, "Partisanship and Group Support," 352–356; Martin Wattenberg, *The Decline of American Political Parties: 1952–1984* (Cambridge, MA: Harvard University Press, 1986).

13. John B. Judis, "The End of Conservatism," *New Republic,* 31 August 1992, 28–30; "The Wilderness Year," *New Republic,* 31 August 1992, 3; Joshua Muravchik, "Why the Democrats Finally Won," *Commentary,* January 1993, 17–22.

14. Bolce et al., "Blacks and the Republican Party," 78.

15. Blacks made up 6 percent of the electorate in California, 10 percent in New York, 13 percent in Texas, 7 percent in Florida, 5 percent in Pennsylvania, 14 percent in Illinois, 10 percent in Ohio, 9 percent in Michigan, 10 percent in New Jersey, and 15 percent in North Carolina.

16. These hypothetical "necessary for Bush to win" black vote shares somewhat overstate the Republican candidate's prospects, for it was assumed that all his increased black vote came exclusively from Clinton. The size of the black electorate and the black share of the electorate figures are drawn from the 1992 VRS presidential exit poll; the actual state votes used in the calculations are from *Congressional Quarterly Weekly Report,* 7 November 1992, 3552.

17. Bolce et al., "Blacks and the Republican Party," 78–79.

18. "Black Republicans and 'The Speech,'" *Washington Post,* 17 November 1992.

─────────────────────Part IV

Gender

The readings in this part concern the relationship between gender, race, and politics. The topic of gender differences among blacks is rarely discussed candidly, and within the black community the plight of black women rarely shares equal billing with the plight of black men. Cornel West, in *Race Matters,* notes that "the claims to black authenticity that feed on the closing-ranks mentality of black people are dangerous precisely because this closing of ranks is usually done at the expense of black women."

The 1991 Clarence Thomas/Anita Hill hearings were a watershed for the politics of race and gender. Anita Hill, a law professor at the University of Oklahoma, accused Clarence Thomas, nominated by President Bush for a seat on the Supreme Court, of sexually harassing her when they both worked at the U.S. Equal Employment Opportunity Commission.

Many blacks accused Hill of betraying the black community—of "airing dirty laundry" in public. On the other hand, more than fifteen hundred black women joined to publish an advertisement in support of Hill, hoping—to no avail—that it would lead to the formation of a black feminist organization.

The politics of race and gender were also present in the 1994 firing of Benjamin Chavis, executive director of the NAACP. Chavis paid $332,000 of NAACP money to Mary Stansel, a former aide, to settle a threatened sexual harassment lawsuit. Chavis failed to receive the authorization of the board of directors for this action—or even to *notify* them. (Chavis was also fired for turning a substantial budget surplus into a deficit, and for developing close relationships with Louis Farrakhan and black gangs.)

Chavis attempted to turn a matter of sexual harassment (and financial impropriety) into a matter of racism. He accused "forces outside the African American community" of conspiring to destroy his leadership.

Many black women, however, had a different view. Julianne Malveaux, a San Francisco economist and syndicated columnist, asked, "Why are women silent as

165

men make excuses about poor judgment?" She said that the failure of black women to "step up to the plate" may be "as indefensible as Chavis' poor judgment." Lulann McGriff, president of the NAACP's San Francisco branch, said that "the men were more concerned with the money than how he might have been treating a woman," and that "none of the men understand that inside the NAACP, women are the ones who build the stage and the men are the ones who dance on it."

The cause of black feminism has created substantial resentment within the black community. Michael Dawson, a political scientist at the University of Chicago, reports that a significant number of African Americans believe "black feminists are dangerous" to the cause of black advancement. A recent national survey of twelve hundred black Americans found that 29 percent felt "black feminist groups just divide the black community." Twenty percent believed black female leaders have "the possibility of undermining the leadership of black men."

This attitude is even held by some black women. Shahrazad Ali created an explosion in the black community with her book, *The Blackwoman's Guide to Understanding the Blackman*, in which she argues that overly aggressive black women are destroying the psyches of black men, leading to the destruction of the black family. She urges black women to be more submissive and supportive in their relations with black men.

If some black feminists feel alienated from the black community as a whole, their relationship is no better with the feminist community. Kimberly Collins, a community activist in Washington, D.C., said that "when I think of feminists, I think of white women fighting for the rights that black women already have," such as employment. "I also think of lesbianism and male bashing."

For this reason, many black women define themselves as "womanists." The term was coined by Alice Walker in her book, *In Search of Our Mothers' Gardens*, to differentiate the set of separate gender issues shared by women of color.

The first reading in this part, by political scientist Jewel L. Prestage, is entitled "In Quest of African American Political Woman." Prestage notes that black women are simultaneously members of two groups that have suffered exclusion from civic life. Her article considers the nature and extent of African American women's political participation, beginning with the slave era.

Three basic contentions underscore Prestage's analysis. The first is that black women, "throughout their existence on the American continent," have been "engaged in political activity, the nature of which has been determined by the legal and cultural circumstances they faced at the time." Second, "African American women's political activities have been directed toward altering their disadvantaged status both as African Americans and as women." Third, black women have "escalated their political activity progressively, moving from a predominance of nontraditional activity to a predominance of traditional activity, and have emerged as prime users of these traditional avenues in contemporary American politics."

Prestage notes, "The holding of political office by African American women is a rather recent experience." Indeed, "the first African American woman elected to a state legislature took office in 1938, the first to ascend to the bench did so in 1939, the first to become a member of the federal bench was appointed in 1966, and the first elected to Congress was elected in 1968."

While black women have come to electoral politics fairly recently, their numbers are almost certain to grow. Currently, black women hold a higher percentage of their race's elective offices than do white women, and black women have higher rates of voter turnout than black men.

The second reading is "Gender, Race, and the State Legislature: A Research Note on the Double Disadvantage Hypothesis." Gary Moncrief, Joel Thompson, and Robert Schuhmann examine the relationship between demographic status and political success, by examining the backgrounds of fifteen hundred state legislators in eleven states. They hypothesize that "black women state legislators must exceed their white female counterparts with regard to certain preparatory background characteristics," and that "black women state legislators must exceed their black male counterparts with regard to certain preparatory background characteristics." The authors found that black women have greater educational and occupational achievement than white women, but that black women and black men had similar educational and occupational backgrounds.

11

In Quest of African American Political Woman

Jewel L. Prestage

The complete history of African American women's participation in American politics must recognize not only their involvement in traditional political acts such as registering, voting, and holding office but also those nontraditional activities in which they engaged long before gaining the ballot. Because African American women are simultaneously members of the two groups that have suffered the nation's most blatant exclusion from the normal channels of access to civic life, African Americans and women, their political behavior has been largely overlooked by political scientists, who have tended to focus primarily on those actions that conform to the more restrictive definitions of politics.[1] Because African American women have only recently been granted access to the political arena as voters and officeholders in significant numbers, there is a paucity of information about them in these roles and even less about their nontraditional actions that predated these roles.[2]

The purpose of this article is to begin a full exploration of the types and extent of political participation and behavior in which African American women have engaged. Utilizing extant social science literature and recent survey research findings by political science scholars, this quest for African American political woman will encompass a historical overview in which traditional and nontraditional political actions will be examined. Three basic contentions will permeate and guide the discussion.

From *Annals of the American Academy of Political and Social Science,* May 1991, pp. 88–103. © 1991 by the American Academy of Political and Social Science. Reprinted by permission of Sage Publications, Inc.

The first contention is that throughout their existence on the American continent, African American women have been engaged in political activity, the nature of which has been determined by the legal and cultural circumstances they faced at the time. The second is that African American women's political activities have been directed toward altering their disadvantaged status both as African Americans and as women. Third is the observation that, historically, African American women have escalated their political activity progressively, moving from a predominance of nontraditional activity to a predominance of traditional activity, and have emerged as prime users of these traditional avenues in contemporary American politics.

In the discussion that follows, four major historical periods will be delineated and the extent and nature of African American women's political activity will be examined in each. The designated periods are preemancipation, Reconstruction, post-Reconstruction through World War II, and the Second Reconstruction. Legal and cultural circumstances of African American women in each period will be summarized, as these are assumed to be the basic impetus for their political actions.

Preemancipation (1619–1865)

While a few held free status, most women of African descent living in the American colonies and in the United States before the Emancipation Proclamation in 1865 were chattel slaves. As enslaved African females, they were the victims of dual oppression, one issuing from race and the other from sex. Subjected to the slave status ascribed to their African male kin, they were further victimized by a body of hostile public policy directed toward them as women. Among the most inhumane and devastating provisions were the lack of legal protection from physical sexual abuse and rape by white males, legally enforced separation from their children, the absence of a legal right to marriage and family life, legally enforced cohabitation with other slaves for breeding purposes, and laws requiring that children born as a result of cohabitation with white males be assigned the slave status of the mother even if the father were white and free, a contradiction of then prevailing common law practices. Abolitionist Frederick Douglass described the African American woman as one " 'consigned to a life of revolting prostitution,' " " 'a mere chattel,' " pointing out that if she even " 'lifted her hand' " in defense of her own innocence she could be lawfully put to death.[3]

The political implications of the physical abuse and rape of African American women have been studied by several social scientists. Angela Davis, for example, argues that rape of slave women was an indirect attack on the slave community as a whole, intended to induce in the African American male doubts about his ability to resist the slave system in any manner whatever since he could not protect the women. For the slave woman, the rape was meant to reinforce her vulnerability as a female.[4]

Most free African Americans of this era, including women, found that their status was not fundamentally different from that of slaves.[5] Restrictive legislation and cultural practices, reflecting the general situation of African Americans and of women, served as a double bind for African American women.

How did African American women respond to their status in the pre-emancipation period? Without the ballot or any other traditional mode of access to the political arena, they resorted to a wide range of other options. Because their nontraditional modes of action were designed to alter public policy provisions and legally condoned cultural practices defining their status and the behaviors mandated for that status, African American women's actions in this period can be appropriately labeled political.[6]

African American enslaved women took leading roles in organizing their community in order to lessen the hostile impact of the slave system on individual and family life. They engaged in physical retaliatory violence on an individual and group basis, systematically refused to carry unwanted children to term and helped others who were so inclined, became runaways whose acumen and skill were cited as unique and superior to those of males, organized and participated in outright slave revolts, and became organizers and operatives—like Harriet Tubman—in the Underground Railroad. They sued for freedom, and in some states they won. During the Civil War, African American slave women escaped to work with the Union Army as laundresses, cooks, and scouts and in other capacities as well.[7]

Free African American women were no less active than their enslaved sisters. Records of antislavery societies, the editorial pages of newspapers and periodicals, available pamphlets, and other records of public discourse reveal the identities of many black women whose attention and talents were devoted to the cause of abolition.[8] In their private capacities, numerous African American free women purchased slaves and granted them freedom, while others went north to find employment to pay for freedom for husbands and other relatives. African American women had their own antislavery societies in addition to being active in the principal abolitionist organizations. It was one of these societies that first defied the prevailing cultural pattern by inviting a black woman feminist and abolitionist, Maria Stewart, to speak to a mixed audience of men and women in Boston in 1832. Women were generally not permitted to speak publicly on an issue as controversial as abolition.[9]

Some other free African American women were active in the women's rights movement in this era.[10] Perhaps the most popular was Sojourner Truth, also a strong force in the abolitionist movement. Author Paula Giddings states that "although the Black woman's contribution to the suffrage campaign is rarely written about, Blacks, including women, had a more consistent attitude toward the vote than Whites, as Blacks had fewer conflicts about women's voting." Furthermore, "one would be hard pressed to find any Black woman who did not advocate getting the vote."[11]

No doubt tensions between women along racial lines within the abolitionist societies and in the women's rights movement, along with the eventual split between the abolitionist movement and the women's movement,[12] had a negative impact on the role of African American women prior to emancipation. While a few African American women whose education and wealth exceeded that of white women were found acceptable as potential members and officers in abolition societies dominated by white women, the question of mass black participation was a matter of bitter conflict.[13] Maria Stewart opined that for black women, race was the priority issue and it was the issue that initially sparked their feminism.[14]

A review of the preemancipation era would seem to suggest that African American women, while deprived of access to traditional channels of political participation, were nonetheless active in a wide range of efforts designed to alter their status as slaves and as women.

Reconstruction

The Emancipation Proclamation, and the constitutional amendments and federal troop occupation of the Southern states that followed, provided the legal changes necessary for African Americans to enter the political arena as full participants for the first time and ushered in the period of Reconstruction. During this period, African American males achieved the right to register and vote, and they were elected and appointed to public office in significant numbers. African American women, like women generally, were excluded from these privileges, however.

How did African American women react to this exclusion? Denied the privilege of personal suffrage, these women are reputed to have found means of influencing the political decisions of their male kin and friends. Accounts from Louisiana provide an interesting group profile. According to one state politician and former state senator, they followed their men from morning to night telling them how to vote, formed a large segment of the audiences at political meetings, and evidenced a deep interest "in all that pertained to" politics.[15] Sensitive to the importance of their exclusion from the suffrage, a New Orleans group published a document in 1878 demanding for themselves, former slave women, "every right and privilege" guaranteed under the United States Constitution to men, and vowed to use every power in their hands to get them.[16]

For African American women, Reconstruction brought other problems, which had roots in the political system. Establishment of family life through marriage, searching for relatives, education of themselves and family members, achieving personal and family economic stability, and developing a consensus concerning the role and status of women in the African American community after emancipation were among the challenges they faced. A disproportionate share of the African American women's energies and organizational efforts was devoted not only to finding solutions to these problems but also to getting the ballot for women. Notable among the African American female suffragettes were three

South Carolina sisters, Frances, Louisa, and Lottie Rollin. Active also were Charlotte Ray and Mary Ann Shadd Cary, in the District of Columbia. Cary actually registered to vote in 1871.[17]

In Louisiana, African American women are credited with organizing the several exoduses that took thousands of African Americans out of the state to the North.

Although Reconstruction did not bring to the African American woman the privilege of traditional political involvement, it did not dull her penchant for the utilization of nontraditional forms of influence. Because the options available to her actually expanded beyond those of the previous era, so did her involvement.

Post-Reconstruction to World War II (1890–1943)

The withdrawal of federal troops from the South facilitated by the Compromise of 1877 proved to be the death knell for Reconstruction and for the African American's maiden voyage into the turbulent waters of American electoral politics. Inherent in the ending of Reconstruction and the return of white control to the southern states were major problems for African American women. Legal constraints on African American political activity in combination with widely used and condoned illegal forms of violence and intimidation instituted by the white power structure resulted in the creation of a very unstable and threatening situation for the race as a whole.

One form of violence of particular concern for post-Reconstruction African American women was the practice of lynching. Although the most frequent victims were African American males, African American women and whites were sometimes targeted also. Lynchings numbered over 2500 between 1884 and 1900 and over 1100 between 1900 and the start of World War I.[18] Disenfranchisement of African American males through newly enacted state laws, lack of adequate educational opportunities resulting from state segregation laws and underfunding of African American schools, racial segregation of all public accommodations, extensive abuse of African American women by white men, and segregation and discrimination in employment were among the other legal and cultural impediments that African American women faced.

Still denied the ballot, these women continued to resort to nontraditional political action. They took the lead in the antilynching movement by staging national and international campaigns that involved meeting with the president of the United States, protest activity in the nation's capital, and even travel outside the United States to generate external pressure on the national government to make lynching a federal crime. Leadership roles in the antilynching campaign were assumed by Ida Wells Barnett and Mary Church Terrell.[19] Also, when the National Association for the Advancement of Colored People (NAACP) was established in 1909 as a general-purpose civil rights organization, African American women were among the principal players. Convinced that the education and social uplifting of women were essential to overall development of the race, women like Mary McLeod Bethune and Charlotte Hawkins Brown operated schools. College-educated African American women formed sororities and clubs with political education and uplifting as goals. Generally, historical accounts of the continuous struggles waged to overturn the plethora of legal and de facto barriers to equality for African Americans reveal the presence and influence of African American women whether the focus is on education, transportation, public accommodations, the right to vote, economic development, or criminal justice.

During this period, relations between the women's movement and African American women ranged from troubled to conflictual. Deckard reports that the women's movement had grown out of the abolitionist movement and that the two had close ties until the Civil War, after which relations deteriorated when the women were not given the vote along with African Americans.[20]

By 1890 the women's movement had dissociated itself from African Americans in an effort to make itself respectable in the eyes of white males. Within a decade its rhetoric and goals had become blatantly racist. Leaders highlighted the potential white outnumbering of total African American voters that would result from the granting of suffrage to white women. White supremacy was touted and appeals to Negrophobia made, out of either expediency or commitment. In a strange turn of events, however, the final congressional arguments against granting the vote to women included expressions of fear that enfranchisement would indeed extend the ballot to African American women. In the bid to achieve ratification of the amendment, Alice Paul, head of the Woman's Party, is quoted as having responded in these words to questions about the possibility of African American women's gaining the vote in South Carolina if the Nineteenth Amendment passed: " 'Negro men cannot vote in South Carolina and therefore negro women could not vote if women were to vote in the nation. We are organizing white women in the South . . . but have heard of no activity or anxiety among the negresses.' "[21]

Efforts to exclude African American women from the mainstream women's political organizations and from the voting privilege sought for white women did not go unchallenged. The NAACP was mobilized by African American women to bring pressure on Alice Paul and her party. In addition, African American women's groups confronted the white women's major organizations with a petition for membership and requests for policy clarification on the question of race and woman suffrage, and the African American groups proved to be effective debaters and negotiators in the foray that emerged in the final stages of the fight for ratification of the Nineteenth Amendment.[22] It was clear even then that African American women were not regarded by their white female counterparts as fully deserving the ballot.

Immediately after the amendment's ratification, African American women were reported to have registered in large numbers in the South. In reaction, Southern states were quick to develop procedures and tactics to slow their registration, including making them wait in line for hours until all white women had registered. Curiously, the enthusiasm for registering to vote displayed by African

American women was not reported for white women.[23] In their fight to eliminate this and other forms of discrimination against them as voters, African American women received no real support from the National Woman's Party, but rather hostility and discourteous treatment.

Overall it seems fair to generalize that African American women found that in their post-Reconstruction push to become full members of the body politic, it was necessary not only to fight the antisuffragists but also to wrestle the ballot from the hands of the white suffragettes. In spite of efforts to the contrary, the success of the tactics used to disenfranchise the entire African American population, women included, is reflected in records from 1940 in Louisiana. There the number of African Americans registered to vote was only 886, while the adult African American population was estimated at 473,562. This pattern was replicated throughout the Southern region, where the majority of African Americans resided.[24]

The Second Reconstruction (1944–Present)

One of the mainstays of white political control in the South, the white primary election, was declared unconstitutional in 1944, creating a more positive environment for African Americans to realize their goal of becoming practitioners of traditional politics. Through individual and group initiatives, African Americans mounted an uphill battle against those legal and cultural norms that had militated against their aspirations in previous eras. African American women were made acutely aware of the irrelevance of the Nineteenth Amendment to their enfranchisement desires and earnestly joined in these race-based strategies.

Nontraditional activities were still necessary in the post-World War II broadside against racial discrimination at the polls. In litigation challenging state laws requiring segregation and discrimination in a variety of areas, including voter registration, and in lobbying for legislative remedies at the national level, African American women played prominent roles. Constance Baker Motley, legal counsel for the NAACP, and Thomasina Norford, lobbyist for the American Council on Human Rights in Washington, D.C., are examples. When the "outside of the courtroom" dimension of the movement emerged in the late 1950s and early 1960s, women again played significant roles in grass-roots organizations in local communities, in national coordination structures, and in confrontations with hostile police officers and anti-integration groups and individuals. Studies of demonstrations by African American college students show that 48 percent of those personally involved in sit-ins and freedom rides were female.[25] A study of participation in protests and more traditional antidiscrimination activity by New Orleans African American adults indicated only minimal overall differences between men and women.[26] Among those persons who achieved high visibility as pioneers in integrating previously segregated higher educational settings were African American women like Autherine Lucy, Ada Sipuel, Edith Jones, Vivian Malone, and Charlene Hunter. Other major activists in the civil rights movement were Rosa Parks, Daisy Bates, Fannie Lou Hamer, and Victoria DeLee. In the NAACP leadership ranks were Margaret Bush Wilson, Althea Simmons, and Jean Fairfax.

Writing about the civil rights movement, Professor William Chafe notes the pivotal, initiating role of African American women in defining issues of sex and race liberation for white women.[27] Within the context of the civil rights movement, African American women experienced and chose to consciously confront the issue of sexism. Through church organizations, women's clubs, sororities, and educational organizations, they provided monetary and moral support for civil rights workers, ranging from those registering voters to those engaged in more revolutionary politics.

Voting

With the passage of the 1965 Voting Rights Act, African American women received their first real opportunity to participate in traditional politics, since both the Fifteenth Amendment, which enfranchised men, and the Nineteenth, which benefited women, had in effect excluded them. Underscoring this is a 1966 publication declaring that African American women were, at the time, "frozen out" of the Southern political scene.[28] Clayton, in 1964, found that only a score or so of these women had achieved "success" in politics and that the "less than a dozen" in political offices across the nation had gained them through political parties.[29]

The 1965 Voting Rights Act was significant empowering legislation for African American women. It produced a remarkable escalation in the levels of African American voter registration and voting, especially in Southern states. For example, in Mississippi registration increased from about 8.0 percent to 62.0 percent between 1964 and 1968. In 1964 in Louisiana only 31.7 percent of the African American voting-age population was registered, but by 1970 over 55.0 percent was and by 1975 the figure had reached almost 67.0 percent.[30] These figures represent total registration of African Americans and comparable figures are not available along gender lines. Later voter-registration projections and voter-participation figures that are available along gender lines, however, lend some credibility to a projection that women were significantly represented among these new voters.

Studies of overall African American voter turnout show that it trailed white turnout from 1960 to 1980 and then surpassed it between 1980 and 1984. The total gain in turnout was 5.3 percent.[31] In fact, reported African American voting in 1984 was 5 percentage points higher than reported white voting when state-level political and contextual variables and demographic characteristics are held constant.[32] Clearly there has been a striking increase in overall African American voter turnout.

When the focus is narrowed to recent voting patterns of African American women, studies show that young African American women voted at a higher rate than did young African American men and that the gap in voting between African American men and women overall was less than the gap for whites. African American women from white-collar and manual occupations had slightly higher turnout rates than did their male counterparts until 1976, when parity emerged. While professional women voted at higher rates than did African American men of similar status, rates for the men in farm occupations were higher than for African American farm women. Regarded as undergirding this pattern of male-female voting differences were egalitarian sex-role orientations and assertive behavior of African American women at both the low and high ends of the economic scale. Feminist orientations were also associated with higher voter turnout. No single explanation was offered for the unusual pattern, however.[33] African American women who expressed the highest levels of political cynicism and the lowest levels of political efficacy increased their voting strength at greater levels than did any of the other race-sex groups.

As of 1988, African American women were reported to be 4 percentage points more likely to cast ballots than were African American men of comparable socioeconomic status. Especially remarkable, in historical context, is the finding that African American women who were heads of their households were 11 percent more likely to exercise the franchise than were white males, after controlling for demographic factors.[34]

Current available information would seem to suggest that African American women, the last group to acquire the ballot, have emerged as its prime users.

Holding Office

The holding of political office by African American women is a rather recent experience. The first African American woman elected to a state legislature took office in 1938, the first to ascend to the bench did so in 1939, the first to become a member of the federal bench was appointed in 1966, and the first elected to Congress was elected in 1968. The first roster of African American women officeholders widely available was prepared by the Joint Center for Political Studies in 1973 and contained 337 names. Table 11.1 reveals the progressive increase in the number of women on the rosters published annually. As of 1989, some 1814 of the 7226 African American elected officials on the roster, or roughly one-fourth, were women.

Probings of the characteristics of African American women officeholders have yielded both selected group profiles and a general profile. African American women state legislators serving in the mid-1970s were found to have mostly Southern origins, to be better educated than their parents and most Americans, to have been elected to office after age 40, to have experienced marriage, and to have children mostly over the age of 18. Most of them had no relative who had held political office. Most had exhibited pre-adult interest in politics, had occu-

Table 11.1

Black Women as a Percentage of Black Elected Officials (BEOs)

Year	BEOs (total)	Female BEOs	Female BEOs as a Percentage of Total	Increase in Number of Female BEOs as a Percentage of Total
1969	N.A.	131	N.A.	N.A.
1970	1,469	N.A.	N.A.	N.A.
1971	1,860	N.A.	N.A.	N.A.
1972	2,264	N.A.	N.A.	N.A.
1973	2,621	337	12.8	N.A.
1974	2,991	N.A.	N.A.	N.A.
1975	3,503	530	15.1	N.A.
1976	3,979	684	17.2	2.0
1977	4,311	782	18.1	1.0
1978	4,503	843	18.7	0.6
1979	4,607	882	19.1	0.4
1980	4,912	976	19.9	0.7
1981	5,038	1,021	20.3	0.4
1982	5,160	1,081	20.9	0.7
1983	5,606	1,223	21.8	0.9
1984	5,654	1,259	22.3	0.4
1985	6,056	1,359	22.4	0.2
1986	6,424	1,469	22.9	0.5
1987	6,681	1,564	23.4	1.0
1988	6,829	1,625	23.8	0.4
1989	7,226	1,814	25.1	1.3

Source: Roster of Black Elected Officials (Washington, DC: Joint Center for Political Studies, published annually).
Note: N.A. = not available.

pations outside the home, and had little prior political experience and yet felt they took office with special advantage in some policy areas. Overall, women's liberation was not opposed, but it was not given high priority. Support of husbands, children, and other family members was considered important and was reportedly given to them to a great degree. All were Democrats representing urban areas.[35]

African American women judges display many of the same traits as do the legislators. Nearly half were born in the South and identified their background as working-class. Almost all reported affiliation with an organized religious denomination. Most were without a lawyer role model in their families, as only one female lawyer was reported among family members. About half were products of historically black colleges and universities, and a quarter of them received legal training at one of the five law schools at these institutions. The vast majority had experienced marriage and a smaller majority were mothers. Husbands were mostly labeled "overwhelmingly supportive," but for nearly half of the women, self-motivation was the source of inspiration for running for office. With reference to age, the majority were in their thirties and forties. Only one of the jurists gained initial office as a result of election. Appointment was the principal facilitator for access.[36]

When a 1983 study compared African American and white women elected officials with each other and with men, it was found that African American women, as a group, were "highly qualified, politically experienced and self-confident, outdoing women officeholders overall, who are themselves outdoing men."[37] They were also more likely than males and than women overall to have attended college, and they were more likely than men to have come from professional, technical, and managerial/administrative positions. While they were less likely than women overall to have political experience, they were more likely to have had staff experience and campaign experience.

Some race-specific differences in the experiences of African American and white women en route to office emerged. One was that groups and organizations were more important in gaining political access for African American women. Another was that, more than white women, the African Americans cited representation of minorities or civil rights issues and the ability to combat discrimination as the main reasons why they ran for office.

In terms of family characteristics, African American women were less likely to be married, less likely to evaluate spousal support as important in decisions to seek office, more likely to be college professors or lawyers, and less likely to have children, but more likely to have children under the age of 12. African American women overall were more likely than white women to be Democrats.

Like African American officeholders generally and women officeholders overall, African American women are concentrated most heavily in local positions. In fact, of the 1814 currently serving, 501 serve on local school boards, and 651 are members of municipal governing bodies, while 1 serves in the United States Congress, and 99 serve in state legislatures. Among the jurists, only 1 serves on a state court of last resort, 88 are on other courts, and 22 are magistrates or justices of the peace.

African American women officeholders seem to have found their major successes in the same electoral settings in which their male counterparts have achieved.

Even after obtaining access to traditional political channels, African American women continue to be involved in a variety of nontraditional activities. For example, they hold leadership positions in civil rights organizations and in interest groups with special relevance for African Americans.

The 1980s brought into being several organizations to accommodate and promote political activity among African Americans in which women have been quite active. Other organizations have been created exclusively for African American women. In the former category are the Congressional Black Caucus and the National Black Caucus of Local Elected Officials. The organizations especially for women include the National Association of Black Women Legislators and the National Political Congress of Black Women. The National Political Congress of Black Women held its first national assembly in 1985, with Shirley Chisholm, the nation's first black congresswoman, at the helm.

Women's Liberation

African American women's relationship to the contemporary women's liberation movement has been a mixed bag. A few African American women have been in the leadership cadre in the major organization, the National Organization for Women, but for most, the women's movement has not been accorded high priority. As early as 1973, the National Black Feminist Organization was formed as an option for African Americans to address feminist issues not dealt with to their satisfaction within the National Organization for Women. Over the last two decades, white women and African American women have worked together when their interests coincided, but, as Deckard points out, "friction does arise."[38] Despite the friction, African American women legislators, as well as African American male lawmakers, have been mostly supportive of women's issues. Curiously, the lack of high-priority status for the women's liberation movement among African American female officeholders has not translated into a lack of membership in women's liberation organizations. Nearly two-thirds of women state legislators who are African American belong to the Women's Political caucus, compared to one-third of all women legislators. NOW membership is held by one-third of African American women, compared to only one-fifth of all women.[39]

Political Parties

African American women's political-party membership and work have increased progressively. While no complete authoritative record is available, the high visibility of Democratic women like Patricia Roberts Harris, Yvonne Burke Brathwaite, C. Dolores Tucker, Barbara Jordan, Cardiss Collins, and Maxine Waters as well as Republicans Jewel LaFontant, Gloria Toote, and LeGree Daniels indicates a change in the role of African American women in the major parties. Shirley Chisholm was the first to seriously contest for presidential nomination, but Charlotta Bass had been the vice presidential candidate on the Progressive Party ticket in 1952.

Political Socialization

Some interesting findings have emerged from studies of the political socialization of African American women, especially of those who hold political office.

For example, the basic assumption undergirding ambition theory is that wanting political office is a prerequisite for winning office.[40] Studies show no significant difference in the political ambition of African American male and female office-holders, in spite of the overall lower social status, educational level, and occupational status of women.[41] Also, among African American women state legislators in the mid-1970s, only one stated unequivocally that she would not seek reelection or aspire to a higher office.[42] Comparisons of political ambition between African American women and white women indicate parity in ambition, but white women's ambition is more closely linked to nontraditional sex-role beliefs acquired early while African American women's ambition is associated more with their current activities.[43] This would seem to lessen the possible impact on African American women of the suppressive legal prescriptions and community practices that prevailed in the period before passage and implementation of the 1965 Voting Rights Act.

Do African American women possess coping skills that separate them from other women officeholders? Work by several scholars indicates that this is true for African American women professionals[44] and for political activists.[45] One scholar even contends that it was the independence of direction and action exhibited by African American women domestic workers that raised the consciousness of their white middle-class employers.[46]

Some African American women scholars have recently addressed the question of African American women's liberation as an issue separate from that of women's liberation, on one hand, and from African American liberation, on the other. Largely because this kind of perspective has been divisive in both the African Americans' and the women's struggles, African American women have generally opted to pursue a two-pronged struggle without taking a radical or self-interested posture in either of the existing movements. Political scientist Shelby Lewis has advised that African American women must construct and implement an independent liberation strategy, as no help can be expected from either of the three other race-sex groups—not even the admission that African American women are oppressed.[47] For either group to do so would acknowledge their culpability in that oppression. Lewis instructs that independence in thought is a prerequisite for independence in action. Given this line of argument, the extent to which there is an African American gender gap equivalent to that reported among white adults takes on special relevance. Research findings to date reveal no comparable division of African American political attitudes along gender lines, however.[48]

Summary and Conclusion

Historical precedence, as examined in this article, suggests that as long as both race and gender remain critical factors in determining life chances, quality of life, and access to what are considered the preferred values in American society,

African American women will continue to respond both as African Americans and as women. The nature of that response will involve creative, innovative structures and strategies if the traditional ones are not available or prove to be ineffective. When and where the traditional channels have opened up, African American women have made optimum use of them. One critical issue that must be subjected to continuing and agonizing reappraisal by these women, however, is the efficacy of the traditional political machinery, to which they have only recently gained access, in the achievement of contemporary social and economic goals. In short, have African American women gained access only to find that access has lost its utility for delivering the resources sought? Are there lessons to be learned from the desertion of the ballot box by white males? Does the existence of powerful single-issue groups signal a fundamental change in American politics to which African American women must adapt?

In the search for indications of African American women's political behavior in the future, it would seem that the contingency orientation that has dominated their political behavior historically, the absence of a gender gap among African American adults, and the finding that race issues rather than gender issues are their priorities provide the best clues.

Notes

1. In Barbara J. Nelson, *American Women and Politics: A Selected Bibliography and Resource Guide* (New York: Garland, 1984), of 1611 entries, only 39 are under "black women."

2. John J. Stucker, "Women as Voters: Their Maturation as Political Persons in American Society," in *Women in the Professions,* ed. Laurily Keir Epstein (Lexington, MA: D.C. Heath, 1975), pp. 97–121.

3. As quoted in Herbert Aptheker, ed., *A Documentary History of the Negro People in the United States* (New York: Citadel Press, 1969), p. 313.

4. Angela Davis, "Reflections on the Black Woman's Role in the Community of Slaves," *Black Scholar,* 3:2–15 (Dec. 1971).

5. John Hope Franklin, *From Slavery to Freedom* (New York: Knopf, 1974), pp. 214–19.

6. For a less restrictive definition, see Harold Lasswell, *Politics: Who Gets What When How?* (New York: McGraw-Hill, 1936). Jewel L. Prestage and Carolyn S. Williams define politics as encompassing "the totality of the power relationships in society as those relationships impinge upon the ultimate use of coercive powers of the society." See Prestage and Williams, "Blacks in Louisiana Politics," in *Louisiana Politics: Festival in a Labyrinth,* ed. James Bolner (Baton Rouge: Louisiana State University Press, 1982), p. 285.

7. Accounts of women's participation in slave resistance are given in John Blasingame, *The Slave Community* (New York: Oxford University Press, 1972), pp. 116–53; Paula Giddings, *When and Where I Enter: The Impact of Black Women on Race and Sex in America* (New York: Bantam Books, 1984), pp. 39–40; Jewel L. Prestage, "Political Behavior of American Black Women: An Overview," in *The Black Woman,* ed. La Frances Rodgers-Rose (Beverly Hills, CA: Sage, 1984), p. 238.

8. Aptheker, *Documentary History,* pp. 126, 253, 380–87, 441–42; Susie King Taylor, *A Black Woman's Civil War Memoirs* (New York: Markus Wiener, 1988).

9. For the content of that speech, see Marilyn Richardson, ed., *Maria W. Stewart: America's First Black Woman Political Writer: Essays and Speeches* (Bloomington: Indiana University Press, 1987), pp. 43–49. Also see Giddings, *When and Where I Enter,* p. 49.

10. Barbara Sinclair Deckard, *The Woman's Movement: Political, Socioeconomic and Psychological Issues,* 3d ed. (New York: Harper & Row, 1983), p. 255.

11. Giddings, *When and Where I Enter,* pp. 119–20.

12. Deckard, *Woman's Movement,* p. 260; Giddings, *When and Where I Enter,* p. 68.

13. Giddings, *When and Where I Enter,* p. 55.

14. Ibid.

15. Aptheker, *Documentary History,* pp. 721–22.

16. Ibid.

17. Giddings, *When and Where I Enter,* pp. 70–71.

18. Prestage and Williams, "Blacks in Louisiana Politics," p. 298.

19. See "Black Women Attack the Lynching System," in *Black Women in White America: A Documentary History,* ed. Gerda Lerner (New York: Vintage Books, 1972), pp. 196–98.

20. Deckard, *Woman's Movement,* pp. 264–66.

21. Giddings, *When and Where I Enter,* p. 160.

22. Ibid., pp. 159–65.

23. Stucker, "Women as Voters," p. 98.

24. Prestage and Williams, "Blacks in Louisiana Politics," p. 299.

25. Donald A. Matthews and James W. Prothro, *Negroes and the New Southern Politics* (New York: Harcourt, Brace & Jovanovich, 1966), pp. 416–19.

26. John Pierce, William Avery, and Addison Carey, Jr., "Sex Differences in Black Political Beliefs and Behaviors," *American Journal of Political Science,* May 1973, 422–30.

27. *Women and Equality* (New York: Oxford University Press, 1977), pp. 108–10.

28. Matthews and Prothro, *Negroes and the New Southern Politics,* p. 68.

29. Edward T. Clayton, *The Negro Politician* (Chicago: Johnson, 1964), pp. 122–48.

30. See the discussion in Jewel L. Prestage, "Black Politics and the Kerner Report: Concerns and Directions," *Social Science Quarterly,* 49: 453–64 (Dec. 1968).

31. Patricia Gurin, Shirley Hatchett, and James S. Jackson, *Hope and Independence: Blacks' Response to Electoral and Party Politics* (New York: Russell Sage, 1989), p. 53.

32. Gerald Davis Jaynes and Robin M. Williams, Jr., eds., *A Common Destiny: Blacks and American Society* (Washington, DC: National Academy Press, 1989), pp. 234–35.

33. See Marjorie Lansing, "The Voting Patterns of American Black Women," in *A Portrait of Marginality: The Political Behavior of the American Woman,* ed. Jewel L. Prestage and Marianne Githens (New York: David McKay, 1977), pp. 379–94; Sandra Baxter and Marjorie Lansing, *Women and Politics: The Visible Majority* (Ann Arbor: University of Michigan Press, 1983), pp. 73–112.

34. *Common Destiny,* pp. 234–35.

35. Jewel L. Prestage, "Black Women State Legislators: A Profile," in *Portrait of Marginality,* ed. Prestage and Githens, pp. 401–18.

36. Jewel L. Prestage, "Black Women Judges: An Examination of Their Socio-Economic, Educational and Political Backgrounds, and Judicial Placement," in *Readings in American Political Issues,* ed. Franklin D. Jones and Michael O. Adams (Dubuque, IA: Kendall-Hunt, 1987), pp. 324–44.

37. Susan J. Carroll and Wendy S. Strimling, *Women's Routes to Elective Office: A Comparison with Men's* (New Brunswick, NJ: Rutgers University Center for the American Woman and Politics, 1983), pt. 1, pp. 141–209.

38. Deckard, *Woman's Movement,* p. 346.

39. Carroll and Strimling, *Women's Routes,* pp. 141–209. See also Susan E. Marshall,

"Equity Issues and Black-White Differences in Women's ERA Support," *Social Science Quarterly,* 71: 299–314 (June 1990).

40. Joseph A. Schlesinger, *Ambition and Politics: Political Careers in the United States* (Chicago: Rand McNally, 1966), p. 1.

41. Pauline T. Stone, "Ambition Theory and the Black Politician," *Western Political Quarterly,* 33:94–107 (Mar. 1980).

42. Prestage, "Black Women State Legislators."

43. Jerry Perkins, "Political Ambition among United States Black and White Women: An Intergenerational Test of the Socialization Model," *Women and Politics,* 6:27–40 (1986).

44. Cynthia Fuchs Epstein, "Positive Effects of the Multiple Negative: Explaining the Success of Black Professional Women," *American Journal of Sociology,* Jan. 1973, pp. 913–35.

45. Chafe, *Women and Equality,* p. 109.

46. Charles V. Willie, "Marginality and Social Change," *Society,* 12:12 (July-Aug. 1975).

47. Shelby Lewis, "A Liberation Ideology: The Intersection of Race, Sex and Class," in *Women Rights, Feminism and Politics in the United States,* ed. Mary L. Shanley (Washington, DC: American Political Science Association, 1982), pp. 38–42.

48. Susan Welch and Lee Sigelman, "A Black Gender Gap?" *Social Science Quarterly,* 70: 120–23 (Mar. 1989).

12

Gender, Race, and the State Legislature: A Research Note on the Double Disadvantage Hypothesis

Gary Moncrief
Joel Thompson
Robert Schuhmann

Numerous studies now exist of women in state/local elective politics in the United States.[1] There are also studies of black officials and the subnational political system.[2] On the other hand, research at the intersection of these topics—black women in subnational politics—is harder to come by. This is especially true in the arena of state legislative politics.

While the subject of black women in state politics has not received much attention, two studies do bear mention. Jewel Prestage interviewed 27 of the 35 black female state legislators serving in the early 1970s, and provided a useful profile of their backgrounds and political ambitions.[3] More recently, Robert Darcy and Charles Hadley compared black and white women delegates to southern state party conventions.[4] They were particularly interested in exploring the *double disadvantage hypothesis:* "Because blacks are at a political disadvantage and because women are at a political disadvantage, black women are doubly disadvantaged."[5]

Darcy and Hadley do not find support for the "double disadvantage" hypothesis; instead they note that the proportion of black legislators who are women is

From *Social Science Quarterly,* October 1991, pp. 481–487. Reprinted by permission of JAI Press.

greater than the proportion of white legislators who are women. In fact, black women seem to fare better than white women (relative to their male racial counterparts) in state legislative, mayoral, and congressional offices.[6] The authors' explanation is that politically active (i.e., delegates to state party conventions) black women are more politically ambitious than their white female counterparts. They conclude that this heightened political ambition is due to the fact that a greater proportion of black than white women political activists have college educations, and are active in civic and interest groups.

Darcy and Hadley provide an important link between background characteristics and political ambition. But it is important to remember the nature of their data set: interviews conducted with delegates to the southern state party conventions. Less than ten percent of those subjects had ever held elective office. This limitation is not due to any shortcoming in the analysis by Darcy and Hadley; it is simply a product of the particular data set with which they worked. Nonetheless, they are trying to explain differences between black and white women in *officeholding* by differences in *political ambition*. Obviously, political ambition is a very important component to holding elective office, but it isn't the only important factor. It is perhaps a necessary condition, but not a sufficient one.

In this note we seek to extend the work of Darcy and Hadley, as well as Prestage, by examining the link between certain background characteristics and state legislative electoral success. By successfully running for the state legislature, all our subjects have demonstrated some threshold level of political ambition. The "double disadvantage" hypothesis leads us to the following propositions:

1. Because they are disadvantaged by *race,* black women state legislators must exceed their white female counterparts with regard to certain preparatory background characteristics.
2. Because they are disadvantaged by *gender,* black women state legislators must exceed their black male counterparts with regard to certain preparatory background characteristics.

The Data

Elsewhere we have presented data relating to state legislators' backgrounds and electoral district characteristics.[7] The data base for those studies was generated by requesting information (usually in the form of state bluebooks and legislative directories) from all fifty states. We received responses from approximately thirty. The amount of information (i.e., the specific array of variables) reported in bluebooks and directories varies. Therefore, we do not have all variables for all respondent states. Our test of the "double disadvantage" hypothesis required that the following information be available for each state in the analysis: race, gender, education, occupation, and the urban/non-urban nature of the electoral district for each state legislator. For this specific array of variables, we have the requisite data for sixteen state legislatures. In five of those states, however, there were no black females in the legislature. Those five states were eliminated, since black females are obviously the focal point of the "double disadvantage" hypothesis. The appropriate data set, then, for this analysis is the states for which we have all the requisite variables, and in which there are at least some black female state legislators. Eleven states met these conditions, and our data set for this analysis consists of over 1,500 state legislators from those eleven states.[8] This represents over twenty percent of the entire population of state legislators in the U.S.

Data Analysis

In Table 12.1 we present data on the educational and occupational achievements of four ascriptive groups (black females, white females, black males, and white males) of state legislators. The number of black women state legislators is small, and therefore our analysis must proceed with caution. While the total number of black females in our data never exceeds twenty-five, it should be recognized that there were fewer than seventy-five black female state legislators in the entire *population* during the 1987-1988 period. In any event, we can note that blacks (both men and women) have slightly higher overall educational levels than white legislators. One of the interesting revelations from these data is that over one-half of black legislators hold graduate degrees. In fact, among state legislators in our study, more black women (54.2 percent) held graduate degrees than did any other group. The disparity between black women and white women state legislators is substantial in this regard (54.2 percent to 31.1 percent).[9]

The same situation holds for the occupational data. Again, a higher proportion of black females (56.3 percent) hold jobs perceived to be "high prestige," followed by black males (52.0 percent), white males (49.5 percent), and white females (39.7 percent). Because of possible gender-bias in the prestige categories (e.g., housewife appears as a "low-prestige" occupation, but one which is traditionally assigned to women), it is perhaps unfair to compare these occupational data across gender. But *within* a gender category (i.e., among women only), we find a substantial (but not statistically significant) difference again between black and white. Black female state legislators are far more likely than their white counterparts to hold high prestige occupations, and far less likely to hold low prestige occupations.

The data in Table 12.1 are consistent with our first proposition, that black women state legislators would exhibit achievement characteristics different from those of white women state legislators. But there is little or no evidence in support of the second proposition—that black female state legislators would

Table 12.1

Educational and Occupational Status of State Legislators by Race and Gender (Figures Represent Percentages)

	Males		Females	
	White	Black	White	Black
Education (n =)	(1,233)	(88)	(193)	(24)
H.S. or less	13.1%	8.0	6.2	8.3
Post-Secondary	18.4	21.6	26.4	16.7
College Graduate	26.8	20.5	36.3	20.8
Graduate Degree	41.7	50.0	31.1	54.2
Occupation: (n =)[a]	(1,049)	(75)	(156)	(16)
High Prestige	49.5	52.0	39.7	56.3
Moderate Prestige	32.2	41.3	35.9	31.3
Low	18.3	6.7	24.4	12.5

[a]Occupational Prestige designations:
High: Attorney, physician, engineer, professional, college professor.
Moderate: School teacher, banker, businessperson, insurance, real estate, clergy.
Low: Blue collar, farmer/rancher, housewife, student, other.
Not Included: Retired, legislator.
Adapted from: National Opinion Research Center, *General Social Surveys, 1972–1983: Cumulative Codebook* (Chicago, 1983): 338–349.

exhibit greater achievement characteristics than black male state legislators. In the education category, black men and women exhibit very similar attainment levels (e.g., 54.2 percent females and 50 percent males hold graduate degrees). These figures are substantially higher for blacks (regardless of gender) than for whites.

Elsewhere we have noted that the nature of the electoral constituency may have a particularly biasing effect on state legislative data.[10] This is because certain groups are more likely to be elected in certain types of electoral districts (e.g., blacks in urban districts, women in multimember districts). Since a large proportion of white males is elected from rural states, and since those states tend to have lower per capita education levels (and more farmers/ranchers, a low prestige occupation), it is possible that the lower achievement levels of white state legislators are really an artifact of our sample of states. To put it another way, almost all the black legislators are from urban districts, and urban constituencies may be more likely to elect individuals (regardless of gender or race) with higher educational and occupational status. To test for this bias, we present data in Table 12.2 only for state legislators representing urban districts.

Eliminating the nonurban legislators from the analysis does boost both white

Table 12.2

Educational and Occupational Achievement of Urban State Legislators, by Race and Gender

	Males		Females	
	White	Black	White	Black
Education (n =)	(843)	(82)	(140)	(23)
H.S. or less	9.8%	8.5	4.3	8.7
Post-Secondary	16.6	23.2	28.6	17.4
College Graduate	28.2	22.0	36.4	21.7
Graduate Degree	45.3	46.3	30.7	52.2
Occupation: (n =)	(1,049)	(75)	(156)	(16)
High Prestige	53.5	50.0	39.4	56.3
Moderate Prestige	31.4	42.6	35.8	31.3
Low	15.1	7.4	24.8	12.5

male and white female state legislators, but not very much. On the education variable, we find some closing of the gaps between groups, but it is not substantial, and no changes occur in the relative positions of the groups.[11] Nor do we find any significant changes in the occupational variable. White men actually fare slightly better than black men, but the differences are small. More black women still hold higher prestige jobs than any other group. Black female state legislators still exhibit markedly higher education (especially postgraduate education) and occupational prestige levels than their white counterparts. While black women still demonstrate higher educational and occupational achievement than black men, the differences are small and statistically insignificant. In fact, when controlling for urban/rural nature of the electoral district, we find a good deal of similarity in the educational and occupational achievement characteristics of black women and men *and* white men. In short, there is nothing in Table 12.2 to cause us to recant our analysis in Table 12.1.

Conclusion

Here we have presented evidence from our state legislative biographical data set which bears on the "double disadvantage" hypothesis. That hypothesis suggests that because of both their race and gender, black women will find it especially difficult to compete successfully in electoral politics in the United States. In regard to our particular data set, the double disadvantage hypothesis would lead us to expect that successful black female state legislative candidates would have to achieve significantly higher levels of educational and occupational status. This would be true in comparison to (a) white female, (b) black male, and (c) white male state legislators. We find evidence that the hypothesis is borne out in relation to white females, but not in regard to the other two groups. Especially when we control for the urban or rural nature of the electoral district, there are only minor differences in educational and occupational status levels of black female, black male, and white male state legislators.

In their study, Darcy and Hadley found no support for the "double disadvantage" hypothesis. They base this conclusion on the fact that a larger proportion of black than white elected officials are women. Based on their analysis of state party delegates, they explain this phenomenon by noting that black political activists are more likely to possess the qualities (such as higher educational attainment and prestigious occupations) associated with political ambition.

In our analysis of backgrounds of state legislators, we also find that black females have higher educational and occupational attainment levels when compared to white females. But it seems unlikely that the black women in *our* data set would be appreciably more ambitious than the white women in our data set. After all, both groups are comprised of elected state legislators, and therefore have exhibited a significant level of political ambition already. If political ambition is not the causal factor in this instance, how then do we account for the fact there are *proportionately* more black female state legislators than white female state legislators? We think the answer may lie in the recent history of electoral redistricting.

Darcy and Hadley point to the "political opportunities resulting from the Voting Rights Act of 1965 and subsequent judicial challenges which led to the creation of black majority political districts."[12] Charles Bullock III makes a similar argument, noting that some districts were reallocated from the rural to urban and suburban areas during the "reapportionment revolution," and that this reallocation created some electoral opportunities for blacks.[13] These new districts became essentially open-seats, in which blacks (including black females) could contest an election without challenging a male incumbent. Since there was no incumbency advantage to overcome, it would be easier for a female (black female, in this instance) to be elected. If this scenario is indeed true, the "electoral advantage" of black women relative to white women is unlikely to increase. As Bullock notes, the major adjustment from rural to urban districts through reapportionment is now complete.[14] Interestingly, it is possible that the recent movement toward term limitations for state legislators could have a positive short-term effect on black *and* white female candidates, similar to the electoral opportunities afforded black candidates during the "reapportionment revolution." By limiting the legislative terms an incumbent can serve, more seats would become open-seat contests. Since most incumbents (especially those serving six years or more) are male, fewer female challengers would have to face male incumbents in an election.[15]

Notes

1. See, for example, Robert Darcy, Susan Welch, and Janet Clark, *Women, Elections, and Representation* (New York: Longman, Inc., 1987); Susan Carroll, *Women As Candidates in American Politics* (Bloomington: Indiana University Press, 1985); Susan Welch, "Recruitment of Women to Public Office: A Discriminant Analysis," *Western Political Quarterly,* 31 (1978): 372–380; Susan Welch and Albert Karning, "Correlates of Female Office Holding in City Politics," *Journal of Politics,* 41 (1979): 478–491; Janet Clark, Charles Hadley, and Robert Darcy, "Political Ambition Among Men and Women State Party Leaders," *American Politics Quarterly,* 117 (1989): 194–207; Paula J. Dubeck, "Women and Access to Political Office: A Comparison of Female and Male State Legislators," *The Sociological Quarterly,* 17 (1976): 42–51; Susan Welch, Margery Ambrosius, Janet Clark, and Robert Darcy, "The Effect of Candidate Gender on Election Outcomes in State Legislative Races," *Western Political Quarterly,* 38 (1985): 464–475; Carol Nechemias, "Changes in the Election of Women to U.S. State Legislative Seats." *Legislative Studies Quarterly,* 12 (1987): 125–141. Wilma Rule, "Why More Women Are State Legislators: A Research Note," *Western Political Quarterly,* 43 (1990): 437–448.

2. For example, Charles Bullock III, "Redistricting and Changes in the Partisan and Racial Composition of Southern Legislatures," *State and Local Government Review,* 19 (1987): 62–67; Richard Engstrom and Michael MacDonald, "The Effect of At-Large Versus District Elections on Racial Representation in U.S. Municipalities," in *Electoral Laws and Their Consequences,* edited by B. Grofman and A. Lijphart (New York: Agathon Press, Inc., 1986); Susan MacManus, "City Council Election Procedures and Minority Representation: Are They Related?" *Social Science Quarterly,* 59 (1978): 153–161; and Jeffrey S. Zax, "Election Methods, Black and Hispanic City Council Membership," *Social Science Quarterly,* 71 (1990) 339–355.

3. Jewel Prestage, "Black Women State Legislators: A Profile," in *A Portrait of Marginality: The Political Behavior of Women,* edited by M. Githens and J. Prestage (New York: McKay, 1977).

4. Robert Darcy and Charles Hadley, "Black Women in Politics: The Puzzle of Success," *Social Science Quarterly,* 69 (1988): 629–645.

5. Darcy and Hadley, op. cit., p. 630.

6. Darcy and Hadley, op. cit., p. 633.

7. Joel A. Thompson and Gary Moncrief, "Residential Mobility of American State Legislators." Paper presented at the 1988 annual meeting of the American Political Science Association (Washington, DC) and Gary Moncrief and Joel A. Thompson, "Electoral Structure and State Legislative Representation: A Research Note," *Journal of Politics,* 54 (1992, Forthcoming).

8. These states are Arizona, Florida, Illinois, Indiana, New Jersey, North Carolina, Pennsylvania, Tennessee, Vermont, Virginia, and Wyoming. This represents a reasonable cross-section of states by population, legislative professionalism, and region, with the possible exception of the west, where only two states are represented. The total n varies in the tables due to missing cases on the education, occupation, and electoral district variables. The data are from the 1987–1988 directories and/or bluebooks.

9. The Chi-Square test for differences between white and black women on the educational variable yields the following results: $X^2 = 5.8$; df = 3; $p \le 13$ for a 4 × 2 table. If we collapse the categories to three (H.S. or less; attended/graduate from college; post-graduate degree) the results are $X^2 = 5.8$; df = 2; $p \le .056$. For occupation, the $X^2 = 1.9$; df = 2; $p \le .38$.

10. Moncrief and Thompson, op. cit.

11. $X^2 = 5.6$; df = 3; $p \leq .13$ for 4×2 table; $p \leq .058$ for 3×2 table. For occupation, $X^2 = 1.9$; df = 2; $p \leq .38$.

12. Darcy and Hadley, op. cit., p. 642.

13. Charles Bullock III, "Minorities in State Legislatures," in *Changing Career Patterns in State Legislatures,* edited by G. Moncrief and J. Thompson (Ann Arbor: University of Michigan Press, 1992, forthcoming).

14. Bullock, op. cit., p. 74.

15. For a further exploration of this argument, see Gary Moncrief and Joel A. Thompson, "The Move to Limit Terms of Office: Assessing the Consequences for Female State Legislators," Paper presented at the 1991 annual meeting of the Western Political Science Association; Seattle; March 21, 1991.

Part V

Congress

This part considers the relationship between blacks and Congress. Congressman Ron Dellums notes that blacks won seats in Congress "only with the enforcement of the Reconstruction Act of 1867 and the ratification of the Fifteenth Amendment."

Three blacks have served in the United States Senate. Hiram Revels of Mississippi took his seat on February 25, 1870. Edward Brooke, a Republican from Massachusetts, was a member of the Senate from 1967 to 1979. In 1992, Carol Mosely Braun of Illinois became the first African American woman to be elected to the United States Senate.

The first black member of the United States House of Representatives was Joseph Rainey of South Carolina, who took his seat on December 12, 1870. Since then, there have been numerous prominent black representatives:

- William Clay, a Democrat from Missouri, author of *Just Permanent Interests: Black Americans in Congress, 1870–1991*
- Shirley Chisholm, a Democrat from Harlem, who ran for president in 1972
- Ron Dellums, a California Democrat who was chairman of the House Armed Services Committee in 1993 and 1994
- William Gray, the former House majority whip, special adviser to President Clinton on Haiti, and currently president of the United Negro College Fund
- Barbara Jordan, a Texas Democrat who came to prominence during the Watergate impeachment hearings
- John Lewis, a Georgia Democrat who was a founding member of the Student Non-Violent Coordinating Committee
- Parren Mitchell, a Democrat from Maryland, a former chairman of the Congressional Black Caucus, and the author of legislation requiring minority set-asides for federal contracts

- Kweisi Mfume, chairman of the Congressional Black Caucus during the 1993–1994 legislative session
- Adam Clayton Powell, a Harlem Democrat and former chairman of the Committee on Education and Labor who was expelled from the House in 1967 for junketeering and absenteeism
- Charles Rangel, a New York Democrat who was chairman of the Select Committee on Narcotics Abuse and Control
- Louis Stokes, an Ohio Democrat who chaired the House Ethics Committee
- Andrew Young, a Georgia Democrat who also served as ambassador to the United Nations and mayor of Atlanta

Prior to the 1992 elections, there were twenty-six African Americans in the House; after that election, there were thirty-nine. After the 1994 election, the figure was forty. (This figure includes the black delegate from the Virgin Islands, who has the same voting privileges as the delegate from the District of Columbia.) Almost every black member of Congress comes from a safe, largely black district.

The 1992 congressional elections were notable in a number of respects. In 1992, blacks won their first House seats since the 1800s in Alabama, Florida, North Carolina, South Carolina, and Virginia. In Illinois, Southside Chicago voters overwhelmingly elected city alderman and former Black Panther leader Bobby Rush. Georgia sent its first black woman to Congress, Cynthia McKinney (a single mother). In Florida, Alcee Hastings won election to the House, after having been impeached as a federal judge for soliciting a bribe from a drug dealer.

Several black Senate candidates have suffered defeat. In 1988, Harvey Gantt, the former mayor of Charlotte, lost in the general election to North Carolina Republican Senator Jesse Helms. Initially, polls predicted a Gantt victory. However, in the last days of the campaign, Helms broadcast a television ad attacking affirmative action. The ad featured a white man receiving a rejection slip for a job application. The narrator intoned, "You needed that job. But it had to go to someone else, because of the color of their skin." This ad was perhaps not surprising, given Helms' history of race-baiting. (Similarly, in 1993, Helms voted against Roberta Achtenberg's confirmation as assistant secretary of housing and urban development because "she's a damn lesbian.")

In 1992, black activist Al Sharpton ran for the Democratic Senate nomination in New York. Surprisingly, he finished third, ahead of former Representative Elizabeth Holtzmann. In Maryland, Alan Keyes, a black conservative Republican, lost badly to Barbara Mikulski, the incumbent Democratic senator. (Keyes lost to Maryland's other Democratic senator, Paul Sarbanes, in 1990.)

The 1992 elections also increased the congressional representation of other minority groups. The number of Hispanic representatives grew from eleven to seventeen. Most notably, Nydia Velasquez of New York became the first Puerto

Rican woman in Congress. In addition, Congressman Ben Nighthorse Campbell of Colorado became the first Native American to win election to the United States Senate. Also, Jay Kim, a Republican from California, became the first Korean American member of Congress. In addition, the 1992 elections increased the number of black women in Congress from four to ten.

Perhaps the most powerful black member of Congress is Kweisi Mfume of Maryland. Mfume was elected to the House from Baltimore in 1988, and headed the Congressional Black Caucus in 1993 and 1994.

Born in 1948, Mfume's name at birth was Frizzell Gray. By the time he was 22, he had fathered five boys, by five different women. He did not marry any of the women, but he continues to provide financial support to the sons, who are now in their twenties.

Congressman Mfume and the Congressional Black Caucus worked with President Clinton on several issues. The caucus played a critical role in extending the earned income tax credit (which reduced federal taxes on millions of poor people), as well as passing the Mickey Leland Hunger Act. President Clinton's aggressive policy toward Haiti was strongly influenced by the caucus.

On several fronts, though, President Clinton and the Black Caucus have not seen eye to eye. Congressman Mfume was incensed when Clinton withdrew the nomination of Lani Guinier to be assistant attorney general for civil rights. The Black Caucus wanted a provision in the 1994 crime bill to allow death row inmates to challenge their sentences on the basis of racial discrimination. Also, Mfume stated that his "bottom line" on health care was universal coverage—a commitment that President Clinton eventually backed away from.

While Congressman Mfume undoubtedly increased the power and visibility of the caucus, one of his actions was highly controversial. In 1993, Mfume and the caucus signed a "sacred covenant" with Louis Farrakhan, leader of the Nation of Islam. Mfume praised Farrakhan's leadership on criminal violence and black self-help. However, critics protested when Khallid Abdul Muhammad (then Farrakhan's chief aide) gave a speech denouncing Jews, homosexuals, Catholics, and the pope.

The 1994 elections dramatically changed the political landscape for black members of Congress. The Republican takeover of the House meant that black Democrats had to surrender three committee chairmanships and seventeen subcommittee chairmanships. Some analysts fear that the Black Caucus will become a nonplayer. Also, new House Speaker Newt Gingrich *abolished* the Congressional Black Caucus, as well as other "legislative service organizations" (such as the Steel Caucas and the Women's Caucus).

The first reading in this part, "The Congressional Black Caucus Revolution," is by William Clay, a Democratic congressman from Missouri. It is taken from his book, *Just Permanent Interests: Black Americans in Congress, 1870–1991.*

Congressman Clay presents a spirited defense of the Congressional Black Caucus. He argues that the caucus, conceived in 1971, has thwarted the efforts of Presidents Nixon, Ford, Carter, Reagan, and Bush to "reverse the social, political, and economic gains black people attained during the sixties." In particular, he gives the Black Caucus credit for preserving the food stamp program.

Clay calls on the Congressional Black Caucus to continue its aggressive promotion of black interests. He says, "In order for our lives to have meaning and relevance, we must continue the struggle, the crusade for racial justice and economic equality." He calls the formation of the caucus "one of the few occasions in history when members of the black race experienced an exhilarating sense of reachable freedom, a renewed self-worth, a recommitment to struggle."

The second reading "Strategies for Increasing Black Representation in Congress," is by Carol Swain, a political scientist at Princeton University. It is taken from her book, *Black Faces, Black Interests: The Representation of African-Americans in Congress.* Swain considers the politics of racial gerrymandering. Three strategies have been used to enhance or reduce the representation of specific racial groups: *cracking* (dispersing minority populations across several districts to dilute their voting strength); *stacking* (combining large concentrations of minority voters with white populations to create districts with white majorities); and *packing* (placing minority voters in districts with already-high minority populations).

While the Republican Party favors stacking (so that more districts will have overwhelmingly white majorities), Swain contends that this strategy simply lessens minority voting strength. She concludes, "The statistics on the distribution and concentration of blacks in the population reveal a need to look beyond the creation of majority-black political units as a way to increase political representation of African Americans. Blacks have already made the most of their opportunities to elect black politicians in congressional districts with black majorities." She argues that black politicians should develop biracial appeal (to win election in majority-white districts), and that black voters should be prepared to vote for sympathetic white candidates.

The next reading, "What Color Is Your Gerrymander? The Constitution and White Minority Districts," is by Lani Guinier, a professor at the University of Pennsylvania Law School. She was President Clinton's original nominee to be assistant attorney general for civil rights.

Guinier's nomination evoked a storm of controversy. Conservatives labeled her "the quota queen," and questioned her commitment to representative democracy. With growing opposition from Senate Republicans, President Clinton decided to read Guinier's writings for himself (something he had not done before submitting his nomination). Clinton then announced that he was withdrawing the nomination, because he did not share Guinier's views.

Clinton's action created a great deal of bitterness. Some of Clinton's supporters were upset that he nominated someone without bothering to discover her views. Others were aggravated because Clinton seemed to back down from a fight. Still others were disturbed because Clinton seemed to betray an old friend (someone he went to law school with, whose wedding he attended).

This selection by Guinier is a summary of her views on black political representation. She addresses the Constitutional and political issues involved in drawing lines for congressional districts.

Guinier notes that the Voting Rights Acts of 1965 and 1982 both require state legislatures and courts to draw congressional lines so as to maximize minority political strength. However, the Supreme Court ruled in June 1993 that congressional districts may not discriminate against white minorities.

In *Shaw v Reno,* a group of white plaintiffs from North Carolina's 12th Congressional District brought suit, arguing that the bizarre district lines followed no logic—other than to elect a black congressman. (The district was of an indescribable shape; at certain points it was as wide as a highway lane.) The Court ruled that the district violated the equal protection clause of the Constitution. While the Court left open the possibility that legislatures could indeed create voting districts that deliberately give blacks and other minority groups a numerical advantage, the Court ruled that such districts must have some basis in geographical reality as well. Associate Justice Sandra Day O'Connor wrote that racial gerrymandering reinforces the stereotype that "members of the same racial group, regardless of their age, education, economic status or the community in which they live think alike, share the same political interests and will prefer the same candidates at the polls." O'Connor also asserted that the same political process that created North Carolina's 12th District had been used for decades to disenfranchise black voters. Such maneuverings, wrote O'Connor, "are by their very nature odious to a free people whose institutions are founded upon the doctrine of equality." She called race-conscious gerrymandering "political apartheid."

Guinier strongly disagrees with the Court's reasoning. She argues that using race as a criterion in constructing congressional districts is no more arbitrary than using political party affiliation (which has long been used). She sarcastically notes that the Supreme Court's discovery of the right to "color-blind elections" is of recent vintage.

Guinier reviews the alternatives for creating congressional districts. She rejects the first option, majority-black districts, because it *wastes* black voting strength rather than enhances it.

The second possibility is at-large elections. The problem with this approach is that the white majority is likely to win all the seats. According to Guinier, "for the racial minority, not to district at all is not to be represented at all."

Guinier then presents her own proposal, "cumulative voting." Under this scheme, each voter would be allotted multiple votes in a congressional election—the same number as there are congressional seats in that state. In other words, a voter in North Carolina would receive twelve votes; a voter in California would receive fifty-two votes. Voters would be free to allocate their votes however they wish. A voter in North Carolina could give all twelve votes to one candidate, or one vote to each of twelve different candidates, or anything in between.

The rationale for this procedure is to allow racial (and political) minorities to maximize their voting power. Under this plan, members of a "politically cohesive minority" could elect their candidates to office. Guinier notes that "women, environmentalists, or Republicans could all vote strategically to form 'districts of the mind.'"

Guinier's proposal (which did not originate with her) is highly creative. However, there are serious problems. One is voter confusion. Voters in California would face a daunting task in deciding how to allocate their fifty-two votes (possibly among 104 major-party candidates, as well as third-party and independent candidates). Also, cumulative voting would greatly complicate campaigns, since candidates could have scores of opponents, not one. Indeed, candidates from the same political party would become *enemies* instead of *allies,* since they would be competing for the same multiple, non-districted votes. Finally, Guinier's system could lessen a citizen's sense of representation in Congress. Voters who decided to "write their congressman" would first have to decide who their congressman *is,* since voters in all but the smallest states would have *many* representatives.

In summary, Guinier's proposal for cumulative voting could lead to the splintering of political interests and the destruction of the two-party system. Of course, this may be her ultimate objective, given that such a system would probably place greater emphasis on *minority rights* rather than *majority rule.*

13

The Congressional Black Caucus Revolution

William Clay

Those who profess to favor freedom and yet deprecate agitation are men who want crops without plowing up the ground. They want rain without thunder and lightning. They want the ocean without the awful roar of its waters. This struggle may be a moral one, or it may be a physical one, or it may be both moral and physical, but it must be a struggle. Power concedes nothing without demand. It never did, and it never will. Find out just what people will submit to, and you have found out the exact amount of injustice and wrong which will be imposed upon them; and these will continue till they are resisted with either words or blows, or with both. The limits of tyrants are prescribed by the endurance of those whom they oppress. . . .[1]

These are the words of Frederick Douglass, an ex-slave who, in 1857, advocated revolution, a violent one if necessary, to throw off the shackles of racial oppression. In the late sixties and early seventies, a somber and impassioned black America attempted a nonviolent political revolution just as deliberate as the one envisioned by Douglass. The Congressional Black Caucus, along with scores of black mayors, state representatives, and city councilmen, was an integral part of the revolution: Gus Hawkins' telling President Nixon that "unless he faces up to the problems of black Americans, there will be chaos," articulated the

Reprinted from William L. Clay, "The CBC Revolution," in Clay, *Just Permanent Interests: Black Americans in Congress, 1970–1992,* pp. 339–354. Published by Amistad Press, 1992. Permission granted by the publisher.

angry mood of black Americans. Charles Diggs' acknowledging that blacks were increasing in numbers within the political arena and were coalescing with other deprived groups for the "purpose of enhancing strength" was truly seeing the facts of life. Louis Stokes' suggesting a boycott of the president's State of the Union address indicated the depth of dissatisfaction with current government policy. Parren Mitchell's admonition that "the black community has [not] been blackjacked into silence or lulled into apathy," gave notice of a people determined to be involved. Charles Rangel's warning, "Where there are causes that can benefit by coalition politics, we shall coalesce," forecast the Caucus's willingness to work with other groups to achieve our goals. My call in 1971 for black communities to "develop the same degree of political sophistication as others" was therefore not farfetched. It did not appear to be the case then, but urging a new, tough approach to solving the problems of racism and discrimination was realistic.

An Effective Voice for the Disadvantaged

Tough talk and tough actions motivate the establishment to sit up and take notice and are necessary stratagems for winning respect and recognition from the movers and shakers of politics and government. Once the agitators are recognized, which lends respect to their concerns, the process for resolution of many community problems is on a solid footing.

Through legislative initiatives, Caucus members have sternly resisted efforts by the administrations of the last five presidents—Nixon, Ford, Carter, Reagan, and Bush—to reverse the social, political, and economic gains black people attained during the sixties. It was the Caucus that stood in opposition to Nixon's total assault on the Great Society programs and successfully waged battle to save most of them by refocusing goals and changing agency names. The public impression was that the president had abolished the many programs that the "silent majority" deemed expendable, but the Caucus kept them alive. It was the Caucus that challenged the conservative ideologies of the Ford, Carter, Reagan, and Bush administrations and preserved vital domestic programs that affected the economically disadvantaged when everything else was being sacrificed in the name of increased defense spending.

How would the poor have survived had it not been for programs preserved by the Caucus when President Reagan offered his slashing budget proposals and phony "safety net"? The 23.5 million (one in ten Americans) receiving food stamps owe this modest assistance to the Congressional Black Caucus, which insisted on no further cuts in the program. More than 50 percent of food stamp recipients lived in households with gross incomes of less than $400 a month. The Reagan administration wanted to make them ineligible for food stamps. Unquestionably, the Caucus has remained the strongest advocate in government for the poor.

We admirably documented the need for preserving the programs designed to feed hungry children, house their families, and provide jobs or unemployment benefits for their parents. The Caucus did not surrender to political expedience, nor did we lose our political integrity. We understand the mandate imposed by the Constitution on those who govern—namely, to promote the general welfare.

In order for our lives to have meaning and relevance, we must continue the struggle, the crusade for racial justice and economic equality. Black members of Congress cannot afford to abandon their agenda for improving the social, economic, and political lot of 32 million black Americans. Despite the vigorous attacks on the concept of affirmative action from numerous and powerful quarters, we must continue to promote set-asides in government contracts based on race; favor scholarships for economically and educationally disadvantaged black students; support on-the-job training for minorities; and insist on goals and timetables for placing blacks on a par with the larger society in every aspect.

This effort must continue until black college graduates no longer earn, on the average, less than white high school graduates; until black males are no longer employed at only half the rate of white males; until black babies no longer die of rat bites at a rate four times that of white babies. Affirmative policies and aggressive politics will be essential as long as black workers earn 56 cents for every dollar earned by white workers; until black mothers no longer die in childbirth at a rate five times greater than white mothers.

Under present circumstances, it is too much to ask that black people proceed respectfully and passively while white America still pursues a course of stubborn resistance to racial and economic justice. Heeding the call of black conservatives and white reactionaries to judge each person on individual merit without considering the past, studying the present, or assessing the future, is too much to ask of a people who have witnessed no realistic programs to deal with their oppression and repression.

Those individuals and groups, conservative and liberal, Democrat and Republican, black and white, who accuse the Congressional Black Caucus of having "outlived its usefulness" or of "being out of touch with their black constituents" would be well advised to ponder seriously one essential question: Where would black Americans be politically, economically, and educationally if there had not been a Congressional Black Caucus?

Sufficient time has expired for most to determine if the Congressional Black Caucus has been able to reach the high standards and fulfill the original expectations of black people in the early seventies. I believe we have made a difference and that we must continue to make a difference. Today, many of the advances developed and supported by the Caucus are being eroded. Elements in society—black and white—are attempting to belittle us as unrepresentative of the black community. The age-old ploy of divide and conquer is used to dilute our strength because our enemies know that the Caucus is the only organization with the potential to mobilize the black community on a national basis for a political cause.

Attacks from within the Black Community

In the beginning, it was white liberals, white conservatives, white labor leaders, and white members of the media who led the attack on the Congressional Black Caucus. In recent years, it has been black social scientists, black educators, and black members of the media who are spearheading the criticism.

Many of the blacks who have benefited most from the aggressive, militant demands of black elected officials seem to recognize that fact the least. They now refer to themselves as "black conservatives" and spend an inordinate amount of time excoriating black leaders and denouncing programs established to give our people an equal footing in jobs, housing, and education. Most of them pretend that they arrived where they are because of unquestioned talent and recognized ability. They allege to be offended because some whites accuse them of being admitted to a prestigious school or getting a top job in corporate America because of preferential treatment accorded through affirmative action policies. The ugly truth is that, talented or not, they and other blacks did not make it to the top because of personal ability, although that may have played a part. Credit must be given to the hordes of nondescript, angry, uncompromising black men, women, and children who laid their bodies and sometimes their lives on the line to change racist policy and racist attitudes. Langston Hughes, the poet, points out the dilemma of the black bourgeois who deny their heritage.

> So I am ashamed for the black poet who says, "I want to be a poet, not a Negro poet," as though his own racial world were not as interesting as any other world. I am ashamed, too, for the colored artist who runs from the painting of Negro faces to the painting of sunsets after the manner of the academicians because he fears the strange un-whiteness of his own features. An artist must be free to choose what he does, certainly, but he must also never be afraid to do what he might choose.[2]

One group of Negroes more unappreciative of efforts of black elected officials than any other is those earning the big bucks in television, radio, and print. To prove their complete acceptance of the one world, one race, one people theory and to display their total dissociation from other blacks, they feel compelled to attack, demean, and degrade black leadership and black organizations that "constantly carp and complain" about racial injustice. Their attacks, however, have failed to negate the accomplishments of the Caucus or to persuade our followers to reject our leadership. Somehow, this new breed of reporter, ignoring the direct pressures applied by the Caucus on the communications industry to hire blacks, perceives itself as possessing awesome powers of persuasion in influencing television producers, station managers, and editors.

Typical of the ever increasing crescendo of criticism leveled against the Caucus are the following statements of black educators, reporters, and television commentators:

Traditional African-American leaders are out of line with what the common black man, woman and family are thinking today. . . . So often (these groups—CBC, NAACP, National Association of Black Lawyers) speak for black people, they don't speak to black people.[3]

—Floyd Hayes, professor at Purdue University

The Congressional Black Caucus weekend is the most glaring evidence of a two-decade-old saga of ineptness, mismanagement, lack of accountability and vision of our so-called leaders.

. . . After 20 years of CBC weekends, the most obvious evidence of black leadership having been on Capitol Hill are thousands of empty Scotch bottles, a slew of chicken bones and a host of white merchants rushing to the bank to deposit the one-half billion dollars they receive each year from CBC hotel rents and the sale of Scotch and hot Buffalo wings.[4]

—William Reed, columnist

These guys [black leaders] are sitting there watching the destruction of our race while arguing about Ronald Reagan. . . . Ronald Reagan isn't the problem. Former president Jimmy Carter was not the problem. The lack of black leadership is the problem.[5]

—Clarence Thomas, as chairman of the
Equal Employment Opportunity Commission

Civil rights leaders . . . bitch, bitch, bitch about the administration . . . they create a narcotic of dependency, not an ethic of responsibility and independence. They are at best an irrelevance, covering up some real problems and inevitably a stigma.[6]

—Clarence Thomas, as chairman EEOC

[The CBC is] demanding that blacks be politically correct. . . . They're looking at life through an elitist perspective.[7]

—Robert Woodson, executive director of
Neighborhood Housing Services

The trashy misrepresentations of the Caucus Weekend and the total distortion of the many valuable contributions imparted throughout the workshops, brain trusts, and networking of the occasion were reprinted from coast to coast by more than fifty black-owned weekly newspapers. They were then repeated by several columnists, including Courtland Milloy of the *Washington Post.* Syndicated columnist Tony Brown, who has become fanatical in his attacks on black organizations, did not miss the opportunity to attack the CBC again. He used the article by Reed almost verbatim in his column.

Either these individuals do not realize or they refuse to accept the fact that it was the CBC who orchestrated and pressured the national news media to hire blacks at all levels in their industry. It was members of the CBC who met countless times with officials of the Department of Defense in the early seventies and negotiated the deal whereby minority-owned newspapers would automatically get a percentage of the agency's huge budget for advertisement. Prior to this arrangement, they had received none of the funds for recruitment solicitation or announcements of bids for contracts and materials. Legislative set-asides for minority-owned businesses, sponsored by CBC members in the Highway Bill, Alaskan Pipe Line Construction Bill, and the Surface Transportation Act, have provided access to millions of dollars in advertisement funds for black-owned newspapers and radio stations.

In addition to black media personalities attacking us, a new breed of black spokesperson has emerged to do battle with black elected officials and heads of civil rights organizations. This cadre of "created" black leaders—people without any discernible black followers (and hence, political eunuchs)—are often referred to as the "new conservatives." It is disheartening to hear these antebellum visionaries speak of "a colorblind society," of "pulling yourself out of the quagmire of poverty and deprivation by hard work and self-reliance," of "affirmative action for black people being unfair to white males," and of "getting the government off our backs."

The Caucus has not been deterred by these attacks. We have remained steadfast in pursuit of our original goals. We have also attempted to deal logically and forcefully with the foolishness of our critics.

The CBC Fight for a Pro-active Government

Possessing an in-depth knowledge of and a keen perception of American history, it was not necessary for Caucus members to conduct extensive research to reach the conclusion that hard work and self-reliance alone have never enabled a race of people to pull itself up by its own bootstraps. Our comprehension, intelligence, and awareness inform us that it has been a combination of hard work and direct government assistance that has improved the living conditions of the average American citizen. In order to change basic, pervasive deficiencies in any society, government has always played a major role.

It has been government in partnership with enterprising citizens that enabled white Americans to make progress. After World War II, the government recognized that our cities were in shambles, that the buildings were deteriorating, that pollution from smokestack industries was taking its toll, that automation was a thing of the future. And it was government that took the lead in addressing these problems. Government decided that millions of acres of land surrounding the cities were desirable for development. It was not enterprising, hard-working, self-reliant entrepreneurs. It was government policy makers. It was the government that made resources available, including tax monies to build roads, schools, and libraries on this vacant land to make it conducive to and attractive for living. The government established a policy to guarantee loans to developers to build shopping centers and middle-income housing with front lawns and backyard swimming pools—hardworking, self-reliant, enterprising white businessmen cannot take the credit. Government policy created the Federal Home Loan Assistance Program, which subsidized the purchase of houses for middle-income Americans and guaranteed that bankers who financed those homes would not lose on their investment. The government passed laws that allowed the purchasers to deduct interest payments on home mortgages from income tax liability. So hardworking, self-reliant Americans have not done all of those wonderful things on their own—have not achieved such great heights by themselves. Government played the key role in their Horatio Alger success stories.

The big problem with this scenario is that black people were left out of the equation. We were excluded from this great American experiment launched to expand opportunity, this great program designed to lift 100 million poverty-stricken white Americans from the Hoovervilles, shanty towns, and tobacco roads and place them in the middle class with sufficient buying power. Let us be honest about it. We, black Americans, were denied an opportunity to share in this great government-financed "operation boot strap." We were not allowed to ascend the ladder in tandem with other citizens of like circumstances. We were handicapped, victimized not by accident, not by oversight, but by deliberate, conscious acts of government.

Let us not be evasive or polite in explaining what happened. It was not racial segregation or separation of the races that prevented us from taking advantage of the benefits offered by the government's policy of expansion—these are merely phrases coined to make more plausible and more acceptable the most inhumane kind of treatment one group of people can inflict on another. Simply put, it was racist policies and racist laws and racist customs enacted, employed, and enforced by racist individuals that kept us out of "operation boot strap." But more important, these insurmountable impediments were sanctioned by a racist government existing in a racist society. Any other explanation is an attempt at historical revision and denigrating to those of us who have suffered the consequences of these uncivilized, bigoted acts.

If twenty-six black members had been in Congress instead of only two, Powell and Dawson, when these post–World War II measures were enacted, benefits allocated under those programs probably would have been distributed more fairly to include black people.

The mandate of the Congressional Black Caucus, as I perceive it, is to ensure that government now becomes a partner with our people to rectify three centuries of unfair, immoral treatment. Our role must be to educate black people that there is nothing shameful about petitioning the government for financial and economic assistance in order to right these past wrongs. We should not apologize for expecting our government to correct longstanding inequities and to abolish unequal treatment based on race. White America did not get where it is without substantial financial and economic government help. And we are not going to rebuild our inner city neighborhoods, close the wide gap in income between white and black workers, or effectively deal with intolerable joblessness in our communities by resorting to the juvenile nickel-and-dime self-help programs proposed by the so-called new black conservatives.

We need the same kind of massive dollar infusion that built suburbia. We need government policy that guarantees insurance companies will insure our properties at reasonable and fair premiums; that forces banks to lend black property owners money for rehabilitation and remodeling under the same terms and at the same interest rates as whites. We need a government that seeks out and aggressively prosecutes those who violate our laws against discrimination in employment, just as it does those who rob banks.

Finally, the Caucus must orchestrate a campaign to reverse the psychological hangups that make the poor, and black people in particular, fearful, wary, and apprehensive about accepting government assistance. The misleading slogan "Get government off our backs" is designed primarily to keep government from assisting those most in need so that those least in need, those who now get the bulk of the benefits, will not have to share. Citizens at the bottom of the economic ladder must have government on their side, and the Caucus must continue to serve as a catalyst for fostering policies that deliver services and goods to them.

Ever mindful of the history of aggressive acts against black elected officials in the nineteenth century and the continuing massive opposition to their attempts to legislate fairly, we must never relax or relent in our quest for equal standing in society. Just 100 short years ago, twenty-two black members had served in the United States Congress. Surely they and their constituents, ex-slaves or poor men and women only one generation removed from slavery, thought this nation well on the way to atoning for its sins against humanity. Who among them would have guessed in 1892 that seven years later not a single black would be left sitting in Congress?

Certainly Senators Revels and Bruce from Mississippi, who championed restoring unrepentant southern rebels to citizenship with full voting rights, did not envision what eventually happened. I am sure that early freedom fighters and dedicated statesmen like the very militant Alonzo J. Ransier of South Carolina and the Civil War hero Robert Smalls, also of South Carolina, never imagined that Reconstruction would end so abruptly and that within thirty years after the first black was elected to Congress, none would serve in that august body for another twenty-seven years.

It is evident that Robert Brown Elliott had no idea what brutal repression was in store for the black race when he uttered these optimistic remarks on the floor of Congress in 1872:

> We trust the time is not far distant when all our fellow citizens—whether they be native born or whether they first drew the breath of life on the banks of the Rhine; whether they sprang from the Orient or the Occident—no longer controlled by the teachings of false political faith, shall be touched with the

inspiration of a holier sentiment and shall recognize the "universal fatherhood of God and the brotherhood of man."[8]

To prevent the kind of isolation experienced by those early black members of Congress, it was important and logical that an entity such as the Congressional Black Caucus be formed. No one has so clearly defined the role that the Caucus has played in serving as the catalyst for the important advances made by blacks as Congressman Julian Dixon:

> The Caucus has been the cutting edge opposing administration policies of Nixon, Ford, Carter, and Reagan. We were the first to speak out against the nominations of G. Harold Carswell and Clement Haynesworth as Supreme Court justices, and Edwin Meese as attorney general, and to question their commitments to justice for all.
>
> On the floor of the Congress, in committee hearings, before the press and across America, we have spoken out against policies which undermine the enforcement of civil rights and civil liberties, respect for law and order, disregard for personal rights of privacy, and attempts to infringe on the rights of free speech. Whether it was a president's assault on the Civil Rights Commission, a proposal for a youth sub-minimum wage, efforts to weaken federal contract compliance, to lessen the effects of full-employment legislation, or to eliminate minority set-asides, the Caucus was there to respond. Yet, perhaps it is these very challenges which have helped energize the black community to seek change through political empowerment. In the streets of our communities we have seen the damage of presidential economic policies.
>
> The momentum among black voters must peak, in conjunction with that of other denied groups, so that the direction of this nation can change as we restore America's commitment to fairness and justice for all.[9]

The challenges of which Congressman Dixon speaks are the same ones that members of the CBC have consistently faced. While white leaders were joyously celebrating America's two hundredth anniversary as a nation in 1976, the Congressional Black Caucus was reminding them that the struggle for decency and justice was not over. Black leaders were addressing the sad truth of America's pitiful beginnings—a country conceived in sin, born in corruption, and continuing to live out the lies, contradictions, and hypocrisies embodied in the Declaration of Independence and the Bill of Rights.

That glorious document, the United States Constitution, which is the subject of so much fanfare and brouhaha, denied women the right to own property and to vote; defined blacks as non-persons and so sanctioned "cruel and unusual punishment" against them. But despite the imperfections in the legacy of our founding fathers, the Congressional Black Caucus—because it is in our permanent interest—has directed its efforts to perfecting the union and providing for the general welfare by working to eliminate poverty, sexism, and racism.

Lesser men and women may have been willing to accept the fate imposed by a system in which they were the constant victims, but black legislators have always fully realized, as did Frederick Douglass before, that "The hypocrisy of the Nation must be exposed; and its crimes against God and man must be denounced."[10]

Marguerite Ross-Barnett, in a scholarly article, poses what I consider a factual analysis and a fair critique of the Congressional Black Caucus. She establishes a reasonable yardstick for measuring the good and the bad of the Caucus:

> . . . two overarching considerations must be kept in mind in drawing conclusions about the CBC. The CBC can be isolated for analytical purposes but in a political sense it is part of larger systems and subsystems. It is an intrinsic part of the black community. It can only be as powerful inside Congress as the black community is outside Congress. Its weaknesses, failures and flaws, as well as its successes, strengths and assets, should not be attributed solely to individual CBC members but should be seen in the broadest political and social context. Greater CBC accountability, philosophical coherence, political innovativeness, and so on, are changes that must reflect a transformed black political culture.
>
> The second consideration is the difficult task faced by the CBC as it attempts to use the political system to bring about economic change. . . . Transformation of CBC potential into positive political realities will depend on a variety of factors, only some of which are in the direct control of the black members of Congress.[11]

The potential for the CBC, indeed for black elected officials generally, to transform political actions into political realities depends very much on unified support in our individual districts, but to an even greater degree depends on the will and determination of those in black communities to insist that their white elected officials support the programmatic agenda of the Caucus.

It's Time to Recognize Black Political Maturity as Well as Black Rights

The process of complete political independence in black communities began in earnest in the mid-sixties when an increasing number of blacks started agitating for control of positions that affected their daily lives. The rising tide of racial consciousness enabled them to assess the problem clearly and see the enemy more lucidly. That enemy was not always white officialdom *per se;* oddly enough, more often it was indifference on the part of blacks who tolerated the lackluster leadership of white elected officials.

The politics of a militant black community took almost twenty years to reach fruition. Many suffered and agonized during the period of evolution but considered the results worth the pain. One man standing almost alone at first, Jesse Jackson, is due a great deal of credit for opening the eyes and unlocking the minds of a complacent black electorate. His campaign for the presidency of the United States in 1984 went one step farther than any program our race had ever pursued and was in line with the permanent interests of black people. He unshackled the chains of political bondage to an indifferent political system and severed the long-held psychological dependence of those who had relied exclusively on whites to give leadership at the highest level of government. His foray into the realm of the heretofore politically impossible convinced the average black person that Jackson towered head and shoulders over the other seven Democrats in the race. And most believe in their heart that if Jackson were white, the Democratic nomination would have been his for the asking.

The issues Jackson promoted and the style in which he did so, would, in a "colorblind society," have guaranteed him the privilege of being the standard-bearer of the Democratic party. However, make no mistake, we still live in a society blinded by color rather than color-blind.

Jackson's campaign provided a basis for awakening a constituency from a mental complacency. The platform objectives of the Rainbow Coalition jogged the memory of many too closely aligned to the Democratic party. Jackson did for blacks in this country what John F. Kennedy did for Catholics. Kennedy dispelled the myth that Catholics could not get elected to the highest office. Jackson shattered the ill-founded belief that a black person cannot be taken seriously when aspiring for the presidency. It is merely a matter of time before a black will be the standard-bearer or the vice-presidential candidate of one of the major political parties. What was considered comical in the beginning, lightly covered by the media and grudgingly accepted by some black leaders, blossomed into a full-fledged campaign.

Although Jackson did not win, we can also say he did not lose, because black people and the new black politics did not lose. In reality, we lost the battle and won the war. We won because we found ourselves politically, proudly acknowledging our worthiness. The country lost because it was once again revealed that its people were still steeped in racial prejudice against dark-skinned citizens regardless of their talents.

For sure, our people and our politics have come a long way since that afternoon in 1971 when the Congressional Black Caucus was first conceived. The gathering at the first annual CBC dinner on that June night in 1971 was one of the few occasions in history when members of the black race experienced an exhilarating sense of reachable freedom, a renewed self-worth, a recommitment to struggle. For one fleeting moment—more accurately, for several fleeting hours—the revolutionary spirit of Frederick Douglass, W. E. B. DuBois, Paul Robeson, Angela Davis, and Stokely Carmichael meshed into a beautiful symphony of unified determination to achieve pride of race and equality of citizenship. In a sense, Lorraine Hansberry's *Raisin in the Sun,* Richard Wright's *Native Son,* and James Baldwin's *The Fire Next Time* collided with all the other angry black artistic geniuses to produce an amalgamation of the black man's American dream. That night 2,700 participants witnessed Denmark Vessey and Nat Turner as decorated national heroes; W. C. Handy and Nikki Giovanni as space ships orbiting the world of art; Jackie Robinson and Buddy Young quietly smiling as they destroyed Americanized Aryan myths of racial superiority.

Here were 2,700 black people cheering for another 25 million at a fashionable hotel in the nation's capital—finding the soul, if not the heart of America; celebrating the memories of ancestors who advanced the hopes of a people as they marched gallantly through the ravages of the eighteenth, nineteenth, and twentieth centuries to bring us to this point in time.

They also remembered that no other group of legislators has had to endure as many hardships, suffer as many indignities, or win so little appreciation as the sixty-seven black men and women who have served in the United States Congress.

These pioneers for justice and equality, some of whose character was honed in slavery, all victims of discrimination, all schooled in the hard knocks of reality, were unwavering in their faith in mankind. They believed more deeply in the promises of democracy than did the framers of the Constitution, who viewed them as less than human. They embraced the essence of the Constitution as did no other group in America, perhaps because they had no other choice, as their very survival depended on adherence by the majority to the tenets embodied in that document.

It may be too much to expect all elements of the black community to understand and appreciate the accomplishments of the Congressional Black Caucus. However, of this I am certain: While many have contributed to efforts to lift our people from bondage, the Caucus has been the single most effective political entity we have had in articulating, representing, protecting, and advancing the interests of black people in this nation over the past twenty years. In its twenty-year history, the Congressional Black Caucus has reflected on the injustices existing in American society and has pursued a course of action designed to rid this nation of the scourge of racism.

The Congressional Black Caucus fully understands that the "man with the plan" for resolution of these problems must adhere to the dictates of several political axioms. One of the more important of these was enunciated by Ossie Davis at the first Congressional Black Caucus dinner in 1971: "[The] name of the game is power, and if you ain't playing power, you're in the wrong place."[12]

The Congressional Black Caucus, playing a leadership role in this power game, is reeling under the stress and strain of a staggering federal budget deficit that threatens programs vital to our constituents. A spineless Congress concentrates primarily on the politics of reelection and an uncaring Bush administration is attuned only to big business and the wealthy; both expect the poor and dispossessed to do with even less than they already have.

Poverty, despair, despondence, and hopelessness, the four horsemen of racial discrimination, are galloping ever faster, and the poor can no longer rely on the president to publicly defend their rights, the Congress to aggressively protect their rights, or the courts to fairly interpret their rights.

In this period of chaos, the Caucus is flexing its collective muscle and judiciously using its ofttimes balance-of-power position on many close votes, deciding key issues that affect those who have been denied. The Congressional Black Caucus has succeeded because we heeded the words of Lerone Bennett, Jr., who in 1972 advised us to disengage ourselves from white people's arguments and redefine all concepts and associations in terms of the fundamental interests of black people. We have succeeded because we understand that the destiny of each of us is inextricably bound to the destiny of 32 million other black brothers and sisters, and that their struggle and our struggle are irrevocably tied one to the other.

We have survived and will continue to succeed in protecting our interests because we have adhered to the most important political principle of all, the official motto of the Congressional Black Caucus:

BLACK PEOPLE HAVE NO PERMANENT FRIENDS,
NO PERMANENT ENEMIES,
JUST PERMANENT INTERESTS.

Notes

1. Frederick Douglass, in a speech given August 4, 1857, cited in *Before the Mayflower: A History of Black America,* by Lerone Bennett, London: Penguin Books, 1984, pages 160–161.
2. Langston Hughes, "The Negro Artist and the Racial Mountain," *The Nation,* volume 22, number 3181, June 23, 1926, page 694.
3. Floyd Hayes.
4. William Reed, in the *Capital Spotlight,* a black-owned newspaper.
5. *The Washington Post,* October 25, 1991.
6. *The Washington Post,* July 2, 1991.
7. *USA Today,* July 19, 1991.
8. *Congressional Globe,* 42nd Congress, second session, 1872, page 492.
9. Congressman Julian C. Dixon, "Annual CBCF Legislative Weekend Souvenir Program Book," September 1984, page 75.
10. Frederick Douglass, cited in *The Negro Almanac—The Afro American,* New York: The Bellwether Company, 1976, page 107.
11. *The Crisis* magazine, April 1981, page 131.
12. Ossie Davis in his keynote speech at the Sheraton-Park Hotel, Washington, D.C., June 18, 1971.

14

Strategies for Increasing Black Representation in Congress

Carol Swain

Some time in the past it was necessary to have black faces in Congress to serve as role models for other young people who would aspire to be elected officials, to be at the table so that our voices would be heard, to insure that we were not overlooked. But at some point, we have to question the creation of districts in which the election of a black person is an end within itself. I believe that it is not an end in itself, it's a means to an end, and the end to be accomplished is to win. It takes a majority of the votes, 218, to win in Congress.

> —Interview with Representative Craig Washington,
> October 22, 1991

What will happen to black representation in Congress when courts and state legislatures can no longer draw new districts with black majorities? Do blacks have any other means of increasing their congressional representation? Can more blacks be elected from majority-white districts?

Factors Influencing Black Political Gains in Congress

African Americans have made unmistakable progress in Congress. In 1991, the 435 members of the House included 24 black Democratic representatives and 1 black Republican (see Table 14.1). Forty percent of the black representatives

---

Reprinted by permission of the publishers from BLACK FACES, BLACK INTERESTS: THE REPRESENTATION OF AFRICAN-AMERICANS IN CONGRESS by Carol M. Swain, Cambridge, Mass.: Harvard University Press, © 1993 by the President and Fellows of Harvard College.

Table 14.1

Congressional Districts Represented by Blacks, 1991

Representative	District	Principal city	BVAP 1980s	HVAP 1980s	Total minority
Franks (R-CT)	5	Waterbury	4	3	7
Wheat (D-MO)	5	Kansas City	20	2	22
Dellums (D-CA)	8	Oakland	24	6	30
Dymally (D-CA)	31	Compton	31	21	52
Dixon (D-CA)	28	Los Angeles	37	24	61
Washington (D-TX)	18	Houston	39	27	66
Clay (D-MO)	1	St. Louis	46	1	47
Flake (D-NY)	6	Queens	47	8	55
Towns (D-NY)	11	New York	47	34	81
Rangel (D-NY)	16	New York	49	35	84
Ford (D-TN)	9	Memphis	51	1	52
Waters (D-CA)	29	Los Angeles	51	32	83
Jefferson (D-LA)	2	New Orleans	52	3	55
Espy (D-MS)	2	Greenville	53	1	54
Payne (D-NJ)	10	Newark	54	12	66
Stokes (D-OH)	21	Cleveland	58	1	59
Collins (D-IL)	7	Chicago	60	4	64
Lewis (D-GA)	5	Atlanta	60	1	61
Conyers (D-MI)	1	Detroit	66	2	68
Savage (D-IL)	2	Chicago	66	7	73
Collins (D-MI)	13	Detroit	67	3	70
Mfume (D-MD)	7	Baltimore	70	1	71
Gray (D-PA)	2	Philadelphia	76	1	77
Owens (D-NY)	12	Brooklyn	78	9	87
Hayes (D-IL)	1	Chicago	90	1	91

Sources: Linda Williams, ed., *The JCPS Congressional District Fact Book,* 3rd ed. (Washington, D.C.: Joint Center for Political Studies, 1988); *Congressional Quarterly,* November 10, 1990, vol. 48, n. 45, pp. 3822–3823.

Note: BVAP = Black voting-age percentage of district population; HVAP = Hispanic voting-age percentage of district population.

were elected from districts that were less than 50 percent black in their voting-age populations.

Increases in the number of black representatives have resulted from changes in the nature of political opportunities in the United States, particularly changes in the country's demography and in the electoral system. During the Reconstruction era, federally facilitated black voter registration and educational programs led to the election of black politicians at all levels of government. During the twentieth century black representation has been influenced by urban migration and by voting-rights legislation that led to competition for the black vote. In some areas African Americans were rewarded with congressional seats once the black population reached a certain percentage and the white incumbent left Congress. The Voting Rights Act of 1965 was one watershed for blacks; the decision of the Supreme Court to enter the "political thicket" of reapportionment and redistricting was another.

The history of congressional reapportionment in the twentieth century is well known.[1] The requirements for reapportionment and redistricting are based on Article 1, Section 2, of the U.S. Constitution. Reapportionment is the redistribution of the nation's 435 congressional seats among the fifty states, and this is done on the basis of successive decennial censuses.[2] Redistricting is the actual redrawing of district lines within the individual states. Officials of the states concerned draw the lines. The process is highly political, and the outcome is often based on which party controls the legislature in a state.[3]

Redistricting and changes in black representation in the twentieth century have been very much a function of key court decisions. After refusing to enter the apportionment arena in the case of *Colegrove v. Green* in 1946, the Supreme Court in 1961 decided to hear *Baker v. Carr*, which involved state legislative districts in Tennessee that had not been redistricted since 1901. By a vote of six to two the court declared the issue worthy of litigation but offered few guidelines about what would be a fair apportionment; political observers were left to grapple with the meaning of the decision. *Reynolds v. Sims* followed in 1964, resulting in more representation for urban areas and an increase in the number of African-American politicians in state legislatures—positions that have traditionally been stepping stones to Congress.[4] *Wesberry v. Sanders* (1964), a Georgia case, extended the principle of "one person, one vote" to the congressional arena.[5] Many of the subsequent cases have involved clarifications of what constitutes fair apportionment. *Kirkpatrick v. Preisler* (1969), *White v. Weiser* (1973), *Wells v. Rockefeller* (1969), and *Karcher v. Daggett* (1983) are cases in which a strict population standard was applied to congressional redistricting.[6]

Since the case of *Kirksey v. Board of Supervisors of Hinds County, Mississippi*, in 1977, courts have leaned toward a rule that directs mapmakers, wherever possible (that is, in areas with large minority populations), to create districts in which minorities make up at least 65 percent of the population.[7] The 65 percent rule takes into account lower voter turnout among racial minorities, and it assumes a racially polarized electorate in which white voters opt for white candidates and black voters for blacks, but it is not rigid.[8] Whether or not the 65 percent rule is adhered to may depend on factors such as the size of the minority population in a given area, its past turnout rate, party cohesion, and similar issues.[9] On court order, Georgia's fifth district was redrawn so that it became 65 percent black *after* it had already elected a black representative, Andrew Young, when it was majority-white. After the court had increased the size of the district's black population, the independent-minded electorate responded by electing Wyche Fowler, a white representative. Georgia's fifth district did not need a 65 percent black population to elect a black politician with biracial appeal. What happened after the court's intervention illustrates that electorates do not always vote in a racially predictable and straightforward manner.

Much of the reasoning for drawing congressional districts to ensure the descriptive representation of minorities can be found in the case of *Thornburg v. Gingles* (1986), which involved a challenge to North Carolina's multimember state legislative districts. The court devised a three-part test for discrimination that focuses on an analysis of the local political situation, its openness to minorities, and the ability of minority groups to elect the representatives of their choice. *Thornburg v. Gingles* mandates the creation of a maximum number of minority districts whenever a geographical area contains a large, politically cohesive minority group (that is, one that votes en bloc for minority candidates) whose choices of minority candidates have been defeated on a regular basis in the past by a bloc of white voters.[10] The decision in this case moved the nation one step closer to requiring proportional representation for racial and ethnic minorities.[11]

By 1992 compliance with the *Thornburg* decision had led to the creation of contorted computer-drawn districts that resembled spiders, masses of bacteria, pitchforks, and worse. . . . It is a major feat to determine where such a district begins and ends. One can only imagine the havoc that these twisted districts create for members of Congress as they campaign for election and reelection, and for voters as they seek constituency service.[12] If confusion is too great, all constituents in such districts may be ill served. Certain racial gerrymanders, however, are now sanctioned by law.

Racial Gerrymandering

Gerrymandering is the manipulation of district lines for political advantage. Racial gerrymandering occurs when district lines are drawn to enhance or reduce the representation of particular racial groups.[13] Its major forms are known as "cracking" (a significant minority population is dispersed across several districts to dilute its voting strength), "stacking" (large concentrations of minority voters are combined with white populations to create districts with white majorities), and "packing" (minority voters are put in districts that already have high minority populations).[14] Although it has ruled against cracking and stacking, the Supreme Court has not yet considered packing to be worthy of legal remedies (see *Wright v. Rockefeller,* 1964).[15]

Seven of the fifteen majority-black districts in Table 14.1 appear to be packed beyond what is needed to elect black politicians. The most egregious cases from the 1980 census were the first district in Illinois, which had a black voting-age population of 90 percent, and New York's twelfth district and Pennsylvania's second district, which both had black voting-age populations of 78 percent. Four remaining districts were also more than 65 percent black: Maryland's seventh

(70 percent), Michigan's thirteenth (67 percent), and Illinois's second and Michigan's first district (both with 66 percent).

Black politicians consider packing less harmful than the other two forms of racial gerrymandering, because it adds to the safeness of their districts. At the Congressional Black Caucus legislative weekend in September 1990, Ronald Walters, chairman of Howard University's political science department, spoke of some of the dangers that redistricting might pose for John Conyers, representative of Michigan's first district: "[It is] an important national question because he chairs the Committee on Government Operations. . . . It's a black question in that the way he got his seniority is through black political power, black voters returning to him over and over."[16] Echoing his concerns was Bernard Anderson, a representative of Philadelphia's Urban Affairs Partnership, who said that although decreased black population density did not necessarily mean that black congressmen would not be reelected, "it does mean the congressman then has to deal with a wider variety of issues, and perhaps become . . . less directly [involved] with racial interests. It's likely we'll see more black elected officials like [Virginia Governor L. Douglas] Wilder than the CBC members of the past."[17] Many blacks would consider this a negative outcome, and many minority leaders would prefer to be dependent only on the votes of members of their own racial group.[18]

Only a minority of black politicians oppose the packing of black voters. Representative Craig Washington, a Texas Democrat, is among them, and he is outspoken in his views: "If you take 20 percent of those blacks who are in a 90 percent district and put them in an adjoining district that is probably 75 or 80 percent white, you'd get the white percentage down to where the impact of the black community is a lot greater. Instead of one district with black influence, you can have two."[19] Representative Washington argues that isolating black voters in overwhelmingly black districts places them in a situation where their policy preferences can be more easily ignored. "We shouldn't warehouse black people in districts," Washington declares. "You don't need a threshold of 90 percent in order to allow blacks to elect someone black. My district is 30 percent black. I would like to hope that it keeps the same ethnic breakdown after the 1991 redistricting."[20]

Washington is not alone in questioning the wisdom behind drawing overwhelmingly black districts. The legislative expert Phil Duncan points to the irony of the existing remedy: "Let's just suppose someone suggested that the United States adopt a policy of segregating blacks for the purpose of providing them congressional representation. . . . A shocking suggestion? In fact, just such a separatist approach to congressional redistricting is widely and favorably discussed by many politicians and legal scholars who regard themselves as vigorous advocates of minority rights."[21] Similarly, Mississippi's Mike Espy told me: "Although nothing's guaranteed, I think that the need for a 65 percent black population has been disproved. Look at Doug Wilder [Governor of Virginia], look at David Dinkins [Mayor of New York], look at Norm Rice [Mayor of Seattle]—black men and women all over the nation are running and winning in areas that are not predominantly black. And, in the deep South, we've got a lot of successful examples, too."[22] As redistricting approached after the 1990 census, Espy argued for keeping his biracial coalition intact; black leaders in the district fought for a 60 percent black population so that any black candidate could win with black support only.[23]

Among the examples of blacks who have been elected to Congress from districts that fell short of being 50 percent black are: Ron Dellums (1970, Berkeley, California), Andrew Young (1972, Atlanta, Georgia), Harold Ford (1974, Memphis, Tennessee), Alan Wheat (1982, Kansas City, Missouri), Katie Hall (1982, Gary, Indiana), and Gary Franks (1990, Waterbury, Connecticut). This list is remarkable in that it goes far beyond the traditionally liberal constituencies in Massachusetts that elected Senator Edward Brooke and those in California that we might expect to be liberal. Since the early 1970s, a much larger group of black representatives, including Barbara Jordan (1972, Houston, Texas), Julian Dixon (1978, Los Angeles, California), Mervyn Dymally (1980, Los Angeles, California), Mickey Leland (1978, Houston, Texas), Floyd Flake (1986, Queens, New York), and Craig Washington (1990, Houston, Texas), have been elected from districts in which no racial group constitutes a majority. Others, such as William Clay (1968, St. Louis, Missouri) and Charles Rangel (1970, Harlem, New York), have been able to hold on to their seats as their once majority-black constituencies have become either majority-white or majority-other.

That districts with black majorities are clearly not the black politician's only route to Congress refutes the logic behind the belief that a minority must constitute at least 65 percent of the population to guarantee descriptive representation.[24] Each election of a black candidate from a non-black-majority district, such as Gary Franks's 1990 election from a 4 percent black district, further weakens this argument.

Thus far the Supreme Court has not been sympathetic to the pleas of white voters who complain about racial gerrymanders that crack and stack their populations in order to make way for minority districts. The case of *United Jewish Organizations v. Carey* in 1977, for example, involved white voters who complained about a redistricting plan that split two Hasidic Jewish communities in order to create a district with a black majority. Undeterred by their arguments, Justice White, writing for the majority, argued that a group can be represented by legislators elected outside its district lines. He declared that "the white voter who as a result of the 1974 plan is in a district likely to return a nonwhite representative will be represented, to the extent that voting continues to follow racial lines, by legislators elected from majority white districts."[25]

Why Question the Strategy?

When African Americans question the common strategy of drawing legislative districts with large black majorities, they are sometimes viewed by other blacks with suspicion and regarded as "enemies of the group." Yet the electoral demography of the United States favors such a policy. The statistics on the distribution and concentration of blacks in the population reveal a need to look beyond the creation of majority-black political units as a way to increase political representation of African Americans. Blacks have already made the most of their opportunities to elect black politicians in congressional districts with black majorities. In 1991 the only states providing real prospects for new minority-majority districts were Alabama, Florida, Georgia, Louisiana, Maryland, Mississippi, North Carolina, South Carolina, Texas, and Virginia.[26] The creation of a new district in Alabama would require combining the city of Birmingham with the city of Tuscaloosa and several rural areas, and this would result in another odd-shaped district. Some experts suggest that African Americans and Hispanics might be able to find twelve to fifteen new districts for themselves after the 1990s redistricting. Beyond that, and in years to come, we can expect severe limitations on what can be achieved by relying on the creation of black districts to ensure the election of black politicians.[27]

Consider the problem of gaining adequate congressional representation for blacks from the South, who account for 60 percent of the nation's African-American population and who will account for an even greater percentage if a recent trend toward reverse migration continues. Although 67 percent of the nation's black elected officials are from the South, the region contributes only 20 percent of the black representation on Capitol Hill.[28] Bernard Grofman and Lisa Handley have shown that the underrepresentation of southern blacks in Congress appears to result not from the factors that might be first suspected, such as white racism, lack of campaign funds, or low black turnout, but from the geographical dispersion of southern blacks. Most black representatives are elected from large cities in which the black population is 300,000 or more (the setting in which it is most feasible to create black districts), but there are few southern cities that match this criterion.[29]

Not only is the strategy of carving out predominantly black districts from urban areas with dense concentrations of blacks unlikely to encourage adequate black representation in the South, but it is also likely to become ineffective in the future in the Northeast and Midwest, which are presently the largest "producers" of black members of Congress. Of the seventeen black-represented districts that lost population in 1980, 29 percent lost more than a fifth of their population (see Table 14.2). Seventy percent lost more than a tenth. Although the overall population losses were smaller between 1980 and 1990, districts with significant black populations were usually the most seriously affected. Some of the greatest losses occurred in northeastern and midwestern districts.[30] Illinois, Michigan, New York, Ohio, and Pennsylvania have continued to lose congressional representation.[31] In states losing seats, courts and state legislators have promised to preserve the black districts; it may not be possible to do this, however, while at the same time complying with the equal-size guidelines established by the Supreme Court.

Table 14.2

Population Change for Black-represented Congressional Districts

District	1970–1980 Percentage change	1980–1990 Percentage change
Michigan–13	37.3%	–23.2%
New York–12	31.4	+10.6
Ohio–21	24.7	–10.9
Missouri–1	23.9	–10.0
Illinois–1	20.0	–20.4
Illinois–7	19.8	–14.2
Michigan–1	15.9	–12.3
Pennsylvania–1	15.3	–8.3
Missouri–5	14.2	–4.7
Maryland–7	13.8	–5.9
New Jersey–10	10.8	–11.5
Tennessee–9	–9.4	–8.7
Georgia–5	–8.7	–1.8
Texas–18	–8.4	–14.7
California–8	–5.1	+6.8
New York–6	–4.3	+1.9
New York–11	–3.5	+4.8
California–31	0.0	+13.9
Illinois–2	+.02	–11.9
California–28	+.09	+14.1
Louisiana–2	+1.7	–11.1
Mississippi–2	+4.6	–6.2
California–29	+5.2	+3.5
Connecticut–5	+7.3	+7.8
New York–17	+13.2	+22.2

Sources: "Urban Districts Suffer Big Population Losses," *Congressional Quarterly Weekly Report,* April 25, 1981, pp. 646–649; "Official 1990 Count by District," *Congressional Quarterly Weekly Report,* May 18, 1991, pp. 1309–1312.

The experiences of George Crockett (D-MI) and his successor, Barbara Rose Collins, point to some of the specific problems of seeking to expand black congressional representation by creating predominantly black districts. Crockett, who had already seen his black-majority district diluted with the addition of conservative white suburbs, told me that he expected the 1990 redistricting to reduce further the ratio of whites to blacks in the district. He commented: "They're going to have to redraw my district lines, because I have lost almost 100,000 residents. I am told that my congressional district has lost more people than any other congressional district in the country."[32] He was correct; the district lost 185,000 residents. It will be preserved, however, by a further expansion into the white-dominated suburbs. This effort to preserve the seats of black members occurs at a time when the state is losing two congressional seats.

Other black representatives, such as Mike Espy (D-MS) and William Clay (D-MO), are convinced that census data showing their districts to have black majorities are flawed.[33] Espy believes that his district is really majority-white. Clay, whose district is majority-white in voting-age population, considers himself the beneficiary of a black undercount that works in his favor because it misleads the potential opposition.[34] According to one of Clay's staffers, white opponents who take Clay on quickly learn that the district is really majority-black. At any rate, confusion about the size of black districts and the decline in their black populations further signal the limitations of electoral strategies based solely on the creation and preservation of districts with black majorities.

Even when it is feasible to create or maintain heavily black districts, it may be undesirable. Large concentrations of poor black voters, who normally elect black politicians, are often plagued by high crime rates, drug abuse, and other ghetto problems. This makes areas less attractive to all inhabitants, leading to both black and white flight. Research has shown that attitudes on racial segregation in housing are such that most whites are willing to live in neighborhoods with some integration.[35] As the percentage of black residents increases, however, so does the percentage of whites who leave the area or decide not to move into the neighborhood. Even black residents indicate a preference for more integrated neighborhoods, with two-thirds to three-quarters preferring mixed neighborhoods to those composed mostly of blacks.[36] A more heterogeneous population might elect a more racially diverse group of politicians, and this can lead to broad coalition building across racial groups and therefore to improvements in the district, including a higher tax base, which might stem the tide of out-migration.

There are other ways in which less overwhelmingly black districts could have a positive effect on black representation of blacks. Black representatives would have to work harder at increasing voter turnout in their districts. Voter turnout in historically black districts is now abysmally low. Turnout, for example, was 13 percent in Major Owens's (D-NY) 78 percent black district in 1986. Lowered black population in such districts might mean that black representatives would have to compete actively for white as well as black voters and would therefore become more responsive to all of their constituents. Race relations suffer when "electoral remedies" favor one racial group over another or in environments where candidates can engage in racially polarizing tactics without fear of defeat.[37]

At present, few black representatives have any incentive to tackle the problems that lead to high population losses in their districts. They know that they are protected by a legacy of court decisions. *Beer v. United States* (1974 and 1976) led to the establishment of a "no retrogression rule," mandating that a redistricting or electoral change cannot leave minority voters worse off. Black federal and state legislators know that the district lines are likely to be drawn to capture the voters who have fled into outlying suburbs.[38] Regardless of high population losses, black representatives can rest assured that their states will maintain the districts of black members. They are not, however, necessarily guaranteed a

district with a black majority. In 1991 officials at the Justice Department began
to question what enforcement of the no retrogression standard actually entails.
According to John Dunne, the head of the department's Civil Rights Office:
"The law doesn't endow anyone with a right to office. . . . It may be appropriate
to reduce the percentage of the non-white population in a majority-black or
Hispanic district without violating the [retrogression standard that prohibits the
dilution of minority votes]."[39] Violating the no retrogression standard might
entail lowering the black population percentage in certain historically black congressional districts.

As we have seen, building a biracial coalition does not mean that black
politicians have to "sell out" the interests of their group to gain the white support
needed. Some black representatives from historically black districts have done
an excellent job of representing whites without neglecting the interests of blacks.
Representative Louis Stokes (D-OH), for example, expects a population that will
be 45 percent white after the 1990s redistricting. He has already made changes in
his outreach services. After the 1980s redistricting, he added another district
office in a newly annexed white suburb. He described to me how these changes
affect what he does:

> There's been a shift in what we have to do congressionally. I don't know that
> we work any harder. That is, we work hard as it is, but in the suburban part of
> my district the problems are different. In the central city I've got all these
> problems related to crime, inadequate health facilities, housing problems re-
> lated to public housings, things of that sort. But suburban problems are differ-
> ent. I deal more with people who have personal problems related to
> immigration and trade—things of that nature. We address all the problems of
> anybody in our district without any reference to their race, ethnicity, or color.
> We realize that the problems in the predominantly white community are differ-
> ent from, and not as magnified as, the problems related to the inner city. But
> we address them all, whether it is the person who calls up and says, "Hey,
> we're having trouble getting a visa or a passport," or a person who calls up and
> says, "They've shut the gas off at my house because I haven't been able to
> pay." It means a transfer of application of time to a totally different series of
> problems.[40]

Stokes has effectively combined outreach to whites with mobilization efforts in
the black community. His observations about the different nature of the constituency requests are similar to those made by Floyd Flake and others. He does not
seem afraid of redistricting, because he knows that he has biracial appeal.

Black Representation and the Republican Party

The quest to increase minority representation took a new twist during the early
1990s when the Republican National Committee combined redistricting with its

outreach program to minorities. Republican leaders have zealously urged the creation of the maximum number of "safe" black and Hispanic districts. In doing so they have encouraged unrealistic goals. Benjamin Ginsberg, chief counsel for the National Committee, for example, declared: "If I were a member of the Congressional Black Caucus, it wouldn't be unreasonable to think that my membership ought to be doubled after the 1992 elections if I got a fair shake in the redistricting process."[41] The Republican position on minority districts may seem surprising, given that Republicans have gained so much political mileage by opposing affirmative action quotas. Why would Republicans want more minority-elected officials, if most are likely to be Democrats? Why do Republicans care about the number and size of black districts?

The answers would appear to be simple. It is in the Republican interest to want large black districts. To the extent that the black Democrats are concentrated in legislative districts, it is easier for Republican candidates to win more seats overall. The creation of a newly black district is likely to drain black voters from other districts, many of them represented by white Democrats. The more "lily-white" the districts so drained become, the easier it is for Republicans to win them.[42] In short, by adopting such a redistricting strategy, Republicans give African Americans the opportunity to increase their descriptive representation but, quite possibly, at the expense of their substantive representation.

Representative Craig Washington described such a process and explained how blacks could lose ground: "If you have four districts in a state like Alabama, for example, with a sufficiently large black population to neutralize Republicans on some issues, and if you can create one black district by gathering up all the blacks in such a fashion that they could elect a black person to Congress, and in the process you lose the leverage that you had in the three other districts, then that's foolish to me. Every time the one person votes for the things that I'm for, and that the black community is for, the other three from the state will probably vote against them."[43]

In Washington's view, Republican efforts to encourage predominantly black districts are part of the larger question of how Republican policies relate to the interests of blacks:

> Ninety percent of the Republicans vote against things that are centrally important to blacks, like the Civil Rights Bill, Family Medical Leave Act, the Child Care Act, things that by and large will benefit the broad cross-section of American people, including large segments of the black community, not because Republicans are targeting for or against them, but because blacks happen to be in the lowest socioeconomic groups. Republicans are against most of the programs that are designed to help people who happen to fit the strata in which 90 percent of black people fall. . . . It doesn't take a fool twenty years to be able to figure out that [Republicans] are against what I stand for.[44]

Many white liberal Democrats have a big stake in how redistricting is done.

Representative Martin Frost (D-TX), for example, who stood to lose many of his minority voters, questioned what he was hearing from voting rights advocates: "There are some in the civil rights community who say they don't care; let the chips fall where they may. I do not believe that represents the majority view. Their larger agenda cannot be enacted unless there are both [minorities and supportive whites in Congress]."[45] A sympathetic Alan Wheat (D-MO) noted the difficulties of achieving the goals of both white incumbents and civil rights activists without causing some "individual tragedies" that most representatives would prefer to avoid.[46]

The Republicans are not united with regard to their position on minority districts. The inconsistency of the party's opposition to affirmative action quotas on the one hand and its eagerness to extend such quotas to minorities for reasons relating to electoral politics on the other has been pointed out by a number of prominent Republicans, most notably the former Reagan Administration drug czar William Bennett.[47] The eagerness of Republicans to help blacks on redistricting issues, but not on other equally important issues, makes them especially vulnerable to charges by Democrats that they are wolves in sheep's clothing. Fortunately for those who seek to increase African-American representation, there is no need to rely on the growth of black Republicanism and the ostensibly benign intervention of the party. Other possibilities abound. . . .

Notes

1. Some of the more relevant literature on reapportionment and redistricting includes Nelson Polsby, ed., *Reapportionment in the 1970s* (Berkeley: University of California Press, 1971); Robert Dixon, Jr., *Democratic Representation and Reapportionment in Law and Politics* (New York: Oxford University Press, 1968); Bruce Cain, *The Reapportionment Puzzle* (Berkeley: University of California Press, 1984); Timothy C. O'Rourke, *The Impact of Reapportionment* (New Brunswick, N.J.: Transaction Books, 1980); Charles Bullock III, "Redistricting and Congressional Stability, 1962–1972," *Journal of Politics,* 37 (1975), 569–575; Keith E. Hamm, Robert Harmel, and Robert J. Thompson, "Impacts of Districting Change on Voting Cohesion and Representation," *Journal of Politics,* 43 (1981), 544–555.

2. In December 1991 the Supreme Court agreed to hear a challenge to the 1941 federal law that provides a formula for the allocation of congressional seats. A federal district court in Montana ruled that the 1941 law ignored "the goal of equal representation for equal numbers of people." If the court sustains the Montana ruling, congressional districts allocated after the 1990 census to 18 states will have to be reassigned. See "High Court to Weigh Redistricting Case," *New York Times,* December 17, 1991.

3. Q. Whitfield Ayres and David Whiteman, "Congressional Reapportionments in the 1980s," *Political Science Quarterly,* 99, no. 2 (Summer 1984), 303–314.

4. *Reynolds v. Sims,* 377 U. S. 533 (1964).

5. *Wesberry v. Sanders,* 376 U. S. 1 (1964).

6. *Kirkpatrick v. Preisler,* 394 U. S. 526, 531 (1969), *White v. Weiser,* 412 U. S. 783, 790 (1973), *Wells v. Rockefeller,* 394 U. S. 542 (1969), and *Karcher v. Daggett,* 462 U. S. 725 (1983).

7. *Kirksey v. Board of Supervisors of Hinds County, Mississippi,* 544 F. 2d 139 (1977); see also *Ketchum v. Byrne,* 740 F. 2d 1398 (1984).

8. Kimball Brace, Bernard Grofman, Lisa Handley, and Richard Niemi, "Minority Voting Equality: The 65 Percent Rule in Theory and Practice," *Law and Policy*, 10, no. 1 (January 1988), 43–62; Bernard Grofman and Lisa Handley, "Minority Population Proportion and Black and Hispanic Congressional Success in the 1970s and 1980s," *American Politics Quarterly*, 17, no. 4 (October 1989), 436–445; "Creating Black Districts May Segregate Voters," *Congressional Quarterly Weekly Report*, July 28, 1990, p. 2462.

9. Bernard Grofman, Michael Migalski, and Nicholas Noviello, "The 'Totality of Circumstances Test' in Section 2 of the 1982 Extension of the Voting Rights Act: A Social Science Perspective," *Law and Policy*, 7, no. 2 (April 1985), 199–223.

10. *Thornburg v. Gingles*, 478 U. S. 30 (1986).

11. Charles Bullock III, "Redistricting and Changes in the Partisan and Racial Composition of Southern Legislatures," *State and Local Government Review* (Spring 1987), 62.

12. "Monster Map," editorial, *Wall Street Journal*, October 18, 1991; "North Carolina Computer Draws Some Labyrinthine Lines," *Congressional Quarterly Weekly Report*, July 13, 1991, pp. 1916–1917; "Democrats' Ties to Minorities May Be Tested by New Lines," *Congressional Quarterly Weekly Report*, June 2, 1990, pp. 1739–1742.

13. Robert C. Smith provides a useful discussion of the major court cases involving blacks in his article "Liberal Jurisprudence and the Quest for Racial Representation," *Southern University Law Review*, 15, no. 1 (1988), 1–51.

14. Frank Parker, "Racial Gerrymandering and Legislative Reapportionment," in Chandler Davidson, ed., *Minority Vote Dilution* (Washington, D.C.: Howard University Press, 1984); Frank Parker, *Black Votes Count: Political Empowerment in Mississippi after 1965* (Chapel Hill: University of North Carolina Press, 1990).

15. *Wright v. Rockefeller*, 376 U. S. 52 (1964).

16. Dr. Ronald Walters, as quoted in "Changing Horizon for Black Caucus," *Philadelphia Inquirer*, September 26, 1990.

17. Bernard Anderson, as quoted in "Changing Horizons for Black Caucus."

18. See Robert C. Smith, "Recent Elections and Black Politics: The Maturation or Death of Black Politics," *PS*, 22 (June 1990), 160–162.

19. Interview with Craig Washington, Washington, D.C., October 22, 1991.

20. Ibid.

21. "Creating Black Districts May Segregate Voters," p. 2462.

22. Interview with Mike Espy, Washington, D.C., June 14, 1990.

23. "Race and Politics: A Border Clash," *Washington Post National Weekly Edition*, December 23–29, 1991, p. 13.

24. Brace et al., "Minority Voting," pp. 42–62; Grofman and Handley, "Minority Population Proportion," pp. 436–445.

25. *United Jewish Organizations v. Carey*, 430 U. S. 144 (1977), p. 166, n. 24; see also Robert Weissberg, "Collective v. Dyadic Representation in Congress," *American Political Science Review*, 72 (1978), 535–547.

26. Blacks and Hispanics are sure to fight over a new district to be drawn in the Dallas, Texas, area that will jeopardize white Democratic incumbents such as Representatives Michael Andrews and Martin Frost; see "Endangered Species: 'Anglo Democrats,' " *International Herald Tribune*, May 22, 1991.

27. See "Minority Mapmaking," *National Journal*, April 7, 1990, pp. 837–839; "Democrats' Ties to Minorities May Be Tested by New Lines"; "Maps That Stand Up in Court," *State Legislatures*, September 1990, pp. 15–19; "Mapmakers Must Toe the Line in Upcoming Redistricting," *Congressional Quarterly Weekly Report*, September 1, 1990, pp. 2786–2794; "Pushing for More Black House Seats," *National Journal*, January 5, 1991, p. 34; "Minority Poker," *National Journal*, May 4, 1991, pp. 1034–1039.

28. African Americans currently make up 20 percent or more of the voting-age popu-

lation in Mississippi (31 percent), Louisiana (27 percent), South Carolina (27 percent), Georgia (24 percent), Maryland (24 percent), Alabama (23 percent), and North Carolina (20 percent). Furthermore, blacks constitute sizable minorities in New York (15 percent), Illinois (14 percent), Michigan (13 percent), New Jersey (13 percent), and Ohio (10 percent). See *Blacks and the 1988 Democratic National Convention* (Washington, D.C.: Joint Center for Political Studies, 1988), pp. 5–6; *Black Elected Officials: A National Roster,* 18th ed. (Washington, D.C.: Joint Center for Political Studies, 1989), p. 1. See also "Race and the South," *U.S. News and World Report,* July 23, 1990.

29. Bernard Grofman and Lisa Handley, "Black Representation: Making Sense of Electoral Geography at Different Levels of Government," *Legislative Studies Quarterly,* 14, (May 2, 1989), 267–268; Grofman and Handley, "Minority Population Proportion," pp. 436–445.

30. "1990s Big Winners: California, Texas, Florida; Northeast and Midwest Seen Losing Seats," *Washington Post,* February 26, 1988, p. 21.

31. David Huckabee, "House Apportionment: Preliminary Projections," *Congressional Research Service Report,* August 1988, pp. 88–567.

32. Interview with George Crockett, Washington, D.C., June 14, 1990.

33. Interview with Epsy.

34. Personal communication with William Clay's district administrator, September 20, 1990.

35. Gerald D. Jaynes and Robin M. Williams, Jr., eds., *A Common Destiny: Blacks and American Society* (Washington, D.C.: National Academy Press, 1989), pp. 140–144.

36. Ibid.

37. Carol M. Swain, "Some Unintended Consequences of the Voting Rights Act," in Chandler Davidson and Bernard Grofman, *Minority Voting: The Voting Rights Act in Twenty-Five Year Perspective* (Washington, D.C.: Brookings, forthcoming).

38. *Beer v. United States,* 374 F. Supp. 363 (D.D.C. 1974), rev'd 425 U. S. 130 (1976).

39. John Dunne, as cited in "Minority Poker," p. 1038.

40. Interview with Representative Louis Stokes, Washington, D.C., June 14, 1990.

41. Benjamin Ginsberg, as quoted in "Minority Mapmaking," p. 837.

42. Kimball Brace, Bernard Grofman, and Lisa Handley, "Does Redistricting Aimed to Help Blacks Necessarily Help Republicans?" *Journal of Politics,* 49 (1987), 169–185; Charles Bullock III, "The Election of Blacks in the South: Preconditions and Consequences," *American Journal of Political Science,* 19, (November, 1975), 727–739.

43. Ibid.

44. Interview with Washington.

45. "Democrats Court Minorities to Counter GOP's Pitch," *Congressional Quarterly Weekly Report,* May 4, 1991, p. 1104.

46. Ibid.

47. Daniel Wattenberg, "The GOP Divides to Conquer," *Insight on the News,* 7, no. 22 (June 3, 1991), 12–19.

15

What Color Is Your Gerrymander? The Constitution and White Minority Districts

Lani Guinier

Nicetown, Fishtown, Germantown. These are neighborhoods in Philadelphia, the city in which I now live. Names from a distant century, they barely capture the checkerboard city Philadelphia has become. The City of Brotherly Love now ranks in the top 10 of the country's most racially segregated municipalities.

But within this city of racially distinct neighborhoods, there are a few racially neutral spaces. These are public areas in which no group feels it owns or controls the space. Here people of different racial and ethnic identities come together to enjoy public festivals or leisurely Sunday afternoons. Here blacks, whites, Asians and Latinos leave their homogeneous neighborhoods behind and enjoy and celebrate their identity as Philadelphians.

From the example of Philadelphia's public spaces we might learn how to rethink one of the trickiest legal and racial issues facing the federal courts and state legislatures: how to draw the lines for congressional districts. And in doing so, we might find a useful model for transcending other aspects of America's racial division.

The imperative for rethinking the nature of congressional districts comes from the Supreme Court and the Congress. In enacting the Voting Rights Act in 1965 and subsequently amending it in 1982, Congress said the courts must act affirmatively to assure all citizens the opportunity and capacity to participate in their own government. But in the court's *Shaw v. Reno* decision handed down last June, a bare majority of justices called into question congressional districts that are drawn with the purpose of increasing black representation.

These majority-black districts are the political equivalent of the ethnically homogeneous neighborhood. They are a safe haven for members of that group, a bit of turf that one ethnic group controls, a place where its voice is pre-eminent. In her majority opinion, Justice Sandra Day O'Connor said that race-conscious gerrymandering, however well-intentioned, smacked of "political apartheid" and was thus constitutionally suspect.

The legal reasoning of O'Connor's opinion (signed by four of her colleagues, including the court's only African-American member, Clarence Thomas) is certainly open to criticism. But the political implications of the decision are clear: The high court is challenging elected officials, lower courts and the American people to do for their democracy what the city planners have done for Philadelphia: define and design racially neutral space.

The difficulties of this task should not be underestimated. Take the example of North Carolina, where the *Shaw v. Reno* case originated. The white majority had dominated every congressional district in every election in the state from the beginning of the century until 1990. The state's population is 24 percent black but had been represented by an all-white congressional delegation since Reconstruction. No blacks were elected to many statewide or local offices, even where blacks were a sizable minority of the voters. Ten years ago, the Supreme Court found voting in the state to be so racially polarized that 82 percent of white voters would not vote for a black candidate. Political campaigns, the court noted, had been dominated by explicit racial appeals, in which black candidates were targeted because of, not in spite of, their race.

The traditional answer to remedying such voting rights abuses is to acknowledge the exclusion and then to give those whom the court finds to have been excluded their own safe space—in short, race-conscious districting. The 12th congressional district in North Carolina, the subject of *Shaw v. Reno,* was one result. The district snakes around the state to create a constituency that is 54 percent black and 46 percent white. The district proved offensive to the court in large measure because of its bizarre shape.

Lawyers for black voters in North Carolina acknowledged the district's strange outline but said it was a justifiable way to redress previously exclusionary practices. Shouldn't we be more worried, they asked, about the composition of North Carolina's congressional delegation than the appearance of any one district?

In *Shaw* the Supreme Court seemed to answer this question in the negative. The court said race-conscious districting may stigmatize blacks and violate the rights of whites to participate in colorblind elections. Such an approach, the court implied, won't lead us to race-neutral political space comparable to Philadelphia's public parks.

In discovering this new right (previously undetected in the Constitution) to participate in colorblind elections, the court overlooked the reality of drawing congressional districts. The court seemed to imply that there is some racially neutral way to establish the geographic boundaries of voting districts. But all districts, regardless of the race of their constituency, are drawn by someone to eliminate or disadvantage the political influence of someone else. Using race as a criterion in drawing up congressional districts is no more arbitrary than using party affiliation, a practice as old as the Republic itself, which the court did not object to. More important, the court failed to address the harsh but unmistakable reality that without some government intervention, public spaces like the North Carolina congressional delegation have been, in fact, racially segregated.

In its unwillingness to bless race-conscious districting, the court neglected to tell us how else to integrate the parks, i.e., to create racially neutral political space accessible to all.

One alternative would be not to district at all in North Carolina, to elect all members of Congress at-large. There is nothing in the constitution that requires the states to create congressional districts; in fact, congressmen were elected at large in Alabama and Hawaii in the early 1960s. At-large congressional elections would eliminate the race-conscious districting that the court is skeptical about. The problem, of course, is that if voting is racially polarized then this option is effectively "racially neutral" for only one group: the group with the most votes. Where whites won't vote for blacks, and whites are a majority, this option would effectively assure the white majority control of all congressional seats. For the racial minority, not to district at all is not to be represented at all.

Still another choice might be to make as many as possible of the 12 congressional districts competitive, which is usually defined as a district in which no group has more than 55 percent nor less than 45 percent of the voters. In a competitive district, the outcome of the election cannot be predicted based on simply on the relative numerical strength of the more dominant group. In a competitive district, the majority is fluid or majority status is at least within reach of the minority if it plays its cards right. The minority can presumably attract defectors from the majority and become part of the next governing coalition.

This approach is race conscious. Indeed, the 12th Congressional District in North Carolina is drawn to maximize the possibility of black representation in the district while at the same time creating maximum incentives for candidates from the majority to appeal to white voters. This attempt was not sufficient for the white plaintiffs, or for the five justices. The white minority, according to depositions taken of some of the plaintiffs in the case, does not feel it can win over members of the black majority. In their eyes, the black majority of the district is monolithic and likely to remain so, even if only by a narrow margin.

In other words, the problems with the race conscious solution is that it simply reproduces the racial polarization at the heart of North Carolina politics, this time to the disadvantage of a white, not a black, minority. The political justification for the disadvantaged position of whites in this district is that whites, as a majority in 10 of the 12 other districts, have the advantage in electing the congressional delegation statewide.

Yet another alternative, the subject of my much-maligned writings, is cumulative voting. This is a non-districted racially colorblind solution that lowers the threshold for representation by giving each voter multiple votes to cast based on the number of open seats. If North Carolina elected 12 representatives statewide, each voter would get 12 votes. Voters could put all their votes on one candidate or spread their votes out among any number of the other candidates. If all the members of a politically cohesive minority cast votes for the same candidate, that candidate could get elected even under the most adverse circumstances. Women, environmentalists or Republicans could all vote strategically to form "districts of the mind."

Some will fear the empowerment of politically cohesive minorities. Citing the example of Israeli politics, skeptics will worry about the possibility of reinforcing group identities in ways that lead to political paralysis and disproportionate influence of narrow interests. The Israeli electoral system, though, is an extreme example, because parties with as little as 1.5 percent of the vote are entitled to seats in the legislature. North Carolina's current system of district elections is another extreme, because any majority with 51 percent of the vote gets total power, potentially excluding even substantial 49 percent minorities. Cumulative voting is a compromise between these two extremes. It allows representation of substantial minority viewpoints, while assuring that the majority gets most of the power.

In some ways this cumulative voting alternative is ideal because it responds to the issues raised by both black and white voters in North Carolina at the same time that it is colorblind. It does not arbitrarily label voters by drawing districts based on assumptions about race or ethnicity. People are represented based on the way they cast their ballots, not on where they happen to live. Finally, although 60 percent of North Carolina black voters do not live in either of the two currently designated majority black districts, under this alternative every African-American voter would have a chance to elect representatives of their choice.

Whatever the preferred alternative, it should be measured by its ability to remedy—and not to reproduce—the prior discrimination in which majority rule became majority tyranny. The larger challenge is to make sure that collective decision-making about our common destiny occurs within a legislative body or political space in which all voters feel represented. If we fail to meet this challenge we shall never design racially neutral political spaces comparable to Philadelphia's parks. And if we fail, we shall be hard pressed to ask those who feel consistently excluded to keep faith with our democracy.

Part VI

The Presidency

This part examines the relationship between race and the American presidency. The first reading, "The Politics of Race: From Kennedy to Reagan," is by Edward Carmines and James Stimson, political scientists at Indiana University and the University of Minnesota, respectively. It is taken from their book, *Issue Evolution: Race and the Transformation of American Politics*, which won the Gladys Klammerer award from the American Political Science Association in 1990 for the best book on American politics. Carmines and Stimson contend that race "has had a profound impact on American politics." Their essay reviews the politics of race during the presidential administrations of John Kennedy, Lyndon Johnson, Richard Nixon, Gerald Ford, Jimmy Carter, and Ronald Reagan.

Carmines and Stimson contend that 1964 was the watershed year in American racial politics. The Civil Rights Act of 1964 heightened the importance of race in American national politics, and the racial conservatism of Republican presidential candidate Barry Goldwater redefined the racial politics of each party. The post-1964 racial liberalism of Hubert Humphrey, George McGovern, Walter Mondale, and Jimmy Carter helped to destroy the New Deal coalition. The Goldwater candidacy laid the intellectual groundwork for the Reagan presidency—which tried to weaken the Voting Rights Act, deemphasized school desegregation, and supported tax breaks for segregated schools.

The second reading is by Thomas Byrne Edsall, a political reporter for the *Washington Post*, with Mary D. Edsall. It is taken from his best-selling book, *Chain Reaction: The Impact of Race, Rights, and Taxes on American Politics*. In "The Reagan Attack on Race Liberalism," Edsall considers the racial politics of the Reagan administration, focusing on the 1984 presidential election. Edsall contends that President Reagan was able to use the politics of race to lessen white support for the Democratic Party. The Reagan administration saw itself as a bulwark against affirmative action and redistributive liberalism. During the 1980s, according to Edsall, the Democratic Party came to be identified with "such benefit-hungry groups as welfare recipients, feminists, black militants, illegal immigrants, gays, addicts seeking drug treatment, AIDS victims, and members of the underclass." A survey of white, blue-collar workers in Macomb County, Michigan, found that many Reagan voters were disaffected Democrats who "express a profound distaste for blacks, a sentiment that pervades almost everything they think about government and politics."

Edsall's book attracted much attention from the American political community. Many analysts regarded *Chain Reaction* as Bill Clinton's guide to racial politics in the 1992 presidential campaign. Harvard University government professor Martin Kilson said *Chain Reaction* "spooned up a lot of cynical formulations regarding the racial issue that almost amounted to advising Democratic candidates to 'Willie Hortonize' their way back into the White House."

16

The Politics of Race: From Kennedy to Reagan

Edward Carmines and James Stimson

[Our theory of issue evolution] specifies the sources, processes, and outcomes of issue competition. The theory is necessarily dynamic; issues do not appear fully developed on the political agenda. Instead, they evolve through time as they initially emerge, develop, mature, and are sometimes resolved. But not all issue conflicts have long-lasting, much less consequential life histories. Most are as fleeting as they are inconsequential. The vast majority of issues becomes extinct as quickly as the issues appear on the political scene, and, as a consequence, they lack capacity for transforming the political system.

Given this situation, it is not surprising that our attention as political analysts is directed to the few exceptions to the rule, to the tiny number of issue conflicts that truly matter to the long-term development of the political system. Race . . . clearly falls within this category. Over its long history it has had a profound impact on American politics.

Our purpose in this chapter is to trace the life history of this issue, especially its partisan evolution since the New Deal. Elite party actors, notably presidents and presidential contenders, play prominent roles in this history. We shall examine their roles in the evolution of race, focusing on the policy initiatives of presidents and the rhetoric of presidential candidates. We are especially interested in the changing racial positions of the parties as revealed in party platforms. How did party leaders respond to the growing salience of racial concerns? . . .

America's tragic struggle with the cause of racial equality did not, of course, begin with the New Deal. It has been a recurring theme in American history. After the painful resolution of the earlier slavery issue, it became a particularly salient national concern during Reconstruction, as white America first confronted the black man as a free, independent citizen. The early successes but ultimate failure of this first encounter set the stage for the later evolution of race. Thus, it is important to examine this earlier period, albeit briefly, so that the later reemergence of race as a national political issue can be seen in historical perspective. . . .

Kennedy, Johnson, and the Crisis of Civil Rights

The 1960s witnessed the full maturation of the struggle for racial equality. As both parties groped to find a way to deal with this highly divisive issue, the country itself was becoming increasingly polarized by antithetical racial forces. Civil rights leaders turned to protests and mass demonstrations to press their political claims. From the Montgomery bus boycott in 1955, to the lunch counter sit-ins in the late 1950s, to the Freedom Riders in 1961, to the Birmingham demonstration and the great March on Washington in 1963, to the Montgomery march in 1965, the country was faced with a mass civil rights movement that would no longer accept second-class status and treatment for black Americans. But the segregationist forces would not give in without a protracted struggle. Their protests were conducted in the halls of Congress and were reflected in the brutal manner of local police using fire hoses and attack dogs to quell nonviolent demonstrators.

The campaign of the 1960 presidential election was conducted in this atmosphere of heightened racial concerns. Both parties and their respective candidates took progressive positions on civil rights. Whereas the civil rights plank in the 1956 Democratic platform was written in compromise language so as to not offend southern Democrats, the 1960 plank contained strong and specific support for civil rights. Senator Sam Ervin of North Carolina introduced motions to the platform committee to delete portions of the proposed platform that called for establishing a permanent FEPC, continuing the Civil Rights Commission as a permanent agency, granting the attorney general the power to file civil injunction suits to prevent desegregation, and setting 1963 as the deadline for the initiation of school desegregation plans, but his motions were overwhelmingly defeated by the platform committee. A minority report by nine southern state delegations calling for the elimination of the platform's civil rights plank was similarly defeated on the convention floor (*Congressional Quarterly* 1983, 99–100). Democrats were determined to adopt a strong civil rights plank even if it meant overriding the strong objections of the southern wing of the party and possibly leading to a new split in the New Deal coalition.

But the Republicans would not be outdone on civil rights. Led by Senator

John Tower of Texas, the platform committee initially adopted a fairly weak civil rights plank that did not express support for civil rights demonstrations or promise federal efforts to gain job equality for blacks. But Richard Nixon and Nelson Rockefeller met during the convention and reached consensus on several major policy issues. Their agreement, informally dubbed the "compact of Fifth Avenue," included a much stronger civil rights plank on which Nixon threatened to wage a floor fight if it were not accepted by the platform committee. The committee adopted the stronger plank by a margin of fifty-six to twenty-eight (*Congressional Quarterly* 1983, 101). The final plank included an extensive array of civil rights' commitments, including support for equal voting rights, establishment of a Commission on Equal Job Opportunity, and a prohibition against discrimination in federal housing and in the operation of federal facilities.

> We oppose the pretense of fixing a target date 3 years from now for the mere submission of plans for school desegregation. Slow-moving school districts would construe it as a three-year moratorium during which progress would cease, postponing until 1963 the legal process to enforce compliance. We believe that each of the pending court actions should proceed as the Supreme Court has directed and that in no district should there be any such delay. (Johnson 1978, 619)

"Although the Democratic-controlled Congress watered them down," the GOP platform also stated, "the Republican Administration's recommendations resulted in significant and effective civil rights legislation in both 1957 and 1960—the first civil rights statutes to be passed in more than 80 years" (Johnson 1978, 618). In short, the Republican platform statement on civil rights was at least as progressive as its Democratic counterpart.

During the campaign itself John Kennedy and Richard Nixon followed their parties' leads, adopting progressive and almost identical civil rights positions. The most dramatic event of the campaign—and the single symbolic event that gave Kennedy a closer identification with the cause of racial equality—was his well-publicized telephone call to Coretta Scott King inquiring about the status of her recently arrested husband (Brauer 1977; Oakes 1982).

While the 1960 Democratic platform called for strong action on civil rights, President Kennedy initially took a very cautious approach to racial issues. Like Roosevelt before him, civil rights was not a deep moral concern for the new president. Nor was he about to sacrifice his domestic and economic programs on the altar of civil rights. Kennedy initially decided that he would not sponsor a civil rights bill after all, and, although he made a number of symbolic gestures in support of civil rights, he was unwilling to bring racial concerns within the legislative scope of his "New Frontier." His strategy, so reminiscent of Franklin Roosevelt's, may have worked if civil rights had been a normal political issue, its outcome determined largely by the interplay of political forces in Washington.

But civil rights was not an ordinary political issue, and it could not be resolved within the confines of the Potomac. It was an all-consuming, passionate concern both for those who wanted to see segregation ended a generation earlier and for those who wanted it to last forever. And the nation was caught up in this unfolding political drama.

Kennedy's go-slow approach to civil rights continued into his third year in office. In February 1963 he submitted a modest civil rights bill to Congress asking mainly for legislation to broaden the existing laws to protect blacks' voting rights. Civil rights leaders were unimpressed and stepped up action to put greater pressure on the federal government. The result was a national domestic crisis in which demonstrations and boycotts spread to the entire country, North and South. By the end of the year, demonstrations had taken place in 800 cities and towns. In the aftermath of one of the most dramatic of these confrontations—in which Birmingham's Commissioner of Public Safety, Bull Connor, employed dogs, clubs, and fire hoses to quell a nonviolent demonstration against the city's segregation policies—Kennedy finally acted. On June 11 he delivered the most memorable speech of his presidency, placing his administration squarely on the side of the civil rights forces. He concluded his televised address with an emotion-filled plea:

> We are confronted primarily with a moral issue. It is as old as the scriptures and is as clear as the American Constitution. . . . If an American, because his skin is dark, cannot eat lunch in a restaurant open to the public, if he cannot send his children to the best public school available, if he cannot vote for the public officials who represent him, if, in short, he cannot enjoy the full and free life which all of us want, then who among us would be content to have the color of his skin changed and stand in his place? Who among us would then be content with the counsels of patience and delay? . . .
>
> Are we to say to the world, and much more importantly, to each other that this is a land of the free except for Negroes; that we have no second-class citizens except Negroes; that we have no class or caste system, no ghettos, no master race except with respect to Negroes? (Kennedy 1964, 469–70)

On June 19, Kennedy sent a comprehensive civil rights bill to Congress, following through on his nationwide address. In it, he asked for legislation to guarantee blacks access to public accommodations, allow the national government to file suit to desegregate schools, allow federal programs to be cut off in any area that practiced discrimination, strengthen then existing machinery to prevent employment discrimination by government contractors, and establish a community relations service to help local communities resolve racial disputes. Here, at last, were the legislative proposals that civil rights advocates had demanded and expected since Kennedy's inauguration.

But it was one thing to propose such far-reaching legislation, and it was quite another for it to become the law of the land. For this to happen the proposals would have to work their way through that mine field known as the United States Congress. All the major civil rights groups believed that massive public pressure would be necessary in order to force Congress to enact the administration's civil rights bill. In this situation, the March on Washington planned by A. Phillip Randolph, president of the Negro American Labor Council, to protest the treatment of black citizens took on a larger meaning. Although Kennedy initially tried to persuade the civil rights leaders to call off the March, arguing that it might lead to violence and undermine public support for the bill, he reluctantly supported the action. The March on Washington was a resounding success in bringing together the diverse elements of the civil rights movement and demonstrating the extent to which racial issues had touched the moral soul of the nation. Whether it improved the bill's chances of getting through Congress was more difficult to determine. Administration strategists decided that the bill should first be passed in the House before coming to the full Senate and facing an expected filibuster. The House Judiciary Subcommittee initially agreed on a bill that went well beyond the scope of the administration's proposal, especially in the areas of public accommodations and the greatly expanded powers of the Justice Department to file suits in civil rights cases. The administration opposed the stronger bill, believing it would not command the necessary Republican votes to pass the full House. A compromise bill, stronger than the administration's original proposal but milder than the judiciary subcommittee's initial draft, was approved by the full House Judiciary Committee on October 29, 1963.

Within a month Kennedy was assassinated, and Vice-President Lyndon Johnson had assumed the presidency. Johnson's record on civil rights was mixed. When he ran for Senate in 1948, he made clear his opposition to civil rights in racially conservative Texas by declaring:

> The civil rights program is a farce and a sham—an effort to set up a police state in the guise of liberty. I am opposed to that program. I have voted against the so-called poll tax repeal bill; the poll taxes should be repealed by those states which enacted them. I have voted against the so-called anti-lynching bill; the state can, and does, enforce the law against murder. I have voted against the FEPC; if a man can tell you whom you must hire, he can tell you whom you can't hire. (Miller 1980, 118)

But Johnson's position on civil rights had moderated considerably by the time he became Senate majority leader. In fact, his moderate, compromising approach to civil rights together with his ability to deal with Republicans, liberal Democrats, and southern Democrats allowed him to play a pivotal role in the passage of the 1957 and 1960 civil rights acts. But his compromising stance raised questions in the minds of liberal Democrats concerning the extent of his personal commitment to civil rights. Would he now, as president, seek a compromise on the pending civil rights bill, trading its stronger features for possible southern Democratic support? As civil rights friends and foes were soon to learn, President Johnson would show no signs of hesitation; he quickly grasped the mantle of civil rights leadership.

"We have talked long enough in this country about equal rights," said Johnson in his first address to Congress on November 27. "We have talked for one hundred years or more. It is time now to write the next chapter, and to write it in the books of law" (Johnson 1965, 9). Johnson made it clear that enactment of the civil rights bill would be a top legislative priority, representing a living memorial to the slain president: "No memorial oration or eulogy could more eloquently honor President Kennedy's memory than the earliest possible passage of this bill for which we fought so long."

Having publicly committed himself to the pending civil rights legislation, Johnson was now determined to see it enacted into law. Using the full powers of the presidency and his own legendary political skills, he pressed Congress to action. On February 10, by a margin of 290 to 130 the House passed a bipartisan civil rights bill. Democrats supported the bill 152 to 96. Their vote revealed a sharp regional split; northern Democrats voted 141 to 4 in favor of the bill while southern Democrats voted 11 to 92 in opposition. Of the 177 Republicans, 138 voted for the bill and 34, including 12 southern Republicans, against.

Attention now shifted to the Senate where the key question was not whether there existed sufficient votes for passage of the actual bill, but whether the bill would ever come to a vote. To invoke cloture to end a filibuster, a two-thirds majority was then required. Such a majority had never before been produced on civil rights legislation. But on June 10, 1964, after months of legislative maneuvering, the Senate voted 71 to 29 to cut off debate on the civil rights bill; 44 Democrats and 27 Republicans voted in favor of cloture while 23 Democrats and 6 Republicans opposed the motion. The cloture paved the way for the bill's approval on June 19 by a 73-to-27 roll-call vote.

The Civil Rights Act of 1964 was comprehensive in coverage. Its eleven sections barred discrimination in public facilities and accommodations, granted the attorney general the power to initiate suits against public schools that practiced segregation, forbade job discrimination by employers or unions, extended efforts to assure the right to vote, allowed the Justice Department to sue to desegregate state and local facilities, and provided that federal funds would be withheld from any federally funded program or activity that practiced discrimination. Speaking before a nationally televised audience at the signing of the bill, President Johnson concluded his address with the ringing assertion: "Our Constitution, the foundation of our republic, forbids it [racial discrimination]. The principles of our freedom forbid it. Morality forbids it. And the law I will sign tonight forbids it" (Johnson 1965, 108).

Passage of the Civil Rights Act of 1964 signified two major and interrelated developments in American politics. First, it demonstrated that the national government could play a major role in bringing about equal rights. The mild and largely ineffective 1957 and 1960 civil rights laws had led many to believe that opponents of civil rights were too powerful to allow the national government to exert significant influence in this area. The 1964 civil rights act proved that this was no longer the case. Passage of this legislation also revealed just how far the Democratic party had come on civil rights. The party had finally taken up the challenge issued by President Truman in 1948. Democrats had altered their historic position on this issue and become the principal defenders of black civil rights. And they had done so not only with rhetoric and proposals but also with action.

The Goldwater Response

But would the Democratic party continue to champion civil rights, and what would the political implications be if it did so? Obviously not all Democrats had embraced the cause of racial equality. Quite the contrary. The party was sharply and, it seemed at the time, irrevocably divided on this issue: northern Democrats against southern Democrats, integrationists against segregationists. The national Democratic party had now chosen to ally itself with the former groups, leaving the latter to either change their racial attitudes to accommodate this new reality or find more appropriate parties and candidates to reflect their racial views.

Into this political void marched Barry Goldwater and the modern conservative movement of the Republican party. Neither Goldwater nor the conservative movement he led had their origins in America's racial crisis. Indeed, both candidate and movement were largely unconcerned with the specific issue of racial segregation. Goldwater and his followers were motivated by their fundamental belief in conservative principles, one of which was that the national government should play only a minimalist role in domestic matters. Not only was this principle a key element of the conservative ideology, but it was also mandated by the conservative understanding of the Constitution.

Goldwater derived his position on desegregation directly from his conservative ideology. Goldwater was neither a racial bigot nor, in principle, a segregationist. "I believe," he said, "that it is both wise and just for negro children to attend the same schools as whites, and that to deny them this opportunity carries with it strong implications of inferiority" (Goldwater 1960, 38). But his conservative ideology would not allow him to support government ordered desegregation policies:

> [T]he federal Constitution does not require the States to maintain racially mixed schools. Despite the recent holding of the Supreme Court, I am firmly convinced—not only that integrated schools are not required—but that the Constitution does not permit any interference whatsoever by the federal government in the field of education. . . .

> The problem of race relations . . . is best handled by the people directly concerned. (Goldwater 1960, 35, 38)

Although Goldwater was thus neither racist nor segregationist, his racial conservatism had a powerful appeal to anti-civil rights forces that had been deserted by the national Democratic party. In Goldwater, they found a presidential candidate who was willing to let states and localities continue their segregationist policies and practices, unaffected by the intrusion of the federal government. His vote against the Civil Rights Act of 1964, one of only eight from outside the South, was fully consistent with his ideology, and it reinforced his appeal to southern whites.

Goldwater was no Republican aberration. The conservative movement he led controlled the 1964 Republican convention and dominated the platform committee. Republican Senator Hugh Scott from Pennsylvania introduced an amendment on the convention floor to strengthen the weak civil rights section of platform: increasing the enforcement authority of the Justice Department, setting specific compliance dates for desegregating school districts, guaranteeing voting rights in federal and state elections, and requiring federal commitment to ending employment discrimination. The amendment was resoundingly rejected (*Congressional Quarterly* 1983, 103–4). The platform's brief civil rights plank did call for "full implementation and faithful execution" of the 1964 Civil Rights Act but went on to state that "the elimination of any such discrimination is a matter of heart, conscience and education, as well as of equal rights under the law" (Johnson 1978, 683). Clearly, the Republican platform did not endorse racism. Nor did it call for segregation. But it embodied a racial conservatism that had great appeal to southern whites. The Republican party was to go "hunting where the ducks are"—a strategy that sent them right to the heart of Dixie.

In the ensuing election Goldwater suffered an overwhelming defeat, winning the electoral votes of only six states. But five of those states were in the Deep South, and Goldwater won each of them by large margins: 87 percent of the vote in Mississippi, 70 percent in Alabama, 59 percent in South Carolina, 57 percent in Louisiana, and 54 percent in Georgia. Republican presidential candidates had not carried these states since Reconstruction, again demonstrating the potency of Goldwater's appeal to southern white constituencies.

Although Goldwater's attraction to southern whites was impressive, his candidacy proved disastrous for the party's long-term relationship with black voters. Historically, as we have seen, blacks had had a close tie to the Republican party—a tie that had not been broken until the presidency of Franklin Roosevelt when millions of northern blacks became "Roosevelt Democrats." But the Republican party continued to be a viable alternative for black voters, often capturing a sizable if minority proportion of their votes. Approximately 40 percent of blacks had voted for Eisenhower in 1956, and about one in three voted for

Figure 16.1. **Vote for Democratic Presidential Candidates in the Black Precincts of Twenty-four Southern Cities, 1952–1972.**

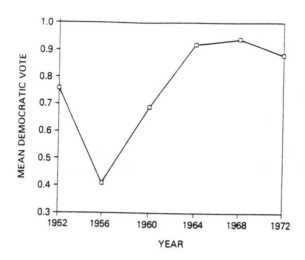

Source: Bartley and Graham (1978).

Richard Nixon in 1960. But Barry Goldwater in 1964 won the support of less than 10 percent of black voters. Blacks had gone from being solidly to overwhelmingly Democratic in casting their presidential ballots.

Figure 16.1 indicates the dramatic nature of this change. It shows the mean proportion of the vote for Democratic presidential candidates in the black precincts of the twenty-four largest southern cities from 1952 to 1972. Stevenson in 1952 and Kennedy in 1960 did well in these precincts, capturing roughly 76 and 70 percent of their votes, respectively. But Eisenhower cut deeply into the metropolitan black southern vote in 1956, winning a clear majority in these precincts. The Johnson candidacy in 1964, however, represents the fundamental break in the series. Johnson won more than 90 percent of the votes in these black precincts: that figure was slightly exceeded by Humphrey in 1968 and almost matched by McGovern in 1972.

The 1964 presidential election thus marked the decisive turning point in the political evolution of racial issues. With the nomination of Goldwater the Republican party—the party of Lincoln and emancipation—turned its back on one hundred years of racial progressivism and instead undertook a strategy designed to attract the support of racially disaffected Democrats. At least this aspect of Goldwater's electoral strategy was clearly successful, marking the end of the "solid Democratic South" in presidential elections. But this strategy also led to severing the historic ties between the Republican party and the black electorate.

Conversely, the Democratic party, historically the party of slavery and segregation, had now become the home of racial liberalism, representing the views of the desegregationist forces in the struggle over civil rights. In so doing, it had strengthened its ties to blacks and white liberals but severely strained them with southern whites. The Roosevelt Democratic coalition, which counted upon southern electoral votes, was shattered beyond recognition. Not for many years would the full effects of this election work their way through the American party system. But it was already clear, in retrospect, that the 1964 presidential election had set into motion political forces that would transform the nature of American politics.

The Post-1964 Period

Several things could have happened in the post-1964 period that would have reversed or at least halted the political transformation marked by this election. The 1964 presidential election may have been a critical moment in the partisan evolution of racial desegregation. But if the moment had not been reinforced by future developments, its effects may have been temporary and thus ultimately inconsequential. Three developments in particular seem crucial in understanding the long-term significance of the 1964 election: Johnson's actions after the election, the racial orientation of the Democratic party in the post-Johnson era, and the response of Republicans to the Goldwater candidacy.

One possible course of action for Johnson after his overwhelming victory in 1964 was to be conciliatory toward the white South—to moderate the strong stand he had taken on civil rights. Johnson, of course, did nothing of the kind. Instead he pressed for congressional action in a new area of civil rights—black voting rights. The 1964 civil rights act had touched on voting rights, but it had not challenged a system in which millions of southern black citizens were being denied this fundamental political right. The immediate impulse for the Voting Rights Act of 1965 was the march from Selma to Montgomery led by Martin Luther King, Jr., to protest racial voting discrimination. As the nation watched in horror, state troopers, acting on orders from Governor George Wallace, used tear gas, night sticks, and whips to halt the peaceful marchers. As a result of this action Johnson not only put 700 federal troops on alert to protect the marchers from further violence, but he also called on Congress to pass a far-reaching voting rights act. Speaking before the Congress in a nationally televised address on March 15, the president bluntly told his fellow southerners: "To those who seek to avoid action by their National Government in their own communities, who want to and who seek to maintain purely local control over elections, the answer is simple: open your polling places to all your people" (Johnson 1966, 287).

Within a week of this address Johnson submitted a comprehensive voting rights bill to Congress, and on August 4 Congress approved the final bill. The

Table 16.1

Proportion of Blacks Registered to Vote in Southern States, 1960–1970

	1960	1964	1970
ALABAMA	0.137	0.230	0.640
Arkansas	0.377	0.544	0.716
Florida	0.390	0.637	0.670
GEORGIA	NA	0.44	0.636
LOUISIANA	0.309	0.320	0.618
MISSISSIPPI	0.061	0.067	0.675
North Carolina	0.382	0.468	0.548
SOUTH CAROLINA	NA	0.388	0.573
Tennessee[a]	0.641	0.694	0.765
Texas[b]	0.337	0.577	0.847
Virginia	0.230	0.457	0.607

Source: Congressional Quarterly (1967; 1970).
Note: States in small capital letters cast their electoral votes for Barry Goldwater in 1964.
[a]The 1960 proportion for Tennessee is based upon data from 63 counties.
[b]The 1960 proportion for Texas is based upon data from 213 counties.

main provision of the Voting Rights Act of 1965 gave the attorney general the power to appoint federal examiners to supervise voter registration in states and localities where a literacy test was in force and where fewer than 50 percent of voting-age residents were registered or cast ballots in the 1964 presidential election. Seven states would be subject to this federally funded and directed registration process: Alabama, Alaska, Georgia, Louisiana, Mississippi, South Carolina, and Virginia.

The 1965 Voting Rights Act dramatically increased registration among blacks in southern states, as shown in Table 16.1. In Mississippi, for example, the proportion of blacks registered to vote increased from 0.067 in 1964 to 0.675 in 1970. There were similar, if less spectacular, increases in the other southern states as well. The increases were especially impressive in precisely those five deep southern states that had voted for Goldwater in 1964. There was a certain logic to this pattern, of course. These states were most angered by the racial policies of Kennedy and Johnson and found a sympathetic voice in Goldwater. These were also the states in which racial discrimination was most deeply entrenched; consequently they had the lowest levels of black voting participation prior to 1965. Given the opportunity, large numbers of blacks in these states registered to vote for probably the first time in their lives.

The Voting Rights Act also made sense from the perspective of Democratic party strategy. It was clear from the voting results in 1964 that Democratic presidential candidates could no longer count on winning the electoral votes of the Deep South. Indeed, given the scale of the defeat, the opposite seemed more likely; the party would not be able to win electoral votes in this region for the foreseeable future. One possible way to alter this outcome was to add large numbers of likely Democratic voters to the voting population, trying to offset defections among white voters—precisely the effect of the voting rights act. That this strategy ultimately did not succeed says less about the wisdom of the strategy itself than about the disdain with which white southerners now held the national Democratic party.

The Civil Rights Act of 1964 and the Voting Rights Act of 1965 had dealt with most important areas of civil rights except one: housing discrimination. In 1966 Johnson asked for legislation to ban discrimination in housing. The legislation passed the House but with a much more narrow margin than the earlier civil rights bills: 259 favored the legislation, and 157 opposed. The winning margin was provided by 183 Democrats and 76 Republicans, who were opposed by 95 Democrats and 62 Republicans. The voting pattern revealed a substantial decline in support for civil rights among Republican congressmen. Whereas the 1964 and 1965 legislation had received overwhelming support among House Republicans, the party membership was sharply split on the 1966 bill.

This bill was never enacted into law because it was subject to an intense and successful Senate filibuster. The Senate was unable to cut off debate because southern Democratic senators were joined by a large group of Republicans in opposing cloture. In 1964, forty-four Democrats and twenty-seven Republicans had voted for cloture; in 1965, forty-seven Democrats and twenty-three Republicans supported the cloture motion. But in 1966, the forty-two Democrats were joined by only twelve Republicans in voting to cut off debate while twenty-one Republicans and twenty-one Democrats opposed cloture. An almost two-to-one majority of Republican Senators opposed cloture, a sharp departure from previous years. The lack of Republican support for the Civil Rights Act of 1966 was due partly to the specific content of this legislation. Northern Republican senators and representatives, who had been willing to end segregation and voting discrimination in the South, were much less willing to end housing discrimination prevalent in the North as well as the South. But the lack of Republican support probably also reflected the growing racial conservatism of the GOP.

Johnson, however, would not be dissuaded. In 1967, he again asked for housing legislation, and again the legislation was approved by the House. On the fourth cloture vote minority leader Dirksen was able to produce just enough Republican votes to end the Senate filibuster, and the bill was subsequently passed by the Senate. On April 11, 1968, Johnson signed the bill into law. In sum, Johnson could have tread softly on racial issues after 1964 in an effort to bring white southerners back into the Democratic fold. That he chose to do just the opposite further solidified the Democratic party's relationship with blacks but strained even more the party's now extremely tenuous ties to the white South.

The Post-1964 Democratic Party

If Johnson would not be conciliatory toward the racial views of white southerners, perhaps his successors would be. As we have seen, Stevenson, in a similar situation, had made a supreme effort to rebuild relations with the white South in the post-Truman era. Perhaps Johnson's successors would do the same. But the Democratic party, having moved toward the racial left under Kennedy and Johnson, stayed there. Three of the party's post-1964 presidential candidates—Humphrey, McGovern, and Mondale—came from the programmatic liberal wing of the party. Their racial liberalism was outspoken and uncompromising. None showed the slightest inclination to retreat from Johnson's stand in support of civil rights.

Nor did the party itself retreat from racial liberalism. Instead of downplaying the racial policies of the Johnson administration, the 1968 Democratic platform spoke in glowing terms about those policies:

> The Civil Rights Act of 1964 . . . and the Voting Rights Act of 1965, all adopted under the vigorous leadership of President Johnson, are basic to America's long march toward full equality under the law. We will not permit these great gains to be chipped away by opponents or eroded by administrative neglect. (Johnson and Porter 1973, 734)

The 1972 Democratic platform, the most consistently liberal statement ever made by a major American party, contained a section on civil rights that spoke of a renewed effort to bring about greater racial equality:

> The Democratic Party in 1972 is committed to resuming the march toward equality; to enforcing the laws supporting court decisions and enacting new legal rights as necessary, to assuring every American true opportunity, to bringing about a more equal distribution of power, income and wealth and equal and uniform enforcement in all states and territories of civil rights statutes and acts. (Johnson and Porter 1973, 790)

Moreover, in one of its most controversial statements the 1972 platform offered support for busing as a means to eliminate school desegregation: " 'Transportation of students is another tool to accomplish desegregation. It must continue to be available . . . to eliminate legally imposed segregation' " (Johnson and Porter 1973, 804).

Jimmy Carter's candidacy in 1976 is especially revealing, for it confirmed the new reality of Democratic politics in the post-1964 period. Carter was a politician of the deep South. His speech, religion, and character were firmly rooted in rural southern political culture. Southerners were justly proud of him not only because he was one of their own but because he had won the Democratic presidential nomination against great odds.

But Carter was part of the new breed of southern Democratic politicians. He was a racial liberal whose political success depended upon putting together a coalition of blacks with a segment of mainly working-class white voters. He won the 1970 general election for the Georgia governorship with this coalition and there his chances for the presidency in 1976 rested. In the ensuing election, Carter carried the South but won only 46 percent of southern white votes compared to 53 percent who voted for Gerald Ford. Carter's victory margins in the South were due to the overwhelming support he received among black voters. Thus, in spite of Carter's close identification with the white South, he was unable to win a majority of the southern white vote. Carter's candidacy both confirmed the new direction of the Democratic party on issues of race and demonstrated the continuing estrangement between the Democratic party and the white South.

Our point is simple and straightforward: the post-1964 Democratic party showed not the slightest remorse concerning its past support for civil rights and indicated no hesitation about present and future support. The Democratic party had gradually but unmistakably become the home of racial liberalism.

The Post-1964 Republican Party

But if the Democratic party had turned permanently leftward on race, what about the Republican? Would it now disavow Goldwater's racial conservatism and return to its tradition of racial progressivism? Or was the move to the racial right to be lasting?

There is no simple answer to this question. Clearly, Richard Nixon and Gerald Ford were not Goldwaters; neither embraced racial conservatism to that extent. But one can say with a fair degree of certainty that Republican presidential nominees in the post-1964 period were always more conservative on racial issues than their Democratic counterparts, and often strikingly so.

It is particularly instructive to compare the Richard Nixon of 1960 with the Richard Nixon of 1968 and, especially, of 1972. As we saw, Nixon in 1960 not only ran on a racially progressive platform, but he made a major personal effort to win black votes. Nixon's candidacy in 1960, in short, was still part of the racially progressive tradition of the Republican party. But in 1968 Nixon was far more interested in appealing to southern whites than to blacks. The day before the balloting for the Republican presidential nomination Nixon met with southern delegations to assure them that he was sympathetic to their racial situation. He told them that "he would not run an administration which would 'ram anything down your throats,' that he opposed school busing, that he would appoint 'strict constitutionalists' to the Supreme Court and that he was critical of federal intervention in local school affairs" (*Congressional Quarterly* 1983, 107).

In contrast to the Democratic platform of 1968, the Republican platform made no mention of the recently-enacted civil rights statutes. Indeed, the Republican platform did not include a full section on civil rights, offering but a single phrase on the topic: " 'We pledge . . . energetic, positive leadership to enforce statutory and constitutional protections to eliminate discrimination' " (Johnson and Porter 1973, 749).

In 1968 Nixon won the presidency with only a small proportion of black votes but with a number of states from the once-solid Democratic South in his electoral column. He proceeded to pursue a course of action on racial issues that had great appeal to white southerners. During his first term, he nominated three southern conservatives to the Supreme Court, forced the liberal chairman of the Civil Rights Commission to resign, opposed the extension of the Voting Rights Act of 1965 in its original form, and directed the departments of Justice and Health, Education, and Welfare to request a federal court to postpone the desegregation of Mississippi's public schools.

In 1972, Nixon followed these steps by requesting that Congress place a moratorium on school busing orders by federal courts. The Republican platform of that year echoed Nixon's position, stating that " 'we are irrevocably opposed to busing . . . we regard it as unnecessary, counter productive and wrong' " (Johnson and Porter 1973, 862). Nixon, in sum, made a special effort to court the white South in his comeback bid in 1968 and especially in his reelection in 1972, when he pursued a visible "southern strategy." His actions as president, moreover, more than fulfilled his promise to white southerners that " 'If I'm president of the United States, I'll find a way to ease up on the federal pressures forcing school desegregation—or any other kind of desegregation' " (Murphy and Gulliver 1971, 2).

Although Nixon and later Ford were not Goldwaters in the extent of their racial conservatism, Ronald Reagan's racial views closely match those of the Arizona senator. On the one hand, Reagan, like Goldwater, is clearly no racial bigot or segregationist, declaring: "I am opposed with every fiber of my being to discrimination" (Reagan 1982–1983, 38). On the other hand, Reagan's racial views parallel Goldwater's in his assertion that the federal government should do little or nothing to bring about desegregation. He opposed the Civil Rights Act of 1964, the Voting Rights Act of 1965, and the Fair Housing Act of 1968 (Dugger 1983, 197–98).

During the Reagan administration, the federal government has put hundreds of school desegregation cases on hold, tried to weaken the Voting Rights Act, supported tax breaks for segregated schools, and molded the Civil Rights Commission, always before a bastion of racial liberalism, into an open opponent of it. In short, Reagan has been a chief apostle of contemporary racial conservatism, breathing new life into the Republicans' southern strategy. After winning the electoral votes of the southern states by very narrow margins over Carter in 1980, Reagan scored a landslide in the region against Mondale in 1984. At the same time, he received the lowest percentage of black votes of any Republican presidential candidate for which we have voting statistics and, quite likely, the lowest of any Republican candidate in American history.

Thus, political developments in the post-1964 period tended to reaffirm the historic partisan transition that had taken place in the 1964 presidential election itself. President Johnson continued to be a strong advocate for civil rights, further aligning the Democratic party with the cause of racial equality. The Democratic nominees who succeeded Johnson, moreover, kept the party on the racial left by adopting tough pro–civil rights stands on a variety of racial issues. The Republican party, by contrast, having moved to the racial right in 1964, more or less stayed there after 1964. Republican party elites learned at least one crucial lesson from Goldwater's 1964 candidacy: there are millions of southern white votes to be won by positioning the party to the right of the opposition.

A More Systematic Look at the Party Platforms

We have traced to this point the changing responses of the Democratic and Republican parties to racial concerns by examining the rhetoric and actions of presidents and presidential candidates since FDR. In this effort, we have quoted liberally from the racial statements found in party platforms. We turn now to content analyses of these same platform materials. Quantitative indices from content analysis speak crudely to be sure, but they limit subjectivity, the analyst's ability to find what fulfills preconception and then quote it selectively. Figures 16.2 and 16.3, differing from one another in measurement strategy, report the results of this more systematic analysis of the racial content of the platforms.

One simple measure of the importance of a topic is the space devoted to it. In Figure 16.2 we examine in the Democratic and Republican platforms from 1932 to 1980 the number of paragraphs that focus on racial concerns. The figure indicates the emphasis given to race by the two parties during this period, which, in general, is very little for both parties before 1960 and a great deal after that. That comes as no surprise, although it is worth noting that the surge in party attention to race, indeed its high point, comes in 1960, before the civil rights revolution of the early 1960s. Of more interest are the interparty differences. Before 1960, with the notable exception of 1948, Republican platforms always gave at least as much, and usually considerably more, attention to racial concerns than Democratic platforms. This pattern changed abruptly and permanently in 1964; after that Democratic platforms uniformly accorded more importance to racial issues than their Republican counterparts.

A second measure of the subtle concept "importance" is where, in the list of competitors for attention, an item gets mentioned. We assume that position in the program is an indicator, albeit a crude one, of relative priority among issue domains. We define a "priority index" as 1.0 minus the number of the paragraph

Figure 16.2. **Number of Paragraphs on Race in Party Platforms, 1932–1980.**

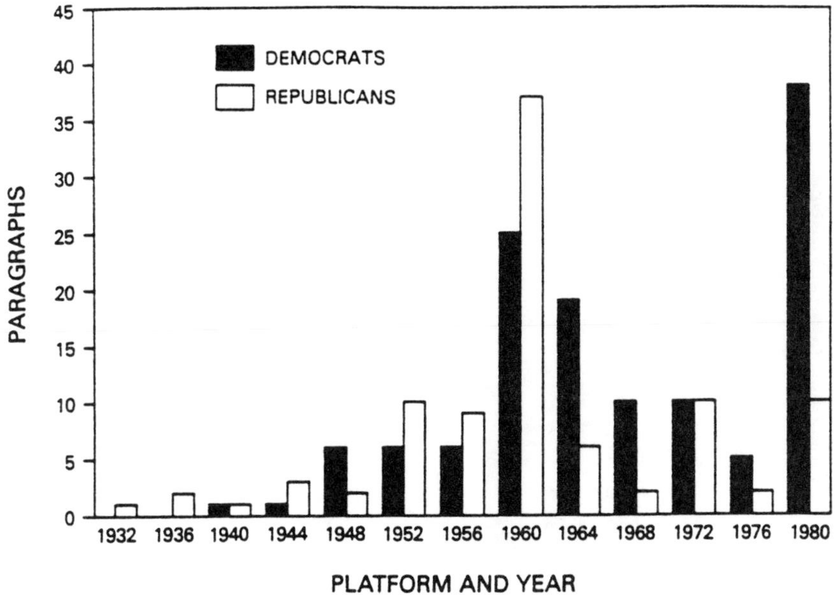

PLATFORM AND YEAR

Source: Computed by the authors from Johnson (1978, 1982) and Johnson and Porter (1973).

containing the first discussion of racial policy (i.e., the number of paragraphs in the platform preceding the first race paragraph) divided by the total number of paragraphs in the platform. Thus, the index is at its maximum value when race is at the very beginning of the program and declines to smaller values as it moves toward the end. If the issue is not mentioned at all, we give the index a zero.

Looking at the priority index of race in the Democratic platforms in Figure 16.3, one sees a clear and obvious pattern. Before 1964 racial concerns were positioned at the end of the party platforms. Beginning in 1964 and continuing through 1980 issues of race moved to the forefront. Racial issues, in other words, were given a great deal more emphasis in Democratic platforms beginning in 1964.

Comparing the relative position of race in the Democratic and Republican platforms, one can see that prior to 1964 Republicans gave relatively more emphasis to racial concerns. In each of the eight platforms 1932 to 1960, race is placed consistently more toward the end of Democratic platforms than Republican. Again this pattern changes dramatically and permanently beginning in 1964. Although the post-1960 Republican party gives relatively more emphasis

Figure 16.3. **Racial Priority Index of Party Platforms, 1932–1980.**

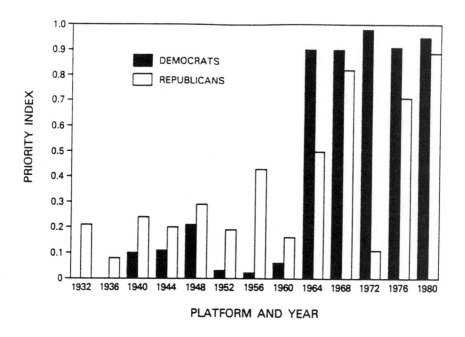

Source: Computed by the authors from Johnson (1978, 1982) and Johnson and Porter (1973).

to race than the pre-1960 Republican party, it always places race in a secondary position to the post-1960 Democratic party. That is, in 1964 and in each succeeding year, Democrats accord race a more prominent position in their platforms than Republicans do in theirs.

This quantitative analysis of the racial content of party platforms confirms the picture that emerged from our earlier, mainly qualitative assessment of these documents—namely, that 1964 was a critical moment in the partisan evolution of racial issues. It was critical not merely because it marked a fundamental change in the parties' response to issues of race but, more important, because the transition was permanent.

It is difficult to overestimate the significance of Barry Goldwater in this partisan transformation. Before Goldwater, the Republican party was dominated by candidates and party leaders committed to racial progressivism. The party's history and lack of support in the South made this a natural stance. But a party committed to progressive racial ideas and policies was not going to be able to take advantage of the growing split between the national Democrats and white southerners. In this case, racial conflict would lie outside the two-party system, leading the white South to support third-party efforts as in 1948. Goldwater's candidacy fundamentally altered the likelihood of this possibility, not because he was a racist or a segregationist but because his racial conservatism struck a responsive chord among racially disaffected southern Democrats. Goldwater showed how Republicans could develop a powerful appeal in the white South without becoming outright segregationists.

No one individual represents the transformation in the Democratic party in the way Goldwater does for the Republican party. Truman, Kennedy, Johnson—all were key figures who moved the party toward racial liberalism, as was Carter, who sustained it at a moment of possible reversal. But if the change were more protracted in the Democratic party, it was no less significant. The party altered its historic position on race, becoming the home of racial liberalism.

The American party system, in sum, was fundamentally transformed during the mid-1960s. The progressive racial tradition in the Republican party gave way to racial conservatism, and the Democratic party firmly embraced racial liberalism. These changes unleashed political forces that permanently reshaped the contours of American politics. . . .

Bibliography

Anderson, J.W. 1964. *Eisenhower, Brownell, and the Congress.* University: University of Alabama Press.

Berman, William C. 1970. *The Politics of Civil Rights in the Truman Administration.* Columbus: Ohio State University Press.

Brauer, Carl M. 1977. *John F. Kennedy and the Second Reconstruction.* New York: Columbia University Press.

Congressional Quarterly. 1983. *National Party Conventions, 1831–1980.* Washington, DC: Congressional Quarterly Press.

Dugger, Ronnie. 1983. *On Reagan.* New York: McGraw-Hill.

Duram, James C. 1981. *A Moderate Among Extremists.* Chicago: Nelson-Hall.

Freidel, Frank. 1965. *F.D.R. and the South.* Baton Rouge: Louisiana State University Press.

Goldwater, Barry. 1960. *The Conscience of a Conservative.* New York: Hillman Books.

Johnson, Donald Bruce, and Kirk H. Porter. 1973. *National Party Platforms, 1840–1972.* Champaign: University of Illinois Press.

Kirby, John B. 1980. *Black Americans in the Roosevelt Era.* Knoxville: University of Tennessee Press.

Martin, John Frederick. 1979. *Civil Rights and the Crisis of Liberalism.* New York: St. Martin's Press.

McCoy, Donald R., and Richard T. Ruetten. 1973. *Quest and Response.* Lawrence: University Press of Kansas.

Miller, Merle. 1980. *Lyndon.* New York: C.P. Putnam's Sons.

Morgan, Rush P. 1970. *The President and Civil Rights.* New York: St. Martin's Press.

Murphy, Reg, and Hal Gulliver. 1971. *Southern Strategy.* New York: Charles Scribner's Sons.

Oakes, Stephen B. 1982. *Let the Trumpet Sound.* New York: Harper and Row.
Pritchett, C. Herman. 1984. *Constitutional Civil Liberties.* Englewood Cliffs, New Jersey: Prentice-Hall.
Rubin, Richard L. 1976. *Party Dynamics.* New York: Oxford University Press.
Sitkoff, Harvard. 1971. "Harry Truman and the Election of 1948: The Coming of Age of Civil Rights in American Politics." *Journal of Southern History* 37: 597–616.
Stampp, Kenneth M. 1965. *The Era of Reconstruction.* New York: Random House.
Stevenson, Adlai E. 1953. *Major Campaign Speeches of Adlai E. Stevenson, 1952.* New York: Random House.

17

The Reagan Attack
on Race Liberalism

Thomas Byrne Edsall with Mary D. Edsall

Traditional Democratic liberalism reached a political nadir in the election of 1984. For the first time in twenty years, the leadership of core Democratic party constituencies—from organized labor to feminists, from old-line city clubs to reform liberals, along with much of the black leadership—coalesced behind the nomination of one candidate, Walter F. Mondale. The intention and the fundamental strategy of these core constituencies was to restore the Democratic coalition, to capitalize on the recession of 1981–82, and to revive Republican liability as the party of Herbert Hoover and of the Great Depression. When the ballots were counted on November 6, 1984, however, it was Mondale, the Democratic standard bearer, who replicated Hoover's performance—losing the majority-party vote to Reagan by exactly the same margin that Hoover lost to Franklin Delano Roosevelt in 1932, 59.2 percent to 40.8 percent.[1]

The 1984 election marked a major shift in the movement toward the Republican party in presidential elections. From 1968 to 1980, the white South had been the driving force in the realignment of presidential politics, the leading indicator of a national trend. In 1984, the precincts in white, working-class neighborhoods in the urban North joined the South in propelling a presidential realignment, as the eroding Democratic loyalty of these voters transformed itself from ambivalence to outright rejection. The 1984 election demonstrated that the policy

Reprinted from CHAIN REACTION, The Impact of Race, Rights, and Taxes on American Politics, by Thomas Byrne Edsall with Mary D. Edsall, by permission of W. W. Norton & Company, Inc. © 1991 by Thomas Byrne Edsall with Mary D. Edsall.

agenda developed by the Reagan administration once in office—an agenda designed to sustain the racial and economic polarization that had emerged in force in the 1980 election—had worked to nurture and enlarge the Republican presidential voting base established in 1980.

For the Democratic party, Reagan's success in expanding his support in northern, working-class white neighborhoods was a body blow. Mondale was the incarnation of the traditional New Deal Democratic party, unlike either Carter or McGovern, but his candidacy produced a severe Democratic setback among precisely those constituencies to which a regular Democrat ought to appeal.

Among white blue-collar workers, once the core of the party, Democratic identification fell 15 points between the 1980 and 1984 elections, four more points than among professionals and managers; among white high school graduates, Democratic identification fell by 18 percentage points, twice the nine percentage point drop among college graduates.[2] Hostility to the Democratic party and its nominee had grown most among just those voters essential to the restoration of an economically based, biracial coalition of the center-left.

For the Republican party, the 1984 election was an opportunity to test the degree to which the conservative revolution of 1980 had become institutionalized. The election affirmed not only that the GOP had reinforced the loyalty of key elements of the new voting majority in presidential elections—through governance and through political strategy—but also that the Reagan administration and the GOP had restructured the terms of the political debate to establish a contrast debilitating to the Democratic party, a contrast that the Democratic party in some instances actively reinforced despite the damaging consequences.

At the core of this restructured debate was the adamant opposition of the Republican party to raising taxes, a stand that in both real and symbolic terms carried a much broader message: that the GOP would stand as a bulwark against, and as an adversary of, all costs imposed by the liberal agenda of race, rights, and taxes. The symbolic significance of the anti-tax message was repeatedly given specific reinforcement by the drive of Reagan loyalists, particularly those in the Justice Department, to end racial preferences, to end affirmative action, to take the government out of the business of enforcing racial integration, and to define "reverse discrimination" as the symbol of liberalism run amok.

Throughout his tenure in office, Reagan explicitly and implicitly affirmed this broad commitment to stand tall against redistributive liberalism: in his successful repopulation of the federal judiciary with ideological conservatives; in his racially conservative appointments to the Department of Justice; in his pointed efforts to force a retrenchment of the welfare and regulatory state; and in the major alteration of the federal tax code during his years in office. Even when the specifics of Reagan's policies were opposed by majorities of the electorate—his attack on environmental protection, for example, or his acceptance of a tax hike in 1982—Reagan's larger commitment to block the tide of liberalism, and the conversion of this commitment into Republican orthodoxy, prevented majority public opinion from turning against him.

More importantly, this broader commitment by both the president and the Republican party established the basis for the strengthening and servicing of the conservative, top-down majority coalition that had come to dominate presidential elections. One of the most consistent themes of the politics of the 1980s was the qualitative difference between the capacities of the Republican and Democratic parties to strengthen their bases of constituent support; to modify strategies to accommodate changing public opinion, ideology, and demography; and to develop strategies to reward the loyal and to penalize the opposition. The Republican party had an inherent advantage in this contest. Rising international economic competition undermined the ability of the Democratic party to service such constituencies as labor and blacks through traditional protective programs—mandatory union-scale wages on federal contracts, and affirmative action hiring, for example—programs that worked best when competition was limited by national borders.

Continued suburbanization, in turn, strengthened natural Republican voting bases, while the share of the national vote cast in Democratic urban strongholds declined. Throughout these transitions, the huge resource advantage of the GOP in terms of money, poll data, consultants, computerized voter lists, phone banks, etc.—particularly in the new technology of politics—provided information and material essential to the fine-tuned tactical and strategic adjustments necessary to staying ahead of the opposition.

In the aftermath of the Democratic defeat in 1984, Reagan received much of the credit for producing the radical shift of voter allegiance reflected in the 1984 outcome. In fact, while Reagan's role was indisputably critical, he was more a principal agent within—rather than the prime mover of—a sea change involving forces substantially more profound and extensive than the fortunes of the two political parties or of their candidates. To see Ronald Reagan as the cause of an ascendant conservatism minimizes the significance and consequence of large-scale social and economic transformations—developments beyond the power of any single political player to determine. Major elements of this sea change include the following:

- For many white voters who had experienced severe hardship in the economic upheaval of the prior decade, and who had also been on the front lines of racial conflict, the Democratic Party in 1984 virtually lost its voice. For these voters, particularly in and surrounding major northern cities, Democratic party messages began to be read and interpreted through a "racial filter"—a filter changing the meaning of traditional Democratic messages and destroying their effectiveness. "Working class voters were persuaded that if you hitched your wagon to the poor, every time the poor moved up a rung on the ladder, they are going to take you down a rung. If you hitched your wagon to the rich, every time they move up a rung, they'll take you up a step. It was a sea change in American politics," contended Mondale campaign manager Bob Beckel, looking back on the 1984 race.[3] Among these voters, Reagan administration policies restricting the scope of affirmative action, busing, and other civil rights remedies; the concerted administration drive to reconstruct a once-liberal judiciary; the consistent administration effort to cut back the means-tested programs of the welfare state; and the encompassing Republican anti-tax stand, all worked as powerful coalition-building tools to produce higher Republican voting margins in 1984 than in 1980.

- The power of the Democratic party to revive the Herbert Hoover-Great Depression image of the GOP—as the party of the rich and of an unraveling economy—was eclipsed in 1984 when many voters perceived the collapse of key sectors of American industry as rooted in the Democratic administration of Jimmy Carter. This collapse had become visible for the first time to the public during the late 1970s, at a time when Democrats were in full control of Congress, and when organized labor was dominant in both the steel and auto industries. For crucial groups within the industrial working class, the period from 1978 through 1982 represented a second Great Depression, a depression whose inception was associated not with Republicanism, but with Democratic party rule, and with a period of trade union hegemony. For ranks of workers in heavy industry, the 1981–82 recession was not a discrete event tied to the Reagan administration, but a continuation of the industrial decline begun under Carter. For the Republican party and the Reagan administration, the success in assigning responsibility for the economic deterioration of 1978–1982 to a history of misguided Democratic policy decisions represented a major ideological victory, strengthening public—and elite—receptivity to the conservative argument for restricting and reshaping domestic interventions by the federal government.

- The divergence in the underlying values and images associated with the two parties—a divergence driven by the agenda of race, rights, and taxes—reached new heights in 1984. For the GOP, religiosity (measured by church attendance) took its place, by 1984, within a loose alliance of other conservative or "traditional" values, now increasingly clustered on the right and claimed by the Republican party: belief in hard work, in the nuclear family, in self-reliance, in personal restraint, in thrift, foresight, and self-denial; belief in doctrines of individual responsibility, in obedience to the law, in delayed gratification, in respect for authority, and in a more repressive (or less self-expressive) sexual morality. This fusion of values, beliefs, reactions, and commitments—increasingly perceived by key segments of the white electorate to be more persuasively upheld by the party of the right—served, in turn, to strengthen the powerful advantage of the Reagan campaign in television-spot dominated campaigning—a form of campaigning far more amenable to the triggering of submerged values and fears than to the presentation of substantive issues or policy positions.

- Conversely, the identification of the Democratic party with previously subordinate groups—groups making new claims and demands on the majority for rights, for authority, for status, for centrality, for political power, and for money—intensified in 1984. This identification strengthened the perception of the Democrats, by crucial numbers of voters within the white electorate, as the party of victims, of redistribution to victims, and of a public ethos skirting the issues of individual responsibility, fiscal discipline, and social obligation. The accumulated history of Democratic ties to the rights revolution—particularly as amplified and exploited by the campaign messages of the GOP in 1984 (and in 1988)—produced a linkage in public perceptions between the national Democratic party (whose most famous spokesman was now Jesse Jackson) and such benefit-hungry groups as welfare recipients, feminists, black militants, illegal immigrants, gays, addicts seeking drug treatment, AIDS victims, and members of the underclass. The word "groups" in GOP hands would soon come to connote just these constituencies.

The complex of connections between the national Democrats and these newer entrants to the competition for public resources severely restricted the competitive ability of the Democratic party and of its presidential nominee in the mainstream "values marketplace" of politics.

- Benefiting from demographic and ideological trends—and from access to a huge reservoir of financial support—the presidential wing of the Republican party in 1984 in addition moved a quantum jump ahead of the Democratic party in terms of its mastery over the technology, over the nuts-and-bolts tactics, and over the broader strategy of national elections. Vast quantities of Republican cash financed the maintenance of a semipermanent cadre of campaign specialists who were either employed by the three major Republican committees or served as consultants to them. These specialists became, in turn, increasingly adept in the control and manipulation of a tri-level strategy for victory: the "air war" on television; the "ground war" of high-tech direct mail, phone banks, polls, focus groups, and computerized voter lists; and the effective political use of government policy itself to build election-day majorities. The careful separation of the air and ground wars permitted the Reagan campaign to conduct an essentially centrist campaign on television, while using the far less visible tactics of the ground war to mobilize support among groups with more divisive, and potentially threatening, agendas—including fundamentalist Christians and anti-abortion activists.

This ability to keep some constituencies off of center stage was in sharp contrast to the Democrats, whose negotiations, jousting, and mobilization of minorities, peace activists, feminist organizations, homosexual-rights groups, and a host of other controversial interests were generally conducted in full public view, often on the evening news. In the arena of government policy itself, the Reagan administration was committed to stressing, consistently and visibly throughout its first term, adamant opposition to Democratic-endorsed racial preferences, quotas, goals, and timetables. The repeated raising of the issue of affirmative action—and the high profile of the Reagan Justice Department in this effort—gave added power to Reagan's campaign theme in white, working-class neighborhoods and in the South, a theme captured by the slogan aired repeatedly throughout the 1984 campaign: "You haven't left the Democratic Party, the Democratic Party left you."

The isolation of the national Democratic party during the 1984 campaign was dramatically reflected in the ease with which the Reagan team and the Republican party were able to polarize the electorate along racial and economic lines through simple assertions of "middle-class values and goals." The political success of such Republican assertions signaled that the public perceptions of the two parties had become dangerous to Democratic ambitions. For a crucial segment of the white electorate, to be middle class, to hold traditional values, to endorse work, family, responsibility, achievement and the like, meant not supporting the presidential wing of the Democratic party.

The insularity of the national Democratic party—its ignorance of the power and potential for conservative exploitation of the "values" issue—grew out of the coexistence of its liberalism and idealism with its distance from the concerns of pivotal numbers of working and middle-class white voters. These pivotal voters felt that public resources once securely within their own province were being rapidly diluted, stretched, and redirected—redistributed to people often unfamiliar, "different," and often sharply critical of or dissident from majority values. This Democratic insularity provided a point of attack for the 1984 Reagan campaign. Among the principal Republican strategic responses to Democratic vulnerability was the initiation of a major extension of the language of politics—the enlargement of a television language empowering the Republican party and its candidate to reach voters through a set of majoritarian "values-oriented" images and phrases that, for key segments of the electorate, set the GOP apart from the Democratic party. This television language was most fully expressed in 1984 in the series of campaign commercials collectively known by the phrase from one of them, "It's morning again in America."

Two sets of forces combined to provide the Republican party with the opportunity to dominate the values marketplace, the first of which were the schisms within the Democratic coalition. The second was the adoption by the GOP of a comprehensive, resilient ideology focused on conservative egalitarianism, an ideology revolving around "equal opportunity" rather than "equal outcomes";

around the idea that market mechanisms functioned most effectively to allocate scarce resources; and around the linkage of merit and status, and of reward and effort. It was an ideology that used opposition to federal tax burdens to unite the rich and the working class, as opposed to the use of federal spending to unite the poor with the middle class, an ideology purged of overt bias, tinged—in the wake of twenty years of unprecedented social change—with nostalgia, and with an implicit but stern admonition to life's losers.

"You persuade by reason, but you motivate people by tapping into values that run much deeper," said Richard Wirthlin, Reagan's pollster, in discussing the strategy underpinning both the conduct of the 1984 election and the conduct of the Reagan presidency: "[You] measure attitudes toward the issues and attitudes toward the candidate, but go beyond that and see if those could be linked in any reasonable rational fashion to people's values. And again it's in this higher level of values and emotions that you really do understand what things are driving behavior."[4] This appeal to values and emotions was conducted both in the campaign, through superficially "inclusive" messages, and through governance, where policy and programs helped to polarize the electorate by race and by class.

At the core of the 1984 campaign strategy was the recognition that televised images—Reagan filmed at the Daytona 500, surrounded by bleachers of white working-class southerners; Reagan, beer in hand, among the working-class regulars in a Boston bar—could now be used to project the values Republicans were successfully appropriating. These painstakingly staged television events, in combination with phrases carefully tested in focus groups for voter resonance—"ours is a chosen land," "a triumph of hope and faith," "a celebration of the new patriotism"—were used to focus viewer/voter attention on a value-laden conception of both conservatism and of the Republican party. This conception was designed to contrast sharply with a Democratic party painted as estranged from the mainstream; a party which, in Reagan's words, "sees people only as members of groups."[5]

The success of Republican strategy required not only the complicit, if unknowing, cooperation of the Democratic party and of its own liberal cadre, but, even more importantly, it depended on a genuine resonance with the voters. The Republican party by 1984 had gained a powerful internal coherence based on factors far more substantial than the manipulation of televised images. By 1984, Republican identification with "traditional values" and with the advocacy of a conservative egalitarianism had significantly increased working and middle-class support for a party already closely associated by many voters with the so-called "Protestant ethic."

The 1984 election marked the solidification of a parallel trend functioning to the advantage of the GOP: the voting patterns of the religious and the nonreligious. Religiosity (defined in terms of regular church attendance) became by the mid-eighties an identifying characteristic of white voters who aligned themselves with the Republican party. Among Catholics, union members, southerners, and white northern Protestants, regular churchgoers in 1984 were 11 percentage points more Republican than Democratic, while those who never attended church were 8 points more Democratic.[6] In a parallel finding, when voters in 1984 were asked about the degree of their belief in the authenticity of the Bible, the only group of those surveyed who said they intended to cast a majority of their votes for Mondale, 55–45, were those who agreed that the Bible "was written by men who lived so long ago that it is worth very little today." Mondale lost by a slim, 49–51, margin among those who agreed that the Bible "is a good book because it was written by wise men, but God has nothing to do with it," and he was crushed, 40–60, among those who believed either that the Bible "is God's word and all it says is true," or that the Bible was "inspired by God but it contains some human errors."[7]

Republican dominion over the terrain where religious conviction, the work ethic, backlash over social reform, conservative egalitarianism, anti-black feeling, and racial conservatism met, gave the GOP, by 1984, a decisive advantage in the competition over values, providing access to both a general election majority and to those specific groups of white voters most directly affected by conflicts over race. This complex interaction is best reflected in the contrast between the central public themes of the 1984 Reagan campaign on the one hand, and the actual perception of the content of the political conflict by key segments of the electorate on the other. While the 1984 campaign ostensibly portrayed competition between Democratic and Republican agendas and values in race-neutral terms, in actuality, urban, working-class whites saw (or read) those same partisan divisions as structuring a race-freighted competition for the "direction of the country," as well as for increasingly contested diminishing national resources. In a sense, *explicitly* accessing or tapping voter convictions and anxieties about values and economic status allowed *implicit* access to anxieties and resentments about race.

Reagan campaign strategists sought to define the choice in 1984 as between two alternative visions of America, one Republican, the other Democratic. In a heavily used 1984 commercial—devoid of explicit racial content, but with strong implicit messages about "the kind of country" Democrats were responsible for—pictures of rusting farm and factory equipment, and a shot of an elderly woman walking bent with a cane, alone are first shown with a Reagan voice over:

> This was America in 1980. A nation that wasn't working. Huge government spending gave us the worst inflation in 65 years, interest rates were at an all-time high. The elderly were being forced out of their homes. People were losing faith in the American dream.

The picture then changes to scenes of farmers loading seed, an arc welder at work in a machine plant, autoworkers entering a factory gate, and a family bringing home a newly purchased living room rug, with Reagan's voice now extolling a restored America:

So we rolled up our sleeves and showed that by working together there is nothing Americans can't do. Today, inflation is down and interest rates are down. We've created six and a half million new jobs. Americans are working again. So is America. If the dream that built America is to be preserved, then we must not waste the genius of one mind, the strength of one body or the spirit of one soul. Now it's all coming together. With our beloved nation at peace, we are in the midst of a springtime of hope for America.

The Reagan television spot was notable not only for the utter absence of bias, but for its conflation of an idealized, homogeneous Republican "hometown" with an evocation of economic success—reminding voters of what was arguably the most important dimension to them of the first Reagan administration: that the country had entered the second year of a substantial economic recovery after experiencing the most severe recession since the 1930s. Simultaneously, the portrayal in the T.V. spot of two visions of America, one Democratic, the other Republican, reinforced a far more conflict-ridden perception of America held by key swing voters.

The central battleground in 1984 was in fact for the support of besieged members of the most vulnerable sector of what remained of the New Deal coalition, the white working and lower-middle class. Not quite the balance of power, these voters were, rather, at the fulcrum of power: not only were their votes important numerically, but they were essential to the ideological coherence of each party. For the Democratic party, their support was critical to the maintenance of an economically based coalition made up of majorities of voters at or below the median income. For the Republican party, these voters were essential to the strengthening of the doctrine of conservative egalitarianism that had become the hallmark of the GOP.

Macomb County, for example, is a largely white, working-class suburb on the northeast border of Detroit, a bastion of United Auto Workers and assembly-line retirees, one of the constituencies that had absorbed the brunt of the collapse of the auto industry in the late 1970s and early 1980s. Before the civil rights revolution moved north, this county had been bedrock for the Democratic party. In 1960, Macomb County voters cast one of the highest margins of any major suburban county for the Democratic candidacy of John F. Kennedy, 63 to 37 percent. Even in the midst of the civil rights and anti-war battles of 1968, Macomb County voters cast a solid 55 percent of their votes for the Democratic nominee, Hubert Humphrey, compared to just 30 percent for Nixon, and 14 percent for Wallace. Democratic allegiance was severely eroded in the early 1970s, not only by the conversion of Detroit to a black-majority city, but also by the threat of forced busing between Macomb County and Detroit, a proposal rejected by the Supreme Court in 1974, but one that significantly altered established voting patterns. In 1976, Gerald Ford, a Michigan native son, carried the county by a 52–48 margin; four years later, Reagan beat Carter countywide by a 56–44 margin.

In 1984, however, the bottom fell out for the Democratic party in Macomb county. In a working-class area hard-hit by the recession, in neighborhoods with a deep tradition of union loyalty, Mondale, a labor stalwart, lost to Reagan by a margin of 67–33, precisely reversing Kennedy's 1960 victory over Nixon. Even worse for the Democrats, the GOP picked up half of the county's state legislative seats. The outflow of Democratic defectors, which had accelerated in 1980, became, by 1984, a flood—not only in Macomb County, but in similar areas across the country, areas like Southwest Chicago; Parma, Ohio, outside of Cleveland; and Northeast Philadelphia, where precincts that twenty years earlier had yielded decisive Democratic majorities, voted for Reagan over Mondale in 1984 by 2–1 margins.

The Michigan Democratic party, facing the prospect of losing its base not only in Macomb County but in all of the state's white, working-class suburbs, financed a study of Democratic defectors in the county. The study, conducted by a major Democratic polling firm, was based on five separate focus-group sessions in early 1985. Stanley Greenberg, president of the Analysis Group, summarized the findings:

> These white Democratic defectors express a profound distaste for blacks, a sentiment that pervades almost everything they think about government and politics. . . . Blacks constitute the explanation for their [white defectors'] vulnerability and for almost everything that has gone wrong in their lives; not being black is what constitutes being middle class; not living with blacks is what makes a neighborhood a decent place to live. These sentiments have important implications for Democrats, as virtually all progressive symbols and themes have been redefined in racial and pejorative terms. . . . The special status of blacks is perceived by almost all of these individuals as a serious obstacle to their personal advancement. Indeed, discrimination against whites has become a well-assimilated and ready explanation for their status, vulnerability and failures. . . . Ronald Reagan's image [was] formed against this [Democratic] backdrop—disorder and weakness, passivity, and humiliation and a party that failed to speak for the average person. By contrast, Reagan represented a determined consistency and an aspiration to unity and pride.[8]

While extreme in their willingness to make their views known, the voters of Macomb County were not exceptional among the white working class. Findings parallel to those of the Analysis Group were produced by a $250,000 study commissioned by the Democratic National Committee in 1985, a nationwide poll involving 5,000 voters and thirty-three separate focus groups targeting key Democratic constituencies, including white liberals, blacks, public employees, white urban ethnics, and white southern moderates. The DNC study, conducted by CRG Communications of Washington, D.C., found that race was a divisive issue among all of these groups, but that it was most intense among the white ethnic voters (primarily Irish and Italian) and among southern Democratic moderates. These white voters, according to the CRG study, believed "the Democratic Party has not stood with them as they moved from the working to the middle class. They have a whole set of middle-class economic problems today, and their party is not helping them. Instead it is helping the blacks, Hispanics and the poor. They feel betrayed." These voters "view gays and feminists as outside the orbit of acceptable social life. These groups represent, in their view, a social underclass. . . . They feel threatened by an economic underclass that absorbs their taxes and even locks them out of the job, in the case of affirmative action. They also fear a social underclass that threatens to violate or corrupt their children. It is these underclasses that signify their present image of the Democratic Party. . . . The Democrats are the giveaway party [and] 'giveaway' means too much middle-class money going to blacks and the poor. . . ." Affluent liberals and such groups as "blacks, gays, hispanics, feminists and labor" were effectively "trad[ing] the party between themselves, leaving the 'common man' out of the picture."[9]

The attitudes among white voters found by the CRG study were diametrically opposite to the views found among a substantial majority of black voters, as expressed in other contemporary surveys. The divide between blacks and whites on the issue of government responsibility to provide jobs and a decent standard of living remained huge in 1984, with a massive 58-percentage point spread between black support for government intervention and white opposition to such intervention.[10] In response to a related question—whether government should provide fewer services, even in health and education, in order to cut spending, or whether government should provide more services—whites were effectively split down the middle, while blacks were in favor of expanded services by better than a two to one margin, 69–31.[11]

"The issues that concern working-class minorities comprise the traditional 'fairness' agenda of jobs, housing, welfare, and education. They want more benefits for themselves and their children," the CRG voter study found. These working-class minority voters "*strongly assert the validity of the 'fairness' theme* [emphasis added]. They believe that they are entitled to certain governmental benefits and view the diminishment of those benefits as a betrayal of a trust." For the white voters of Macomb County, in contrast, the Analysis Group found that "*conventional Democratic themes, like opportunity and fairness, are now invested with all the cynicism and racism* that has come to characterize these sessions [emphasis added]. In effect, the themes and Party symbols have been robbed of any meaning for these Democratic defectors. On hearing the term 'fairness,' these voters recall, on the one hand, 'racial minorities' or 'some blacks kicking up a storm,' and on the other hand, 'only politics' or politicians who are 'lying.' It never occurred to these voters that the Democrats were referring to the middle class."[12]

In essence, the Democratic message by 1984 was viewed by one sector of the white electorate—a crucial sector in terms of presidential votes—through what might be called the prism of race; traditional liberal messages were passed through a racial filter; the word "fairness" was read in racial terms, even when no explicitly racial content was intended. For the Democratic message to be heard by key numbers of white voters as favoring blacks and as preempting the rights and customary privileges of whites was fatal to the Mondale candidacy; the more so since "fairness" by the 1980s, had become a central Democratic theme. The 1980 Democratic platform declared that "In all of our economic programs, the one overriding principle *must be fairness.*"[13] Four years later the 1984 platform asserted that "A nation is only as strong as its commitment to justice as equality. Today, *a corrosive unfairness* eats at the underpinnings of our society."[14]

While the tensions between factions of the Democratic party made it possible for Reagan and for the Republican party to establish in 1984 a seemingly race-neutral political language which in fact accessed—that is, implicitly evoked—submerged racial and cultural conflict, that year's election represented the clearest signal that the voice of the national Democratic Party no longer reso-nated with a voting majority. For one segment of the old Roosevelt coalition—10 to 15 percent of the white voters, by rough estimate—the "fairness" message of the Democratic party now jarred, incongruent in the context of a harsh worldview. In this view, life was dominated by a bitter struggle for limited resources; in this view, blacks, like whites, were responsible for their own well-being. This view held that the history of legal oppression and discrimination against blacks had been remedied, and was no longer to be compensated for by government "handouts"; and that if blacks wanted the rewards of American society, they would have to compete, unaided, as whites felt they themselves did, armed only with whatever advantages or disadvantages were dealt to them at birth. For white voters who construed fairness in this manner, braced before what they regarded as a grueling social and economic competition, the Democratic party had come, in the course of twenty-five years, to represent, not their own interests, but instead, those of their adversaries.

The worldview of such white voters—voters vital to a party dependent on lower-income biracial majorities—had the effect of scrambling Democratic messages, of superimposing 'racial' interpretations on traditionally liberal economic messages. Mondale's call for a tax hike on workers earning more than the median income in order to finance a restoration of Reagan budget cuts, and Mondale's promise to revive "fairness" in the distribution of the tax burden, were not heard by these white voters in terms of a Democratic candidate seeking to improve the lot of the average white working man and woman. Instead, Mondale and the Democratic party were heard by these key voters as advocating a redistribution—*from* whites *to* the black and Hispanic poor. By the time of the 1984 presidential election, the national Demo-cratic party had lost its encompassing voice for this key constituency.

Notes

1. Richard M. Scammon and Alice V. McGillivray, *America at the Polls 2* (Washing-ton, D.C.: Congressional Quarterly, 1988), 3 and 29.

2. CBS News/New York Times exit poll data as developed by James L. Sundquist, "The 1984 Election: How Much Realignment," *The Brookings Review* (Winter 1985): 10.

3. Robert Beckel [Democratic consultant], interview with author, February 5, 1990.

4. From an interview with Richard Wirthlin by Bill Moyers, broadcast on "The Public Mind," a public affairs television program.

5. Remarks accepting the presidential nomination at the Republican National Convention in Dallas, Texas, August 23, 1984, in the official papers, *Administration of Ronald Reagan, 1984*, page 1,174.

6. Frederick T. Steeper and John R Petrocik, "New Coalitions in 1988" (Paper supplied by the authors June 1987), Figure 4.

7. Santa A. Miller and Warren E. Traugott, *American National Election Studies Data Sourcebook* (Cambridge: Harvard University Press, 1989), 325.

8. Stanley B. Greenberg, *Report on Democratic Defection* (Washington, D.C.: The Analysis Group, April 15, 1985), 13–18, 28.

9. Milton Kotler and Nelson Rosenbaum, "Strengthening the Democratic Party through Strategic Marketing: Voters and Donors" (A confidential report for the Democratic National Committee) (Washington, D.C.: CRG Research Institute, 1985).

10. Miller and Traugott, *American National Election Studies,* 181.

11. Ibid., 183.

12. Kotler and Rosenbaum, "Strengthening the Democratic Party"; Greenberg, "Report on Democratic Defection," 24–25.

13. *1980 Congressional Quarterly Almanac* (Washington, D.C.: Congressional Quarterly Inc., 1981), 91-B.

14. *1983 Congressional Quarterly Almanac* (Washington, D.C.: Congressional Quarterly Inc., 1985), 89-B.

Part VII

The Judicial System

The readings in this part consider the role of race in the American judicial system. Many advocates of racial equality have regarded the courts as the best hope for bringing about the constitutional goal of "equal protection." Federal judges have lifetime appointments, and are thus freed from political pressures.

The first reading in this part is "The Constitution, the Supreme Court, and Racism: Compromises on the Way to Democracy." William J. Daniels, professor of political science at the Rochester Institute of Technology, contends, "The Constitution has not been color blind; the justices of the Supreme Court have not been color blind; and the people of the United States have not been color blind. There is a persisting legacy of racism."

Daniels argues that "there can be no doubt" that slavery was condoned by the Founding Fathers in 1787. Article I, Section 2 of the Constitution provided that "Representatives . . . shall be apportioned among the several states . . . by adding to the whole number of Free Persons . . . three-fifths of all other Persons." This compromise meant that each free black in the North only counted for three-fifths of a person for purposes of Congressional apportionment.

Race has been at the core of several landmark Supreme Court rulings; until recently, the Court always ruled against the interests of blacks. The first major case was the *Dred Scott* decision of 1857. The Court ruled that the Missouri Compromise of 1820 (to overcome the nation's division on slavery) was not constitutional, since Congress lacked the power to "confer the rights of citizenship on them or their descendants." The Court said that Congress had no right to prevent citizens from owning a certain type of property—slaves.

In 1896, in *Plessy v Ferguson,* the Supreme Court gave judicial sanction to the "separate but equal" doctrine. The Court held that mandatory racial segregation on passenger trains was within Louisiana's police powers, and did not violate the Equal Protection Clause of the Fourteenth Amendment. The *Plessy* decision legitimated racial segregation in transportation, public education, voting, public accommodations, and employment.

In 1944, the Supreme Court struck a blow for racial equality by holding that the Southern "white primary" violated the Fifteenth Amendment. In the 1940s, victory in a Southern Democratic primary was tantamount to election, because of the weakness of the Republican Party. Southern Democratic leaders had prevented blacks from joining the party (and thus voting in the primary), on the grounds that a political party was a private association, not subject to legislative or judicial regulation. In *Smith v Allwright,* the Court rejected this reasoning.

In 1954, the Supreme Court reversed the "separate but equal" doctrine of *Plessy v Ferguson.* In *Brown v Board of Education,* the Court ruled that segregated public schools were inherently discriminatory. It ordered the school district of Topeka, Kansas, to proceed "with all deliberate speed" toward school integration. The *Brown* decision gave rise to mandatory school busing (mainly of black students to schools in white neighborhoods), a major controversy in the 1970s.

The Supreme Court issued another major race-related ruling in 1962. The Court decided in *Baker v Carr* that the state of Tennessee must reapportion its state legislature according to the principle of "one person, one vote." Tennessee had not redistricted itself since 1901, thereby allowing the state legislature to be dominated by rural interests, to the detriment of blacks in urban areas.

The Supreme Court has also ruled on affirmative action. In 1978, Allan Bakke, a white, was denied admission to the medical school at the University of California–Davis. Bakke sued, claiming that the school's policy of reserving sixteen seats (out of one hundred) for minorities was unconstitutionally discriminatory. In *University of California v Bakke,* the Court granted Bakke's appeal. However, the Court also ruled that affirmative action programs that simply took race into consideration (without requiring quotas) *were* constitutional.

After reviewing the role of race in American constitutional development, William Daniels quotes Thurgood Marshall's observation that the United States Constitution should be viewed in terms of "hopes not realized and promises not fulfilled."

The second reading in this part, "The New Supreme Court and the Politics of Racial Equality," is by Christopher E. Smith, a political scientist at the University of Akron. Smith worries that "the new Supreme Court" rejects a role for the Court in protecting and extending civil rights.

Smith argues that the Supreme Court played a proper role under Earl Warren, who was chief justice from 1953 to 1969. The "Warren Court" extended rights to criminal defendants and prisoners, required state legislatures to be apportioned under the principle of "one person, one vote," and required the nation's school districts to proceed "with all deliberate speed" toward racial desegregation. Associate Justices William Brennan and Thurgood Marshall played critical roles on the Warren Court.

Smith maintains that the retirements of Warren, Brennan, and Marshall marked a transformation from "judicial activism" to "judicial restraint." Under judicial restraint, judges should restrict themselves to determining the "original intent" of the Founding Fathers, rather than extending the principle of equal protection. Supporters of judicial restraint assert that judicially imposed remedies (such as mandatory school busing) exceed a court's legitimate authority.

Smith reviews the Reagan administration's strategies to "undo programs and policies beneficial to historically victimized political minorities," including lax enforcement of civil rights laws. He notes that the new Supreme Court (dominated by justices appointed by Presidents Reagan and Bush) has struck down minority set-asides for government contracts, increased the burden of proof on plaintiffs in employment discrimination cases, and failed to rule that racially discriminatory application of the death penalty is unconstitutional.

The third reading concerns the police as a component of the judicial system. In "Beyond the Rodney King Story: Police Conduct and Community Relations," the NAACP reports on its investigation into police brutality. This study was sparked by the beating of Rodney King by four Los Angeles police officers, which was recorded by an amateur photographer. The acquittal of the four policemen by a nearly all-white jury in suburban Simi Valley, California, incited rioting in Los Angeles from April 29 to May 3, 1992. Forty-seven people died in the riots, and property damage was estimated at $1 billion—making it the largest civil disturbance in American history. The most brutal incident in the rioting was the beating of Reginald Denny, a white truck driver, by four black youths, in full view of live television.

After hearing witnesses in six cities, the NAACP concluded, "It is impossible to study the police in this country without studying race." The report contends that racism is the central motivation of police brutality, that many police officers regard all African Americans as criminals or potential criminals, and that excessive force against blacks has become a standard part of the arrest process. Blacks are often subjected to brutal beatings, attacks by police dogs, police shootings, and verbal harassment. The report calls on police departments to increase the number of black police officers, to expand the power of civilian review boards, and to require cultural sensitivity training.

18

The Constitution, the Supreme Court, and Racism: Compromises on the Way to Democracy

William J. Daniels

The 200th birthday of the U.S. Constitution has been the occasion both for celebrating its long life and for criticizing some aspects of that long life. Professor Forrest McDonald of the University of Alabama, for example, concluded that the Constitution was the product of "America's Golden Age, the likes we shall not see again." Supreme Court Justice Thurgood Marshall was uncomfortable with the thought that bicentennial celebrations "invite a complacent belief" in the perfection of the work of the framers. Given Justice Marshall's skepticism as a point of departure, this essay uses this time of reflection to review the role of Supreme Court decisions in interpreting the Constitution on conflicts that involve race.

This republic began with support for the "peculiar institution" of slavery, and the Civil War ended that support. The matter of race, however, continues to be one of the most pressing issues on this nation's political agenda. Thurgood Marshall maintains that the Constitution was flawed and defective particularly because of the way in which slavery was handled in that document and the subsequent history of this country that flowed from this fact. However, one might argue that the framers made compromises about slavery and race that may not be apparent from a superficial reading of the Constitution.

Aristotle had written that slavery was part of a universal natural pattern:

From *National Political Science Review* 1 (1989), pp. 126–132. © 1989 by Transaction Publishers. Reprinted by permission of Transaction Publishers.

whether or not it is a just and better thing for one man to be a slave to another, or whether all slavery is contrary to nature . . . Neither theoretical discussion nor empirical observation presents any difficulty. That one should command and another obey is both necessary and expedient.

Of the nearly 400,000 blacks in the colonies in 1765, all but a handful were slaves. Clinton Rossiter notes that there was no place for blacks in the American definition about the rights of man and that the mental climate was hostile to "the assumption that the Negro was a whole man."

Nonetheless, against this theoretical and practical background, the framers did not use the terms *Negro* or *slave* in the Constitution but refer always to the *person*. Consistent with natural law, "persons" are equal by nature or by God in a self-evident sense. This usage would have allowed justices of the Supreme Court in later years to interpret in favor of full equality had they not been acting within the social context of their time.

There can be no doubt, however, that slavery was condoned by passage of the Three-Fifths Compromise. Nonetheless, Herbert Storing suggests that the support for slavery that stems from this passage, when placed in the proper context, may be ambiguous. Briefly, he contends that the compromise did not signify that slaves possessed less humanity than whites, because it was the slave holders who argued most strenuously for the counting of slaves as whole persons. Rather, it was the leaders in the free states who maintained that slaves, because they were prevented from becoming citizens, should not be counted as full persons for the purpose of representation.

Of course, the question of citizenship for blacks did eventually surface in the celebrated case of *Dred Scott v. Sanford* in 1857. The Constitution had not defined the term *citizen* but had recognized a distinction between federal and state citizenship and, by implication, assumed that federal citizenship was derived from state citizenship. The Constitution specified that the president be a natural-born citizen and that the citizens of each state be entitled to the privileges and immunities of citizens of the several states.

The political issue at the time was that few states were willing to consider the extension of the benefits of the federal courts to blacks with concomitant privileges and immunities of U.S. citizenship. Hence, the decision in *Dred Scott* did not build on the auspicious language nor grasp the natural law significance attached to the term *person* that the framers had placed in the Constitution.

Instead, Chief Justice Taney, writing for the majority of the Court, held that blacks were not and could not become citizens of the United States; they were not entitled to any privileges and immunities. Justice Taney had taken advantage of the fact that the federal government had not bestowed citizenship on free blacks when the Constitution was adopted (Dred Scott was not the descendant of a free black) and combined this fact with an acceptance of discriminatory legislation found in many states that blacks were not regarded as constituent members of the body politic when the Union was formed. Therefore, no free blacks nor slaves were citizens of the United States. Justice Taney concluded his opinion and added remarks that indicated that the social context was perhaps more influential than his legal reasoning: blacks were "beings of an inferior order, and altogether unfit to associate with the white race, either in social or political relations; and so far inferior, that they had no rights which the white man was bound to respect."

All blacks had been debilitated by *Dred Scott.* Following the inevitable Civil War, three amendments were added to the U.S. Constitution to free the black slaves, grant the freed blacks citizenship, and protect their right to vote. In addition to these constitutional provisions, Congress provided support to the struggle for civil rights for blacks by passing seven civil rights acts during the Reconstruction era. The first, passed in 1866 over the veto of President Andrew Johnson, overturned the *Dred Scott* decision by providing blacks the "full and equal benefit of all laws and proceedings . . . as is enjoyed by white citizens," especially the right to sue and be sued and to own property. The Fourteenth Amendment was intended to provide additional constitutional protection to these legislative provisions.

The next two acts, passed in 1866 and 1867, respectively made it a crime to "kidnap or carry away any other person, whether negro, mulatto, or otherwise, with the intent that such other person shall be sold or held in involuntary servitude, or held as a slave" and "to abolish and forever prohibit the System of Peonage in the Territory of New Mexico and other parts of the United States."

The fourth of the civil rights acts was known as the Enforcement Act of 1870. This act imposed criminal sanctions for those who interfered with the right of the franchise as granted in the Fifteenth Amendment. The Ku Klux Klan Act, the sixth passed by Congress in 1871, made it a crime to use "force, intimidation or threat" to deny any citizen the equal protection of the law. The final Reconstruction civil rights act was passed by Congress in 1875 and was known as the Public Accommodations Act. This act stipulated that

> all persons within the jurisdiction of the United States shall be entitled to the full and equal enjoyment of the accommodations, advantages, facilities, and privileges of inns, public conveyances on land or water, theatres, and other places of public amusement; subject only to the conditions and limitations established by law, and applicable alike to citizens of every race and color, regardless of any previous condition of servitude.

The justices of the U.S. Supreme Court began to interpret and dismantle this massive array of constitutional and statutory protections. The first interception of the Fourteenth Amendment, the *Slaughter House Cases* in 1873, produced an extremely narrow reading of one of its provisions, namely: "No state shall make or enforce any law which shall abridge the privileges or immunities of citizens of the United States."

On the surface, the case had nothing to do with the rights of blacks. The litigants were employees in several slaughterhouses who argued that they had been deprived of their privileges and immunities (jobs) because of a state contract with other slaughterhouses. The Court ruled that the amendment provision in question referred to citizenship in the United States, conferred no new privileges, immunities, or rights and merely served as a federal guarantee against state abridgement of existing rights. The Fourteenth Amendment, the Court argued, was designed to safeguard those privileges and immunities fixed by state law or those broadly articulated by the Constitution. The problem for blacks was that most of the racial burdens and disabilities they faced were under state law.

The civil rights legislation did not fare well under the review by the Supreme Court. In several cases, Sections 3, 4, 5, and 16 of the 1870 act were invalidated (*Reese*, 1876, *James*, 1903, and *Hodges*, 1906). Essentially, the Court held that: offenses created for interfering with voting rights were not limited to denial on the basis of race; the Fifteenth Amendment did not give anyone the right to vote but merely guaranteed the right to vote under state law; and also that Congress had exceeded its power when it provided penalties for state officials who denied blacks the right to vote.

The 1871 act was held to be unconstitutional in two cases (*Harris*, 1883, and *Baldwin*, 1887). The Court found that the penalties were "directed exclusively against the actions of private citizens, without reference to the laws of the state or their administration by her officials." Finally, in five cases announced as a single decision, the public accommodations section of the Civil Rights Act of 1875 was struck down by the Court. In a literal interpretation of its provisions the Court held that "individual invasion of individual rights is not the subject-matter of the amendment" and concluded that neither the Thirteenth nor the Fourteenth Amendments empowered Congress to enact legislation on private or social actions of citizens or to prohibit discrimination against blacks in privately owned public accommodations. In a review of the amendments respectively, the Court found that private discrimination did not violate the Thirteenth Amendment because an act of refusal has nothing to do with slavery or servitude. The provisions of the Fourteenth Amendment generally prohibited only state-sponsored discrimination and the "last section of the amendment invests Congress with the power to adopt appropriate legislation for correcting the effects of such prohibited state law." These findings of the Court notwithstanding, observes Lois Moreland, "it should be remembered that separation of the races in 1875 was achieved largely by voluntary, private action, not by law" (Moreland, 1970).

These rulings, which relied heavily upon the principle of federalism, had effectively prevented Congress from exercising its perceived authority to protect the rights of black persons. Interestingly, these rulings served to buttress the *Marbury* doctrine, namely that it is the province of the Court and duty of its judges to interpret the Constitution and say what the law is. Thus the decisions also served to increase the power of the Supreme Court. And, consequently, given the Court's role as interpreter of civil rights legislation, the Supreme Court became the most important institution for blacks in pursuit of civil rights in the next century.

The *Slaughter House* principle, effectively that state authorities are to recognize and protect the rights of blacks, was eroded beyond legal recognition by the time of the opinion by the Court in *Plessy v. Ferguson* in 1896. The status of black Americans was spelled out quite clearly when the equal protection clause was interpreted by the Supreme Court to mean substantial equality. The Court held that the Thirteenth Amendment was not intended to abolish distinctions based on color. Furthermore, laws that required or permitted separation of the races were valid and reasonable exercises of the police power of the state. This interpretation of the Fourteenth Amendment was also reasonable, according to the Court, because the amendment could not have, "in the nature of things," been intended to enforce "social" as distinct from "political" equality.

The actions of the Supreme Court between *Plessy* and the school desegregation cases in the area of race relations are highly visible. This is the period when organized black Americans and their associates worked to impress upon the Supreme Court the pernicious effects of the policies it had assisted in creating with its interpretations over the years. The opinion in *Brown* found the Court using "intangible factors" to strike down the tangible "separate-but-equal" doctrine and the tangible injurious effects that segregation had on public education.

Brown and related cases represented an effort by the Court to dismantle the legal framework that had supported separatism and racism. Congress again had joined the struggle by enacting several civil rights acts from 1957 through 1968. Consistent with the thrust of the earlier legislative measures, a major intent of Congress was the desire to protect and enforce the civil rights of black citizens and enhance social justice for the citizens who had suffered the ravages of racism and discrimination.

Again, the Court has been asked to interpret these measures as against the Equal Protection Clause. However, now the Court is weaving concepts of equal justice with requests based on compensatory justice. Whether litigation is based on claims of "reverse discrimination" or "benign discrimination," the key issue is whether racial neutrality will supplant racial affirmative action. The justices of the Supreme Court must sort through their social and legal philosophies and determine whether the remedial use of race is permitted by the Equal Protection Clause and, if so, whether the remedial use of race is allowable under civil rights legislation. The Supreme Court again is exercising its will regarding the Constitution and conflicts involving race.

The Constitution has not been color blind, the justices of the Supreme Court have not been color blind; and the people of the United States have not been color blind. There is a persisting legacy of racism. The disturbing historic role of the Supreme Court in this legacy warrants a special perspective when considering what might constitute acceptable and adequate remedies under the Equal

Protection Clause. Under the color of law, the justices of the Court have not been disinterested, passive instruments of objective justice who have exercised judicial review to counteract the inequities that result from the political process. Clearly, the machinations of judicial interpretation that have mirrored fears and prejudices found in the social context have contributed significantly to the present residue of unclaimed opportunities for blacks.

The Constitution is, nonetheless, a remarkable document, for we yet debate its language, original meaning, and hermeneutics of constitutional interpretation. Justice Marshall again: "[T]he true miracle was not the birth of the Constitution, but its life." And perhaps words of Langston Hughes best describe the process of the first two centuries of its existence: "Those of us engaged in racial struggle in America are like knights on horseback—the Negroes on a white horse and the white folks on a black. Sometimes the race is terrific. But the feel of the wind in your hair as you ride toward democracy is really something."

Under the "color" of law, the Constitution, of course, was flawed. But it is perfectible. We must recognize that, historically, the Supreme Court was part of the racial problem. Now for political, legal, and practical reasons it must be part of the solution. We can admire its birth, praise its spirit, and celebrate its life, particularly when compared with the constitutions of other countries. But let us observe the anniversary of the U.S. Constitution, according to Justice Marshall, with an awareness of the "hopes not realized and promises not fulfilled."

References

Books and Articles

Aristotle. 1981. *The Politics,* rev. ed. New York: Penguin.
Berns, Walter. 1987. "Do We Have a Living Constitution?" *National Forum,* pp. 29–33.
Brest, Paul. 1983. "Race Discrimination." In *The Burger Court,* Vincent Blasi, ed. New Haven: Yale University Press, pp. 113–31.
Cruse, Harold. 1987. *Plural but Equal.* New York: William Morrow and Company.
Daniels, William J. 1987. "Citizenship, Naturalization, and Citizenship," *Encyclopedia of the American Judicial System.* New York: Charles Scribners Sons.
———. "Mr. Thurgood Marshall." In *The Burger Court: Political and Judicial Profiles.* Charles Lamb and Stephen Halpern, eds. (forthcoming).
Hopkins, Vincent C. 1967. *Dred Scott's Case.* New York: Atheneum.
Hughes, Langston. (1958). "The Fun of Being Black." In *The Langston Hughes Reader.* New York: George Braziller.
Marshall, Thurgood. 1978. Concurring opinion in *University of California Regents v. Bakke,* 438 U.S. 265.
Miller, Loren. (1966). *The Petitioners.* New York: Pantheon Books.
Moreland, Lois B. 1970. *White Racism and the Law.* Columbus, OH: Charles E. Merrill, 1970.
Rossiter, Clinton. 1933. *The First American Revolution.* New York: Harcourt Brace Jovanovich.
Storing, Herbert J. 1985. *The Anti-Federalist.* Chicago: The University of Chicago Press.

———. 1977. "Slavery and the Moral Foundations of the American Republic." In *The Moral Foundations of the American Republic*. Robert H. Horowitz, ed. Charlottesville, VA: University of Virginia Press.

Taylor, Stuart, Jr. 1987. "Marshall Sounds Critical Note on Bicentennial," *New York Times*, May 7, 1ff.

Tribe, Laurence H. 1985. Chapter 14, "Dismantling the House That Racism Built: Assessing Affirmative Action." In *Constitutional Choices*. Cambridge: Harvard University Press.

Woodward, C. Vann. 1957. *The Strange Career of Jim Crow*. New York: Oxford University Press.

Legal Decisions

Baldwin v. Franks, 120 U.S. 678 (1887).
Brown v. Board of Education I, 347 U.S. 483 (1954).
Brown v. Board of Education II, 349 U.S. 294 (1955).
Civil Rights Cases, 109 U.S. 3 (1883).
De Funis v. Odegaard, 416 U.S. 312 (1973).
Dred Scott v. Sanford, 60 U.S. 393 (1857).
Firefighters v. Stotts, 81 L. Ed. 2 (1984).
Hodges v. United States, 203 U.S. 1 (1906).
James v. Bowman, 190 U.S. 127 (1903).
Marbury v. Madison, 5 U.S. 137 (1803).
Moose Lodge No. 7 v. Irvis, 407 U.S. 163 (1972).
Plessy v. Ferguson, 163 U.S. 537 (1896).
Regents of the University of California v. Bakke, 483 U.S. 265 (1978).
Slaughter House Cases, 83 U.S. 36 (1873).
Steelworkers of America v. Weber, 443 U.S. 193 (1979).
United States v. Harris, 106 U.S. 629 (1883).
United States v. Reese, 92 U.S. 214 (1876).

19

The New Supreme Court and the Politics of Racial Equality

Christopher E. Smith

During the past three decades, advocates of racial equality have regarded the United States Supreme Court as the primary governmental institution that possesses the inclination and will to effectuate the constitutional ideal of "equal protection." Leading scholars have observed that the Supreme Court "protected and expanded constitutional rights of [B]lack Americans, as well as individuals generally, against governmental authority" and "helped to place racial problems generally on both the formal and informal agendas of other political institutions."[1] The Supreme Court may lack the capacity to guarantee that its decisions advancing equality will be completely implemented. However, Supreme Court decisions facilitate and encourage political mobilization designed to pressure other branches of government to implement "equal protection" principles:

> *Brown [v. Board of Education]* and other decisions were important symbols: they declared that government support for discrimination was constitutionally unacceptable and encouraged other efforts to achieve racial equality. Once the civil rights movement became active, the Supreme Court took extraordinary steps to protect it, striking down the convictions of people arrested in demonstrations and overturning state laws intended to cripple civil rights organizations.[2]

Like other Supreme Court decisions from earlier eras, the twentieth century decisions advancing equality did not spring from the inherent meaning of the Constitution's words. The meaning of the Constitution rests in the hands of the

Reprinted with permission: *Western Journal of Black Studies,* Spring 1991, Washington State University Press.

black-robed judicial officers who are vested with the authority to determine the meaning and effect of the nation's fundamental document. As fallible human beings, these judicial officers cannot avoid having their judgments influenced by their personal attitudes, values, and policy preferences.[3] The Supreme Court played a leading role in altering the society's discriminatory practices and policies because the members of the Court from the 1950s and thereafter gave meaning to the Fourteenth Amendment's provision mandating "equal protection." The justices whose groundbreaking decisions advanced equality in American society are, for the most part, now gone from the Supreme Court. Indeed, the retirement in 1990 of Justice William Brennan, who was regarded by many observers as a primary architect of equalitarian judicial decisions,[4] clearly marked the end of an era for the Supreme Court. The composition of the Supreme Court changed during the 1980s and new orientations toward issues of equality are evident among the new justices. The recent changes in the Supreme Court's membership have changed the dynamics of institutional interactions within the American political system concerning issues of discrimination and racial equality. Although there is uncertainty about how the development of public policy will affect long-standing problems that are the legacy of America's history of discrimination, the recent developments affecting the Supreme Court give strong clues about how various political actors and government institutions will react when confronted with the reality of continued social inequality.

The changes affecting the Supreme Court and the politics of racial equality have their roots in the unhappiness expressed by political conservatives in regard to judicial decisions redressing discrimination. The initial opponents of the Supreme Court's decisions on school desegregation in the 1950s and 1960s soon found that the expression of overtly racist views placed them outside of the political mainstream which had gradually adopted the rhetoric, if not the policies, of racial equality. It became apparent, however, that any specific judicial decisions to redress discrimination generally required a shifting of costs and benefits in society and thereby led majoritarian groups to bear some burden for ensuring that previously victimized minorities shared in opportunities for education, employment, and other societal resources. Thus, political opposition to judicial decisions could be more readily generated by shifting the focus of criticism from the general principle of equality to the specific policies designed to engender equality.

Some critics of the Supreme Court's civil rights decisions may engage in thinly-veiled subterfuge by claiming that their opposition is only focused upon judicial policies and not upon the concept of equality. Klansman David Duke, who has attracted significantly electoral support among White voters in Louisiana, appears to be a prime example of this category of civil rights opponents. Most critics of the Supreme Court's decisions advancing equality genuinely view themselves as advocates of racial equality, despite their vociferous opposition to the specific policy tools, such as school desegregation, affirmative action, and antidiscrimination laws, that are designed to remedy historic inequalities. The Supreme Court itself now contains critics of previous civil rights decisions who fit this second category. Like others who oppose judicial policy making to advance equality, these justices support the concept of racial equality *in the abstract,* but they evince a limited capacity to recognize the continuing existence of racial discrimination against minorities and the need to redress such harms through practical policies.

The opposition to the Supreme Court's role as a policy leader for civil rights focused upon several issues. Conservative lawyers and legal scholars have argued that the Supreme Court has improperly failed to interpret the Constitution according to the original intent of the framers.[5] Despite the apparent legitimacy of their theoretical arguments about how the Supreme Court should interpret the Constitution, these originalists have attempted to rewrite history in order to avoid the inevitable association between their theory of constitutional interpretation and judicial outcomes that reinforce racial discrimination.[6] Other critics have argued that the Supreme Court should not initiate specific remedial policies because the elected branches of government (i.e., Congress, the President, state legislatures) possess the sole legitimate authority to formulate public policies.[7] Such arguments, however, frequently underestimate the risks posed to political minorities' rights when majoritarian interests enjoy policy preeminence: "Elected legislatures and governors' administrations are structured to register current voter preferences and organized interests' desires, and these political forces hinder officials' ability to apply the Bill of Rights' protections for individuals."[8] Other criticisms assert that the practical results of judicial policies are inferior to those of policies produced by other institutions.[9] These arguments generally undervalue the practical limitations upon effective policy formulation and implementation that affect legislatures, executive officials, and other policy makers as well as judges.[10] Because critics of the Supreme Court's civil rights role gained political power during the 1980s, there were new directions in policy development without regard for the strong counterarguments favoring judicial activity to advance "equal protection."

The Reagan administration made great efforts to alter the development and enforcement of laws to advance racial equality. Scholars have documented the myriad of strategies employed by Reagan's associates in their attempts to undo programs and policies beneficial to historically victimized political minorities. These strategies included: failure to enforce aggressively existing civil rights laws;[11] alteration of the Solicitor General's office from respected legal advocate on behalf of the United States to partisan proponent of conservative policies;[12] and advocacy of constitutional theories, such as original intent jurisprudence, which could undercut established precedents advancing equality.[13]

Despite these concerted efforts to reverse such policies as affirmative action and school desegregation, the Reagan administration did not completely succeed. Reagan's efforts paid dividends, however, in slowing and stopping societal initiatives to advance equality. According to Norman Amaker:

> Although [he was] not able to reverse the march of history, Ronald Reagan did succeed in slowing the tempo by creating a climate in which the fact and appearance of retrenchment was possible.[14]

If Reagan's influence had ended with his departure from office, advocates of civil rights could congratulate themselves on the survival of programs advancing equality in the face of eight years of powerful, concerted political opposition. The design of the American constitutional system, however, permits Reagan's influence to continue even after his retirement. Because, under Article III of the United States Constitution, federal judges serve "during good Behaviour," a President can have lingering influence over the development of constitutional law and judicial policy making through appointments to the life-tenured judiciary. The social policy objectives that Reagan could not achieve while he was in office may now come to fruition through the decisions of Supreme Court justices and other federal judges.

According to Sheldon Goldman, the leading scholar on the politics of federal judicial selection, the Reagan administration "engaged in the most systematic ideological or judicial philosophical screening of judicial candidates since the first Roosevelt administration."[15] Candidates for judgeships were screened and selected by officials within the Reagan Justice Department according to their support for the administration's conservative political agenda. If candidates did not indicate that they strongly opposed abortion, affirmative action, and other policies, they frequently were not nominated. This ideological screening has had immediate and continuing consequences for the development of law and judicial policies because of the large number of judges appointed by Reagan. Reagan appointed more than half of the federal judiciary, 377 of the 752 federal judges.[16] Reagan also appointed young judges who will remain on the bench and influence public policies for decades to come. Several empirical studies have already shown the influence of the new judges by demonstrating that Reagan appointees are significantly more conservative than Carter appointees in deciding cases affecting civil liberties and the rights of criminal defendants.[17]

Fateful quirks of history determine a President's influence over the composition of the Supreme Court. Reagan benefited greatly from the uncontrollable events which contributed to his election in 1980 and to the subsequent timing of justices' retirements. For example, Reagan's advisers were well aware that if there had been no lingering Iranian hostage crisis, he might never have won the 1980 presidential election.[18] Although no justice retired during the Carter presidency, three justices retired during the Reagan era, thus permitting him to appoint three new justices and elevate a fourth to the position of chief justice.

Civil rights and equality were not priorities for Reagan and his advisers in making appointments to the Supreme Court. In fact, they preferred justices who would reverse legal trends aimed at redressing America's legacy of discrimination against African Americans and other political minorities. This lack of concern about equality was indicated, for example, in the attempt to appoint Douglas Ginsburg to the Supreme Court. When asked on a judicial questionnaire to describe what he had done to advance equal justice under the law, Ginsburg responded that he had worked to prevent unnecessary government regulation of economic activities. As Herman Schwartz observed, "[r]acial injustice, sexism, poverty—these apparently played no role in [Ginsburg's] thinking about [equal] justice, but only the opportunity to make money without government interference."[19]

Reagan's first appointment to a Supreme Court vacancy won him accolades for placing the first woman, Sandra Day O'Connor, on the Court in 1981. Because she replaced a moderate Republican justice, Potter Stewart, O'Connor's appointment did not dramatically alter the balance of power on the Court. Although Justice O'Connor has demonstrated some sensitivity to issues of gender discrimination,[20] in racial discrimination cases she has generally joined the Nixon and Reagan appointees who have comprised the conservative bloc during her tenure on the Court. The Reagan administration's effect upon the Supreme Court increased significantly in 1986 through the appointment of Antonin Scalia to replace retiring Chief Justice Warren Burger and through the elevation of William Rehnquist to chief justice. With the appointment of Scalia, Reagan had replaced an ineffective but dependable conservative with a dynamic, articulate spokesperson for many conservative causes, including opposition to affirmative action and abortion. Justice Scalia (age 54) is likely to be a powerful voice on the Court for decades to come.[21] Moreover, the elevation of Rehnquist to chief justice placed the justice who is least likely to support recognition of individuals' constitutional rights in the position to lead the justices' discussions of cases and to assign responsibilities for writing opinions.[22]

Although the first Reagan appointments made the conservative voices on the Court more articulate, persuasive, and powerful, the balance of power on the Court was not drastically altered until 1988 when Justice Anthony Kennedy was appointed. The appointment of Kennedy created a new Reagan-influenced majority bloc, usually composed of the four Reagan appointees plus Justice Byron White, which frequently perceives (or fails to perceive) racial discrimination and other civil liberties issues in light of a conservative judicial and social philosophy. Because the conservative Justice Kennedy replaced Justice Lewis Powell, who had been the moderate architect of compromises on many issues, including the famous *Bakke* case upholding the constitutionality of affirmative action in higher education,[23] the Court moved quickly to change legal precedents affecting racial discrimination.

Cases decided by the Court since Justice Scalia's appointment in 1986 are indicative of the accelerating trends in Supreme Court jurisprudence concerning discrimination. For example, Scalia and O'Connor joined three other justices, including Rehnquist, Reagan's choice for chief justice, to demonstrate a complete absence of concern about documented racial discrimination in the application of the death penalty. Scholars utilizing the best available social science methods developed a 230-variable model to examine the application of punishment in 2,000 murder cases in Georgia during the 1970s.[24] The study demonstrated the strong effects of racial discrimination in capital sentencing. Prosecutors sought the death penalty for seventy percent of African American defendants with White victims but only nineteen percent of White defendants with African American victims. Moreover, African Americans who killed Whites were sentenced to death at nearly twenty-two times the rate of African Americans who killed other African Americans, and more than seven times the rate of Whites who killed African Americans.[25] The five-member Court majority said, in effect, "we do not care about obvious, aggregate racial disparities unless you can demonstrate clear discrimination in a particular case." Despite the pervasiveness of subtle discrimination and its attendant harmful effects,[26] the emerging majority on the Court served notice that it would only recognize discrimination as unlawful if it resulted from clearly intentional discriminatory actions—a difficult burden for most victims of discrimination to prove.

Prior to appointment to the federal bench, Justice Scalia demonstrated his vigorous opposition to the concept of affirmative action in his legal writings. In one article, Scalia personalized the affirmative action debate by asserting that his immigrant father and other ethnic Whites were the ultimate victims of affirmative action although they "took no part in, and derived no profit from, the major historic suppression of the currently acknowledged minority groups."[27] He subsequently conceded that "in relatively recent years some or all of these groups have been the beneficiaries of discrimination against blacks, or have themselves practiced discrimination,"[28] but he claimed that they should not bear the burden for remedying discrimination because other Whites have been the most significant oppressors. As legal commentators have noted, Scalia pursues an abstract theory of equal rights that is removed from the realities of history and context.[29] Scalia apparently does not want the remedies for America's history of discrimination to be borne by anyone unless it is proven that they personally and intentionally committed acts of discrimination. Scalia erroneously presumes that without affirmative action, employment decisions would be based upon some idealized conception of merit criteria despite the inherent subjectivity in developing and applying most criteria and despite the role of familial, social, and political connections in maintaining Whites' hegemony over most sectors of the employment market. In refusing to recognize the continuing harms of the legacy of discrimination and in declining to distribute the remedial burden throughout society, Scalia ignores where the burden of the past will fall, or rather continue to fall, if no remedial efforts are undertaken—namely, upon African Americans, women, and other political minorities who have always borne the burden of discrimination.

The addition of Justice Kennedy in 1988 to the Supreme Court's conservative bloc led to changes in the Court's opinions on employment discrimination and affirmative action. The 1988–1989 Supreme Court term generated a wave of decisions altering established precedents as the emerging Reagan-influenced majority asserted its views. The new Court majority undercut local governments' efforts to increase participation of minority-owned businesses in government contracts and public works programs. In 1980 the Supreme Court had approved a federal program reserving ten percent of government contract funds for minority contractors in order to increase participation, remedy past discrimination, and share governmental benefits with broader sections of society.[30] Many states and cities created similar programs. Richmond, Virginia's program reserved thirty percent of city contract funds for minority-owned businesses because, although African Americans comprised fifty percent of the city's population, less than *seven-tenths of one percent* of prime construction contracts were awarded to minority-owned businesses.[31] In rejecting Richmond's program in 1989 over the dissenting opinions of Justices Brennan, Blackmun, and Marshall, the Court declared that Richmond had not justified its program by showing that the substantial statistical disparity in contract awards was caused by racial discrimination. In a concurring opinion evincing superficial reasonableness, Justice Scalia declared that remedial measures would be permissible when implemented on behalf of actual individual victims of proven discrimination. What Scalia and other members of the majority ignored were the long-term, complex elements of history that operated to deprive African Americans and other political minorities of opportunities to start businesses and to compete freely in the open market.

In the area of employment discrimination law, the Supreme Court's new majority drastically altered the established procedures for proving discrimination when employers' policies and procedures have a detrimental impact upon women and minorities. In a case concerning the segregation of employment opportunities and residential facilities in a salmon cannery operation, the Reagan appointees and Justice White comprised a slim five-member majority to create a greater burden of proof to be placed upon plaintiffs alleging the existence of discrimination.[32] Under the previous procedures established in 1971 and utilized for eighteen years prior to this decision, the employers bore the burden of showing an absence of discrimination whenever the plaintiffs provided statistical evidence indicating discriminatory impacts from employment practices. This was an appropriate placement of the legal burden because the employers controlled the internal business documents and other information that could establish whether apparently discriminatory impacts occurred for improper or benign reasons. As a result of the new Court majority's 1989 decision, it is significantly more difficult for victimized plaintiffs to establish the existence of discrimination even in employment settings that appear highly segregated for no explainable reason. The four dissenters in the case, Justices Blackmun, Brennan, Marshall, and Stevens, complained that "a bare majority of the Court [took] three strides backwards in the battle against race discrimination" by undercutting the cannery workers' challenge against "a total residential and work environment organized on principles of racial stratification and segregation, which . . . resembles a plantation economy."[33]

An equally troubling decision by this same, new five-member majority restricted the scope of an established civil rights law affecting racial discrimination in employment and other areas. Without being requested to do so by any attorneys or litigants, the five justices reached out on their own to order reconsideration of the statute permitting lawsuits for racial discrimination in contracts.[34] In response to the new majority's aggressive interest in reversing a civil rights precedent, the attorneys general from forty-seven states, both Republicans and Democrats, filed briefs asking the Court not to tamper with a well-established, effective law for combating racial discrimination.[35] Ultimately, the Court upheld the statute's existence but significantly undercut its effectiveness by ruling, five to four, that the law only applied to the formation of contracts (i.e., hiring) and that it could not be used to redress racial harassment on the job (i.e., the implementation of the contract).[36] As Justice Brennan noted in dissent, "[w]hat the Court declines to snatch away with one hand, it takes with the other."[37] In one employment case, the justices established a statutory precedent to place a great, if not impossible, burden of proof upon discrimination victims. In the other case, they rewrote a statute's meaning after thirteen years of effective application in order to remove any substantive protections against racial discrimination after the initial formation of contracts.

The Court's decision changing the civil rights law concerning contracts had an immediate impact upon lawsuits and potential lawsuits seeking redress for racially discriminatory practices in the execution of private contracts. A study by the NAACP Legal Defense and Educational Fund found that within five months after the Court's decision ninety-six discrimination cases were dismissed by federal judges because of the new, restrictive interpretation of the civil rights law.[38] The Supreme Court has created a situation in which private, nonsectarian schools and private employers can be sued for damages only if they discriminate by race in the initial process of admitting students or hiring employees. There is now an absence of effective remedies for discriminatory treatment that occurs after the initial contract is formed.[39] How will people be protected from racial harassment if they cannot sue for damages and thereby deter such noxious, harmful behavior?

A case in 1990 appeared to reveal a more aggressive attitude among the Court's new majority in rejecting claims of racial discrimination. The four Reagan appointees plus Justice White disagreed with their four more liberal colleagues in rejecting a claim by a White criminal defendant concerning the exclusion of African Americans from his jury.[40] In the majority opinion, Justice Scalia derided the four dissenters' concerns about the existence of racial discrimination in the selection of juries:

> Justice Marshall's dissent rolls out the ultimate weapon, the accusation of insensitivity to racial discrimination—which will lose its intimidating effect if it continues to be fired so randomly.[41]

As a practical matter, Justice Scalia is wrong to assert that practices of racial exclusion on juries are irrelevant when the defendant is white. Social science research on juries indicates that prosecutors disproportionately use their allotted challenges in order to exclude young people and racial minorities from juries.[42] Thus prosecutors frequently manipulate racial considerations to defeat the societal goal of selecting juries that represent a cross-section of a community. This is done in order to generate more conviction-prone juries which can be applied against all defendants. As a result, African Americans and other minority group members are deprived of opportunities to participate in an important governing institution, namely the jury, which provides the context in which citizens' values and opinions shape and determine outcomes within the judiciary. Most importantly, because of the reduced opportunities to participate on juries, African Americans have less ability to assist in preventing any discrimination or other abuses of judicial authority by police, prosecutors, and judges.

One cannot miss the tinge of sarcasm in Scalia's characterization of Marshall as "roll[ing] out the ultimate weapon" by raising the issue of racial discrimination. In addition, Scalia's statement that assertions of racial discrimination will "lose [their] intimidating effect" clearly implies that such considerations improperly deter justices from making the decisions that Scalia believes to be most appropriate. Scalia's claim that the assertions surface "randomly" and the tone of his message, which explicitly scolds his liberal colleagues, appear to indicate that he believes that he possesses a superior ability to identify situations that constitute racial discrimination.

In contrast to President Reagan's efforts to appoint established conservatives to the Supreme Court, President Bush sought to avoid political controversy by appointing a justice whom he believed to be a dependable conservative, but one whose lack of an established record would defuse the mobilization of political opposition to the nomination.[43] Bush replaced retired Justice William Brennan, a forceful advocate of equality, with David Souter, a jurist who spent nearly his entire life in homogeneous New Hampshire, far removed from the issues of racial discrimination which effect much of American society.[44] Souter's sensitivity to issues of discrimination has yet to be tested.

Although President Bush did not seek to appoint a conservative ideologue to the Supreme Court, his lack of concern about civil rights and equality is reflected in his methods for selecting judicial appointees. The Bush administration has continued the methods and priorities of the Reagan administration by appointing conservative federal judges.[45] The judicial appointments by both Reagan and Bush have made the federal courts less hospitable to victims of racial discrimination. Just as Reagan attempted to appoint to a federal judgeship a man who called the NAACP "un-American" and "communist-inspired,"[46] Bush has nominated a judge who shows a disturbing insensitivity to the appropriate role of judicial officers as protectors of minorities' civil rights:

[Bush's nominee] for the 11th Circuit Court of Appeals . . . has favored defendants in civil rights cases 90 percent of the time. After a young [African American] who wasn't charged with a crime was attacked by a police dog, [the Bush nominee] said, "It might not be inappropriate to carry around a few scars to remind you of your wrongdoing." He also, his opponents say, belongs to an all-white golf club.[47]

The recent trends spearheaded by the emerging conservative majority on the Supreme Court have demonstrated to civil rights advocates that the judiciary cannot automatically be regarded as the governmental institution most sensitive to issues of discrimination. The decisions produced by courts are determined by the composition of the judiciary (i.e., judges' party affiliations, values, etc.) and not by fixed constitutional principles. As David Adamany has observed, "[a] continuing retreat on individual rights by the Rehnquist Court would affirm that the Warren Court was an anomaly in a long history of judicial indifference or hostility to disadvantaged minorities."[48] Thus, civil rights advocates must consider strategic alternatives to litigation as the means to advance equality. There is limited potential for effective political action in the legislative and executive policy-making arenas because African Americans and other minorities lack the political and economic power necessary to ensure the passage and implementation of civil rights initiatives. For example, political mobilization generated by the Supreme Court's recent decisions contributed to the passage of Congressional legislation (Civil Rights Act of 1990) designed to reverse the Court's recent statutory interpretation decisions that had limited the scope of established civil rights laws. The legislation passed both houses of Congress by comfortable margins (65 to 34 in the Senate; 272 to 154 in the House),[49] but President Bush vetoed the legislation because he claimed that it would force employers to utilize racial quotas. Without effective influence in both the legislative and executive branches, civil rights advocates cannot implement legislation even when they enjoy support from a majority in Congress.

Bush's assertion that the civil rights legislation would create racial quotas is erroneous for three reasons. First, the legislative provision in question would simply restore employment discrimination law to the form in which it existed from 1971 to 1989 before the new majority on the Supreme Court narrowly managed to increase the burden of proof upon discrimination victims in the Wards Cove case.[50] Yet, from 1971 to 1989 there was neither notable evidence nor public concern that racial quotas were being created. Second, Republican supporters of the legislation ensured that the statute accommodated Bush's expressed concerns by adding explicit language directing that the law not be interpreted to require any quotas. Third, the federal judiciary is now predominantly composed of Republican appointees from the Reagan and Bush administrations. If any issue of quotas was generated by the legislation and subsequently challenged in court, the Republican judges and justices would prevent any quotas as they continue to evince their heightened concern for any governmental actions that might arguably burden Whites or males.

Since there really is no possibility that racial quotas would be created, why then did President Bush veto this legislation aimed at restoring previously established civil rights laws? Strategists within the Republican Party have decided that they will attempt to develop the issue of racial quotas into an effective campaign ploy to attract White voters.[51] Because Jesse Helms apparently succeeded in exploiting White voters' fear of quotas to defeat his African American senatorial opponent, Harvey Gantt, and former Ku Klux Klan leader David Duke has had similar political success with such issues in Louisiana, other Republican politicians are interested in gaining majoritarian political support by fighting against the restoration of civil rights protections for minority victims of discrimination. This partisan exploitation of racial polarization has led the Bush administration to nullify Congressional efforts to hold the new Supreme Court in check.

What does the immediate future hold for Supreme Court decisions concerning discrimination? During Justice Brennan's final term in 1990, he managed to pull together slim 5–4 majorities in two significant cases affecting the pursuit of equality. In these cases, Justice White temporarily abandoned the conservative coalition to cast deciding votes with the liberals to preserve aspects of school desegregation and affirmative action. In *Missouri v. Jenkins*,[52] the slim majority supported a district judge's efforts to facilitate a local tax increase to fund desegregation programs in the Kansas City schools. In *Metro Broadcasting v. F.C.C.*,[53] the liberals preserved a federal government preference program for awarding Federal Communication Commission licenses for radio and television stations which was established in order to combat the historic underrepresentation of minorities in mass media. The Reagan appointees dissented vigorously in both cases and are clearly primed to reverse these decisions in the wake of Brennan's departure if Bush-appointee Justice Souter is willing to provide them with the decisive fifth vote.

The Bush administration's views on civil rights were indicated by its arguments in a case seeking to remove a judicial desegregation order from the Oklahoma City schools. The Bush administration argued that courts should not remedy school segregation that stems from segregated housing patterns.[54] Although federal judges have frequently been receptive to this argument, the argument is based upon the myth that housing segregation is a "natural" phenomenon and it ignores the long history of actions by government, banks, and realtors to confine racial minorities within specific neighborhoods.[55] In this case, which was argued before Justice Souter's confirmation, the four Reagan appointees plus Justice White comprised the five-member majority for a decision which opened the possibility of terminating school desegregation plans.[56] The effects of this decision upon school desegregation programs remain to be seen.

African Americans have not been the only people to experience adverse consequences from the recent trends in Supreme Court decisions. Native Americans, for example, have seen their freedom to engage in traditional religious practices eroded by Supreme Court decisions in 1988 and 1990.[57] These cases do not bode well for future civil rights claims asserted by racial minorities.

The counterattack upon civil rights law mounted by the new Supreme Court majority has elicited a tone of sadness and despair from one of their senior Republican colleagues. Although one might hope that Justice Blackmun has overestimated the extent of racial insensitivity manifested by his colleagues, because he is generally a dispassionate observer and he is so intimately involved in the Court's recent history, one must take seriously his troubling observation that:

> Sadly, [these civil rights law reversals] come as no surprise. One wonders whether the majority still believes that race discrimination—or, more accurately, race discrimination against nonwhites—is a problem in our society, or even remembers that it ever was.[58]

The views manifested by the Supreme Court's emerging conservative majority are a powerful component of regressive political and policy-making forces being asserted throughout the political system. Although it is disturbing to witness the transformation of the Supreme Court away from its role as the protector of victimized minorities, it is all the more troubling to recognize the extent to which other political actors in the 1980s and 1990s are joining the Court's efforts to push American society in a new and undesirable direction.

Notes

1. Lucius J. Barker and Jesse J. McCorry, Jr., *Black Americans and the Political System* (Cambridge, Mass.: Winthrop, 1976), p. 176.

2. Lawrence Baum, *American Courts: Process & Policy,* 2nd ed. (Boston: Houghton Mifflin, 1990), p. 353.

3. See, e.g., James L. Gibson, "From Simplicity to Complexity: The Development of Theory in the Study of Judicial Behavior," *Political Behavior* 5 (1983): 7–49.

4. See, e.g., David A. Kaplan, "A Master Builder," *Newsweek,* July 30, 1990, pp. 19–20.

5. See, e.g., Edwin Meese, "The Battle for the Constitution," *Policy Review,* Spring 1986, pp. 32–35.

6. Christopher E. Smith, "Jurisprudential Politics and the Manipulation of History," *The Western Journal of Black Studies* 13 (1989): 156–161.

7. See, e.g., Jeremy Rabkin, *Judicial Compulsions: How Public Law Distorts Public Policy* (New York: Basic Books, 1989).

8. Christopher E. Smith, "Federal Judges' Role in Prisoner Litigation: What's Necessary? What's Proper?" *Judicature* 70 (1986): 145.

9. See Donald Horowitz, *The Courts and Social Policy* (Washington, D.C.: Brookings Institution, 1977).

10. Stephen Wasby, "Arrogation of Power or Responsibility: Judicial Imperialism Revisited," *Judicature* 65 (1981): 208–221.

11. Norman C. Amaker, *Civil Rights and the Reagan Administration* (Washington, D.C.: The Urban Institute Press, 1988).

12. Lincoln Caplan, *The Tenth Justice* (New York: Vintage Books, 1987).

13. Smith, "Jurisprudential Politics and the Manipulation of History," pp. 156–161.

14. Amaker, p. 163.

15. Sheldon Goldman, "Reagan's second term judicial appointments: the battle at midway," *Judicature* 70 (1987): 326.

16. Aaron Epstein, "Reagan leaving mighty legal legacy," *Akron Beacon Journal,* November 24, 1988, p. G5.

17. Jon Gottschall, "Reagan's appointments to the U.S. courts of appeals: the continuation of a judicial revolution," *Judicature* 70 (1986): 49–54; Timothy B. Tomasi and Jess A. Velona, "All the President's Men? A Study of Ronald Reagan's Appointments to the U.S. Courts of Appeals," *Columbia Law Review* 87 (1987): 766–793; C. K. Rowland, Donald Songer and Robert A. Carp, "Presidential Effects on Criminal Justice Policy in the Lower Federal Courts: The Reagan Judges," *Law and Society Review* 22 (1988): 191–200.

18. Richard L. Kolbe, *American Political Parties: An Uncertain Future* (New York: Harper & Row, 1985), p. 209.

19. Herman Schwartz, *Packing the Courts: The Conservative Campaign to Rewrite the Constitution* (New York: Charles Scribner's Sons, 1988), p. 146.

20. See, e.g., Mississippi University for Women v. Hogan, 458 U.S. 718 (1982): Johnson v. Transportation Agency, Santa Clara County, California, 107 S. Ct. 1442 (1987).

21. See Christopher E. Smith, "Justice Antonin Scalia and the Institutions of American Government," *Wake Forest Law Review* 25 (1990): 783–809.

22. See David J. Danelski, "The Influence of the Chief Justice in the Decisional Process of the Supreme Court," in *American Court Systems,* 2d ed., Sheldon Goldman and Austin Sarat, eds. (New York: Longman, 1989), pp. 486–499.

23. Regents of the University of California v. Bakke, 438 U.S. 265 (1978).

24. McClesky v. Kemp, 107 S. Ct. 1756 (1987).

25. *Ibid.,* p. 1785 (Brennan, J., dissenting).

26. Thomas F. Pettigrew, "New Patterns of Racism: The Different Worlds of 1984 and 1964," *Rutgers Law Review* 37 (1985): 673–705.

27. Antonin Scalia, "The Disease as Cure," *Washington University Law Quarterly* (1979): 152.

28. *Ibid.*

29. Michael Patrick King, "Justice Antonin Scalia: The First Term on the Supreme Court—1986–1987," *Rutgers Law Journal* 20 (1988): 42.

30. Fullilove v. Klutznick, 100 S. Ct. 2758 (1980).

31. City of Richmond v. J. A. Croson Co., 102 S. Ct. 854, 873 (1989).

32. Wards Cove Packing Co. v. Atonio, 109 S. Ct. 2115 (1989).

33. *Ibid.,* p. 754 (Blackmun, J., dissenting).

34. Stuart Taylor, Jr., "Court, 5–4, Votes to Restudy Rights in Minority Suits," *New York Times,* April 26, 1988, p. 1.

35. Linda Greenhouse, "Court Upholds Use of Rights Law But Limits How It Can Be Applied," *New York Times,* June 16, 1989, p. 10.

36. Patterson v. McLean Credit Union, 109 S. Ct. 2363 (1989).

37. *Ibid.,* p. 2379 (Brennan, J., dissenting).

38. NAACP Legal Defense and Educational Fund, "The Impact of *Patterson v. McLean Credit Union,*" November 20, 1989.

39. See Theodore Eisenberg and Stewart Schwab, "The Importance of Section 1981," *Cornell Law Review* 73 (1988): 596–604.

40. Holland v. Illinois, 110 S. Ct. 803 (1990).

41. *Ibid.,* p. 810.

42. Valerie P. Hans and Neil Vidmar, *Judge the Jury* (New York: Plenum Press, 1986), p. 75.

43. See, e.g., Neil A. Lewis, "Souter's Chances of Confirmation Viewed as Strong," *New York Times,* September 15, 1990, p. 1.

44. R. W. Apple, Jr., "Bush's Enigmatic Choice for the High Court," *New York Times,* July 29, 1990, pp. E1, E5.

45. Neil A. Lewis, "Bush Travels Reagan's Course in Naming Judges," *New York Times,* April 10, 1990, p. A1.

46. Harry P. Stumpf, *American Judicial Politics* (New York: Harcourt Brace Jovanovich, 1988), p. 208.

47. "A First," *Newsweek,* February 25, 1991, p. 3.

48. David Adamany, "The Supreme Court," in *The American Courts: A Critical Assessment,* eds. John B. Gates and Charles A. Johnson (Washington, D.C.: Congressional Quarterly Press, 1991), p. 18.

49. Richard L. Berke, "House Approves Civil Rights Bill; Veto Is Weighed," *New York Times,* August 4, 1990, pp. 1, 11; Neil A. Lewis, "President's Veto of Rights Measure Survives By 1 Vote," *New York Times,* October 25, 1990, p. A1.

50. Wards Cove Packing Co. v. Atonio, 109 S. Ct. 2115 (1989).

51. See Eleanor Clift, "Bennett Hits the Hot Button: Is the GOP Looking to Play the Politics of Quotas?" *Time,* December 3, 1990, p. 26; Thomas B. Edsall, "A Political Powder Keg," *Washington Post National Weekly Edition,* January 14–20, 1991, p. 6.

52. Missouri v. Jenkins, 110 S. Ct. 1651 (1990).

53. Metro Broadcasting Inc. v. Federal Communications Commission, 110 S. Ct. 2997 (1990).

54. Linda Greenhouse, "Segregation After Busing: A Puzzling Legal Issue," *New York Times,* October 3, 1990, p. B7.

55. Thomas F. Pettigrew, "A Sociological View of the Post-*Bradley* Era," *Wayne Law Review,* 21 (1975): 828–829.

56. Oklahoma City Board of Education v. Dowell (1991), described in Linda Greenhouse, "Justices Rule Mandatory Busing May Go, Even If Races Stay Apart," *New York Times,* January 16, 1991, pp. A1, B6.

57. See Lyng v. Northwest Indian Cemetery Protective Association, 108 S. Ct. 1319 (1988): Employment Division, Department of Human Resources of Oregon v. Smith, 110 S. Ct. 1595 (1990).

58. Wards Cove Packing Co. v. Atonio, 104 L. Ed. 2d 733, 755 (Blackmun, J., dissenting).

20

Beyond the Rodney King Story: Police Conduct and Community Relations

NAACP

With the Rodney King beating as the catalyst, the NAACP announced at its 1992 annual convention that it would conduct a series of national hearings into police conduct.

As defined by the NAACP, the purpose of the hearings was to provide a public platform for citizens, public officials, community leaders, law enforcement personnel, and experts to detail why they believe there continues to exist a wall of mistrust between African American communities and law enforcement departments, and what positive steps can be taken to correct this dangerous situation.

Six cities, representing a geographical and demographic span, were selected as hearing sites: Norfolk, Miami, Los Angeles, Houston, St. Louis, and Indianapolis. In each of the cities, the panel of NAACP staff members was joined by a representative from a local branch of the NAACP.

Police Conduct and Community Relations: Defining the Problem

While the impetus for this report was the beating of Rodney King on March 3, 1991, that incident is not an aberration. The unique element of the Rodney King

From "Beyond the Rodney King Story: Police Conduct and Community Relations" (Executive Summary), 1993, 22 pp. Reprinted by courtesy of NAACP Public Relations.

incident was that it was *videotaped.* Similar, unrecorded episodes happen in cities and towns all over this country.

Whether or not police misconduct is increasing or consists merely of isolated incidents, it cannot be denied that a wall of mistrust exists between minority groups and the police, and that the relationship between the police and the community has eroded considerably.

Respect for law and order is the cornerstone of a free society. The rule of law is predicated upon the consent of people who believe the laws are administered fairly, thus commanding respect and confidence. Unjust or discriminatory administration of law by excessive force tends only to create distrust and contempt for the law and for law enforcement agencies.

The role of the police is difficult, dangerous, demanding, and often misunderstood. Social pathologies intensify problems, requiring strong community support if police forces are to be maintained at sufficient size with adequate training, equipment, and morale.

In lower income areas—where the problems of unemployment, poor education, inadequate housing, and drugs are rampant—the position of police officers is especially difficult because they are viewed as a symbol of oppression. Police officers are a buffer between disadvantaged groups and the "establishment."

It is impossible to study the police in this country without studying race. It is impossible to understand police conduct in the Rodney King beating—or the daily incidents of police "use of force"—without understanding the history of police-minority relations. Those who claim that the verdict in the Rodney King case can be explained as a verdict that was not racist, but rather "pro-police," should next try to separate land from sea. Can they really say where one ends and the other begins?

The recommendations contained in this report rest on the premise that the police beating of Rodney King is part of a long and shameful history of racially-motivated brutality and degradation that continues to find expression in powerful places.

Findings

Racism Is a Critical Component of Police Misconduct

Racism is an important motivating factor in how police departments perform their law enforcement functions. The use of sweeps through minority areas in the name of crime-fighting, targeting of young black males for stop and frisks, the targeting of young black males for humiliating strip searches (even in public), and the creation of criminal profiles which inevitably focus on African Americans and Latinos have become standard police practice in urban America. Rarely does one find the same extreme measures taking place in white areas, notwithstanding the fact that crime occurs there, too.

There is a growing feeling in the black community that the police regard all

African Americans as either criminals or potential criminals. Police practices in black communities are a direct source of this perception.

Young black men are overrepresented in the criminal justice system. Young black men have come to experience police questioning and harassment as their American way of life.

Citizens Experience Police Abuse in a Wide Variety of Forms

Perhaps the most serious problem facing the minority community is police use of excessive and deadly force in the name of "law enforcement." Excessive force encompasses everything from brutal beatings to the use of police dogs to police shootings. Citizens testified about the brutality employed in many routine arrests. Even in instances when a suspect made clear an intention to surrender, far too often the suspect is physically punished as part of the arrest process.

Public defenders, criminal lawyers, and criminal clinicians in law schools routinely hear descriptions of excessive force when clients recount the way they were arrested. Many if not most African American criminal suspects are handcuffed too tightly, smacked with a nightstick, and/or shoved into a police wagon. Even black professionals are subject to this treatment.

Verbal abuse and harassment are the most common forms of police abuse and are standard police behavior in minority communities. This was the most frequent complaint about police officers in the various cities. Verbal abuse and harassment may occur every time a person is stopped by police officers.

Verbal abuse of African Americans by the police appears to be standard operating procedure. Further, there appears to be little distinction between the type of abuse and harassment that occurs during public encounters and what occurs in private encounters. Many citizens testified about the verbal abuse and harassment they endured in their own homes.

False charges and retaliatory actions against abused citizens frequently follow incidents of abuse. Far too frequently, the citizen who has just been subjected to police abuse is then arrested and charged with a variety of offenses. The common charges are disorderly conduct, resisting arrest, and assaulting a police officer.

Police Departments Have Failed to Address Police Abuse

Representatives of several police departments testified that they had adopted specific policies and procedures to regulate the use of force. According to these officials, their new policies permit the use of deadly force only to protect the officer's life or that of another and/or to stop someone in the commission of a violent felony.

Some police and elected officials described new policies regarding the types of weapons or force which can be used by police officers. Indianapolis Mayor

Hudnut endorsed the use of chemical repellents as an alternative to deadly force, a practice instituted by the outgoing Chief of Police. The Chief of the Chesapeake Police Department testified he had revised the department's firearms policies to standardize both the type of firearm used in the department and training in that particular weapon. He also replaced electric shock weapons and most nonlethal gases with one chemical agent.

Many police departments have inadequate systems for detecting patterns of misconduct by individual officers or for discerning the types of situations in which misconduct most frequently occurs. Citizens in several cities testified that most of the incidents of police brutality involve a minority of officers.

Some testified that the same officers engage in repetitive acts of misconduct against citizens and are known within the police department, yet the department fails to adequately discipline the officers who commit acts of brutality.

Recent surveys of the use of force in particular police departments have found a concentration of complaints against certain officers, accompanied by a departmental failure to monitor and discipline those officers.

Civilians Seldom Prevail in Complaints Against Police Officers

Citizens and representatives of community organizations at each of the hearings testified that many people are afraid to come forward to complain about police misconduct or to testify against officers. There was testimony in several cities that African Americans in particular complain within their community, but often do not file formal complaints with their local police departments.

Some citizens fear a complaint will result in retaliation by the police, ranging from harassment to criminal charges. Those who witness or experience police misconduct fear they will be arrested if they complain about the police.

Because of the fear of coming forward, the number of official complaints made to the police is a small fraction of the number of citizens who have been the victims of police abuse. Even community and legal organizations which assist citizens with filing complaints or lawsuits alleging police misconduct hear about a relatively small portion of the incidents of misconduct.

Those who are willing to file complaints alleging police misconduct face a number of impediments. Elected officials as well as citizens testified that many persons do not know what complaint systems are available to them.

Many people reported that their attempts to file a complaint of misconduct are discouraged by the police. The police discourage complaints by threatening to file criminal charges or civil lawsuits against civilian victims. Those subjected to police misconduct are frequently charged with criminal offenses ranging from disorderly conduct and destruction of property to assault on an officer and resisting arrest.

Citizens in each city described numerous deficiencies in the internal police complaint process, ranging from the initiation stage to the results of the police investigations. Many people rejected the notion that police can police themselves.

The consensus of the citizens and community organizations is that the internal review investigators overwhelmingly side with the police, generally concluding that the officer(s) used proper force. Many who have gone through the internal affairs complaint process felt it was of no help.

Civil suits for personal injuries or false arrest are generally not a viable avenue of redress for victims of police misconduct. Few lawyers will take such cases. First, there are considerable financial disincentives to litigating cases of police abuse. Most victims cannot afford to pay an attorney in advance. Moreover, most attorneys will not pursue these cases unless they are convinced they can recover substantial damages.

Race Plays a Large Factor in Police Misconduct

There seems to be a correlation between the race of the officer, the race of the citizen, and the incidence of police abuse. Witnesses report that white police violence on black citizens is more likely to occur than black-on-white police violence. Many blacks believe that white police officers are far more responsible for abusive conduct toward minorities than any other group.

African American police officers may be under greater pressure than white officers to tolerate instances of police abuse to insure continued employment and promotion opportunities. There was testimony in the hearings about black officers needing to make a good impression on white officers or superiors so they can get ahead.

There Is an "Us vs. Them" Mentality in Police-Community Relations

There appears to be a "code of silence" which protects and insulates police officers from allegations of misconduct. The code of silence is a shared, often unspoken vow taken by police officers to never "rat" on each other.

Many police officers deny that a code of silence exists. Certainly, if officers confirmed the existence of a code of silence, they would be admitting something deeply disturbing about how police departments operate.

Many police officials acknowledged that police departments have traditionally made a lot of arrests in the black community and in low-income areas, with the result that many African Americans grow up under constant surveillance. The Chief of the Virginia Beach Police Department testified that the perception that blacks are more frequently police targets arises in part from a "lack of understanding and apprehension of police," which causes "initial strain."

While most citizens testified that police misconduct is an ongoing and pervasive problem, and that police/community relations in their communities are at a low point, some individuals testified that there has been overall improvement in police/community relations and in the frequency of police misconduct. Some of these officers, however, testified that there are still officers who display a pattern of misconduct.

African American law enforcement organizations also took a leadership role in proposing concrete steps to confront police brutality. According to members who testified at the hearings, the National Black Policemen Association and the National Organization of Black Law Enforcement Executives are committed to speaking up and taking action against police misconduct.

In contrast to civilian witnesses, some police officials denied that any code of silence existed. Other police officials asserted the existence of the code of silence, but claimed that it was not as prevalent as previously, and that it would not be condoned by their police department.

Many of the police departments described the need to move away from the traditional "us vs. them" mentality and the rapid response/crime solving approach to policing. Some conceded the failure of such an approach in combating crime. Police officials at the hearings—even those from rural police departments—endorsed the concept of community policing.

Many police officials emphasized the need for better communication between the police and the community. For some, communication between the police department and the community—and within the police department—bears directly on the effectiveness of the department.

Many of those who testified at the hearings believed that much of the "us vs. them" problem rests with an underrepresentation of minorities on the police force and in decision-making roles in law enforcement. Others went further by demanding that more black and Latino officers be assigned to specific jurisdictions, making assignments to certain neighborhoods by race, if necessary. According to these witnesses, for example, there should be more African American officers assigned to patrol black communities and more Puerto Rican officers assigned to patrol Puerto Rican communities.

A number of police and city officials testified at the hearings that the police must recognize the cultural diversity in their cities and increase representation of minorities and women in the police departments. Some of the departments have affirmative action plans.

African Americans and other minorities are poorly represented in ranks above patrol officer and in the specialized units in many police departments. In the Houston Police Department, white males constitute 97 percent of the captains, 87 percent of the lieutenants, and 81 percent of the sergeants. Only 5.7 percent of the supervisory positions are held by African Americans, and only 7.5 percent are held by Hispanics.

African Americans constituted 22 percent of the command rank in the St. Louis Metropolitan Police Department, while St. Louis has an African American population of more than 47 percent. In the Virginia Beach Police Department, African Americans constituted 8.3 percent of the force in 1992, but only 1.8 percent of those in supervisory ranks. Even where the overall numbers of minorities in the police department have increased substantially, few African Americans have risen far in the ranks. For example, in the Metro-Dade Police Department, only 8.5 percent of the sworn force above the rank of patrolman is black. In the top 65 positions, 77 percent are white, 11 percent are black, and 13.8 percent are Hispanic. In the Los Angeles Police Department, the percentage of sworn officers who are African American is comparable to the percentage of African Americans in the population of Los Angeles, but only 8.5 percent of the officers in supervisory positions are black. Hispanics, who comprise 33.3 percent of the city population, constituted 22.2 percent of all sworn officers and 14.3 percent of the supervisors.

Police Training Programs Are Improving

Police departments are beginning to respond to the needs of the community in police training programs. Citizens, police representatives, and elected officials testified that police departments have begun to provide cultural sensitivity and violence-reduction training.

Recommendations for Change

1. There Must Be Sweeping Change in the Concept of Policing

There must be a sweeping change in the very concept of policing in our cities and towns. The first change must be to do away with the "us and them" dynamic of police/community relations. This drawing of lines only fosters racism and violence and needs to be altered.

There was much testimony throughout the NAACP hearings on police alienation from the community. There was also much testimony about an insular police culture which disparages all outsiders, particularly those in minority communities. There was considerable testimony by members of the African American community about the racial animosity that is intrinsic to the "us and them" mentality.

Police officers must be part of the community they serve. Outsiders with weapons, policing a community they neither know nor understand, perpetuate the notion of police officers as an occupying army. Roots in the community should be an important hiring criterion.

Police officers must be reconceptualized as public servants engaged in social service delivery. Notwithstanding their current paramilitary image and structure, this was the original conceptualization of the police. Police officers have always been urban "helpers," providing information, directing other municipal services to areas of need, and serving as an essential neighborhood resource.

While crime-fighting will always be an important part of police work, it is not the only police function, nor is it necessarily the most important one. In inner city areas, police perform a wide array of services.

Police officers should be viewed as valuable members of the community. Police should be seen as the keepers of the calm, the keepers of safety.

2. There Must Be Greater Police Accountability

Effective management of any large bureaucracy requires systematic, formalized, and comprehensive mechanisms to ensure attainment of the organization's goals and objectives. Among the most important are mechanisms to achieve *accountability*—rewarding and encouraging positive police behavior as well and preventing negative police performance.

3. There Must Be a Renewed Commitment to Diversity in Hiring

There is no question that police departments should reflect the communities they serve, a recommendation made by many who testified at NAACP hearings throughout the country. Almost every police official who testified at the NAACP hearings presented their department's affirmative action plan, emphasizing the successes and apologizing for the failures. There was an almost universal view that diversity in the police ranks was a key to improving police/minority relations and stopping police brutality.

4. Police Departments Must Reevaluate Criteria for Recruitment and Hiring

Police departments should recruit better-educated candidates. The broader the educational background, the broader the perspective.

A special effort should be made to recruit candidates who are less potentially violent. We recommend extensive psychological testing for potential violence, racism, sexism, homophobia, and intolerance of difference. We recommend that the testing include more than a written exam, and that simulations be incorporated into the screening process.

Police departments should learn from the tactics of military recruiting. They should recruit at high school, colleges, shopping districts, recreational centers, ball fields, basketball courts, at the Scouts, at places where gangs hang out.

5. Continuing Training and Education Must Be Offered

It is essential to continue training and education beyond the police academy. If multicultural understanding and alternatives to violence are taught only to new recruits, what they learn will be quickly undone after contact with other officers.

Multicultural education must be an integrated part of training and ongoing educational programs. Those who conduct teaching sessions for the police should come from academia, the minority community, the feminist community, the gay and lesbian community, and the religious community. They should also come from those who work with the homeless, the mentally ill, the drug and alcohol addicted, and the battered.

Education sessions should be held with other urban social service providers whenever possible. The insularity of the police and other aspects of police culture might be altered by exposure to the perspectives of others serving the same urban population.

6. Promotion and Advancement Criteria Must Be Reevaluated

Criteria for advancement and promotion should include a history of nonviolent police intervention, the lack of civilian complaints, ongoing educational achievement, ties to the community, and extraordinary efforts to build community. Preference should be given to those who either come from or who have made themselves part of the community.

7. Some Form of Civilian Review Must Be Adopted by All Police Departments

The NAACP hearings reinforce the view that police misconduct must be taken seriously, and that institutional mechanics must be firmly in place to promptly and adequately discipline offending officers. There is a growing national consensus that some form of strong, independent, civilian oversight is necessary.

Of the 13 largest cities in the country with forms of civilian review, six have wholly *civilian* review, four have boards with a combination of both sworn officers and civilians, and three have parallel review processes (police and civilian) operating at the same time.

There was a strong call from civilians (and some police) at the hearings for an independent review board. For most, the need for independence was based on long, painful experience, which had taught them that the police cannot effectively investigate and discipline themselves. As one Los Angeles witness testified, "The remedy is a Civilian Review Board independent of the police department, independent of an out-of-control department."

The civil review board must have independent investigatory power. Civilian review boards should be composed of a majority of non-law enforcement personnel. Hearings should be open to the public.

8. A Community-Oriented Approach Should Be Adopted by All Police Departments

_____ Part VIII

State and Urban Politics

Blacks have faced momentous obstacles to full participation in American politics: slavery, the three-fifths compromise, poll taxes, literacy tests, and white primaries. Indeed, William Rehnquist, currently chief justice of the United States Supreme Court, was accused of actively discouraging blacks from voting in Arizona in the 1960s.

In addition, many Southern states still require primary candidates to win at least 50 percent of the vote, or face a runoff. This system makes it more difficult for black candidates to win statewide races, since no state has a majority black voting population and because white voters are typically reluctant to vote for black candidates. Black candidates who win a primary with less than 50 percent of the vote are forced into a second, one-on-one primary, very possibly against a white opponent.

In spite of these constraints, black candidates have recently made significant gains in winning state and local elections. In 1970, according to the Joint Center for Political and Economic Studies (a black-oriented think tank in Washington, D.C.), there were 1,469 black elected officials in America, including 623 in municipal offices. By 1992, there were 7,480 black office-holders, including 458 in state legislatures and 3,683 in municipal positions.

Progress has been much slower among the nation's governorships. L. Douglas Wilder, governor of Virginia from 1989 to 1993, is the only black ever elected governor. Wilder, who ran briefly for the Democratic presidential nomination in 1992, was constitutionally ineligible to run for reelection in 1993.

Several black candidates have failed in gubernatorial bids. Los Angeles mayor Tom Bradley lost gubernatorial races in 1982 and 1986, both times to Republican George Deukmejian. In 1982, Bradley was the front-runner throughout the campaign. On election day, exit polls indicated that he would win; it is possible that many white voters were not truthful in their responses to pollsters.

In 1982, Bradley lost, 49.3 percent to 48.1 percent. Four years later, Deukmejian's margin of victory was 60.5 percent to 37.4 percent. Deukmejian ran on the issue of crime, and his campaign ads used the racial code language, "He can represent all Californians."

In addition, Andrew Young failed in his 1990 bid for the governorship of Georgia. Young, who had served in Congress, had been United States ambassador to the United Nations, and had been mayor of Atlanta, lost the Democratic primary to Lieutenant Governor Zell Meller (who went on to win the general election). Many observers believe that Young failed to vigorously court the black vote; some even accused him of "trying to be white."

In the first reading, Raphael J. Sonenshein, a political scientist at California State University, Fullerton, asks, "Can Black Candidates Win Statewide Elections?" He reviews the statewide campaigns of Edward Brooke (former Republican senator from Massachusetts), Tom Bradley (unsuccessful candidate for governor of California), and Doug Wilder (elected governor of Virginia in 1989). Sonenshein concludes that the best conditions for statewide black candidacies are liberal racial attitudes, a "positive political situation," and a flexible campaign strategy. He also states that "the black statewide candidate faces an uphill struggle," given the reluctance of whites to vote for blacks.

Sonenshein is the author of *Politics in Black and White: Race and Power in Los Angeles* (1993), which examines how racial violence coexists with the surprising political linkages between blacks and white liberals (especially Jews). He notes that the racial politics of Los Angeles are much more tranquil than those of New York.

The next three readings in this part involve the linkages between race and urban politics. Most blacks live in major cities, and blacks have had significant success in electing black mayors.

In 1994, there were black mayors in Atlanta (Bill Campbell), Seattle (Norman Rice), New Orleans (Sidney Barthelemy), Cincinnati (Dwight Tillery), Denver (Wellington Webb), Baltimore (Kurt Schmoke), Gary (Thomas Barnes), Cleveland (Michael White), Newark (Sharpe James), Detroit (Dennis Archer), Washington (Marion Barry), Oakland (Elihu Harris), and Birmingham (Richard Arrington). Of these cities, the most surprising outcomes were the election of black mayors in Cincinnati, Denver, and Seattle—cities with overwhelming white majorities.

Several big-city black mayors have attracted attention. One is Kurt Schmoke, mayor of Baltimore since 1987. Schmoke, a Harvard-trained lawyer, generated waves of publicity by advocating the legalization of drugs. Schmoke's reasoning, endorsed by many economists, is that drug legalization would lower the price and profitability of drugs, thereby lessening gang warfare over turf. Also, David Broder, a prominent reporter and columnist for the *Washington Post,* suggested that President Clinton consider nominating Schmoke to the United States Supreme Court.

Certainly the most prominent black mayor is Marion Barry. Barry was first elected mayor of Washington, D.C., in 1978; he was reelected in 1982 and 1986. In 1990, while he was mayor, the FBI videotaped him sucking on a crack pipe in a dimly lit Washington hotel room. He was arrested and convicted of several charges. He spent six months in jail, where he was treated for drug and alcohol problems.

After his release, Barry mounted a comeback. In 1992, he was elected to the city council from Ward 8 (Anacostia)—the poorest, blackest portion of the city. In 1994, Barry ran for mayor. He won 47 percent of the vote in the Democratic primary, against City Councilman John Ray and incumbent mayor Sharon Pratt Kelly (who won only 14 percent of the vote). He won the general election in November 1994, defeating Republican Carol Schwartz, who is white, 50 percent to 42 percent.

During the campaign, Barry stressed his own personal redemption, and at his primary election victory celebration, he sang "Amazing Grace."

Barry's election had a strong racial element. Barry often dresses in African garb, and has been called America's first Afrocentric big-city mayor. Barry received only 5 percent of the white vote in the primary. The day after the primary election, Barry told white voters to "get over" their hangups over having him as mayor. Barry regards Louis Farrakhan, leader of the Nation of Islam, as a friend. Barry won the mayoralty, in large part, because he got thousands of angry young blacks to register to vote.

Barry's election was viewed with horror by many. Newspaper headlines referred to the three-time mayor as "disgraced" or a "convicted felon." Georgia Republican Congressman Newt Gingrich called Barry's election a "sad commentary" on American life and politics. President Clinton's aides reportedly were "chagrined" that the president would be forced to deal with an ex-con.

Others, though, had a different interpretation. Ronald Walters, chairman of the political science department at Howard University, said that Washingtonians voted for Barry in response to "the white power Establishment's attempting to dictate their lives." Mark Plotkin, a political analyst for a Washington public radio station, said that black voters in Washington were providing an "across-the-board, in your face" response to those in Congress who control the city's purse strings.

Two long-term mayors recently retired from office. In Atlanta, Maynard Jackson, mayor from 1974 to 1981 and 1990 to 1993, chose not to run for reelection in 1993. In Detroit, Coleman Young, elected mayor in 1973, decided not to run for reelection in 1993.

Black control of the big-city mayorship may be in danger. In New York, Los Angeles, Chicago, and Philadelphia, black mayors have been replaced by white mayors. Harold Washington, the first black mayor of Chicago, died in office. His temporary successor, Eugene Sawyer (a black), was defeated in his bid for a full term by Richard Daley, son of the legendary Chicago mayor and whose grip on power in Chicago seems firm. Wilson Goode, the first black mayor of Philadelphia, was defeated for reelection in 1987 by Edward Rundell, a white. Goode lost political support because of his decision to bomb the headquarters of the radical activist group MOVE in 1985. In Los Angeles, Tom Bradley served as mayor from 1973 to 1993. He decided not to run for reelection in 1993, because of his age (seventy-five) and because of questions over his handling of the 1992 riots and the performance of police chief Daryl Gates. In the 1992 general election, white businessman Richard Riordan defeated Asian city councilman Michael Woo; there were no major black candidates. In New York, David Dinkins, the city's first black mayor, was defeated for reelection in 1993 by Rudolph Giuliani, a former federal prosecutor. (Giuliani received 48 percent of the vote in the 1989 election.) Dinkins proved to be a disappointment to many white liberals, because of his seeming inability to improve race relations in New York.

African Americans are also increasingly well represented on city councils. There are currently more minority city council members than at any time in the nation's history. Black council representation is highest in central cities with larger councils, and in cities in the Deep South with large black populations. There is little variation in the racial composition of partisan vs. nonpartisan councils. Blacks do slightly better in district elections than in at-large elections.

The next reading in this part, "The End of the Rainbow: America's Changing Urban Politics," is by Jim Sleeper, a columnist for the *New York Daily News,* and the author of *The Closest of Strangers: Liberalism and the Politics of Race in New York* (1990). Sleeper's argument is that the period of black "Rainbow" mayors of large cities may be over.

Sleeper notes the existence of a new pattern in mayoral elections. On the one hand, there is "the liberal candidate, usually a person of color," who "had the mantle of the civil rights movement, the support of a multiracial, multicultural coalition and the endorsement of Jesse Jackson." Such a candidate was pro-choice, anti-death penalty, pro-gay rights, and opposed to restrictions on immigration. On economics, "he may not have much" of a program, "but he branded his white male opponent a closet Reaganite and sounded the trumpet for 'progressive' unity."

The other candidate, typically, "never held elective office, posed as a businesslike reformer, promising to clean house and create new jobs through commercial deregulation, better public safety, less onerous taxation and tougher union contracts."

There are numerous examples of the new breed of mayors: Richard Riordan in Los Angeles, Wellington Webb in Denver, Norman Rice in Seattle, Edward Rundell in Philadelphia, Michael White in Cleveland, Rudolph Giuliani in New York, Bret Schundler in Jersey City, and Steve Goldsmith in Indianapolis. Several of these mayors (Riordan, Giuliani, Schundler, and Goldsmith) are Republicans. Most of the new mayors favor greater privatization of public services, fiscal restraint, getting tough on crime, and restricting school busing.

The third selection is a speech by Bill Bradley, the senior senator from New Jersey. Bradley's speech was delivered on the floor of the United States Senate, and attracted a great deal of attention.

One reason for the newsworthiness of Bradley's speech is his background. After attending Princeton and Oxford, Bradley played for the New York Knicks of the National Basketball Association. As one of the few whites on the team, Bradley came to see New York City "through the eyes of my black teammates, as well as my own."

The other reason that Bradley's speech commanded national interest is his honesty. Bradley calls race "our unresolved dilemma." He notes that "people of different races often do not listen to each other on the subject of race." He also observes that whites typically have a strong fear of "young black men traveling in groups, cruising the city, looking for trouble. . . ."

Much of Bradley's analysis focuses on American *culture*. He complains that television bombards kids "with messages of conspicuous consumption" and that "kids become trapped in the quicksands of American materialism." In this environment, it is increasingly difficult for individuals to defer gratification, stay in school, obtain and keep a job, and assume adult responsibilities.

Much of Bradley's urban policy agenda is traditional liberal fare. He calls for more investment in low-income housing and the urban infrastructure, and expanded funding of the Job Corps.

However, one of Bradley's proposals to break the cycle of poverty is decidedly nontraditional. Along with several leading conservative thinkers (including Charles Murray), Bradley advocates the establishment of fifteen-month houses "for women seven months pregnant who want to live the first year of their life as a mother in a residential setting. Young fathers would be encouraged to participate, too." In addition, Bradley argues that "these fifteen-month houses" need to be combined with full funding for the Women, Infants, and Children program and Head Start, "more generous tax treatment of children, one-year parental leave, tough child support enforcement, and welfare reform that encourages marriage, work, and assumption of responsibility, instead of more children you cannot afford."

The last reading in this part is by Midge Decter, a Distinguished Fellow of the Institute on Religion and Public Life, and a leading neoconservative intellectual. Her husband, Norman Podhoretz, is editor of *Commentary*, the leading Jewish journal in the United States.

In "How the Rioters Won," Decter is extremely critical of the riots following the first Rodney King verdict. She calls Representative Maxine Waters "the star of riot week," with "innumerable talk-show appearances and much press coverage. But as one watched her skipping through the still-smoldering rubble, it was hard to banish the thought that probably never before had she had, and probably never again would she have, quite so good a time." Decter ridicules the rejectionist ideology of black gangs, who are armed with "assault rifles, Uzis, hand grenades, and bulletproof vests." She believes, quoting black economist Glenn Loury, that "the problem of the black underclass is a problem that will only be solved one by one and from the inside out."

Decter's analysis is consistent with her previous writings. In the 1970s, she wrote two books attacking American feminism: *The Liberated Woman and Other Americans* (1971) and *The New Chastity and Other Arguments Against Women's Liberation* (1973). In those books, she contended that the goal of feminists is not freedom from sexual discrimination but freedom from all responsibility.

21

Can Black Candidates Win Statewide Elections?

Raphael J. Sonenshein

While black office-holding has steadily increased at the local level, statewide successes have been few and far between. Edward Brooke, the two-term (1967–1979) Republican from Massachusetts, has been the only black senator in this century. Until Douglas Wilder's 1989 election in Virginia, no black had ever been elected governor. (In 1873, the black lieutenant-governor of Louisiana, P.B.S. Pinchbeck, was elevated to the post of acting governor for forty-three days.) Below these top offices, the dismal record continues. In 1979 there were six statewide black elected officials; by 1985 there were only three. One of these officials, Illinois State Comptroller Roland Burris, called the group "an endangered species."[1] Women and Hispanics have won more top-level statewide offices than blacks. There are currently three women governors and two senators; four Hispanic governors have been elected since 1974. In this century, there have been two Hispanic senators.[2]

A statewide base is a critical factor in attaining national leadership. Excluding generals and vice-presidents, most presidential nominees have previously served as senators or governors. The 1984 and 1988 Jesse Jackson campaigns raised interest in a black presidential candidacy. This article suggests that understanding the intermediate level of statewide black candidacy can shed additional light on the prospects for a winning black presidential campaign.

Are black statewide victories virtually unattainable? Attempting to answer

Reprinted with permission from *Political Science Quarterly* 105 (summer 1990): 219–242.

this question highlights how little research has been devoted to the problem. Perhaps the lack of success has discouraged exploration, or perhaps it is also the lack of terms of reference for undertaking the inquiry. Certainly the excitement of the Jackson presidential campaigns has overshadowed attempts to build a long-range foundation for statewide and national campaigns. There is no real literature on the statewide black candidacy. The only efforts even indirectly to explore the issue have involved analysis of the near-victory by Los Angeles Mayor Tom Bradley in the 1982 California governor's election. And these studies have not moved on to a more general discussion of statewide black candidacies. This article examines the Bradley campaign in light of other statewide black candidacies.

Several studies have contended that Bradley's race was not the central factor in his defeat.[3] Jack Citrin et al. studied pre-election polls of racial attitudes and voting preference. Whites with conservative racial views tended to oppose all Democratic candidates, especially at the top of the ticket. These voters were no more likely to vote against Bradley than against Democratic U.S. Senate candidate Edmund G. Brown, Jr. The relationship between racial attitudes and voting was no stronger in the gubernatorial race than in the senatorial contest. These studies found far higher levels of racial voting in the 1983 Chicago and Philadelphia mayoral elections than in the 1982 California governor's race. Citrin et al. concluded that "it is misleading, then, to say . . . that Californians are not yet ready to tolerate a Black governor."[4]

Others have argued that the main cause of Bradley's defeat was indeed white racist voting. Charles Henry compared votes for Bradley, winning Democratic lieutenant-governor candidate Leo McCarthy, and previous Democratic gubernatorial candidates.[5] In Henry's view, the defection of white Democrats because of race cost Bradley the election. Henry suggested that if a popular moderate candidate like Bradley lost, the prospects for statewide black victories are dim: "Bradley, as a mainstream candidate in a relatively liberal state, represented the best hope. . . ."[6]

The research on the Bradley campaign seems to be polarized between those who deny that racism played a major role and those who see race as a controlling factor beyond influence. The focus has been on voting and survey analysis of the electorate, searching for the degree of racial influence on the results. There has been little discussion of the political dynamics of the election campaign itself, with the exception of a recent study by Thomas Pettigrew and Denise Alston.[7] They examined both the campaigns and election returns of Bradley's 1982 and 1986 races for governor. Their conclusions about the 1982 Bradley campaign— that race was a major factor but that the campaign was potentially winnable—are generally consistent with the analysis presented here. However, like the other studies, the authors do not place the Bradley campaigns within the context of the statewide black candidacy. The Citrin et al. and Stephen Baker and Paul Kleppner studies compared the Bradley case to two big-city elections, not to statewide campaigns.

Fortunately, such a comparative approach is possible. The victories of Edward Brooke in Massachusetts in 1966 and L. Douglas Wilder as lieutenant governor of Virginia in 1985 have been explored both from the standpoint of voting analysis and political dynamics.[8] An analysis of the Bradley campaign can therefore be compared to the Massachusetts and Virginia cases. This study was completed before the Wilder win in 1989, but is suggestive about that historic campaign as well.

The three cases had significantly different outcomes. Brooke won an overwhelming victory, while Wilder was only narrowly elected. Bradley lost to George Deukmejian in one of the closest gubernatorial elections in California history. The difference between Wilder's victory and Bradley's defeat is small. However, underdog Wilder's showing exceeded expectations and was considered a major upset, while Bradley's defeat came as a great surprise to most observers. Why then did Wilder do so much better than expected while Bradley failed to do as well? Why did Brooke do so much better than Bradley? Why were all three campaigns so successful (considering Bradley's near-victory) in light of the low number of statewide black office-holders? What can other statewide black candidates learn from these experiences?

The present study will explore the political dynamics of the statewide black candidacy in light of the continuing impact of race. These dynamics represent the context within which the voting results must be interpreted. The study is based on newspaper and magazine articles, campaign finance reports, public opinion polls, participant observation as a volunteer in the Bradley state campaign headquarters, and several interviews conducted before the election. It is obviously exploratory and even speculative in the hope of raising questions that may encourage further research on an important phenomenon.

The Dynamics of the Statewide Black Candidacy

My first premise is that the dynamics of a statewide black candidacy are qualitatively different from those of the mayoral elections that structure much of the literature on black candidacies. My second premise is that the race of the candidate significantly influences the dynamics of the campaign; race is deeply embedded in the battle itself, not just in the direct evidence of the voting returns. The factors that influence black prospects in statewide elections differ considerably from those in the urban setting. The mass of research on urban racial politics provides a beginning, but the dynamics of statewide racial politics require separate investigation.

Racial politics at the state level differs from the city setting in both demographics and the structure of party competition. While blacks comprise a high percentage of the population in many large cities, they represent a much smaller share in the states. Blacks do not exceed 20 percent of the population in any state outside the South. Within the South, the highest levels of black population are found in the states most resistant to black advances—Alabama, Mississippi, and South Carolina. No state exceeds Mississippi's 35 percent black population.

Without a large base of black voters, black statewide candidates must appeal to a mostly white electorate. The racial attitudes of the white majority can be expected to play a major role in any statewide black campaign, along with the style and issues offered by black candidates.

But it is not just a matter of population percentages; there are also structural differences. Black statewide candidates find themselves in a different relationship to political parties than that faced by black mayoral candidates. While big city politics often centers on the intraparty conflict between party regulars and party reformers, state politics more often involves interparty competition.

In many cities, blacks have attained independent political power by navigating between traditional party organizations and antiparty reformers. Because black mayoral candidates have generally encountered party opposition, blacks have often formed alliances with white liberal reformers against the party organizations. These struggles have occurred *within* the Democratic Party's urban base.

Interparty competition is clearly higher in statewide races than in most big-city elections. The South has usually been cited as the region with the lowest level of two-party competition. However, the ability of southern Republican candidates to win elections for governor and senator has eroded even that bastion of one-party government.[9] According to one measure, nearly half the states experience substantial two-party competition in gubernatorial races, while others have significant, if lesser degrees of competition.[10]

The statewide setting offers new opportunities but also significant limitations for black candidates. While partisan elections seem to create the conditions for reduced racial polarization in voting, this advantage for candidates is offset by the lack of black numbers. The Democratic Party's statewide candidates already draw heavy support from minority and white liberal voters; the marginal increase due to a black candidacy is small. Black candidates cannot afford to run highly publicized minority mobilization campaigns for fear of creating a white backlash. Virtually any white racist voting is likely to come straight off the top of the black candidate's vote. Thus, even when racist voting is small compared to a city election, its marginal impact may be much greater.

A black Democrat whose only white support is from antiparty reformers has little chance of winning a statewide election in a state with a significant level of two-party competition. The black candidate needs the votes of Democrats who might in their own city vote against a black mayoral candidate. Party unity is therefore crucial to black statewide success. Conversely, a black Republican will only succeed if the reluctance of blacks and white liberals to cross party lines is overcome.

I will explore three dynamic elements: racial attitudes of the state electorate, the political situation, and the campaign stance adopted by the black candidate. Through examination of these factors, I will suggest the best environment and strategy for a black statewide victory.

Racial attitudes can be assessed by opinion surveys as well as analysis of the state's social history. Of the three factors, racial attitudes represent the longest-term forces least subject to the control of the black candidate. Political situation includes such current political factors as the popularity and organizational strength of the parties, the quality of the opposing candidate, and the background of the black candidate. The possibilities for control are somewhat higher; the black candidate can choose what office to seek and when, depending on the political situation. Campaign strategy includes the ideological positioning and campaign tactics of the black candidate. What is the message and how is it projected? Of the three factors, this is the most controllable by the black candidate.

Racial Attitudes

California, Massachusetts, and Virginia are widely divergent in black population and voting patterns. Virginia has the largest black population of the three, as well as the most conservative voting record in national elections. It provided bedrock support for massive resistance to integration. Massachusetts is the most liberal and Democratic state in national elections. California, a state that has voted for only one Democratic presidential candidate since 1948, nonetheless has a reputation for racial liberalism.

For this exploratory study, the racial attitudes of each state will be considered as typical of their regions. In surveys of racial attitudes conducted by the Gallup and Harris organizations, clear regional differences have emerged. Generally, the descending order of racial liberalism has been West, East, Midwest, and South. The deep South has been the most conservative. For instance, the 1978 Gallup Poll asked voters if they would vote for a well-qualified black presidential nominee of their own party.[11] While 87 percent in the West and 78 percent in the East said they would vote for the black candidate, only 67 percent in the South and 53 percent in the deep South agreed. A 1971 Harris Poll showed that nearly identical shares of voters (about 30 percent) in the East, Midwest and West agreed that blacks are discriminated against a great deal; in the South the proportion was only 17 percent.[12]

A recent study of party voting in the South argued that the survival of the biracial coalition that supports Democratic candidates virtually depends on keeping blacks from winning statewide nominations on the Democratic ticket. In this view, white hostility to black candidates is so great that such a nomination would ensure Democratic defeat.[13] Wilder's gubernatorial victory thereby seems all the more remarkable.

Thus, the southern social setting would seem to represent the toughest challenge for black statewide candidates, in spite of the larger black population in the individual southern states. Since 1974 the voters of California have elected as many statewide black candidates (a lieutenant-governor and a superintendent of public instruction) as the entire South has since Reconstruction. Victory in a southern state like Virginia requires a favorable political situation and flexible candidate strategies. In an eastern state like Massachusetts or a western state like California, the prospects ought to be considerably better.

Bradley

The 1982 California governor's race began with the decision of two-term Democratic governor Edmund G. Brown, Jr., to seek a seat in the United States Senate. Brown, who had been hugely popular during his first term, ended his governorship in the depths of unpopularity. His public appeal suffered from two presidential campaigns, slowness in dealing with the Medfly infestation, and chaos in the state budget. A 1981 survey revealed that 55 percent of the state's voters had an unfavorable view of Brown.[14] Less than a year later, Democratic voters surveyed on the day of the June 1982 primary gave him a shocking 50 percent disapproval rating.[15]

By contrast, Los Angeles Mayor Tom Bradley brought considerable political strength to his bid to succeed Brown. In his nine years as mayor, Bradley had built a reputation as a unifier of an ethnically diverse city.[16] His steady movement away from his liberal roots to a more moderate stance increased his acceptability to the city's voters.[17] Through his economic development program, Bradley obtained the support of the downtown business community, attracting campaign money for his reelection campaigns. Bradley's favorable public image was reflected in statewide polls; he was the most popular politician in California among the voters of either party.[18] Despite wide recognition, Bradley's name evoked few negative responses.

Backed by an experienced and highly loyal candidate organization of blacks and white liberals,[19] Bradley enjoyed a stature that discouraged other campaigns from getting off the ground. In addition to Bradley's popularity and access to campaign money, no leading Democrat wanted to alienate black voters. As a result, Bradley coasted to an easy victory in the primary with 62 percent of the vote.

Bradley's political situation in the general election was less promising. Californians were not only choosing a governor, but also a senator, members of the assembly and state senate, and six statewide constitutional officers. State voters had several controversial ballot propositions to consider, including Proposition 12—an advisory nuclear freeze initiative—and Proposition 15—a measure to regulate handguns. Bradley supported both. While the ticket brought Bradley into alliance with a well-regarded slate of Democratic candidates for lesser state offices, he was also saddled with the higher visible Jerry Brown and a gun control initiative bitterly opposed by the National Rifle Association (NRA).

Despite his easy primary victory, Bradley was not in a good position to unite his party. His relationship with state party leaders was distant. In Los Angeles, party organizations have traditionally been very weak.[20] Bradley's mayoral coalition united minorities with white liberal reform Democrats who had built their movement out of opposition to the statewide Democratic regulars headed by Assembly Speaker Jesse Unruh in the 1960s.[21] At the state level, regular Democrats were much more powerful than in Los Angeles. The Unruh forces, bearing the scars of the intraparty wars, were unenthusiastic about Bradley.

While Bradley was dominant among minority politicians in Los Angeles, he was alienated from key black and Latino state politicians. Assembly Speaker Willie Brown, the state's highest ranking black elected official, kept his distance from Bradley, as did the legislative allies of Bradley's long-time black rival, Congressman Mervyn Dymally. Latino factionalism emerged as Bradley's urban Latino allies contended with their rural Latino rivals.[22]

These crosscutting factional winds meant that Bradley would be unable to easily unite the already fractious California Democrats. The party was also suffering from an eroding voter base. After the 1980 elections, approximately 300,000 Democrats were dropped from the rolls for non-voting. The party had to undertake a huge registration drive throughout 1982 simply to recoup its strength.[23]

Bradley's mayoral post both helped and hurt him. On the one hand, the image of his record as mayor was one of his greatest strengths, cited most often by voters in pre-election polls as a reason to back him.[24] But big city mayors, whether black or white, have rarely won statewide office.[25] Long-time association with the problems of a big city can counterbalance the high name recognition, even if positive, available to a mayor. A veteran mayor has made many compromises and is held responsible for the city's unsolved problems. The Los Angeles murder rate, for instance, inconveniently set a new record in 1981, causing Bradley severe political damage. As an advocate of his city's interests, the mayor suffers the ire of the rest of the state. This is particularly difficult for a big-city black mayor, because of the association between race and urban conflict. (It did not prevent San Diego Mayor Pete Wilson from defeating Jerry Brown for the U.S. Senate in 1982.)

Finally, Bradley faced a strong opponent in the general election. California Attorney General George Deukmejian, a former state senator from Long Beach, was unlike Bradley's Los Angeles opponents. In three of Bradley's four mayoral races, he had faced Sam Yorty, a maverick Democrat who frequently left the bounds of respectability. By contrast, the dull and cautious Deukmejian duplicated much of Bradley's personal appeal—sober, conscientious, moderate, and clean-living. Bradley had never faced a solid, well-behaved candidate backed by a strong party organization. Unlike his Republican primary opponent, Mike Curb, Deukmejian had few negative evaluations among the voters; his only problem was being unknown.[26]

As a state senator and attorney general, Deukmejian had identified himself with law and order. Having defeated black Democrat Yvonne Brathwaite Burke for attorney general in 1978, he knew how to make subtle racial appeals in a statewide race. The viability of Deukmejian's campaign was enhanced by the likelihood that he would oppose a black candidate. As early as January 1981, one reporter noted:

> Some insiders believe that the recent emergence of GOP Atty. Gen. George Deukmejian as a prospective candidate for governor reflects an assessment by Deukmejian and his chief strategist, Bill Roberts, that Bradley is likely to be the Democratic candidate and that he will be vulnerable to the same kinds of law-and-order arguments they used so successfully in their 1978 campaign against Democrat Yvonne Brathwaite Burke for attorney general. . . . One of the state's leading and most experienced politicians remarked this week, "I don't think Bradley is in the ball game against Deukmejian—a good, tough law-and-order candidate."[27]

Thus, Bradley's political situation was mixed. His high popularity, political style and reputation, solid and loyal political base, and ability to raise money were considerable assets. These strengths helped him preempt Democratic primary opposition and made him a very strong candidate for governor. On the other hand, his race, big-city mayoral post, lack of statewide experience, Democratic factionalism, serious Republican opposition, and association with Jerry Brown and gun control were strong negatives. Finally, he was running for the top executive office, a challenge likely to threaten some whites.[28]

Rather than being the ideal candidate in a perfect situation, as some described him in retrospect after his defeat, Bradley was highly competitive, but not in command. Most observers at the time ignored the negatives. But Pettigrew and Alston wrote in July: "Though Bradley holds a thin edge at this point, it looks as though he may need to use all the political skills he has acquired in his two decades of elected office to become America's first black governor."[29]

Jerry Brown hurt Bradley in several ways. It was bad enough that he left an unpopular Democratic administration to be judged by the voters; he also appeared on the ballot as a candidate for U.S. senator to remind the voters of his shortcomings. The association with Brown meant that Bradley had to persistently define his own independence, thus shaking the momentum of his own campaign. Bradley was even cut off from effective statewide operatives associated with Brown.

Bradley carried Brown throughout the state. Statewide he ran 292,701 votes ahead of Brown. Meanwhile, Deukmejian was being carried by Brown's opponent, Pete Wilson, who outpolled Deukmejian by 141,551 votes. Bradley outperformed Brown in fifty-four of the fifty-eight counties; Bradley won 41,225 more votes than Brown in conservative Orange County. Wilson ran ahead of Deukmejian in forty-one counties and led him by 22,925 votes in Orange County.

In addition to Jerry Brown, Bradley had another ticket partner, Proposition 15. Gun control raised the temperature of the campaign among those voters least likely to support a black candidate. Thus it may have crystallized latent racial feelings. Unlike the purely advisory nuclear freeze initiative, the handgun proposition generated tremendous, highly organized opposition. Proposition 15 opponents, led by the National Rifle Association, fielded 30,000 volunteer workers—more than the two gubernatorial campaigns combined—and spent $5.8 million.[30] The proposition was defeated by a margin of 63–35 percent, losing in all but two of the state's fifty-eight counties. In nineteen counties, the vote was more than 80 percent against the initiative. Turnout was 10 percent higher in rural areas where anti-Proposition 15 sentiment ran high than in the urban areas likely to favor Bradley.[31]

The NRA had as many as 200,000 members in California, and 37 percent of the state's households owned firearms in 1980.[32] An election-day survey indicated that, exclusive of absentee voters, 48 percent of those who voted owned firearms.[33] The NRA lobbied in favor of Deukmejian, who had joined them in opposition to Proposition 15.[34] In early August, Attorney-General Deukmejian issued an advisory opinion sought by the NRA asserting that cities lacked the legal power to limit handguns.[35] Deukmejian also mailed literature directly to conservative households, highlighting his opposition to Proposition 15.[36]

The "normal" racist vote may have been augmented by the outpouring against gun control. People may have come out to vote against Proposition 15 and stayed around to vote against the black candidate.[37] An analysis of exit polls found that about 500,000 Democrats had cast their votes against Bradley rather than for Deukmejian. These anti-Bradley Democrats were typically white males; half owned handguns and 79 percent voted against Proposition 15. Half of them said that Proposition 15 was the most important issue on the ballot, compared to 14 percent of the total voters.[38]

The balance of party organization clearly favored Deukmejian. By comparison to the Republican operation, the labor-based Democratic get-out-the-vote program was unimpressive.[39] Deukmejian was the beneficiary of a brilliant Republican absentee ballot campaign. State Republican leaders sent out absentee ballot applications to all 2.4 million registered Republicans. These mailings had two important elements: a request for funds to cover the mailing's cost and a laser imprint of the voter's name and address. All the voter had to do was sign the application and mail it to party headquarters. There it would be sorted and sent to county registrars. The mailing included a four-page letter from Deukmejian and was followed up by telephone.[40]

There was a significant interest in absentee voting in 1982 to 6.5 percent of all ballots; in 1978 the figure had been 4.5 percent.[41] Deukmejian won 59.6 percent of the absentee ballots. "Had Deukmejian run no better among absentee voters than [Republican gubernatorial candidate] Evelle Younger did against Jerry Brown four years before, he would have lost."[42] The Republicans even recouped much of the project's cost through voluntary contributions from the recipients of the ballot applications.

Brooke and Wilder

Both Brooke and Wilder faced far more auspicious political circumstances. Like Bradley, Brooke possessed enormous popularity in both parties; unlike Bradley, Brooke had statewide experience. As the incumbent state attorney general, he was well known for his investigation of Massachusetts elected officials, which had led to corruption indictments against Democratic and Republican politicians. He was also running for legislative, not executive office in a progressive state.

Despite the large Democratic registration edge in Massachusetts, the Republicans had been doing very well statewide. In the face of the massive national Democratic landslide of 1964, Brooke was reelected attorney general by 350,000 votes, and Republican John Volpe was elected governor. In 1966, an excellent Republican year nationwide, Brooke's senatorial victory was part of a Republican sweep in Massachusetts led by the reelection of Governor Volpe with 63 percent of the vote.[43]

While Wilder lacked the enormous personal popularity of either Bradley or Brooke, he had substantial state experience due to his work as a state senator. Well acquainted with the state's Democratic politicians, he was less alienated than Bradley from the state party leadership. Wilder benefited from the great popularity of outgoing Democratic Governor Charles Robb. Unlike Jerry Brown, Robb had been an extremely popular one-term governor who left office only because of a state law against successive terms. At the time of the election, Robb's public approval exceeded 70 percent.[44] While Robb himself was not running, his popularity assisted the entire Democratic ticket. With 52 percent of the vote, Wilder ran behind his party's gubernatorial (55 percent) and attorney general (61 percent) candidates. Unlike Bradley and Brooke, however, Wilder had personal liabilities, including charges of operating as a slumlord.[45]

Both Wilder and Brooke faced weak opponents in the general election. Brooke ran against former Governor Endicott Peabody, who had been defeated only two years earlier in the Democratic gubernatorial primary. Brooke's polling revealed that many of the state's voters had negative opinions of Peabody, while few held such views of Brooke.[46] Peabody opposed capital punishment, placing Brooke in the enviable position for a black candidate of being more identified with law and order than his white opponent. Furthermore, as a liberal black Republican, Brooke's race was an asset that allowed him to take black and liberal votes from the Democrats. Brooke won 86 percent of black votes, compared to a respectable 39 percent for Volpe.[47]

Wilder's opponent in the general election was John Chichester, a Republican state senator with limited support within his own party. He won the party's nomination as a compromise between bitterly divided party factions.[48] Thus, while the unity factor favored the Republicans in California and Massachusetts, it supported the Democrats in Virginia. Chichester did not have the list of personal negatives associated with Peabody, but he was considered an inept campaigner. Despite considerable encouragement from fellow Republicans, Chichester was unable to effectively use Wilder's personal problems as a campaign issue.[49]

Thus, both Brooke and Wilder had the good fortune to run on strong party tickets in a good year for their state parties. Neither had to defend a big-city mayoralty, and both had extensive state experience. Brooke and Wilder faced weaker opponents than Bradley faced. Both were seeking posts less likely than the governorship to threaten whites. In sum, while Wilder may have faced the least auspicious social setting, Bradley may have confronted the least comfortable political situation. . . .

Can Black Candidates Win Statewide Elections?

Black candidates can win statewide elections, but success will be neither frequent nor easy. There is no wave of victories on the horizon, and there will be many disappointments along the way. The prospects of winning will depend heavily on the context of the election and the strategies used by black candidates in light of that context. The outcome is not fixed, but is subject to luck and design.

Race does not exclude black candidates from contending statewide and even winning. However, race is a central factor throughout the campaign. Women are likely to find the statewide and, by implication, national level substantially easier to enter than blacks. Some research indicates that women candidates have been less limited by bloc voting against their group so much as by the unavailability of seats and candidates.[50] It is unknown what constraints will limit Latinos, since their statewide victories have been generally confined to the Southwest, where their population share is large.

Racial attitudes in a particular state provide a general background for black candidates. Wilder's victory shows that even the most conservative environment can be overcome if the political circumstances are fortunate and the strategies are flexible. However, the optimism engendered by Wilder's success should not obscure the severely constraining context of the South.

The Bradley case indicates that an undesirable political situation in a moderate/liberal state can lead to defeat; only an exceptional strategy in such circumstances can create a victory. But the prospects for black victories in such states may be better than Bradley's defeat indicated. The Brooke case shows that when a black Republican in a progressive state can reach blacks and white liberals, he or she can win a landslide.

Blacks can definitely win statewide nominations. The black electorate, while insufficient to dominate individual states, is often a crucial factor in determining which party wins general elections. This means that even though party leaders may fear that a black candidate will cost the party votes, they cannot afford to oppose him or her publicly. Potential opponents of the black candidate may choose to avoid the primary or nominating convention. Both Bradley and Wilder had easy nomination victories, partly due to this factor. All three black candidates were initially discouraged by party leaders, yet they encountered little effective opposition to their nominations. Since the nomination is obviously the first step to election, the initial opening is apparently available. The Republicans, in fact, have an incentive to nominate blacks for statewide offices even in hopeless races, in order to create conflict among Democrats.

However, the general election is always likely to be hard. Strong Republican opponents will actively seek to run against a black Democrat, perceiving the negative impact of race on the Democrat's chances. Black Republicans will face the deep Democratic loyalty of black and liberal voters, and progressive black Republicans who can be serious candidates must overcome the conservatism of Republican primary voters.

Best Conditions for Statewide Black Candidacies

Liberal Racial Attitudes

States with sufficient black population to command deference, but with liberal racial attitudes are ideal. The first factor eases the route to nomination; the second makes election possible. Sophisticated big states outside the South remain the most inviting targets. Levels of black population are likely to be less important than in black mayoral candidacies. Only a state where blacks are in a majority—and that means Washington, D.C., if it obtains statehood—could sustain a truly black-identified victory. That may help explain Jesse Jackson's interest in statehood for the capital city. The state-by-state focus also indicates that what works in California may not work in Virginia. Ideological positioning of the black candidate must take into account the electorate's views in the particular state—clearly a factor in conservative Virginia.

Positive Political Situation

At the statewide level the health of the party is critical to a black candidate's success. Black mayors can build urban coalitions without or even against the party; black statewide candidates cannot. As Jones noted, "One valuable lesson to be learned from the Wilder victory is the importance of working within the party structure, because without party backing, black statewide aspirations are doomed to political failure."[51] Membership on a popular party slate and a party organization at least as effective as that of the opposition are crucial to a black candidate.

The Brooke case indicates the underrated potential of the Republican option. While Democratic leaders may be reluctant to support statewide black candidacies, Republican leaders in big states may see the potential for symbolic appeals to black voters through supporting black candidacies. While such campaigns may seem quixotic at first, a Brooke-style Republican could find race an asset when combined with Republican identification. Black voters have indeed shown a willingness to cross party lines to reward Republican appeals. In recent years, black support helped Republican governors win in New Jersey and Pennsylvania. Viable black Republican candidacies may place pressure on Democratic leaders to be more responsive to black interests.

Ironically, just as black Democrats need to move somewhat rightward, black Republicans would have to strongly identify themselves as liberal in order to attract blacks and liberals. For the foreseeable future, such Republican candidacies are likely to be confined to those Northeastern states where Republican forces are liberal enough to nominate a black candidate who would be taken seriously outside the party.

Who are the most viable black statewide candidates? Just as an earlier generation of traditional black politicians found it hard to wage mayoral campaigns, black mayors may have important liabilities in statewide campaigns. Atlanta Mayor Andrew Young's campaign for governor of Georgia should provide an illuminating test. Politicians with state experience may be in a better position to unite the state party and to develop state issues. For the top statewide posts, earlier experience in lesser statewide offices is truly helpful. While holding down the post of lieutenant governor, Wilder had strong assets in seeking the governorship.

The prospects for victory depend on the quality of the opponent. Given the inherent liabilities facing black Democrats, stylistic or substantive weaknesses in an opponent are necessary to provide a wedge for campaign charges or to reduce the credibility of the opponent's charges. A strong opponent without substantial liabilities, like Deukmejian, may be able to run a sophisticated campaign that hardly mentions race while subtly drawing on racial feelings. The Deukmejian approach is likely to be studied by Republicans as a model for defeating black Democratic candidates. Any personal weakness is likely to be exploited. Brooke's defeat in 1978 was due in part to a messy divorce. In the same year, California's black lieutenant governor, Mervyn Dymally, was defeated for re-election despite the victory of most of the statewide Democratic ticket; unproved charges of political irregularities hindered his campaign.

Flexible Campaign Strategy

By now, the political style most acceptable to white voters is well known. It is an approach in which the black candidate is highly qualified and middle-class, with a quiet and conciliating style. Bradley is a leading practitioner of the crossover black political style.[52] California's relative success in black statewide candidacies may have been advanced by the presence of a large number of black politicians with this style.

But a "deracial" approach need not mean divorce from the black and liberal agenda.[53] As Jones has asked: "should black candidates seeking political office abandon a progressive agenda which addresses the chronic problems plaguing the black community in order to enhance their electability?"[54] Conservatism on crime, for instance, can coexist with progressive stances on the environment, education, and civil rights. As Wilder has shown, a crossover style can also coexist with an aggressive and assertive campaign.

Black statewide candidates cannot afford to be vulnerable on crime, an issue deeply intertwined with racial feelings. In 1978, black Democrat Yvonne Brathwaite Burke was defeated by Deukmejian for attorney general of California largely on the issue of crime. Even if liberals are alienated by an anticrime strategy, the crime issue left unchecked can devastate a black campaign. The liberal constituency for a statewide black candidate needs to realize that by being black the candidate is already strongly liberal in the minds of many voters.

Black candidates who face a sudden erosion of support or an unusually high number of undecided white voters may be torn between the Brooke and Bradley reactions. A high road approach like Bradley's may work best against a blatant racial appeal when the black candidate is familiar to the voters, but it may be too weak against sophisticated attacks that are not overtly racist. The viewpoint of the media may be very important; in the Wilder case, the media appointed itself as a watchdog looking for racist appeals.[55] In California, Bradley's constant repetition of the theme that race didn't matter may have helped lull the media into ignoring evidence of subtle racial factors. Pettigrew and Alston's advice that the racial issue should be directly confronted seems to be wise.[56]

The dilemma for the black candidate of how to use race as an asset while reducing its liability has yet to be solved. For instance, how low a profile must be kept among liberals and minorities in order to prevent conservative reaction and white backlash? Bradley's careful cultivation of the business community at the expense of an environmental constituency left him with the enthusiastic support of neither. Both Bradley and Wilder avoided black community campaigning, and both experienced a lower-than-average black turnout. Are there ways to solicit minority support without alienating whites?

Implications

The black statewide candidate faces an uphill struggle. While the analysis in this article does not accept the notion that the barriers are insurmountable, it also rejects the notion that black candidates can easily transcend the race question. Blacks remain one group that will not easily gain support from the majority of whites for their candidacies.

The statewide black candidacy carries the evolution of black politics in a logical direction toward higher offices through crossover appeals. Through occasional successes, black politicians can gain entry to higher levels of decision making. In a political system dominated more by media images and political symbols than traditional bargaining, the presence of minority politicians in the visible inner circle of power may be an important factor.

Statewide politics may ultimately allow blacks to navigate within the structure of party competition, creating a potential base of support within both parties.

In light of the tendency of Democratic leaders to take the black vote for granted, such flexibility may force both parties to compete more directly for black voting support. As in urban politics, a new and more forceful relationship to party politics may yield important political benefits.

Finally, the analysis of the statewide black candidacy provides an important opportunity to reconsider the dynamics of a black presidential candidacy. This study suggests that it will be a long time before Americans elect a black president. Statewide success, the first step toward the White House, is still underdeveloped. But we can speculate about what sort of black candidate will someday win that election.

The experience of the Jesse Jackson campaign does not provide the most likely model for an eventual black president. Jackson has built an enthusiastic base through highly progressive appeals, but he faces highly negative evaluations from white voters and is handicapped by lack of office-holding experience. A winning black presidential candidate, by contrast, will probably emerge in an atmosphere of reduced racial prejudice, running against a weakened opponent as a member of a strong and popular party, with extensive office-holding experience and centrist strategies building on highly positive personal evaluations by heavy majorities of the public.

Postscript

In November 1989, L. Douglas Wilder of Virginia became the first elected black governor in the nation's history. This article was largely completed well before election day. What does Wilder's victory mean for the analysis presented here?

As in his 1985 campaign for lieutenant-governor, Wilder demonstrated the importance of a creative, assertive strategy. His effective use of the pro-choice position on abortion, placing his Republican opponent on the defensive, was foreshadowed in 1985 by his emphasis on crime. As in 1985 as well, Wilder touched bases with the southern political culture, cultivating the support of conservative whites.

Wilder's razor-thin margin of victory reemphasizes the vulnerability of the black statewide candidate even when he or she has an outstanding strategy. In both 1985 and 1989, Wilder trailed the other two members of the statewide Democratic ticket; and in 1989, one of those partners was a political unknown. Wilder's close win confirms the view that even when race is not an overt campaign issue, it is deeply embedded in the election.

The obvious question is whether Wilder's election means that the South is a more promising site for statewide black candidacies than my analysis suggests. Even if Virginia has become a less conservative state with the influx of northern liberals in recent years, it is still in the South. Is Wilder an historic exception to the rule or the harbinger of a new southern system? The Andrew Young campaign for governor of Georgia promises to provide a partial answer. It still remains true that Wilder is the only black elected to a statewide office in the South since Reconstruction. His success calls for more attempts in the South, while experience suggests that non-southern states may yet remain the most receptive settings.

In the broadest sense, Wilder's victory ought to help achieve the central goal of this article—to get people thinking about the phenomenon of the statewide black candidacy. For the first time in recent years, it will be possible to focus on a crucial step along a realistic path toward a successful black presidential candidacy.

Notes

1. Roland Burris, "Winning Statewide Office," *Focus* 13 (October 1985): 3.

2. Maurilio Vigil, "Jerry Apodaca and the 1974 Gubernatorial Election in New Mexico: An Analysis," *Aztlan* 9 (Spring-Fall 1978): 133–149; Maurilio Vigil, "The Election of Toney Anaya as Governor of New Mexico: Its Implications for Hispanics," *Journal of Ethnic Studies* 12 (Summer 1984): 81–98; Maurilio Vigil and Roy Lujan, "Parallels in the Careers of Two Hispanic U.S. Senators," *Journal of Ethnic Studies* 13 (Winter 1986): 1–21.

3. Stephen C. Baker and Paul Kleppner, "Race War Chicago Style: The Election of a Black Mayor, 1983," in Terry Clark, ed., *Research in Urban Policy* (Greenwich, Conn.: JAI Press, 1986), vol. 2, 215–238; Jack Citrin, Donald P. Green, and David O. Sears, "White Reactions to Black Candidates: When Does Race Matter?" paper presented at the annual meeting of the Western Political Science Association, 1987.

4. Citrin et al., "White Reactions to Black Candidates," 33.

5. Charles P. Henry, "Racial Factors in the 1982 California Gubernatorial Campaign: Why Bradley Lost," in Michael B. Preston, Lenneal J. Henderson, Jr., and Paul L. Puryear, eds., *The New Black Politics,* 2nd ed. (New York: Longman, 1987), 76–94.

6. Henry, "Racial Factors," 90. An argument along the same lines was made by Robert Staples, "Tom Bradley's Defeat: The Impact of Racial Symbols on Political Campaigns," *Black Scholar* 13 (Fall 1982): 37–46.

7. Thomas F. Pettigrew and Denise A. Alston, *Tom Bradley's Campaigns for Governor: The Dilemma of Race and Political Strategies* (Washington, D.C.: Joint Center for Political Studies, 1988).

8. John F. Becker and Eugene E. Heaton, Jr., "The Election of Senator Edward W. Brooke," *Public Opinion Quarterly* 31 (Fall 1967): 346–358; Charles E. Jones, "Wild About Wilder: The Election of Doug Wilder for Lt. Governor of Virginia," paper presented at the annual meeting of the Western Political Science Association, 1987.

9. Charles J. Barrilleaux, "A Dynamic Model of Partisan Competition in the American States," *American Journal of Political Science* 30 (November 1986): 822–840.

10. C. Anthony Broh and Mark S. Levine, "Patterns of Party Competition," *American Politics Quarterly* 6 (July 1978): 357–384.

11. Gallup Poll, *Public Opinion 1978* (Wilmington, Del.: Scholarly Resources, Inc., 1979), 214.

12. Harris Survey, *The Harris Survey Yearbook of Public Opinion 1971* (New York: Louis Harris and Associates, Inc., 1975), 321.

13. Merle Black and Earl Black, "Democratic Gubernatorial Runoff Primaries in the Modern South," paper presented at the annual meeting of the American Political Science Association, 1987.

14. *Los Angeles Times,* 26 July 1981.

15. *Los Angeles Times,* 9 August 1982.

16. Raphael J. Sonenshein, "Biracial Coalition Politics in Los Angeles," *PS* 19 (Summer 1986): 582–590; Sonenshein, "The Dynamics of Biracial Coalitions: Crossover Politics in Los Angeles," *Western Political Quarterly* 42 (June 1989): 333–353.

17. Maurice Weiner, former deputy mayor of Los Angeles, interview with the author, 6 November 1981.

18. *Los Angeles Times,* 26 July 1981 and 5 August 1981.

19. Raphael J. Sonenshein, "Bradley's People: Functions of the Candidate Organization" (Ph.D. diss., Yale University, 1984).

20. Charles R. Adrian, "A Typology for Nonpartisan Elections," *Western Political Quarterly* 12 (June 1959): 449–458.

21. Sonenshein, "Biracial Coalition Politics in Los Angeles."

22. *Los Angeles Herald-Examiner,* 14 November 1982.

23. Tony Quinn, "The Independent Mood of the California Voter," *California Journal* 13 (September 1982): 347–348.

24. Field Poll, 13 April 1982.

25. Edward Banfield and James Q. Wilson, *City Politics* (Cambridge, Mass.: Harvard University Press, 1961), 35. Theodore J. Lowi, "Why Mayors Go Nowhere," *Washington Monthly* 3 (January 1972): 55–61. For a contrary view, see Russell D. Murphy, "Whither the Mayors? A Note on Mayoral Careers," *Journal of Politics* 42 (February 1980): 277–290.

26. Field Poll, 13 April 1982.

27. *Los Angeles Times,* 16 January 1981.

28. Thomas E. Cavanagh, "Race and Political Strategy," Conference Report of a symposium conducted by the Joint Center for Political Studies (JCPS), *Focus* 11 (June 1983): 1–9.

29. Thomas F. Pettigrew and Denise Alston, "Bradley Wins Gubernatorial Nomination," *Focus,* JCPS, 10 (July 1982): 4–5.

30. Eric Brazil, "A Mixed Bag of Messages From Those Ballot Propositions," *California Journal* 13 (December 1982): 442–444.

31. Ibid.

32. Field Poll, 14 August 1980.

33. Ibid., 1 February 1983.

34. Brazil, "A Mixed Bag."

35. *Los Angeles Times,* 4 August 1982.

36. Tony Quinn, "How Governor Deukmejian Won in the Mailbox, Not the Ballot Box," *California Journal* 14 (April 1983): 148–150.

37. Thomas F. Pettigrew and Denise Alston, "What Happened to the Bradley Campaign?" *Focus,* JCPS, 10 (November-December 1982): 5–8.

38. *Los Angeles Times,* 7 November 1982.

39. Ibid., 25 November 1982.

40. Quinn, "How Governor Deukmejian Won."

41. Field Poll, 1 February 1983.

42. Quinn, "How Governor Deukmejian Won."

43. Becker and Heaton, "Election of Senator Edward W. Brooke."

44. *New York Times,* 6 November 1985.

45. Jones, "Wild About Wilder."

46. Becker and Heaton, "Election of Senator Edward W. Brooke."

47. *New York Times,* 10 November 1966.

48. Jones, "Wild About Wilder."

49. Ibid.

50. R. Darcy, Susan Welch, and Janet Clark, *Women, Elections and Representation* (New York: Longman, 1987).

51. Jones, "Wild About Wilder."

52. Michael Goldstein, "The Political Careers of Fred Roberts and Tom Bradley: Political Style and Black Politics in Los Angeles," *Western Journal of Black Studies* 5 (Summer 1981): 139–146.

53. Charles V. Hamilton, "De-Racialization: Examination of a Political Strategy," *First World* 1 (March/April 1977): 3–5.

54. Jones, "Wild About Wilder."

55. Ibid.

56. Pettigrew and Alston, *Tom Bradley's Campaigns,* 88–90.

22

The End of the Rainbow: America's Changing Urban Politics

Jim Sleeper

On a trip to Israel in July, New York Mayor David Dinkins's eyes welled with tears as he recalled a close friendship with his accountant of many years, the late Abe Nowick, a Jew, in which racial differences had mattered so little that "one didn't know what the other was." It was a moment emblematic of the healer New Yorkers hoped Dinkins would be when they elected him over U.S. Attorney Rudolph Giuliani in 1989, shortly after young whites in Brooklyn's Bensonhurst section murdered Yusef Hawkins, a black youth who had wandered onto their turf to look at a used car. It was emblematic, too, of the promise of black "Rainbow" mayoralties in multiracial cities in the 1970s and 1980s—Tom Bradley in Los Angeles, Harold Washington in Chicago and Wilson Goode in Philadelphia, to name a few.

Yet, just as those other rainbows have faded, the ecumenical side of Dinkins on display in Jerusalem has been eclipsed in the years since his "Vote your hopes, not your fears" victory four years ago. Challenged by Giuliani again this year, Dinkins has been reduced in part to running a "Vote your fears" campaign. A string of recent public claims by Dinkins supporters that Giuliani is backed by the Ku Klux Klan, fascists and Reaganites (although conservatives such as William Bennett and Pat Buchanan denounce Giuliani as a liberal) may coax some voters back into Dinkins' corner. But a victory at this price would hardly repeat the harmonic convergence that was once the rationale for a Dinkins candidacy.

What went wrong? There are two reasons for the decay of Dinkins's rainbow

From *The New Republic,* November 1, 1993, pp. 20–25. Reprinted by permission of *The New Republic,* The New Republic, Inc.

politics, neither peculiar to New York. First, a deep recession and economic upheaval demand a "reinventing" of local government that seems utterly beyond the reach of a mayor whose political style is more common in Europe than in America: that of a social-democratic wheelhorse. Dinkins's failure to articulate a rationale for municipal restructuring, much less attempt it against union and black clubhouse opposition, is one reason his government is torn by racial and other subgroup squabbling over jobs, entitlements and preferments.

Second, Dinkins's failures of leadership during a long, black boycott of Korean stores and amid black rioting against Hasidic Jews in Crown Heights are only the best-known of many abdications to the politics of victimization (among them his year-long delay of a contract for street toilets in deference to activists' demands that each one be wheelchair accessible). Such muddlings highlight the rainbow ideology's tendency to deepen racial and other differences in the name of respecting them: in the zero-sum game of urban governance, identity politics implodes.

Meanwhile Giuliani, the erstwhile altar boy with a Savonarola streak and a mostly-white inner circle, has created a Republican-liberal "fusion" slate, with Herman Badillo, the city's most distinguished Hispanic politician, running for comptroller. They claim they want to subordinate parochial grievances to a single, uniform civic standard. Alluding to the Korean boycott, Giuliani says he wants to convince blacks that "If I were mayor and some Italian-Americans were intimidating a black shopkeeper, I'd come down on them hard and fast. People have to be able to feel confident that they'll be protected, whatever the mayor's color."

It's a familiar pattern. Beyond New York, the Rainbow habit of crying racism has found itself discounted by voters of all colors who want better governance and less rhetoric. Politically centrist mayoral candidates, many of them, ironically, white men, have drawn substantial numbers of nonwhite voters into new coalitions—call them Rainbow II—by touting a can-do pragmatism and a common civic identity that is more than the sum of skin tones, genders, sexual orientations and resentments. The truth they've grasped remains obscure only to some in liberal Democratic circles and the academy: The more genuinely multicultural and racially diverse a city becomes, the less "liberal" it is in the Rainbow I sense of the term.

The pattern emerges from half a dozen donnybrooks of the past three years, including Houston and Philadelphia in 1991 and Los Angeles and Jersey City in 1992. In each, the liberal candidate, usually a person of color, had the mantle of the civil rights movement, the support of a multiracial, multicultural coalition and the endorsement of Jesse Jackson. He was militantly pro-choice, anti-death penalty and in favor of the most expansive gay rights and immigrant rights agendas around. He was applauded in black churches and endorsed by liberal newspapers. He may not have had much of an economic program, but he branded his white male opponent a closet Reaganite and sounded the trumpet for "progressive" unity.

The white male opponent, who typically had never held elective office, posed as a businesslike reformer, promising to clean house and create new jobs through commercial deregulation, better public safety, less onerous taxation and tougher union contracts. Preaching tolerance rather than correctness and touting endorsements from prominent Latinos and other minority leaders who had broken with the civil rights establishment, he vowed to unite the city across racial and partisan lines.

Closer examination turns up telling ironies. In Chicago's 1989 special election to fill out the late Harold Washington's term, Richard M. Daley, a son of—but also a reformer of—his father's infamous machine, trounced alderman Timothy Evans, who claimed the mantle of Washington's paradigmatic Rainbow I coalition and was backed enthusiastically by Jackson. Two years later, against a black former judge running on the Harold Washington party line, Daley carried 80 percent of the city's small but critical Latino vote and 26 percent of the black vote (up from just 7 percent in 1989).

Similarly, in Houston in 1991 Robert Lanier, a wealthy white real estate developer and native New Yorker, took 70 percent of the Latino vote to defeat Sylvester Turner, a black, Harvard-educated state legislator backed solidly by blacks and white Rainbow I liberals tied to former Mayor Kathy Whitmire. The popular Lanier—the first candidate in twenty years to be elected mayor with virtually no support from the 25 percent of the city's electorate that is black—is a shoo-in this fall for another two-year term.

That same year in Philadelphia, Edward Rendell, a Jewish New York native and, like Giuliani, a tough-talking ex-prosecutor, won the mayoralty by preaching fiscal austerity and municipal restructuring in a city facing bankruptcy. Campaigning energetically in the black community, he took 20 percent of the black vote against three black Democratic primary opponents before trouncing a Republican to succeed Philadelphia's first black mayor, Wilson Goode.

In July of this year, Los Angeles's Richard Riordan, another native New Yorker and a Wall Street investor, succeeded five-termer Bradley in the 58 percent nonwhite city by carrying 43 percent of the Latino vote, 31 percent of the Asian American vote, 14 percent of the black vote and 67 percent of the white vote against Rainbow I Democrat Michael Woo, a councilman who had led the opposition against Police Chief Daryl Gates. Riordan's Rainbow II is embryonic, at best, however: 72 percent of those who voted in the election were white. He has responded with high-level appointments of blacks, Latinos, Asians, and gays.

Across the continent in Jersey City, both mayoral finalists this spring were white, yet the Rainbow II scenario was otherwise unchanged. Republican Wall Street investor Bret Schundler, yet another ex-New Yorker, beat a Jackson-backed Democrat by winning 40 percent of the black vote and 60 percent of the Latino vote in that majority nonwhite city. This, even after Jackson warned in radio spots that his candidate represented "the values of the USA—the United

States of America," while a vote for Schundler was a vote for "the values of the USA—the Union of South Africa."

It was, of course, nothing of the kind. Neither was Daley's victory in Chicago—which Jackson tried to prevent by linking Daley to his father's infamous "shoot to kill" order against arsonists in 1968—simply a white racist restoration. The new mayors have won by tapping a growing disillusionment with old-style "civil rights" politics among voters whom the movement has betrayed, and by including new racial minorities who feel excluded by black-led Rainbow I administrations.

The new mayors depart, respectfully but firmly, from the politics of such trailblazing black mayors as Gary, Indiana's Richard Hatcher, Cleveland's Carl Stokes, Atlanta's Maynard Jackson, Detroit's Coleman Young, New Orleans's Ernest "Dutch" Morial, Chicago's Harold Washington and the District of Columbia's Marion Barry. Most of these men were broad-shouldered veterans of elemental, often brutal struggles for racial justice that had honed their leadership qualities and introduced them to class- as well as race-consciousness. Most won narrowly against unyielding white hostility.

In office, they had to outmaneuver scheming white politicians, censorious editorial boards and rebellious subordinates in heavily white municipal work forces. With rhetoric, if not redress, they had to relieve the pent-up frustrations of blacks long exiled from city politics and jobs. Civic elites demanded that they end black crime. Businessmen, taking advantage of the mayors' desperation about economic decay, co-opted them into "big bang" development schemes that siphoned city resources from poor neighborhoods. Detroit's Young became defensive and bitter, Marion Barry dissolute and corrupt. Harold Washington seemed to thrive on frustration, towering over his more parochial black supporters and white adversaries alike, but he died in office. Literally and figuratively, the hearts of black mayors were broken by their divided cities.

At the same time, though, some black trailblazers and their Rainbow I successors have shifted from protecting basic individual rights and mobilizing economic coalitions to touting racial group rights and policies that are gratuitously destructive of traditional families. It's almost as if Rainbow I administrations simply presume, and so accelerate, civic and social balkanization. They often pit blacks against almost everyone else, not just against declining white electorates.

It is here, in the interaction of shifting civil rights strategies and changing urban demographics, that Rainbow I meets its end. In the years after 1970, 10 million immigrants, the vast majority of them nonwhite, entered American cities. Today, 40 percent of Angelenos and 30 percent of New Yorkers are foreign-born. These Mexican and Filipino laborers, Chinese and Puerto Rican seamstresses, Pakistani and Haitian cabbies and Korean and Dominican merchants often bring with them notions of race that are more fluid and ecumenical than those of American blacks or whites. They don't necessarily embrace a Rainbow I agenda of affirmative action and group rights-oriented litigation that presumes victimization by white racism. They rely more heavily on family and communal ties in order to achieve success.

For example, the immigrants of color in New York City's poorest census tracts are three times more likely than their American black and Puerto Rican neighbors to live in two-parent households. They're more likely to work within ethnic niches of the economy and to favor public spending on police and schools rather than on welfare, foster care, homeless shelters and drug treatment. The median incomes of Caribbean blacks and Asian Indians exceed those of American blacks, blunting charges of institutional racism. Chinese and Mexican immigrants' incomes are lower, but their family structures and values point upward. Even the high level of welfare dependency among Soviet refugees only underscores that culture, not racism, is the key variable in urban success.

Polls and voting patterns suggest that most newcomers are wary of the stigma and polarization that often accompany race-based politics and programs such as all-black schools, racial districting, municipal affirmative action quotas and multicultural curricula. In recent New York City school board elections, ten of thirteen Asian candidates, and half of the Hispanic candidates, ran against a liberal "Children of the Rainbow" curriculum, backed by Dinkins, and Giuliani has sometimes led Dinkins in polls of Asians and Latinos.

The future is visible in an editorial in San Diego's Mexican-American newspaper *La Prensa,* cited recently by Jack Miles in *The Atlantic,* that heralds Latinos as the new "bridge between blacks, whites, Asians and Latinos. They [Latinos] will have to bring an end to class, color and ethnic warfare. To succeed, they will have to do what the blacks failed to do: incorporate all into the human race and exclude no one."

Demographic change is also accelerating Rainbow I's passing by diminishing black clout. Latinos, vital to Rainbow II victories, now outnumber blacks in Los Angeles and will do so in New York, Houston and Jersey City by the next census. Latinos have long outnumbered blacks in such Sunbelt and Western cities as Miami, San Antonio and Denver; the last two elected Henry Cisneros and Federico Peña, both now in Clinton's cabinet, an honor shared by no former black mayor. The risk is that the new, multiracial coalitions will be openly anti-black.

Yet Rainbow II politics are by no means off-limits to black mayors, who do well among whites when they abandon a Rainbow I agenda. In 1989 Cleveland's Michael White became Rainbow II's first prominent black mayoral standard-bearer after defeating a "blacker-than-thou" opponent; he is a shoo-in for reelection next month. Denver and Seattle, both about 70 percent white, elected Wellington Webb and Norman Rice, black mayors who defy Rainbow I stereotypes. Both practice fiscal conservatism and reject race-based politics. Similarly, Chester Jenkins, the black mayor of mostly white Durham, North Carolina, credits Jesse Jackson with energizing black voters, but, describing his own campaign, says, "I didn't speak of a rainbow coalition. I'm sure that turns a lot of white people off. People think that when a black person is running, he is going to be a big taxer and spender. I'm not that way." Even in heavily black cities, where the first black mayors have left the field to black candidates hawking everything from nationalist paranoia to race-neutral economic realism, debate is less often foreclosed by charges that any candidate's views are racist.

But it's one thing for Rainbow II mayors to win by arguing that the poor, who want to live decently, and the middle class, which wants to live safely, have a common interest in restructuring government. Actually shifting government's emphasis from bureaucratic compassion to urban reconstruction is harder. A disabled federal government—the legacy of Reaganomics—forces mayors to choose between aiding today's casualties and making investments that might prevent more casualties tomorrow.

There's a flawed Democratic legacy at work here, too: In the 1960s, Great Society funding drove cities to increase the social welfare portions of their budgets from around 15 percent to as much as 30 percent. Today, most cities can't meet their needs merely through tough bargaining, more productivity and privatization. The choices mayors face do follow racial fault lines, imperiling efforts to put civic-consciousness above race-consciousness.

One who seems undaunted by these risks is Edward Rendell, the new mayor of Philadelphia. A city of 1.6 million people, it is about half white, 40 percent black and 6 percent Latino. A son of Manhattan's West Side with a voice like Mel Brooks, he moved to Philadelphia to attend the University of Pennsylvania and served as district attorney before winning the mayoralty in 1991.

The city had become insolvent in the late 1980s under its first black mayor, Wilson Goode. Its bonds had been downgraded, it was borrowing at credit card rates and it was running a structural deficit amounting to 10 percent of its $2.3 billion budget, owing to the collapse of its manufacturing base, federal cutbacks and generous union contracts. Goode, a stiff Wharton manager and a passive subscriber to Rainbow I nostrums, had alienated blacks as well as whites while deferring necessary reforms. His infamous bombing of MOVE headquarters in 1985, which destroyed a block of residential homes, was only a symptom of his lack of command.

With Goode retiring, Rendell decided to run against three black Democratic candidates by presenting himself as a "New Democrat," an apostle of David Osborne's and Ted Gaebler's *Reinventing Government*. When the candidates were asked whether they would accept a strike of city workers if it was necessary to turn the city around, "the other three hemmed and hawed," Rendell recalled in an interview with *Newsday*. "I looked in the camera and said, 'I hope it doesn't become necessary, but there's a decent chance it will. The answer to your question is yes. I don't want a strike, but if a strike's necessary to bring about the type of changes we need, then I'm ready." Rendell's strong personality and the city's desperate straits made the election a referendum on whether Philadelphia could look beyond color for candor about its condition.

Rendell could promise not to roll back blacks' political gains relative to whites' because, thanks to enlightened civil service reforms in the '50s, Philadelphia had long had a municipal work force as black as its population. As early as 1964, its police department had been 22 percent black, while nearby Newark and Detroit were at 5 percent. Equally important, Philadelphia has a 20-year-old black political establishment that predated Goode and doesn't countenance the superheated racial rhetoric common in New York or Detroit. Rendell won an absolute majority in a four-way primary, carrying 20 percent of the black vote against his black opponents. "It's not that the era of the black mayor is over," he reflected. "The era of blacks voting lockstep for black candidates is over."

In office, Rendell forged an alliance with newly elected City Council President John Street. "He handled the transition very smoothly, made deals with the black political leadership," comments *Philadelphia Inquirer* columnist Acel Moore. The city's mayors often have been at loggerheads with its council for institutional, not racial, reasons. Rendell courted Street, giving him an implicit veto on some initiatives.

That meant giving ground on privatization—keeping the new convention center under city management, for example, lest black jobs be lost. Yet Rendell privatized custodial services, prison health services and other functions, and says that similar initiatives will soon save $40 million. He insists that all whose jobs are privatized can be hired by other agencies or private contractors. But the contractors impose steep pay and benefit cuts, the point of privatization being to save money at workers' expense. And, as recent New York City scandals involving asbestos removal and parking ticket collections show, privatization can bring corruption and incompetence. Rendell counters that most city unions can avoid such troubles by changing their own work rules to improve productivity.

Rendell and Street also scaled back, by roughly $100 million, a fat trash collection contract negotiated by Goode. That meant weathering the feared strike. When union leaders cried that "an administration of white guys in suits" was beating up on black employees, the new mayor challenged black voters: "Do *you* get twenty paid sick days on your job? Do *you* get fourteen paid holidays?" The strike lasted less than a day after Rendell gave union leaders face-saving exits.

Philadelphia is still a city in decline. Its large public housing authority, which shelters 10 percent of the populace, is mired in patronage and corruption. Its industrial areas are in ruins. Its tax structure is a mess. But Rendell is at least candid about his city's options. Rainbow I mayors like Goode (and, notably, Dinkins) tend to live in denial, railing at Washington without seriously rethinking their own emphasis on rights and redistributive services. Rendell argues that mayors who want a new federal urban policy will have credibility "only if we come to Washington with clean hands."

Rendell is not the only Rainbow II trailblazer. In Cleveland, Michael White, a self-described street fighter from the city's tough East Side, combines an "attitude" toward powerful elites with a fierce determination to reinforce conservative social values in a distinctively black idiom. He ran for mayor in 1989 as a maverick state senator and won partly on a fluke: the two white candidates in the primary were so equally matched that they canceled out each other, and White squeaked past them into a runoff with the most powerful black politician in town, City Council President George Forbes. For the first time, Cleveland's electorate, half black, half white, faced a choice between two blacks.

White had made the runoff partly on his own steam, too, with a forceful campaign against black crime, school busing and Forbes's penchant for playing the race card, which had enraged many whites. "White articulated a vision and said the same thing on both sides of town," says *Plain Dealer* columnist Brent Larkin. He argued that blacks who opposed busing didn't have to fear saying so just because whites opposed it, too. In an ugly runoff with Forbes, White won with 30 percent of the black vote and 90 percent of the white vote—an inauspicious beginning for a black mayor by Rainbow I standards, but one he soon turned to his advantage among blacks.

Since the rocky reign of its first black mayor, Carl Stokes, in the late 1960s, Cleveland's population has dropped roughly 30 percent, to 505,000. Under a succession of white mayors, including ethnic populist Dennis Kucinich and corporate darling George Voinovich, Cleveland touted itself as a comeback city with a sleek new skyline and, not far off, a $365 million stadium for the Indians that will rival Baltimore's Camden Yards. But more than a third of Cleveland's population lives below the poverty line, and much of its East Side is an inner-city moonscape.

White has tackled some problems that his white predecessors avoided. Although he doesn't run the city's elected school board, he backed a winning, insurgent, biracial slate opposed to busing. He won give-backs, reduced overtime and one-cop patrol cars from city unions. He backed cops in crackhouse evictions and a controversial case involving the death in police custody of a drug-abusing black suspected of car theft.

White has been criticized by blacks and white liberals for these positions and for scolding Jesse Jackson at the 1992 Democratic National Convention in New York, when Jackson criticized Bill Clinton after his nomination was inevitable. White's obvious pride in being black has helped him on the East Side, but "he has consciously attempted not to be a 'black' mayor," Larkin says. "If anything, he makes a conscious effort to be a mayor who happens to be black." Civil rights leaders may not like that, but Cleveland's voters do.

As White's and Rendell's accomplishments mirror one another, Rainbow II moves to the center of urban politics from both sides of the racial divide. This is nowhere more clear than in New York, where a Dinkins defeat would mark the first time that a big city's first black mayor has ever lost a re-election bid. Such a defeat, especially amid the liberal fear-mongering about racism and fascism now underway in New York, would be a telling repudiation of twenty years of misguided racial politics.

But a Giuliani victory would not settle the question of whether Rainbow II administrations can regenerate American cities as places where new products, ideas and people circulate freely across the lines of color and class. Full black participation in that exchange is what the early civil rights movement sought, and what more recent black attacks on the liberal civic culture have repelled. Can new mayors outflank or creatively redirect such assaults?

The challenge ought to be irresistible to Democrats, who bring to cities a sophistication at governing and a love of urbanity. But those who cling to Rainbow I social-welfare spending and identity politics will continue to default to Republican neophytes such as Los Angeles's Riordan, Jersey City's Schundler or, indeed, Giuliani. Only if Democrats follow the example of candidate Clinton, who spoke for those "who work hard and play by the rules," and who rebuffed that consummate Rainbow I phony, Sister Souljah, can they expect to win like Rendell and White. Only if Rainbow II succeeds will cities regain their promise and, not incidentally, nourish the occasional friendship where "one didn't know what the other was."

23

Race and the American City

Bill Bradley

A campaign season should be a time for candid truth as well as a time for partisan charges, and nowhere is this more needed than in the consideration of the issue of race and the American city. I come to the floor today to offer some thoughts on that subject. . . .

Slavery was our original sin, just as race remains our unresolved dilemma. The future of American cities is inextricably bound to the issue of race and ethnicity. By the year 2000, only 57 percent of the people entering the work force in America will be native-born whites. That means the economic future of the children of white Americans will increasingly depend on the talents of non-white Americans. If we allow them to fail because of our pennypinching or timidity about straight talk, America will become a second rate power. If they succeed, America and all Americans will be enriched. As a nation, we will find common ground together and move ahead or each of us will be diminished.

I grew up in a small town located on the banks of the Mississippi River, a multiracial, multiethnic factory town in which most of the people were Democrats. My father was a local banker and a nominal Republican. The town had 1 stop light and there were 96 in my high school graduating class. The big city, St. Louis, MO, was something we were not.

I left that small Midwestern town and went to college in New Jersey in another small town, spending most of my time in an even smaller town, the campus, except to travel to places like Philadelphia, New York, or Providence to play basketball. I graduated and spent 2 years in England at a slightly larger college town and then went to New York where for the first time I lived in a big city.

The city for me was always about race as much as it was about class or power or fashion. Maybe that was because I was a professional basketball player in

New York and was working in a kind of black world. This was before I had any real knowledge about the welfare system, the courts and prisons, the nature of an urban economy, or the sociology of neighborhoods. But if I paid attention, I saw the city through the eyes of my black teammates, as well as through my own.

Above all, the city, to me, was never just what I heard my white liberal friends say it was. In their world, people of color were all victims. But while my teammates had been victimized, their experience and their perception of the experience of black Americans could not be reducible to victimization. To many, what the label victimization implied was an insult to their dignity, discipline, strength, and potential.

Life in cities was full of more complexity and more hope than the media or the politicians would admit, and part of getting beyond color was not only attacking the sources of inequity, but also refusing to make race an excuse for failing to pass judgment about self-destructive behavior.

Without a community, there could be no commonly held standards, and without some commonly held standards, there could be no community.

The question is whether in our cities we can build a set of commonly accepted rules that enhances individuality and life chances but also provides the glue and tolerance to prevent us from going for each other's throats.

But remember, urban America is not only divided by a line between blacks on one side and whites on another. Increasingly, it is a mixture of races, languages, and religions as new immigrants arrive in search of economic promise and freedom from state control. Just think, over 4.5 million Latinos and nearly 5 million Asian-Pacifics have arrived in America since 1970.

In New Jersey, schoolchildren come from families that speak 120 different languages at home. In Atlanta, managers of some low-income apartment complexes that were virtually once all black now need to speak fluent Spanish. Detroit is a city that has absorbed over 200,000 people from Middle Eastern descent. And in San Jose, CA, you see in the phone book residents with the Vietnamese surname Nguyen outnumber the Joneses by nearly 50 percent. And in Houston, one Korean immigrant restaurant owner oversees Hispanic immigrant employees who prepare Chinese-style food for predominantly black clientele.

So, even though our American future depends on finding common ground, many white Americans resist relinquishing the sense of entitlement skin color has given them throughout our national history. They lack an understanding of the emerging dynamics of one world, even in the United States, because to them nonwhites have always been the other.

On top of that, people of different races often do not listen to each other on the subject of race. It is as if we are all experts locked into our narrow views and preferring to be wrong rather than risk changing those views.

Black Americans ask of Asian-Americans, what is the problem? You are doing well economically. Black Americans believe that Latinos often fail to find common ground with their historic struggle and some Latino-Americans agree, questioning whether the black civil rights model is the only path to progress. White Americans continue to harbor absurd stereotypes about all people of color, and black Americans take white criticism of individual acts as an attempt to stigmatize all black Americans. We seem to be more interested in defending our racial territory than recognizing we could be enriched by another race's perspective.

In politics for the last 25 years, silence or distortion has shaped the issue of race and urban America. Both political parties have contributed to the problem. Republicans have played the race card in a divisive way to get votes. Remember Willie Horton? And Democrats have suffocated discussion of self-destructive behavior among the minority population in a cloak of silence and denial.

The result is that yet another generation has been lost. We cannot afford to wait longer. It is time for candor, time for truth, and time for action.

America's cities are poorer, sicker, less educated, and more violent than at any time in my lifetime. The physical problems are obvious—old housing stock, deteriorated schools, aging infrastructure, diminished manufacturing base, a health-care system short of doctors that fails to immunize against measles, much less educate about AIDS. The jobs have disappeared, the neighborhoods have been gutted. A genuine depression has hit cities, with unemployment in some areas at the levels of the 1930s.

Yet, just as Americans found solidarity then in the midst of trauma and just as imaginative leadership moved us through the darkest days of the Depression, so today the physical conditions of our cities can be altered. What it takes is collective will, greater accountability, and sufficient resources.

What is less obvious in urban America is the crisis of meaning. Without meaning, there can be no hope. Without hope, there can be no struggle. Without struggle, there can be no personal betterment. Absence of meaning derived from overt and subtle attacks from racist quarters over many years and furthered by an increasing pessimism about the possibility of justice offers a context for chaos and irresponsibility.

Development of meaning starts from the very beginning of life. Yet, over 40 percent of all births in the 20 largest cities of America are to women living alone. Among black women, out-of-wedlock births are over 65 percent.

While many single women do heroic jobs of raising kids, there are millions of others who get caught in a life undertow that drowns both them and their children. Many of these children live in a world without love and without a father or any other male supportive figure besides the drug dealer, the pimp, or the gang leader. They are thrown out on the street without any frame of reference except survival. They have no historical awareness of the civil rights movement, much less the power of American democracy.

I remember a substitute teacher in New York who once told me that he was assigned *The Autobiography of Malcolm X* when he learned to read and write. In hopes that they would get that same excitement, he remembers assigning *The Autobiography of Malcolm X* to his students, and they wanted to know why the teacher assigned them a book about Malcolm Ten.

To say to kids who have no connection to religious faith, no family outside a gang, no sense of place outside the territory, no imagination beyond the cadence of rap or the violence of TV, that government is on their side rings hollow. Their contact with government has not empowered them but diminished them. To them, government at best is incompetent—look at the schools, the streets, the welfare department—and at worst, corrupt—the cops and building inspectors on the take, the white color criminal who gets nothing but a suspended sentence, the local politician with gross personal behavior. And replacing a corrupt white mayor with a corrupt black mayor will not make the difference.

In such a world, calls to "just say no" to drugs, or to study hard for 16 years so you can get an $18,000 a year job are laughable. Instead of desires rooted in the values of commitment and service to community as expressed through black churches and mosques, desires, like commodities, become rooted in the immediate gratification of the moment. TV bombards these kids with messages of conspicuous consumption, and they want it now. They become trapped in the quicksands of American materialism. The market sells images of sex, violence, and drugs, regardless of their corrosive effects on hard work and caring—values formerly handed down from an older generation. With no awareness of how to change their world through political action and no reservoirs of real self-knowledge, they are buffeted by the winds of violence and narcissism.

The physical conditions of American cities and the absence of meaning in more and more lives come together at the barrel of a gun. If you were to select the one thing that has changed in cities since the 1960s, it would be fear. Fear covers the streets like a sheet of ice. Every day, the newspaper tells of another murder. Both the number of murders and violent crimes has doubled in the 20 largest cities since 1968. Ninety percent of all violence is committed by males, and they are its predominant victims. Indeed, murder is the highest cause of death among young black males. In 1968, there were 394,000 security guards in America. Today, it is a growth industry with nearly 700,000 guards.

For African-Americans in cities, the violence is not new. You do not have to see "Boyz N the Hood" to confirm it. Just visit a public housing project where mothers send their kids to school dodging bullets; talk with young girls whose rapes go uninvestigated; listen to elderly residents express their constant fear of violation; and remember the story of the former drug dealer who once told me that he quit only after he found his partner shot, with his brains oozing onto the pavement.

What is new is the fear of random violence among whites. No place in the city seems safe. Walking the streets seems to be a form of Russian roulette. At the core, it is a fear of young black men. The movie "Grand Canyon" captures the feeling. It sends the message that if you are a white and you get off the main road into the wrong territory, you are a target because you are white. And you are a target for death, not just robbery. And if you stay on the main road, you still might be shot for no apparent reason. Guns in the hands of the unstable, the angry, the resentful, are used. As the kid in "Grand Canyon" says: "You respect me only because I have a gun."

Never mind that in a society insufficiently color blind, all black men have to answer for the white fear of violence from a few black men. Never mind that Asian-Americans fear both black and white Americans, or that in Miami and Los Angeles, some of the most feared gangs are Latinos and Chinese. And never mind that the ultimate racism was whites ignoring the violence when it was not in their neighborhoods, or that black Americans have always feared certain white neighborhoods. Never mind all that.

There are two phenomena here. There is white fear and there is the appearance of black emboldenment. Today, many whites, responding to a more violent reality heightened by sensational news stories, see young black men traveling in groups, cruising the city, looking for trouble, and they are frightened. Many white Americans, whether fairly or unfairly, seem to be saying of some young black males:

> You litter the street and deface the subway, and no one, black or white, says stop.
> You cut school, threaten the teacher, dis' the social worker, and no one, white or black, says, "Stop." You snatch a purse, you crash a concert, break a telephone box, and no one, white or black, says, "Stop." You rob a store, rape a jogger, shoot a tourist, and when they catch you, if they catch you, you cry "racism," and nobody, white or black, says, "Stop."

It makes no difference whether this white rap is the exact and total reality in our cities; it is what millions of white Americans feel is true. In a kind of ironic flip of fate, the fear of brutal white repression felt for decades in the black community and the seething anger it generated now appear to be mirrored in the fear whites have of random attacks from blacks and the growing anger it fuels. The white disdain grows when a frightened white politician convenes a commission to investigate the charges of racism, and the anger swells when well-known black spokespersons fill the evening news with threats and bombast.

What most politicians want to avoid is the need to confront the reality that causes the fear. They do not want to put themselves at risk by speaking candidly about violence to blacks and whites and saying the same thing to both groups. Essentially, they are indifferent to the black self-destruction, and violence only hardens that indifference, not only to the perpetrator, but to all African-Americans.

Physically, more white Americans leave the city. From 1970 to 1990, over 4 million white Americans moved out of our big cities. Psychologically, white Americans put walls up to the increasing desperate plight of those, both black and white, who cannot leave, those Americans who are stuck trying to raise kids in a war zone, holding jobs in a Third World economy, establishing a sense of community in a desert where there is no water of hope and where everyone is out for themselves.

It is not that there is not racism, you understand; it is alive and well. It is not that the police brutality does not exist; it does. It is not that police departments give residents a feeling of security; few do. But when politicians do not talk about the reality that everyone knows exists, they cannot lead us out of our current crisis. Institutions are no better than the people who run them, and because very few people of different races make real contact or have real conversations with each other—when was the last time you had a conversation about race with someone of a different race—the white vigilante groups and the black TV spokespersons educate the uneducated about race. The result is that the division among races in our cities deepens with white Americans more and more unwilling to spend the money to ameliorate the physical conditions or to see why the absence of meaning in the lives of many urban children threatens the future of their own children.

Yet, even in this atmosphere of disintegration, the power of the human spirit comes through. Heroic families do overcome the odds, sometimes working four jobs to send their kids to college. Churches are peopled by the faithful who do practice the power of love. Local neighborhood leaders have turned around the local school, organized the health clinics, or rehabilitated blocks of housing. These islands of courage and dedication still offer the possibility of local renewal, just as our system of Government offers and makes possible national rebirth.

So, the future of urban America will take one of three paths: abandonment, encirclement, or conversion.

Abandonment means recognizing that with the billions of investment in the national highway system which led to suburbia, corporate parks, and the malling of America, and with communications technology advancing so fast that the economic advantages of urban proximity are being replaced by computer screens, in those circumstances, the city has outlived its usefulness. Like the small town whose industry leaves, the city will wither and disappear. Like empires of ancient days, the self-destruction has reached a point of no return and will crumble from within, giving way to new and different forms of social arrangement. "Massive investment in urban America would be throwing money away," the argument goes, "and to try to prevent the decline will be futile."

Encirclement means that people in cities will live in enclaves. The racial and ethnic walls will go higher, the class lines will be manned by ever increasing security forces, and communal life will disappear. What will replace it are deeper divisions, with politics amounting to splitting up a shrinking economic pie into ever smaller ethnic, racial, and religious slices. It will be a kind of clockwork orange society in which the rich will pay for their society, the middle class will continue to flee as they confront violence, and the poor will be preyed upon at will, or will join the army of violent predators. What will be lost for everyone will be freedom, civility, and the chance to build a common future.

Conversion means winning over all segments of urban life to a new politics of change, empowerment, and common effort. Conversion is as different from the politics of dependency as it is from the politics of greed. Its optimism relates to the belief that every person can realize his or her potential in an atmosphere of nurturing liberty. Its morality is grounded in the conviction that each of us has an obligation to another human being, simply because that person is a human being.

There will not be a charismatic leader here but many leaders of awareness who champion integrity and humility over self-promotion and command performances. Answers will not come from an elite who has determined in advance what the new society will look like. Instead, the future will be shaped by the voices from inside the turmoil of urban America, as well as by those who claim to see a bigger picture.

Conversion requires listening to the disaffected as well as the powerful. Empowerment requires seizing the moment. The core of conversion begins with a recognition that all of us will advance together, or each of us will be diminished; that American diversity is not our weakness but our strength, and that we will never be able to lead the world by the power of our example until we have come to terms with each other and overcome the blight of racial division on our history.

The first concrete step is to bring an end to violence, intervene early in a child's life, reduce child abuse, establish some rules, remain unintimidated, and involve the community in its own salvation. As a young man in dredlocks said at one of my recent town meetings, "What we need is for people to care enough about themselves, so that they won't hurt anyone else." That is the essence of community policing—getting a community to respect itself enough to cooperate and support the police so that together security is assured. And our schools can no longer allow the 5 percent of kids who don't want to learn to destroy the possibility of learning for the 95 percent who do want to learn. In addition, we need gun control, draconian punishment for drug kingpins, mandatory sentences for crimes committed with guns, and reinvestment of some defense budget savings into city police departments, schools, and hospitals.

The second step is to bolster families in urban America. That effort begins with the recognition that the most important year in a child's life is the first. Fifteen-month houses must be established for women 7 months pregnant who want to live the first year of their life as a mother in a residential setting. Young fathers would be encouraged to participate, too. Fifteen-month houses would reduce parental neglect or violence by teaching teen-age mothers how to parent. Fifteen-month houses, by offering a program of cognitive stimulation, would prepare a child for a lifetime of learning. These 15-month houses need to be combined with full funding for WIC and Head Start, more generous tax treatment of children, 1-year parental leave, tough child support enforcement, and welfare reform that encourages marriage, work, and assumption of responsibility, instead of more children you cannot afford.

But there is also a hard truth here. No institution can replace the nurturing of a loving family. The most important example in a child's life is the parent, not celebrities, however virtuous or talented they might be. You might want to play golf like Nancy Lopez or play basketball like Michael Jordan or skate like Kristi Yamaguchi or display the wit of Bill Cosby, but you should want to be like your father or mother. And in a world with few involved fathers, mom has a big burden. There are no shortcuts here, only life led daily.

The third step is to create jobs for those who can work—jobs that will last in an economy that is growing. It is only through individual empowerment that we can guarantee long-term economic growth. Without growth, scapegoats will be sought and racial tensions will heighten. Without growth, hopes will languish. How do we get growth? Enterprise zones, full funding of jobs corps, more investment in low-income housing. Yes. Helping to finance small businesses and providing technical assistance in management. Yes. Investment in urban infrastructure such as ports, roads, and mass transit will become a source of jobs and training for urban residents at the same time it builds part of the foundation for private investment. Yes. Allowing pension funds to make some investments in real estate and assessing a very low capital gains tax on the sale of assets that have generated 500 urban jobs for 10 years will attract more investment. Yes.

But no targeted program can overcome the drag of a sluggish national economy. Reducing the deficit, consuming more wisely, increasing public investment in health and education, and avoiding protectionism are essential for long-term growth. Combined with assuring economic opportunity for all, long-term growth can save American cities while taking all Americans to a higher economic ground.

Finally, the political process holds the ultimate key. It has failed to address our urban prospect because politicians feel accountable mainly to those who vote. Urban America has voted in declining numbers. So politicians have ignored them. Voter registration and active participation remain the critical empowerment link. The history of American democracy is a history of broadening the vote: when the Constitution was adopted, the only Americans who had the vote were white males with property. Then, in the 1830s, it was extended to white males without property, in the 1860s to black males, not until the 1920s to women, and finally to young people age 18–21 in the 1970s. That is the history. Yet today, if one-third of the voting-age population in America woke up on election day and wanted to vote, they would not be allowed to vote because they are not registered. Again what is needed is not so much charismatic leadership but day-to-day leadership, truthful leadership, dedicated to real and lasting change. Leadership that has the power within the community by virtue of the community knowing the life of the spokesperson. That is leadership that can get things done, and in the end, for change to come, decisions have to be made, work has to get done, and some group of individuals has to accept collective responsibility for making change happen.

Stephen Vincent Benet once said about American diversity: "All of these you are," all of these racial ethnic religious groups you are, and each one of them, "and each is partly you," and none, not any of them, "and none is false, and none is wholly true."

Another way of saying out of many, one. He was describing America. Whether the metaphor is the melting pot or a tossed salad, when you become an American citizen you profess a creed. You forswear allegiance to a foreign power; you embark on a journey of development in liberty. For those who came generations ago there is a need to reaffirm principles—liberty, equality, democracy—principles that have always eluded complete fulfillment. The American city is where all these ideas and cultures have always clashed—sometimes violently. But all, even those brought here in chattel slavery and subsequently freed, are not African or Italian or Polish or Japanese. They are Americans.

What we lose when racial or ethnic self-consciousness dominates are tolerance, curiosity, civility—precisely the qualities we need to allow us to live side by side in mutual respect. The fundamental challenge is to understand the suffering of others as well as to share in their joy. To sacrifice that sensitivity on the altar of racial chauvinism is to lose our future. And we will lose it unless urgency informs our action, passing the buck stops, scapegoating fails and excuses disappear. The American city needs physical rejuvenation, economic opportunity, and moral direction, but above all what it needs is the same thing every small town needs: The willingness to treat another person of any race with the respect you show for a brother or sister with the belief that together you'll build a better world than you would have done alone; a better world in which all Americans stand on common ground.

24

How the Rioters Won

Midge Decter

In August 1965, the late Bayard Rustin, one of the major civil-rights leaders of that day, traveled to Los Angeles to see for himself the results of the massive outbreak of violence, arson, and looting that was henceforth to be known simply as "Watts." In the course of the melee, 34 people had been killed, more than 1,000 injured, and local businesses and services almost totally wiped out. As Rustin would later write,* during his tour he came upon a street-corner meeting at which a twenty-year-old unemployed black man was shouting, "We won! We won!"

"'How have you won?'" Rustin reported challenging the young man. "'Homes have been destroyed, Negroes are lying dead in the streets, the stores from which you buy food and clothes are destroyed....'"

"'We won,'" came the answer, "'because we made the whole world pay attention to us. The police chief never came here before. The mayor always stayed uptown.'"

Rustin, though no sympathizer with violence, black or any other kind, was persuaded. He most certainly did not condone the behavior of the Watts rioters, but he did in the end conclude that Watts deserved to be dignified as a "manifesto":

> The first major rebellion of Negroes against their own masochism ... carried on with the express purpose of asserting that they would no longer quietly submit to the deprivation of slum life.

Today, some 27 years later, in the wake of a riot in a section of Los Angeles

---

From *Commentary,* July 1992, pp. 17–22. Reprinted by permission of Midge Decter.
*"The Watts 'Manifesto' and the McCone Report," *Commentary,* March 1966.

not all that far from Watts which left nearly twice as many dead and injured, that young man's declaration of victory has taken on more meaning than was ever dreamed of in Bayard Rustin's philosophy.

The story of the many riots which have erupted in the inner cities of America since the mid-60's, including this most recent one in South-Central Los Angeles, is invariably quite simple. First there is a putative "cause." Often the claimed incitement is no more than a soon forgotten attempted arrest, or perhaps an automobile accident; only very rarely is it something as historically weighty as the assassination of Martin Luther King, Jr., or as loaded as, in this case, the acquittal of four police officers known to have brutalized a black man (indeed, seen doing so on videotape by the whole country). Next, some individual or group finds the occasion a sufficient reason for a bit of avenging mayhem in the form of a fire or a broken window or two. And then, as they say, all hell breaks loose: one fire leads to another; broken windows and doors offer the temptation of the goods arrayed behind them; a push leads to a beating which leads to general bloodlust which leads to gunfire; and finally the normally peaceable are drawn irresistibly by the lure of free merchandise, and full-scale looting commences. What brings all this to an end? External force, without doubt, but probably to some extent also sheer fatigue, the goods all carried off, the fires all damped.

Obviously, not all eruptions of the inner city follow this pattern in every precise particular. Neighborhood geography, for instance, is an important influence on both the direction and velocity of a rioting mob. But certain general conditions do usually seem to be present—reasonably warm weather, for example, and a critical mass of young people, particularly young men, hanging around with nothing much to do.

Given that there have been many such riots in the past quarter of a century, it might seem odd that the whole country should have responded to the outbreak of April 29-May 3 in Los Angeles with such a flood of social theory and such a fury of sociological chatter—quite as if everyone, white and black, were being confronted by a new phenomenon in need of fresh explanation.

To be sure, the Los Angeles riot was exceptionally murderous and destructive: perhaps, as has been claimed in a weird parody of local boosterism, this will even turn out to have been the biggest and worst riot ever. Moreover, to reinforce the images of mayhem broadcast night and day on television—pictures of beating and burning, shooting and stealing, coming at the audience with the immediacy that has been made possible by the technology of the camcorder—there has emerged a new cadre of journalists who seem positively blown away by the discovery that all is not well among America's inner-city blacks. Add to this the fact that we are in a presidential election year, a time when politicians, too, are given to unearthing *de novo* each of our very old and long-accustomed problems, and you have the ingredients of an even more voluble round of the ritualistic position-taking which has come to constitute the nation's normal discussion of race policy.

Strangely enough for an event of this kind, there is no dispute about what actually happened. On Wednesday, April 29, at 3:30 P.M., the jury in the trial of the four Los Angeles policemen who had beaten up a young black man named Rodney King brought in a verdict of not guilty on all charges (except for one charge against one defendant, on which they had been deadlocked). "Today the system has failed us," the mayor of Los Angeles, Tom Bradley, declared, and anticipating what might happen, he also pleaded for calm.

Within an hour and a half, however, billows of smoke could already be seen rising from South-Central L.A., and soon after that, also from nearby districts, particularly the one called Koreatown. Before quiet was to be restored, days later, fires would be set, and some looting would be done, in places far beyond the boundaries of South-Central L.A., places as distant and supposedly out of reach as Beverly Hills to the north and Long Beach to the south. But the main violence and damage were confined (as usual) to the slums where the rioters themselves lived and/or did their shopping.

In any case, by Thursday the smoke was so dense that the air-traffic controllers at Los Angeles International Airport had to close all but one runway. Highways were clogged with frightened people trying to get out of town. Bus and train service stopped. Schools and offices and stores were closed throughout the city. In other words, here were the makings of looters' heaven.

Although Mayor Bradley had been apprehensive enough from the first moment to plead for calm, and though things soon got sufficiently out of hand to force him to declare an emergency, the police were amazingly scarce. On the first day, a small contingent of cops made its way to a spot near the now-famous intersection of Normandy and Florence, credited with being the riot's "epicenter," but after a brief scuffle with some gang members, the police retreated. Not until the next day would there be even a semblance of force, which by the end would include California National Guardsmen and federal troops called out by the President. Without the police there could be no firefighting, either; for in accordance with the tradition established in the urban ghettos during the 60s, firemen were assaulted with bricks and bullets as they attempted to go about their work.

It seems reasonable to suppose that at least some policemen, out of solidarity with their four newly-acquitted colleagues, took a certain satisfaction in leaving the cop-hating denizens of South-Central L.A. to fend for themselves. But whether or not their absconding had something in it of *Schadenfreude,* the famously zealous Los Angeles Police Department was absent for a long and what might have been a critically helpful time; and once the cops were in evidence, particularly in the effort to control the orgy of looting which had almost immediately broken out, they were somewhat less than fully energetic and efficient.

Meanwhile the entire nation, which thanks to television news had for months been witnessing and rewitnessing the pummeling of Rodney King, was now, again thanks to television, watching over and over a group of young blacks pull a white truckdriver out of the cab of his truck, throw him on the ground, and attempt first to kick his head in and then to beat it in with a brick. This, along with the pictures of Korean boys with Uzis keeping watch from a rooftop and the shots of several buildings in full flame, constitute the main iconography of the first 36 or so hours of the riot.

Seen with the eyes of television, the riot seemed to fall into three acts. The first was bloody and frightening, so full of running and shouting and the sound of breaking glass that it might almost have been a crudely overstated scene directed by one of those new young black film-makers.

The second act was quieter, and not without its deeply bitter amusements. This was the period devoted to the theater of looting—men, women, and children coming into view from behind various shapes and degrees of wreckage carrying anything they had been able to get their hands on, from cooking utensils to furniture to rolls of toilet paper and disposable diapers. Girls were seen dragging whole racks of dresses, and of course sneakers—those great emblems of ghetto status—were hanging off the arms of young and old alike.

This was also the act in which the district's representative in Congress, Maxine Waters, who had flown in from Washington, could be observed rushing around in high spirits, cameramen in tow, crying out to her constituents how much she cared for them and exhorting them to trust her in return. Representative Waters was subsequently to become the star of riot week, with innumerable talk-show appearances and much press coverage. But as one watched her skipping through the still-smoldering rubble, it was hard to banish the thought that probably never before had she had, and probably never again would she have, quite so good a time.

If the second act was not without its moments of involuntary comedy, the third act—clean-up time—provided a number of outright laughs. This was the moment of intervention from Hollywood. As calm at last returned and burned-out storekeepers and residents of the neighborhood tearfully began to dab at the charred ruins where their businesses and homes had once stood, there appeared on the scene a troop of movie stars bearing brooms and speaking soulfully to the cameras about "bringing us all together."

Movie stars, we know, have become a solemn lot who regularly take themselves and are taken for the heroes they play: Jack Klugman testifies to Congress as Quincy the medical examiner; Meryl Streep becomes a reborn Karen Silkwood, this time warning the authorities against the poisons of alar; and Edward James Olmos, brilliant portrayer in *Stand and Deliver* of a real-life teacher who got children in a Latino slum to master calculus, arrives in South-Central L.A. to save the children there. But viewers were never to discover just how long Mr. Olmos and his glittering companions stayed around or how much debris actually gave way before them.

As to that debris, no one knows for sure just how much of it was created or how much, in dollars or time, will be required to clear it away. Estimates of property damage vary from $750 million to $1 billion. And even numbers as gigantic as this do not and cannot by themselves tell the whole story, since they do not and cannot include any calculations of the value of the future that has now been wiped out—future efforts, future profits, future salaries. In Watts, undone by a riot more than 25 years ago, few businesses have been restored, or new ones started up, to this very day. Indeed, as a New York *Times* reporter pointed out (in another bit of inadvertent humor), the boys of Watts, deprived in so many other ways, were now also denied their fair share of the looting, because there were no businesses left in *their* neighborhood to loot.

The worst damage was suffered by the Koreans, who were deliberately singled out by the blacks for special ruin. But neither were all black-owned businesses spared, not from the torch and certainly not from the looters. One of the more vivid televised vignettes was that of a young black businessman entering his fried-chicken restaurant which had been gutted of just about everything, including even the stoves, as two teen-age girls were rummaging around for some leftovers to carry off. "Hey," he called to them in shock and bewilderment, "you're not supposed to take from a brother!" They shrugged, and giggled, and walked off a little sheepishly with a couple of pans.

By Friday, May 1, the rioting and looting had spread to a variety of places in the United States, big cities, small cities, and suburbs—Atlanta (which once advertised itself as a "city too busy to hate"), Seattle, Las Vegas, Minneapolis, Miami, San Francisco, New Rochelle. All these copycat riots were ostensibly set off by the acquittal of Rodney King's tormentors, and all were almost completely confined to the rioters' own neighborhoods. In Las Vegas, nighttime violence was to continue for weeks.

In Manhattan, the news that the ubiquitous black demagogue, the Reverend Al Sharpton, would be leading a protest march down Broadway triggered alarmist rumors that virtually shut the city down by 3:00 P.M. on Friday, and sent an unprecedented torrent of traffic to choke the bridges and the tunnels that are the island's only avenues of escape. Sharpton had called for a peaceful demonstration, and the police had been both plentiful and highly visible, surrounding the marchers like so many sheepherders. Thus only a small breakaway group got out of control, smashing "only" a few store windows, overturning "only" a few cars, and leaving "only" one Korean shopkeeper paralyzed for life. A bit of violence was also reported in Harlem, but again "only" one shooting and one stabbing, neither fatal.

In the days following, the city's press and officialdom were beside themselves with pride in this achievement, heaping praise on the mayor, on the police chief, and above all on the demonstrators, who had managed to come through such a difficult pass without destroying too much property or killing anyone.

If it was to take three or four days of military patrolling, as well as nights of strict curfew, to bring the violence in Los Angeles to a final halt, it took hardly more than 24 hours for the pundits and editorialists, not to mention the politicians and the professional black leaders, to commence offering their explanations of what the Los Angeles riot—and, by extension, the others—was really about.

The overwhelming thrust of the comment was simultaneously to deplore and to justify the rioting. George Bush himself more or less took this tack, but that did not prevent his (and Ronald Reagan's) alleged responsibility for the disorders from becoming a steady subtheme of the justifiers. Naturally, the presidential campaign had something to do with the bruiting of this theme: the Democratic hopeful, Jerry Brown, for instance, found the opportunity on a talk show hosted by his fellow Democrat, Jesse Jackson, to announce that ". . . ten years of building more prisons than ever before, more erosion of civil liberties, more urine testing, more police work, and at the same time exporting millions of jobs, this is what you get."

For others somewhat more focused than Brown, the charges against the Republicans came down roughly to two. First and most pervasive was the direct connection drawn between the condition of the black slums and the supposed withdrawal of federal funds from the cities. And second was the Bush campaign's use in 1988 of the notorious Willie Horton commercial, which had encouraged whites, as Michael Kramer of *Time* wrote, "to demonize blacks."

But aside from such exploitations of this wonderful opportunity to gain a little fortuitous partisan advantage, there was an instantaneous and wide consensus about the deeper causes of the riot. These were almost universally identified under the quick and handy rubric of "rage and frustration"—the latter, for those inclined to psychological theory, inevitably creating a breeding-ground for the former. "Rage and frustration"—the words were on the lips of everyone from the lowliest local reporter and newscaster to the most esteemed academic and social and political commentator.

Blacks across the spectrum, from Al Sharpton and Jesse Jackson to the columnists Carl Rowan and William Raspberry to the *Today*-show host Bryant Gumbel, harped continuously on the idea that the people, particularly the young men, of the ghetto had been neglected for too long. According to Rowan, the big cities have been given short shrift under Reagan and Bush because the people who live there, especially blacks, vote Democratic. According to Raspberry, ghetto blacks are "people who don't register on society's screen except when they are hurting someone else, or threatening to." And according to Gumbel, "Maybe [the riot] might help in putting race relations on the front burner, after they've been subjugated [*sic*] for so long as a result of the Reagan years."

If Gumbel was, characteristically, a touch muddled, most of the black contributors to a special report, "America on Trial," published in *Newsweek* (May 11), were quite clear about the role of racism in this neglect. As Norman Amaker, professor of law at Loyola University, bluntly put what many others obviously felt: "African-Americans will draw from this the lesson we've always known. Our lives aren't worth shit."

Interestingly enough, however, when it came to justifying the violence in Los Angeles as a response to racist oppression, whites, and especially certain white journalists, were even more outspoken than their black counterparts. In a column in *Newsday,* for example, the much-lionized Sydney Schanberg asked:

> Why do so many white Americans hail protests against human-rights abuses in distant countries and fail to understand the grievances of their own black neighbors?

In a similar vein, David Broder of the Washington *Post* cautioned both George Bush and his Democratic challenger Bill Clinton that

> There is no more important test of character for an American President than what he does to heal the scars that slavery and racism have left on this society. That is the curse that is killing us, and everything else is secondary.

And on the same day, in another column in the Washington *Post,* Hobart Rowan seconded Broder's analysis:

> America is really two nations, divided along rigid class lines—the privileged who have jobs and the underclass who are denied hope because they were born with skin of the wrong color. This ugliness has been festering for a long time: too many of us turned our faces away from the obvious and refused to look at the reality of racism.

So, too, Anna Quindlen, winner of the 1991 Pulitzer Prize for her New York *Times* column, confessed that she had first thought of proposing that we wear ribbons of the kind worn for hostages and AIDS victims, to "repulse racism." But then she realized how naive this was:

> It's as naive as thinking that because African-Americans go to Harvard and sit in the next booth at Burger King, it cancels out the neon sign that blinks "Nigger" in white minds.

In an effort, presumably, to force us to confront the reality from which we have "turned our faces away," the ever-enterprising Ted Koppel of *Nightline* provided a group of young black gang members from Los Angeles with a rich opportunity to make themselves heard and understood in millions of American homes.

Now, as has been so colorfully depicted in several movies and innumerable television dramas, the minority neighborhoods of Los Angeles are riven with violent youth gangs. Their tables of organization, so to speak, as well as their relation to one another, are highly complex. There seem to be two overarching gangs, called the Bloods and the Crips, broken down into subdivisions, and subdivisions of those. Basically what these gangs do is hang out and kill one another's members, in some longstanding round of retribution and counterretribution whose mythic origin lies back in the mists of history. (One of the reasons the authorities had difficulty at first in calculating the number of deaths attributable to the riot is that a certain number are considered "normal" each week as the wages of gang warfare.)

The gang, or subgang, invited to appear on *Nightline* was the one involved in sparking the riot, the 8-Trey Gangster Crips. When Koppel asked the boys about the white truck driver who had in full view of the nation been pulled from his truck and beaten, one of them replied, "He knew better. He saw what was happening." Said a second, "It was a CIA." A third pointed out, "They saying that, well, we burning down our own community. I mean, we don't own none of these liquor stores."

Yet another, named Time Bomb, was surprised that Koppel had never heard of him, "because of my background and my crime." At Koppel's urging, Time Bomb began to expand on that background—his years in prison for shooting, breaking and entering, and attempted murder. The member known as Li'l Monster complained that the spotlight was always on them for drive-by shootings or the killing of an innocent victim, "but what about that fly-by the United States just did on Iraq?" The conversation continued in this vein, with Li'l Monster explaining that his father had to be a criminal because he couldn't feed his family, and now he, Li'l Monster, must be a criminal, and he would in turn hand on his father's legacy to his son.

Many people were offended by this program, with its suggestion that these young thugs had a genuine case to argue. Yet there was something truly interesting to be learned from Time Bomb and Li'l Monster and the others. And that was how very much they have managed to pick up from the high-toned academic and political generalizations that have for so long served as an excuse for them and their lives. They could speak coolly in one breath of breaking and entering and killing, and in the next of their rage and frustration at the lack of jobs in their community. Or they could explain how, unlike their predecessors in 1965, they had assault rifles, Uzis, hand grenades, bulletproof vests—"not a generation of asskicker takers but . . . giving out asskickers now"—and in the same moment justify themselves by referring to the CIA and the Gulf War.

Thus does liberal ideology make its way to the streetcorners of South-Central Los Angeles.

If, then, the solemn attention which has been paid to the rioters is any measure, they too can claim, as the Watts rioters did to Bayard Rustin in 1965, that they have "won." By the same measure, the great losers in 1992 are the Koreans, about whom very little has been said.

Ted Koppel did bring up the Koreans in his conversation with the gang members, and so did Tom Morganthau of *Newsweek*. With a few notable exceptions, however, the Koreans served mainly to introduce into the discussion mournful considerations of just how, in Morganthau's words, "infinitely sensitive, infinitely complicated" is the relation of race and ethnicity to poverty.

But very far from complicated is the hatred of the Koreans on the part of many blacks in South-Central L.A. It is the hatred felt for the enterprising immigrants in their midst by individuals living month to month on government checks, unable to do for themselves or by themselves. To account for these immigrant shopkeepers and small businessmen, a paranoid fantasy has been invented, that the government and/or the banks offer the Koreans special favors—an explanation the fantasists must know in their heart of hearts not to be true. (On the other hand, the complaint that the Koreans look down upon their black customers *is* very likely true.)

But the point is that among all the predictable cries that something must be done either for or about the black underclass—from Head Start to drug rehabilitation to reconstituting the Civilian Conservation Corps to a tough new clamping-down on crime—one would be hard put to find a suggestion that anyone should pass the hat for the burned-out citizens of Koreatown.

This refusal of empathy with the Los Angeles Koreans on the part of America's liberal publicists has very deep roots—as does the strange denial involved in the liberal culture's entire response to the riot. Denial, to be sure, might seem a curious choice of word for such a deal of coverage and scrutiny and such a throaty exploration of meaning. And yet for all the wrapping-up and summing-up to which the world has been treated, the very heart of the matter, staring everyone in the face, has been evaded and obscured.

Leaving aside the hope of taking some partisan political advantage of a crisis—all too easy to understand but under the circumstances despicable—how can so many people with the utmost sincerity have said the things they said about this riot?

How is it possible that anyone, black or white, in speaking of the black underclass should in this day and age use the word "neglect"? After all, there has not been a month or a week or a day since Daniel Patrick Moynihan wrote his 1965 report on the disintegration of the black family in which diagnoses of the problems of the urban black community and prescriptions for healing them have not filled the American air. That most of these prescriptions have themselves in turn created iatrogenic diseases is irrelevant here: whatever the failures that have followed upon it, attention has certainly been paid—and paid and paid and paid again.

How is it possible that anyone in good conscience should claim that too little money has been spent in, or on, the cities, when more than a trillion dollars has in one way or another been allocated to them by Washington since the 60s? How is it possible to go on declaring that what will save the young men of South-Central L.A., and the young girls they impregnate, and the illegitimate babies they sire, is jobs? How is it possible for anyone to look at these boys of the underclass—to look at them literally, with one's own eyes, and actually *see* them—and imagine that they either want or could hold on to jobs? How is it possible to think that Time Bomb and Li'l Monster, and their counterparts in Chicago, Detroit, New York, are angry and frustrated at the unemployment rate in their communities?

In short, how is it possible to persist in refusing to recognize that the condition of those young men is beyond the reach of government—that, indeed, the efforts of government have done much to undermine their capacity to take charge of their own lives? Yet taking charge of their own lives is the *only* thing that will save them. As Glenn Loury, the black [economist], recently remarked, "The problem of the black underclass is a problem that will only be solved one by one and from the inside out."

This is not so very difficult an idea to grasp and it has become an ever more difficult one to deny. It is equally difficult to continue denying that to hold blacks responsible for themselves would be a mark of respect that has heretofore, despite all passionate protestations, been withheld from them in liberal thought.

Difficult—but not, it would appear, impossible. For not even a quarter of a century of failure has been enough to dislodge the belief that society at large must furnish the means—the magic program or school curriculum or legal reform—to make everything all right for the black underclass. And the reason this belief cannot be shaken when it comes to blacks is that giving it up for them would force the liberal culture to give it up for everyone else as well.

Assuming responsibility for one's life, for one's everyday choices as well as for one's moral conduct, is a practice that has been eroding in American life for a long, long time: every private weakness is by now regarded as a legacy of parental misbehavior, every discomfort as an injustice, every wrong turn as an enforced imposition from outside, every defeat as a malfunction of "the system." From something as fatal as AIDS to something as nebulous as acquaintance rape, the slightest suggestion that the consequence might be connected with one's own behavior has become anathema.

This is what accounts for the absurd hue and cry over Vice President Dan Quayle's disapproving remark about the decision of a TV-sitcom heroine to have a child out of wedlock. Full-page headlines were devoted to this attack on Murphy Brown by the Vice President; talk-show guests shouted at one another about it. People attempted to charge Quayle with triviality, but their very passion in doing so belied their intention. Quayle was suggesting that both the producers and the more privileged consumers of American popular culture have a house of their own to put in order. But this stuffy message, which is to say, this truth, is what the main managers of our public discourse can least bear to hear—never mind the cost to those poor blacks whose interests they have for so long and with such self-exculpating gratification appointed themselves to serve.

Part IX

Public Policy

The readings in this section concern the relationship between race and public policy. There is a strong racial element to many public policy issues, including welfare, crime, illegitimacy, education, and affirmative action. For example, while there are more whites than blacks on welfare, blacks comprise a disproportionate percentage of welfare recipients. Similarly, crime, the police, and the criminal justice system are major issues for African Americans. Young black males commit an undue amount of crime in America—most of which is perpetrated against blacks. In addition, one survey indicates that one-fourth of all American black males between the ages of eighteen and twenty-nine are either in jail, on probation, or on parole.

The first reading is by Paul E. Peterson, Henry Shattuck Professor of Government at Harvard University. In "The Urban Underclass and the Poverty Paradox," Peterson examines the persistence of poverty in the United States, in spite of massive federal expenditures.

Peterson reviews four explanations for the continuation of poverty. The first is an inadequate welfare state. This argument points to America's lack of a strong labor movement, a vigorous socialist party, or "a coherent set of national bureaucratic institutions that could administer an integrated welfare system." Peterson notes that there is much evidence for this viewpoint. The American welfare state is much less extensive than social welfare programs in European countries, and the social changes created by the Great Society are far less consequential than is often claimed by conservatives. The "inadequate welfare state" thesis is used by political liberals and radicals who favor expanded social welfare programs, and do not blame the underclass for their condition.

The second explanation of the poverty paradox is the culture of poverty. This perspective is based on anthropological and sociological analyses of ghetto life, such as *Tally's Corner,* by Hylan Lewis (1967). Individuals in the culture of poverty fail to exhibit customary middle-class values, such as self-sacrifice, industriousness, and future orientation. Peterson summarizes this viewpoint as follows: "In a world where jobs are dull, arduous, or difficult to obtain and hold, it is more fun to hang out, make love, listen to and tell exaggerated stories of love and danger, plan parties and escapades, and exhibit one's latest purchases or conquests."

The third explanation, perverse government incentives, is complementary to the culture of poverty thesis. This argument, advanced by Charles Murray in *Losing Ground: American Social Policy, 1950–1980* (1984), holds that the urban underclass lifestyle is actually quite rational. According to Murray, the increasing size and availability of federal welfare programs has created a new set of incentives for America's poor. The current welfare system makes single motherhood preferable to marriage, and receiving welfare assistance preferable to work.

Peterson observes that Murray's thesis "resonated well with the political climate of the early 1980s." Murray's analysis blamed big government, the welfare state, and welfare recipients for illegitimacy, unemployment, crime, drugs, urban violence, and racial tension.

However, Peterson offers several criticisms of Murray's propositions. Peterson contends that the work ethic is deeply ingrained in all parts of American society, that most studies show little relationship between welfare assistance and willingness to work, and that most research shows that welfare benefit levels do not affect the incidence of out-of-wedlock births.

Peterson then analyzes a fourth explanation for the poverty paradox, "the inner city in a changing economy." This argument has been advanced by William Julius Wilson, in *The Declining Significance of Race: Blacks and Changing American Institutions* (1978) and *The Truly Disadvantaged: The Inner City, the Underclass, and Public Policy* (1987). In *The Truly Disadvantaged,* Wilson argues that America's growing urban underclass is the result of "the shift from goods-producing to service-producing industries, the increasing polarization of the labor market into low-wage and high-wage sectors, innovations in technology, the relocation of manufacturing industries out of the central cities, and periodic recession." Wilson contends that "any significant reduction of the problem of joblessness will call for a far more comprehensive program of economic and social reform than what Americans have usually regarded as appropriate or desirable." He maintains that the problems of the underclass are mostly the consequence of economic dislocations. While he does not deny the persistence and significance of racism in America, he contends that economic factors have greater consequence.

In *The Declining Significance of Race,* Wilson maintains that the United States is in a period of transition from racial inequalities to class inequality, and that racial conflict is a special manifestation of class conflict. He discusses the harmful effects of changes in the modern American economy, such as uneven economic growth, increasing automation, industrial location, and the decline of high-wage, low-skill jobs. He calls for a policy of full employment and reindustrialization.

While generally sympathetic to Wilson's analysis, Peterson asserts that this theory "makes only a modest contribution to our understanding of the poverty paradox," due to the fact that it applies only to those neighborhoods in which poverty is particularly concentrated. Peterson states that a comprehensive theory of the urban underclass needs to focus on "the increasing numbers of female-headed households, the declining earnings and labor force participation of young men from minority backgrounds, and the shift in poverty from rural areas to central cities."

Peterson outlines a program to reduce poverty in the United States. Besides a growing economy, he recommends reform of the health care system (so that low-paid workers have access to health insurance) and improving inner-city education (by giving parents the right to choose schools for their children).

Daniel Patrick Moynihan, the senior United States Senator from New York, is the author of the second reading, "How the Great Society 'destroyed the American family.'" Moynihan has long been involved in American racial politics. During the Johnson administration, he was assistant secretary of labor for policy planning and research, where he wrote "The Negro Family: The Case for National Action." The opening line of the "Moynihan Report" was that "the United States is approaching a new crisis in race relations." The report sounded an alarm over the deteriorating status of the black family, and raised a storm of controversy over the effects of slavery, economic decline, and the welfare system upon adult black males.

Moynihan was also a controversial figure in the Nixon administration. While serving as President Nixon's chief domestic adviser, he urged adoption of a national "guaranteed annual income" plan to replace the existing welfare system. He reviewed the debate over this proposal in *The Politics of a Guaranteed Annual Income: The Nixon Administration and the Family Assistance Plan* (1973). Later, Moynihan urged Nixon to adopt a policy of "benign neglect" toward blacks. Moynihan's argument was that an excessive emphasis on the problems of minorities and the poor was serving only to heighten expectations among blacks and discontent among whites.

In the reading reprinted in this part, Moynihan notes that the condition of the black underclass has worsened since the publication of the "Moynihan Report" in 1965. There is growing black illegitimacy, increasing rates of welfare dependency, and a massive deterioration of black society.

There is also a growing public resentment over welfare spending and social welfare liberalism. Indeed, William Barr, attorney general in the Bush administration, claimed that crime and family breakdown were the "grim harvest of the Great Society." Moynihan responds that "this is manifestly absurd. The breakdown was there in the data before the Great Society, just as the welfare system was there before the Great Society."

The third reading, "The Clinton Administration and African-Americans," is by Monte Piliawsky, a political scientist at Penn Valley Community College in Kansas City and the author of *Exit 13: Oppression and Racism in Academia.*

Piliawsky argues that black support of the Democratic Party is overwhelming, due to Republican stands on busing, states' rights, "welfare queens," affirmative action, and Willie Horton. However, he argues that this allegiance to the Democrats has come at the price of being taken for granted.

In 1992, presidential candidate Clinton wooed middle-class Reagan Democrats, campaigned extensively in white suburbs, and ignored the urban black population. Clinton stressed welfare reform and opposition to crime, "issues with strong racial overtones."

Piliawsky takes exception to Clinton's "New Covenant" social philosophy. He calls Clinton's emphasis on individual responsibility "profoundly conservative." He objects to Clinton's support of "workfare" (which he terms "punitive"), and he opposes Clinton's proposals for boot camps, metal detectors in public schools, and drug sweeps in public housing.

He also criticizes Clinton for several racial incidents during the 1992 presidential campaign. In one such episode, Clinton was photographed on the front page of the *New York Times* (with Georgia Senator Sam Nunn) overseeing a group of black boot camp prisoners. Jesse Jackson commented that Clinton and Nunn looked like slave masters.

Clinton also comes under attack for several symbolic actions during his presidency, such as sending his daughter, Chelsea, to a private school. Further, Piliawsky complains that Clinton's black cabinet appointments are from the wealthy strata of society.

Piliawsky's arguments are consistent with old-fashioned liberalism. He calls for a public works program to "rebuild the decaying sections of our cities." He says, "The key to eradicating black poverty is for the national government to provide meaningful jobs for African-Americans."

Piliawsky's views are almost certainly outside the political mainstream—including the black mainstream. In an era when most voters are interested in federal deficit reduction, a massive public works employment program is not high on the national agenda. In spite of Piliawsky's criticisms, Clinton's "conservative" views on crimes and welfare reform have wide public support—even among blacks.

One of Piliawsky's arguments is somewhat odd. He notes that the Clinton administration "boasts of a cabinet that is the most diverse ever assembled—four African-Americans and two Hispanics among its fourteen members. . . ." However, this is insufficient for Piliawsky, because the black Cabinet members (heads of the Agriculture, Commerce, Energy, and Veterans Affairs Departments) are not in the right places. He approvingly quotes Howard University political scientist Ronald Walters, who points out that no blacks are in charge of Housing and Urban Development, Health and Human Services, or Education, "where the pain is greatest, where the greatest number of our people are suffering."

What is striking about this argument is that it assumes that there are "black" departments in the cabinet. Indeed, prior to the Clinton presidency, the Department of Housing and Urban Development was the "black" cabinet, having been headed by Robert Weaver (under President Johnson), Patricia Roberts Harris (under President Carter), and Samuel Pierce (under President Reagan). The only other black cabinet officials have been William Coleman (secretary of transportation under President Ford) and Louis Sullivan (secretary of health and human services under President Bush). Many observers *applauded* the fact that Clinton's African American cabinet officers cover a wide range of (non-traditional) territory.

25

The Urban Underclass and the Poverty Paradox

Paul E. Peterson

The urban underclass is at once a characterization of a fragment of American society, a statement about the interconnections among diverse social problems, and an attempt to theorize about the paradox of poverty in an affluent society. The term is powerful because it calls attention to the conjunction between the characters of individuals and the impersonal forces of the larger social and political order. "Class" is the least interesting half of the word. Although it implies a relationship between one social group and another, the terms of that relationship are left undefined until combined with the familiar word "under." This transformation of a preposition into an adjective has none of the sturdiness of "working," the banality of "middle," or the remoteness of "upper." Instead "under" suggests the lowly, passive, and submissive, yet at the same time the disreputable, dangerous, disruptive, dark, evil, and even hellish. And apart from these personal attributes, it suggests subjection, subordination, and deprivation. All these meanings are perhaps best brought together in Richard Wagner's *The Ring of the Nibelung*. Wotan goes under the earth to wrest the ring from the malicious Alberich, who had used it to enslave a vile and debased subhuman population.

Because of these diverse meanings, underclass is a word that can be used by conservatives, liberals, and radicals alike. It is a fitting term for conservatives who wish to identify those people who are unable to care for themselves or their

From *The Urban Underclass,* edited by Christopher Jencks and Paul E. Peterson (Washington, D.C.: The Brookings Institution, 1992), pp. 3–27. Reprinted by permission of The Brookings Institution.

families or are prone to antisocial behavior. But underclass, like lumpen proletariat, is also a suitable concept for those who, like Karl Marx, want to identify a group shaped and dominated by a society's economic and political forces but who have no productive role. And underclass is acceptable to some liberals who somewhat ambiguously refuse to choose between these contrasting images but who nonetheless wish to distinguish between the mainstream of working-class and middle-class America and those who seem separate from or marginal to that society. But, above all, the concept has been called back into the social science lexicon because it offers an explanation for the paradox of poverty in an otherwise affluent society that seems to have made strenuous efforts to eradicate this problem.

Two recent analyses of the urban underclass, Charles Murray's *Losing Ground* (1984) and William Wilson's *The Truly Disadvantaged* (1987), have generated the most vigorous research effort on the poverty paradox since the proliferation of urban studies spawned by the civil rights movement during the 1960s. Indeed, this renaissance of social science investigation into the connection between the urban underclass and the paradox of poverty in the late 1980s is, on the whole, simply a picking up of the intellectual pieces that were left scattered in the early 1970s by the acrimonious debate over the existence and nature of the culture of poverty, Daniel Moynihan's study of *The Negro Family* issued by the Labor Department, and the Nixon administration's family assistance plan.[1] The objectivity of research, the effect on scholarship of the racial background of social science investigators, and the hidden agendas of protagonists in the debates all became a matter of considerable disputation. Amidst this turmoil, college students and younger scholars turned their attention elsewhere, foundation and government agencies reoriented their research priorities, and universities closed down their urban studies programs.

The research and analysis reported in *[The Urban Underclass]* is just one sign among many that at least for the moment the urban studies tide has begun to flow back in. Motivated by an effort to test some of the many hypotheses set forth in Wilson's book, it brings together research by sociologists, economists, political scientists, and policy analysts that allows us to make some empirically based assessments of the validity of various claims about the origins and significance of the urban underclass. The collection is hardly definitive, for research on this topic is today vigorous enough that new insights and findings are emerging with a rapidity quite unthinkable in the recent past. . . .

The Paradox of Continuing Poverty

When Lyndon Johnson declared the War on Poverty in 1964, he had good reason to believe that the federal government could succeed in ridding itself of the paradox of widespread poverty in the world's wealthiest country. The poverty rate in the United States had been declining steadily since 1940 even without any self-declared government effort to address it. In 1940 some 34 percent of the population was living in poverty; by 1960 this had decreased to 15 percent and by 1970 to 11 percent. Among black Americans the decrease had been even steeper: from 71 to 32 percent. Among Hispanics the rate fell from 55 to 23 percent.[2]

The specific battle plan drawn up by the Johnson administration for the War on Poverty failed to match the rhetorical artillery the president employed. The effort was little more than a call for citizen participation combined with a hodge-podge of hastily designed educational, job training, and neighborhood service programs that had little internal coherence and only limited financial backing. It was more important as a vehicle for involving blacks and other minorities in local political processes than as a mechanism for redistributing wealth. When the Office of Economic Opportunity, the high command for the official poverty war, was finally disbanded in the early 1970s, few noticed the difference.[3]

But a focus on the conduct of the official War on Poverty is misleading. If the war effort is understood instead as the sum total of Great Society programs enacted and enhanced during the Johnson and Nixon administrations, then the transformation of a broad range of social welfare programs in the late 1960s and early 1970s can, in comparison with previous government efforts, truly be declared a full-scale war. The elderly, for whom the poverty risk in 1960 was higher than one in three, obtained easy access to low-cost medical services and greatly improved retirement benefits. Cash assistance to the blind, deaf, and disabled was increased, funded more completely by the federal government, and indexed to changes in the cost of living. Eligibility restrictions were relaxed on aid given to needy families with dependent children, and food stamps and medical assistance were added as supplements to the cash assistance these families received. Special education programs for the disadvantaged and the handicapped were enacted. Head Start was provided to very young children, and job training programs were offered to those entering the labor market. The amount and variety of housing subsidies available to qualifying families also increased.

The most conservative way of estimating the growth of these programs is to consider the percentage of the nation's gross national product used to fund them. This estimate controls not only for inflation but also for any change in the size of the economy that occurs as a function of growth in the size of the labor force or improved economic productivity. By this conservative measure the nation doubled its social welfare effort in the fifteen years between 1965 and 1980, increasing the share of GNP allocated to social security, welfare assistance, medical services, and food stamps from 5 to 10 percent.[4] Nor did the conservative climate and fiscal crises of the 1980s cut deeply into the size and scope of these programs. As Robert Greenstein points out ... the Reagan administration's effort to cut back the welfare state was frequently checked by strong congressional supporters of existing programs. Thus it might be said that as a result of its war on poverty, the nation now seems finally committed to meeting the biblical requirement that a tenth of income be set aside for those in need.

This war on poverty did not fail in any absolute sense. Although the poverty rate no longer continued to decline, it remained fairly stable at the level it had reached in the late 1960s. Among whites the official rate leveled off at about one-eighth of the population; among blacks the [poverty population] remained about one-third.[5] The poverty rate among older Americans continued to decline. Whereas one-quarter of those aged sixty-five or older had an income below the poverty line in 1970, only one-eighth did in 1987. Social security programs had been extended to include virtually all workers, benefit levels had been increased and indexed at a new, higher level, and medicare insured against most poverty-inducing illnesses. For this group at least, the effort to eradicate poverty had been a resounding success.

Yet in recent years there has been a gnawing sense that poverty, instead of disappearing, has become worse. Not only has the poverty rate for the population as a whole stabilized at around 13 percent, but the risk of becoming poor has increased in disconcerting ways. First, the official poverty rate among Hispanics increased from 28 to 39 percent between 1972 and 1987. It is not clear, however, how much of this apparent change actually occurred. The Bureau of the Census broadened its definition of Hispanic during this period, making comparisons over time suspect. In addition, it is not clear whether any increases that have occurred have been caused by changes that have taken place within the states. Both the legal and illegal immigration of many low-income Latinos from Mexico, Puerto Rico, the Caribbean, Central America, and South America may have contributed to the increased rate. However, increases in Hispanic poverty before 1980 were as large among longer-term residents as among recent immigrants.[6] Whether that remained the case in the 1980s, when the number of immigrants increased sharply, is not yet clear. It is thus not certain to what extent the poverty rate has increased among Hispanics who are not recent immigrants to the United States.

Young families have also experienced a steadily increasing chance of being poor. Although the poverty rate among the elderly was cut by one-half between 1970 and 1986, the probability that a child under the age of eighteen would be living in a poor family increased from 15 to 20 percent.

The heightened risk of poverty has shifted from people in rural areas to those living in central cities. In 1960 about 28 percent of the rural households were poor, as compared with 14 percent in the nation's central cities and 10 percent in the suburbs. By 1987 the rate in rural America had fallen to 14 percent, while in the central cities it had climbed sharply from its low of 10 percent in 1970 to 15 percent (Table 25.1). This change, it should be stressed, was not the result of any movement in the overall population from rural America to the central cities. In fact, the percentage of the nation's nonpoor population living in central cities was smaller in the late 1980s than in 1960.

Finally, the poor today are living in female-headed families more often than ever before. Whereas 25 percent of the poor were living in female-headed fami-

Table 25.1

Households with Incomes below the Poverty Line, Selected Years, 1960–87
(Percent)

Year	Central city	Suburb	Nonmetropolitan
1960	13.7	9.6	28.2
1970	9.8	5.3	14.8
1980	14.0	6.5	12.1
1987	15.4	6.5	13.8

Sources: Bureau of the Census (1972), table 3; (1982), p. 445; and (1989), table 17.

lies in 1960, by 1980 about 35 percent were, and by 1987 perhaps 40 percent were. That female-headed families were somewhat more likely to be poor in 1987 than they were in 1970 (an increase from 50 to 55 percent) provides part of the explanation. But more important was the increase in the percentage of all families that were headed by women. As Christopher Jencks points out . . . , the percentage of female-headed families has increased rapidly among all racial and occupational groups. Between 1970 and 1987 the percentage among whites increased from 8 to 13 percent and among blacks from 28 to 42 percent.

In short, the poverty paradox continues even after a major increase in the government's commitment to the welfare state. And not only has the overall poverty rate refused to fall in the 1970s and 1980s in the way that it had in earlier decades, but the risk of poverty grew greater among Hispanics, children, residents of urban areas, and those living in female-headed families (itself a growing percentage of the population).

Nor is it just the recent trends in poverty rates that are disconcerting. The poverty paradox is even more apparent when the United States is compared with other industrial societies. With the U.S. government's official measure of poverty as a standard, comparative data were collected for eight industrial countries—Australia, Canada, Norway, Sweden, Switzerland, the United Kingdom, the United States, and West Germany—for 1979–82. Australia had a slightly higher poverty rate than the United States, while the United Kingdom's rate was 1 percentage point less. But the average poverty rate in the other countries was 5 points lower. The differences were even more dramatic when the rates of children in poverty were calculated: the United States scored higher (that is, worse) than did any other country. Its rate was only slightly higher than Australia's, but it was more than 6 percentage points higher than the rate in the United Kingdom and 10 percentage points higher than the average of the other five countries. Only among the elderly did the poverty rate in the United States not appear exceptional; it ranked fourth after the United Kingdom, Australia, and Norway, and was only slightly higher than the rate in West Germany. In other words, cross-national comparisons reinforce the impression one obtains by examining changes in the incidence of poverty within the United States over time. The poverty rate in this affluent society seems exceptionally high, and young people are especially at risk.[7]

The Underclass-Poverty Connection

The relationship between this poverty paradox and the urban underclass has been a subject of considerable debate. Many poor people are clearly not members of any underclass. The elderly poor, widows, orphans, the severely sick and disabled, and the simply unlucky can find themselves suddenly plunged into poverty without warning. Similarly, many people who engage in activities said to be characteristic of the underclass are hardly poor. Indeed, some of the most celebrated instances of an underclass style of life—laziness, unreliability, unrestrained attachment to fancy clothes and high fashion, episodic romantic attachments, drug addiction and alcohol abuse—are to be found among the very rich.

Indeed, for some analysts the poverty paradox is only one manifestation of a much more general deterioration in American society and culture. The major problem is the way in which a spreading underclass culture is undermining the country's productive capacity, family life, social integration, and, ultimately, its political stability.[8] Other analysts see virtually no relationship between the poverty paradox and the existence of an urban underclass. Often they object to using the word underclass, and if they accept the concept, they argue that an underclass, to the extent that one exists, is small, heterogeneous, and not growing. They argue that it constitutes no more than a minor portion of the low-income population, and that overall poverty levels have little to do with the activities of this segment of the population.[9]

From these varying views on the urban underclass, one can differentiate four quite separate explanations for the poverty paradox: the incomplete extension of the welfare state, the culture of poverty, the perverse incentives provided by welfare assistance, and the disproportionate effects of changes in the international economy on the core areas of cities. Each explanation implicitly or explicitly addresses the way in which the urban underclass has contributed to a poverty paradox, and each offers policy recommendations designed to resolve that paradox.

An Inadequate Welfare State

The standard interpretation, at least in liberal intellectual circles, is that the United States has always been an inegalitarian society in which the myth of equal opportunity has obscured a reality of submerged class conflict, racial discrimination, and tolerance of economic inequality. Compared with European societies, the United States has never had a strong labor movement, a vigorous socialist party, or a coherent set of national bureaucratic institutions that could administer an integrated welfare state.[10] Americans have instead relied on great natural resources, a decentralized governmental system, a large internal private market, and dynamic economic growth to resolve their social tensions. Extremes of wealth and poverty have emerged side by side, and although some efforts to ameliorate these extremes developed in the wake of the Great Depression of the 1930s and the civil disorders of the 1960s, the country is too committed to individual liberty, too suspicious of big government, and too divided by race and ethnicity to redistribute wealth in such a way as to meet the needs of the poor adequately.

Although the United States made greater progress toward creating a welfare state during the Great Society years than at any other time in its history, the argument continues, the result is still a patchwork of programs and institutions that fails to provide for the needs of the poor in a comprehensive manner. The most elaborate and expensive of Great Society innovations were the elaboration of the social security program and the institution of medicare, both of which addressed the economic and social needs of the elderly. Not surprisingly, it is precisely this group for which the appellation poverty paradox seems no longer appropriate. As Theda Skocpol points out . . . , social innovation was much more modest for other demographic groups. Although the "deserving" poor—the blind, deaf, and disabled—were placed within a new, nationally funded program that materially improved their welfare, the government was still reluctant to address the needs of the "undeserving" poor—those who many people thought could and should earn a living for themselves. Aid to families with dependent children remained a program administered by the states. When the federal government supplemented this cash assistance with food stamps, the cash assistance provided by state governments declined, leaving poor families no better off than they had been.[11] "Undeserving" men and women in households without dependent children were eligible only for state general assistance programs, which varied greatly from one part of the country to the next and in most places provided only the most token assistance. The amount of this assistance also declined in value when federally funded food stamps became available.[12] Admittedly, medicaid helped reduce the extreme disparity in medical services between the middle class and the poor, but housing subsidies reached only a small minority, and increased educational services were too marginal and too fragmented to have much effect.

For the most part the liberal view attributes the poverty paradox to the inadequate development of the welfare state rather than to any changes in society or to specific characteristics of an urban underclass. But there is one strand of thinking within the liberal tradition that at least has implications for understanding the urban class phenomenon—the discussion of social rights and citizenship that has evolved out of the writings of the British social theorist, T. H. Marshall. From this perspective, the United States has a larger, more threatening underclass than most European countries because it has done so little to incorporate marginal groups into the social and political mainstream. The United States has a dual economy, a social world divided along racial and ethnic lines, and large numbers of people who are politically apathetic and uninvolved. Any society that does not treat all its citizens as valued members of the political community encourages marginal citizens to think of themselves as political outsiders who share in neither the benefits nor the responsibilities of the social and political community. If an underclass exists, it is because the state has created a group of outcasts that are denied their social and political rights.

There are at least three major pieces of evidence that support the liberal view: the welfare state in the United States is much less uniform and comprehensive than it is in many European countries; the elderly have done much better in the past two decades than have other social groups; and the changes in public policy wrought by the Great Society have been less significant than has often been claimed. But if these pieces of evidence support the liberal interpretation, another points in another direction. Poverty in the United States had been declining steadily between 1940 and 1960, two decades in which the welfare state expanded hardly at all. Yet when the welfare state expanded in the 1970s, progress toward eliminating poverty came to a halt. What is more, poverty increased among young families and inner-city residents.

The Culture of Poverty

The cultural explanation, perhaps the classic statement of the relationship between the underclass and the poverty paradox, holds that the style of life to which the urban poor has become attached is self-perpetuating. Street life in the ghetto is exhilarating—at least in the short run. In a world where jobs are dull, arduous, or difficult to obtain and hold, it is more fun to hang out, make love, listen to and tell exaggerated stories of love and danger, plan parties and escapades, and exhibit one's latest purchases or conquests. Gangs provide young people thrills, protection, mutual support, friendship, prestige, and enough income to allow them to buy fashionable clothes, alcohol, and drugs. When men cannot earn enough to support their families adequately, they avoid enduring relationships with their female companions. Women respond by becoming self-reliant, domineering, and mutually supportive. But without an adult male figure in the household, they are unable to protect their children from the alluring street life that promises short-term excitement, if not much hope for a prosperous future.[13]

There is little consensus on the origins of the culture of poverty in American society. Some theorists have attributed it to the inequalities of economic power in the larger society, others to processes of urbanization that undermined the mutual interdependence of family members characteristic of traditional societies. John Ogbu has recently used an imaginative reconstruction of the cultural thesis to account for the contrasting experiences of various ethnic groups in American society.[14] Those groups—American blacks being the extreme case—who were compelled to come to or were forcefully incorporated into the United States and, once there, were subjected to poverty, discrimination, and slavery, constructed for themselves a conflictual understanding of the country's social and political institutions. Members of these forcefully incorporated groups explained personal disappointments and affronts as the product of broad social forces—class dominance, racial prejudice and discrimination, cultural exclusiveness—over which they, as individuals had little control. It was hopeless to fight the system; instead, one might as well rip off and enjoy as big a piece of it as one could. As New Yorkers would say, "Take a bite of the Big Apple." But this explanation of their experiences, Ogbu suggests, would often become self-fulfilling—both for the individual minority member and the group as a whole. The more one rejects the system, the less one is willing to study or work and the more one is rejected by the societal mainstream.

Voluntary immigrants to America experienced many of the same disappointments, affronts, and rejections, but when they compared their experience in the United States with their experience in their homeland, they found opportunity much greater in the United States. They thus explained their limited success as a function of their own shortcomings, and they believed that if their children acquired the advantages of language and education they could succeed in the new world. These voluntary immigrants worked hard, told their children to take advantage of the opportunities available to them, and, once again, often found their prophecy self-fulfilling.

Whatever the causes of ghetto social practices, anthropological studies of the culture of poverty continue to provide troubling accounts of urban underclass life. . . . Elijah Anderson shows the processes by which teenage girls decide to keep their babies to term and raise them, the joys a young child brings to a single parent, and the sorrows and troubles that later emerge. . . . David Greenstone discusses the ways in which these commitments to street life can be understood both as a rational response to immediate circumstances and as a product of a distinctive cultural milieu. He then suggests, along lines similar to those developed by Ogbu, that only by reducing the distance and conflict between mainstream institutions and ghetto culture can policymakers find the mechanisms for transforming it.

If the emphasis on a cultural milieu helps explain immediate choices in poor urban neighborhoods, it is by itself too static a concept to be a satisfactory explanation for the poverty paradox. Indeed, many of those who describe the culture of poverty locate its origins in social relationships in the wider society, whether these be characterized in terms of class conflict, racial discrimination, cultural distance, or social dislocation. At its best, the explanation warns against expecting rapid change in urban neighborhoods in response to broader economic and political change. At its worst it blames the victims for their problems. In all cases, it is most satisfying when linked to other, more structural interpretations.

Perverse Government Incentives

The third interpretation of the relationship between the underclass and poverty, propounded most compellingly by Charles Murray, identifies the Great Society programs as the most important structural factor affecting inner-city culture. While accepting the description of ghetto life elaborated by cultural anthropologists, Murray claims that members of the urban underclass, far from being irrationally bound by a cultural milieu that is as self-debilitating as it is unchangeable, are quite rational in the way they live their lives. He attributes the increase in male unemployment and female-headed households not to a spreading underclass culture but, ironically enough, to the Great Society programs that were expected to eliminate the poverty paradox.[15] Murray argues that the increasing size and availability of cash assistance, disability insurance, food stamps, medicaid insurance, housing subsidies, and other government aids to the poor inadvertently created a new set of incentives for marginal members of American society. It was no longer necessary to work in order to survive; indeed, full-time employment in an unpleasant, entry-level position at times yielded less after-tax, take-home pay than the income one could receive in benefits from a multiplicity of government programs. And marriage could be economically painful. The old shibboleth that two could live more cheaply than one no longer held. Instead, a single woman with children could receive more from the government than from the earnings of her potential husband. It was better—and more fun— for both if they lived apart; she could share her welfare check with him, and he could earn through episodic or part-time employment enough to sustain an adventurous street life. The result was an increase in the poverty rate in the later years of the 1970s.

Murray's explanation resonated well with the political climate of the early 1980s. Americans were suspicious of big government, the welfare state, and the political demands made by minority spokespersons. Murray's analysis blamed government for the rising percentages of children born out of wedlock, the rising percentages of unemployed young males, the seemingly pervasive crime, drugs, and violence in cities, and the continuing sharp racial tensions in American life. If most Americans were unwilling to dismantle the welfare state altogether, they certainly accepted limits on its further expansion.

Murray's critique has nonetheless been subjected to relentless criticism.[16] Some have argued that the work ethic is deeply ingrained in all parts of American society and that the dignity that comes from an earned income is something most people strongly prefer to welfare assistance. They have pointed out that most studies show little, if any, effect of welfare assistance on willingness to work. Neither do they show much effect of welfare benefit levels on the incidence of out-of-wedlock births.[17] Others have argued that inasmuch as cash assistance to welfare recipients was diminishing in terms of real dollars throughout the 1970s, it was peculiar for Murray to argue that increases in these benefits could be causing poverty to increase. As Greg Duncan and Saul Hoffman show . . . , the income loss to a young woman who has a child out of wedlock or does not finish high school has actually increased in recent years. Still others have taken issue with his finding that the poverty rate was in fact increasing, noting that the apparent increases could be accounted for by errors in the way changes in the cost of living were being measured.

In defending his interpretation against these criticisms, Murray has pointed out that whatever the measurement problems are, it is certainly clear that the poverty paradox is not withering away. He has argued, moreover, that efforts to discredit his analysis are based on studies that focus on small variations in welfare policy from one state to another. More important than minor variations, he has claimed, is the major national increase in the level of welfare provided in the late 1960s as well as the greater ease with which the poor could receive it. If cash assistance diminished after 1975, the loss has been offset by the food stamp program, medicaid, housing assistance, and other benefit programs.[18]

The Inner City in a Changing Economy

It was in this context that a fourth interpretation of the poverty paradox was developed by William Julius Wilson. In a series of essays that resulted in *The Truly Disadvantaged,* he developed an explanation for continuing poverty that accepted the accuracy of anthropological studies of the urban underclass but explained its existence not as the result of government handouts, but as the social by-product of a changing economy whose uneven impact was leaving inner cities with extraordinarily high levels of unemployment.

Wilson's thesis contains the following propositions:

— In the face of increasing competition from foreign countries, the United States has been moving from a unionized, oligopolistic, manufacturing economy to a more competitive, less unionized, service economy in which hourly earnings are falling while skill requirements are rising.

— These changes are having a disproportionate effect on urban minorities because the loss of manufacturing jobs has been greatest within large cities, and most of the new, high-technology service industries are locating in smaller cities or on the fringes of the metropolitan area. Urban minorities do not have ready access to the new jobs because the jobs are difficult to reach and educational requirements are high.

— As a result, the percentage of urban, working-age minority men who are employed in stable, reasonably well paid jobs has fallen dramatically.

— Without a decent job, men are undesirable marriage partners, and the number of female-headed households has as a result increased rapidly.

— These changes have been aggravated by the increasing social isolation of the inner-city poor caused by the outward migration of middle-class whites and blacks, who are moving to suburbs in pursuit of jobs, better houses, and more effective schools.

— Thus there are growing concentrations of low-income minorities in the inner cities, within which dysfunctional social behavior becomes contagious. Lacking middle-class adult role models, local places of employment, adequate public services, or community institutions that support traditional family values, these core areas become breeding places for sexual promiscuity, crime, violence, drug addiction, and alcohol abuse. It is here that one finds the people who are properly called the urban underclass, because they are isolated from the mainstream social, occupational, and political institutions of the society.

— To counteract these trends, Wilson advocates policies that will guarantee a full-employment economy; federal policies that provide unemployment insurance, family allowances, and other social services to all citizens; greater race and class desegregation within metropolitan areas; and revitalization of community institutions in the urban core. . . .

If there is no single, simple explanation, certain policy conclusions can nonetheless be drawn from the four interpretations I have summarized. Wilson is correct in emphasizing that unless the United States remains strong, growing, and economically competitive, nothing is likely to reduce the poverty rate significantly. But the experience of the 1980s shows that a steadily growing economy will not by itself eliminate the poverty paradox. In addition, as liberal theorists point out, the income transfer system needs to be restructured so that government responds to the needs of working-age adults and families in as humane a way as it does to the needs of the elderly. As both Theda Skocpol and Robert Greenstein suggest, this will require a much more centralized, comprehensive, and integrated welfare system than the nation currently has.

Adopting such a policy does not entail the rejection of Charles Murray's argument that our present welfare system discourages participation in the mainstream economy. There is something wrong about a health care system that provides assistance to the nonworking indigent but will not help those in low-paid jobs whose employers do not provide health insurance. There is also something wrong about a system in which the movement from welfare to work must be abrupt and expensive. An integrated, comprehensive national welfare policy could provide a more flexible public response to those who move in and out of low-skilled, low-paid employment.

Finally, the United States needs a much more flexible and adaptable educational system in the core areas of cities, a system that can enhance the country's human capital, strengthen the institutional position of the family, and reduce the alienation between minority youth and the mainstream institutions of society.

The current expensive, bureaucratically controlled, hierarchical, rule-bound, stratified, gang-infested system of urban education needs to be drastically changed. We need to redesign our urban school systems to give families more choice and more control, provide harbors for young people seeking to escape the neighborhood peer culture, and create a learning environment that respects the culture of the low-income, minority community. If the civil rights movement wants to shed its middle-class bias and address the critical problems of the poor that became of increasing concern to Martin Luther King, it should make educational choice for urban residents and an integrated welfare system its most important concerns.

Notes

1. Office of Policy Planning and Research (1965). On the controversy, see Rainwater and Yancey (1967).
2. Smith (1988), p. 143. Smith's measure of poverty is not quite the same as the measure of poverty used by the Bureau of the Census. It is a measure that instead weights absolute and relative definitions of poverty equally. Absolute measures of poverty would show a steeper downward trend before 1960.
3. On the politics of the war on poverty, see Sundquist (1968), pp. 111–54; Moynihan (1969); and Peterson and Greenstone (1977).
4. Peterson and Rom (1988), p. 217.
5. For whites it was 9.9 percent in 1970, 10.2 percent in 1980, and 10.5 percent in 1987; for blacks the percentages were 33.5, 32.5, and 33.1.
6. National Council of La Raza (1989).
7. Smeeding, Torrey, and Rein (1988), pp. 96–97. International comparisons of poverty levels are not easily made. I report here the indicators of absolute, not relative, poverty. If relative measures were used, the United States would look even worse.
8. On these themes, see Mead (1986); Bloom (1987); and Murray (1988). Earlier versions of these themes can be found in Durkheim (1951); Bell (1963); Kornhauser (1959); and Riesman (1953).
9. Various estimates of the size of the underclass population have emphasized that it is much smaller than the poverty population taken as a whole. See Ricketts and Sawhill (1988); Reischauer (1987); and Adams, Duncan, and Rodgers (1988).
10. Skowronek (1982); Shefter (1978); Lipset (1977); Hartz (1955); and Weir, Orloff, and Skocpol (1988).
11. Peterson and Rom (1990).
12. Rossi (1989), pp. 190–94.
13. This summary of the anthropological descriptions of the culture of poverty draws on Hannerz (1969); Lewis (1961, 1966); Liebow (1967); and Rainwater (1970).
14. Ogbu (1978, 1988).
15. Murray (1984). I am using Murray's argument as shorthand for a broader literature advancing a similar line of interpretation. See Mead (1986); Glazer (1988); Banfield (1969); Lenkowsky (1986); and Anderson (1978).
16. See Danziger and Gottschalk (1985); and Ellwood and Summers (1986).
17. McLanahan, Garfinkel, and Watson (1988); Ellwood and Bane (1985); Moore (1980), but see Plotnick (1989).
18. Murray (1985, 1986).

References

Adams, Terry K., Greg J. Duncan, and Willard L. Rodgers. 1988. "The Persistence of Poverty." In *Quiet Riots: Race and Poverty in the United States,* edited by Fred R. Harris and Roger W. Wilkins. New York: Pantheon.

Anderson, Martin. 1978. *Welfare: The Political Economy of Welfare Reform in the United States.* Stanford: Hoover Institution Press.

Banfield, Edward C. 1969. "Welfare: A Crisis without 'Solutions.' " *Public Interest* 16 (Summer), pp. 89–101.

Bell, Daniel, ed. 1963. *The Radical Right: The New American Right, Expanded and Updated.* Garden City, N.Y.: Doubleday.

Bloom, Allan. 1987. *The Closing of the American Mind: How Higher Education Has Failed Democracy and Impoverished the Souls of Today's Students.* Simon and Schuster.

Bureau of the Census, 1972. "Characteristics of the Low Income Population, 1971." Series P-60, no. 86. Department of Commerce.

———. 1982. *Statistical Abstract of the United States: 1982–83.* Department of Commerce.

———. 1989. "Poverty in the United States, 1987." Series P-60, no. 163. Department of Commerce.

Danziger, Sheldon, and Peter Gottschalk. 1985. "The Poverty of *Losing Ground.*" *Challenge* 28 (May–June), pp. 32–38.

Durkheim, Emile. 1951. *Suicide: A Study in Sociology.* Glencoe, Ill.: Free Press.

Ellwood, David T., and Mary Jo Bane. 1985. "The Impact of AFDC on Family Structure and Living Arrangements." In *Research in Labor Economics* 7, edited by Ronald G. Ehrenberg. Greenwich, Conn.: JAI Press, pp. 137–207.

Ellwood, David T., and Lawrence H. Summers. 1986. "Is Welfare Really the Problem?" *Public Interest* 83 (Spring), pp. 57–78.

Glazer, Nathan. 1988. *The Limits of Social Policy.* Harvard University Press.

Hannerz, Ulf. 1969. *Soulside: Inquiries into Ghetto Culture and Community.* Columbia University Press.

Hartz, Louis. 1955. *The Liberal Tradition in America: An Interpretation of American Political Thought since the Revolution.* Harcourt Brace.

Kornhauser, William. 1959. *The Politics of Mass Society.* Glencoe, Ill.: Free Press.

Lenkowsky, Leslie. 1986. *Politics, Economics, and Welfare Reform: The Failure of the Negative Income Tax in Britain and the United States.* Washington: American Enterprise Institute for Public Policy Research.

Lewis, Oscar. 1961. *The Children of Sanchez: Autobiography of a Mexican Family.* Random House.

———. 1966. *La Vida: A Puerto Rican Family in the Culture of Poverty—San Juan and New York.* Random House.

Liebow, Elliot. 1967. *Tally's Corner: A Study of Negro Streetcorner Men.* Boston: Little, Brown.

Lipset, Seymour Martin. 1977. "Why No Socialism in the United States?" In *Sources of Contemporary Radicalism,* edited by Seweryn Bialer and Sophia Sluzar. Boulder, Colo.: Westview Press.

McLanahan, Sara, Irwin Garfinkel, and Dorothy Watson. 1988. "Family Structure, Poverty, and the Underclass." In *Urban Change and Poverty,* edited by Michael G. H. McGeary and Laurence E. Lynn, Jr. Washington: National Academy Press.

Mead, Lawrence M. 1986. *Beyond Entitlement: The Social Obligations of Citizenship.* Free Press.

Moore, Kristin. 1980. *Policy Determinants of Teenage Childbearing.* Washington: Urban Institute.

Moynihan, Daniel P. 1969. *Maximum Feasible Misunderstanding: Community Action in the War on Poverty.* Free Press.

Murray, Charles A. 1984. *Losing Ground: American Social Policy, 1950–80.* Basic Books.

———. 1985. "Have the Poor Been 'Losing Ground'?" *Political Science Quarterly* 100 (Fall), pp. 427–45.

———. 1986. "No, Welfare Isn't Really the Problem." *Public Interest* 84 (Summer), pp. 3–11.

———. 1987. *In Pursuit of Happiness and Good Government.* Simon and Schuster.

National Council of La Raza. 1989. *Hispanic Poverty: How Much Does Immigration Explain?* Proceedings from the National Council of La Raza's Poverty Project Roundtable. Washington.

Office of Policy Planning and Research. 1965. *The Negro Family: The Case for National Action.* Washington: Department of Labor.

Ogbu, John U. 1978. *Minority Education and Caste: The American System in Cross-Cultural Perspective.* Academic Press.

———. 1988. "Diversity and Equity in Public Education: Community Forces and Minority School Adjustment and Performance." In *Policies for America's Public Schools: Teachers, Equity, and Indicators,* edited by Ron Haskins and Duncan MacRae. Norwood, N.J.: Ablex Publishing.

Peterson, Paul E., and J. David Greenstone. 1977. "Racial Change and Citizen Participation: The Mobilization of Low-Income Communities through Community Action." In *A Decade of Federal Antipoverty Programs: Achievements, Failures, and Lessons,* edited by Robert H. Haveman. Academic Press.

Peterson, Paul E., and Mark Rom. 1988. "Lower Taxes, More Spending, and Budget Deficits." In *The Reagan Legacy: Promise and Performance,* edited by Charles O. Jones. Chatham, N.J.: Chatham House.

———. 1990. *Welfare Magnets: A New Case for a National Standard.* Brookings.

Plotnick, Robert D. 1989. "Welfare and Out-of-Wedlock Childbearing: Evidence from the 1980s." Paper prepared for the Conference on the Urban Underclass, Northwestern University.

Rainwater, Lee. 1970. *Behind Ghetto Walls: Black Families in a Federal Slum.* Chicago: Aldine Press.

Rainwater, Lee, and William L. Yancey. 1967. *The Moynihan Report and the Politics of Controversy.* MIT Press.

Reischauer, Robert D. 1987. "The Size and Characteristics of the Underclass." Paper prepared for the Research Conference of the American Public Policy and Management Association.

Ricketts, Erol R., and Isabel V. Sawhill. 1988. "Defining and Measuring the Underclass." *Journal of Policy Analysis and Management* 7 (Winter), pp. 316–25.

Riesman, David. 1953. *The Lonely Crowd: A Study of the Changing American Character.* Garden City, N.Y.: Doubleday.

Rossi, Peter H. 1989. *Down and Out in America: The Origins of Homelessness.* University of Chicago Press.

Shefter, Martin. 1978. "Party Bureaucracy and Political Change in the United States." In *Political Parties: Development and Decay,* edited by Louis Maisel and Joseph Cooper. Beverly Hills: Sage.

Skowronek, Stephen. 1982. *Building a New American State: The Expansion of National Administrative Capacities, 1877–1920.* Cambridge University Press.

Smeeding, Timothy, Barbara Boyle Torrey, and Martin Rein. 1988. "Patterns of Income and Poverty: The Economic Status of Children and the Elderly in Eight Countries." In *The Vulnerable,* edited by John L. Palmer, Timothy Smeeding, and Barbara Boyle Torrey. Washington: Urban Institute.

Smith, James P. 1988. "Poverty and the Family." In *Divided Opportunities: Minorities, Poverty, and Social Policy,* edited by Gary D. Sandefur and Marta Tienda. Plenum.

Sum, Andrew, Neal Fogg, and Robert Taggart. 1988. "Withered Dreams: The Decline in the Economic Fortunes of Young, Non-College Educated Male Adults and Their Families." Paper prepared for the William T. Grant Foundation Commission on Family, Work, and Citizenship.

Sundquist, James L. 1968. *Politics and Policy: The Eisenhower, Kennedy, and Johnson Years.* Brookings.

Weir, Margaret, Ann Shola Orloff, and Theda Skocpol, eds. 1988. *The Politics of Social Policy in the United States.* Princeton University Press.

Wilson, William Julius. 1987. *The Truly Disadvantaged: The Inner City, the Underclass, and Public Policy.* University of Chicago Press.

26

How the Great Society "destroyed the American family"

Daniel Patrick Moynihan

What we are seeing in the inner city [is] essentially the grim harvest of the Great Society . . . because we are seeing the breakdown of the family structure, largely contributed to by welfare policies. . . . We now have a situation in the inner cities where 64 percent of the children are illegitimate, and there's a very small wonder that we have trouble instilling values in educating children when they have their home life so disrupted.

> —Attorney General William P. Barr, appearing on "This Week with David Brinkley," April 26, 1992

This election year will be the first in American history in which the issue of welfare dependency has been raised to the level of presidential politics. Not, that is, the issue of persons who are out of work, but rather of persons who, typically, are not in the work force. At the outset of the year there were 4,719,000 AFDC cases with a total of thirteen million recipients. By contrast, in January there were some eight million persons unemployed.

President George Bush set the pattern in the following passage of his January 1992 State of the Union address:

Ask American parents what they dislike about how things are in our country, and chances are good that pretty soon they'll get to welfare.

Reprinted with permission of the author and *The Public Interest*, No. 108 (Summer 1992), pp. 53–64. © 1992 by National Affairs, Inc.

Americans are the most generous people on earth. But we have to go back to the insight of Franklin Roosevelt who, when he spoke of what became the welfare program, warned that it must not become "a narcotic" and a "subtle destroyer" of the spirit.

Welfare was never meant to be a lifestyle; it was never meant to be a habit; it was never supposed to be passed from generation to generation like a legacy.

It's time to replace the assumptions of the welfare state, and help reform the welfare system.

As we later learned, out in Arlington Heights, Illinois, White House strategists assembled a focus group with hand-held Perception Analyzers, each with a dial hooked up to a computer. Viewers were told to turn up to 100 or down to 0 as they approved or disapproved parts of the speech.

The address wasn't that much of a hit. The declaration that "The Cold War didn't end. It was won," left the focus group, well, cold. There were, however, two big scores. "This government is too big and spends too much" came in at 94. "Welfare was never meant to be a lifestyle . . . passed from generation to generation like a legacy" hit 91. Had the President declared, "This government is too big and spends too much on welfare," the Perception Analyzers might have gone into meltdown.

The President took up the theme of welfare reform with yet greater insistency in a Rose Garden press conference on April 10. He announced that he was granting a waiver to the state of Wisconsin to cut benefits to welfare mothers who had a second or third child, which the Congressional Budget Office estimates would come to a third of all AFDC children nationwide.

Whilst all this was taking place, various Democratic candidates were setting forth welfare proposals, notably Governor Bill Clinton, who led the alliance of governors that helped conceive the Family Support Act of 1988. Not to be overlooked, H. Ross Perot ended a question-and-answer session at the National Press Club with an analogy to the fate of the American Indians. "Nothing ever stopped them," he said, "until we put him on the reservation." Then this: "Don't ever put anybody on the reservation again. Our current welfare system puts people on the reservation."

All this was associated with a long recession in which welfare dependency rose markedly. The week following Mr. Bush's press conference, *U.S. News & World Report* published a thoughtful article on the subject by David Whitman entitled "War on Welfare Dependency." Cutting back was one theme:

As public resentment toward welfare crests, presidential candidates and other politicians have started pressing for benefit cutbacks that would have been unthinkable a few years ago. . . . All told, 31 states froze AFDC benefits last year—and nine more actually trimmed benefits for some or all families. Next year, financially stressed states will likely seek more cutbacks.

There was also a second theme:

In practical terms, those numbers amount to a kind of social crisis: One in 7 American children is now on relief and roughly 2,000 more are joining the rolls every day.

That same week the *New York Times Book Review* carried a notice of two books on this same subject, *Rethinking Social Policy: Race, Poverty, and the Underclass* by Christopher Jencks, and *The New Politics of Poverty, The Nonworking Poor in America* by Lawrence M. Mead. Both books speak of a crisis. The reviewer, Dennis H. Wrong, notes that one of these describes it as "an American crisis comparable to the Civil War, even as a threat to the basic values of Western Civilization."

A Crisis Foretold

As it happens, this is precisely the crisis I forecast in a policy planning paper written in the U.S. Department of Labor just twenty-seven years earlier. This paper, sent to the President, began with a one-sentence paragraph:

The United States is approaching a new crisis in race relations.

The crisis would be associated with the social structure of inner-city black communities. This was in March 1965. In September of that year, in the Jesuit journal, *America,* I put the proposition more graphically:

From the wild Irish slums of the nineteenth-century Eastern seaboard, to the riot-torn suburbs of Los Angeles, there is one unmistakable lesson in American history: a community that allows a large number of young men to grow up in broken families, dominated by women, never acquiring any stable relationship to male authority, never acquiring any set of rational expectations about the future—that community asks for and gets chaos. Crime, violence, unrest, disorder . . . that is not only to be expected; it is very near to inevitable. And it is richly deserved.

Let me set forth the simple background of the report, entitled "The Negro Family: The Case for National Action." I was then Assistant Secretary of Labor for Policy Planning and Research. This was a new position; part of the style of government in the New Frontier. I had a small but exceptionally able planning staff, some half dozen persons in all. I also had a nominal supervisory relationship to the Bureau of Labor Statistics.

In 1963, we had set about trying to develop correlations between unemployment data of various sorts and other indicators of social disorder. We began to find strong correlations between "manpower" data (as we would have said at that time) and family indices of various kinds. Most striking was the relationship between the nonwhite male unemployment rate and the number of AFDC cases opened. Between 1948 (when the present unemployment data series begins) and 1961 we found a correlation, as I recall, of .91. Whereupon the correlation, having already weakened, went negative. The unemployment rate went down, the number of new AFDC cases went up. James Q. Wilson has called this "Moynihan's scissors." It persisted through the decade.

As I later showed in a paper in the Annals of the American Academy of Political and Social Science, this "scissors" occurred over a considerable range of subjects. Thus the percent of nonwhite married women separated from their husbands continued to rise even as nonwhite male unemployment dropped. *Something* was happening.

I must be clear. I did not know *what.* I was well beyond my methodological depth. You ought to have known a lot more than I did to feel comfortable telling the President of the United States that the nation was "approaching a new crisis in race relations." Yet we were not alone in sensing trouble. At this time, for example, Kenneth Clark was writing of the "massive deterioration of the fabric of [black] society and its institutions," of "the tangle of pathology" in what we would come to call the inner city, of "protest masculinity," and so on. What we added was the sense of impending instability, the possibility, as I would write in *Commentary* in 1967, "that the situation had begun feeding on itself." In any event, as President Kennedy would say, to govern is to choose. If we were wrong, I thought, no great harm could come of it; I chose to bet that we were right.

As it turned out, we were right enough in our forecasts. Let me be spare in the particulars. Something did snap in the early 1960s. The illegitimacy ratio among blacks rose from 24 percent to a current 63.5 percent. Of black children born between 1967 and 1969, 72.3 percent were on welfare before reaching age eighteen, which is to say they were paupers; not a pretty word but not a pretty condition. Census data show that in 1964 some 75 percent of black children under age six were living in a married-couple family. By 1990—in a steady descent—this ratio had dropped to 37.4 percent.

Alan Wolfe of the New School for Social Research sums up the situation in a recent *New Republic* review essay:

> Whatever progress has been achieved for middle-class blacks . . . the condition of the urban black poor has deteriorated over the past quarter century, to the point where it threatens all the other gains in race relations that were realized during the same period.

This, of course, is precisely as forecast.

However, I was absolutely wrong in thinking that no harm would come of this work. Possibly great harm was done. This was not clear at the outset. Rather the contrary. In a hurried sequence in early June, 1965, President Johnson decided to make the strengthening of the black social structure, specifically family structure, the theme of a major address at Howard University. On a Thursday, I wrote a first draft, overnight the White House turned out a second, and the speech was given on Friday afternoon, June 4. The response was overwhelmingly positive. The policy paper remained well in the background.

Controversy

The paper became public in the aftermath of the urban roots in the Watts section of Los Angeles some three months later. On August 17, 1965, Bill Moyers, then presidential press secretary, gave out copies to a baffled White House press corps. The next day, August 18, Evans and Novak recounted the findings in a column entitled, "The Moynihan Report."

The report soon became available and evoked, for the most part, indignation and denial. In retrospect, it is not hard to see why. Social science is not rocket science. The opening chapter of the report stated:

> There is no very satisfactory way, at present, to measure social health or social pathology within an ethnic, or religious, or geographical community. Data are few and uncertain, and conclusions drawn from them, including the conclusions that follow, are subject to the grossest error.

No one would launch a spacecraft on the basis of an engineering report that warned of the possibility of "the grossest error" in design. There was, and is, no institutional capacity to review the data and the conclusions, such as exists, say, for papers published in the *New England Journal of Medicine*. The report should have been published, but the thesis ought never to have been raised to the level of presidential pronouncement. Even though, to repeat with a measure of insistence, we turned out to be accurate in our forecast.

Sociologist Lee Rainwater undertook to examine the ruckus along with a young colleague, William Y. Yancey. *The Moynihan Report and the Politics of Controversy* was published two years later in 1967. It opens with this passage from Louis Wirth's Preface to Karl Manheim's 1936 work, *Ideology and Utopia:*

> The distinctive character of social science discourse is to be sought in the fact that every assertion, no matter how objective it may be, has ramifications extending beyond the limits of science itself. Since every assertion of a "fact" about the social world touches the interests of some individual or group, one cannot even call attention to the existence of certain "facts" without courting the objections of those whose very *raison d'être* in society rests upon a divergent interpretation of the "factual" situation.

In feverish times—and those were feverish times—this normal disposition can become pathological in itself. One is reminded of Hannah Arendt's observation that the tactical advantage of the totalitarians in Europe in the 1920s and

1930s derived from their ability to turn every statement of fact into a question of motive. I was everywhere attacked in this mode, being charged with "blaming the victim."

In 1968, rummaging through the data of the Coleman report, I came upon what seemed to me further evidence that family structure, a surrogate for class, would become increasingly significant. Coleman and his associates had obtained information from students as to family composition. In the still caste-segregated schools of the rural South, this circumstance had at most a slight influence on achievement. Ninth graders scored at fifth-grade levels regardless. By contrast, in the urban North, black family structure was associated with almost one year's difference in grade level. For whites the difference was even more pronounced. So, clearly, this was the direction in which things were heading.

The Great Society's Legacy

In retrospect, my assessment would be that had the policy paper never been written, or never risen to the level of presidential pronouncement, the social changes it forecast would have come about in any event, and would have gradually been recorded and acknowledged. That would have made it easier for them to be accepted in the political world, and might have given social scientists the opportunity to sort it all out.

The problem was that the constituency groups whose support and involvement was needed to carry forward policies directed to the problem could not accept the problem as we had defined it. And so it came to pass that a generation later it was defined by persons with quite different political sympathies. In the spring of 1992, Attorney General William P. Barr had no qualms on the matter. Family breakdown, which was the source of crime, was the "grim harvest of the Great Society," largely the result of "welfare policies." This is manifestly absurd. The breakdown was there in the data before the Great Society, just as the welfare system was there before the Great Society.

And yet, the Attorney General had a point. Or may have had a point. For a brief time, the Great Society gave great influence in social policy to viewpoints that rejected the proposition that family structure might be a social issue. Accordingly, even if social policy might have produced some effective responses, no such policies were attempted. In that sense, the current crisis is indeed a "grim harvest of the Great Society."

The reaction to the Moynihan report effectively banished the subject from the academy. That period may now be easing, however. In 1984 William Julius Wilson and Kathryn Neckerman picked up those "scissors" and began to puzzle anew over the subject. In 1986 they published an analysis showing that the crossover disappears when the number of AFDC cases is charted against the nonwhite male labor force *non-participation* rate. This and other work has led Wilson to fruitful insights into the role of male employment and earnings in the central city—the issues at the heart of our research in the Department of Labor a generation ago.

More recently, economists Richard Freeman and Paul Osterman have looked into the natural experiment of the 1980s, when employment rose dramatically. They found that a tight labor market sharply lowered the official unemployment rate, but did nothing to reverse "the trend toward single-parenthood, to lower the inner-city crime rate or to appreciably reduce the proportion of men who had stopped working." The lesson, according to Freeman, is that full employment "is necessary but not sufficient." All this is consistent, or so I would think with Wilson and Neckerman's 1986 analysis and with the 1965 report. The problem then as now is that no one has a clue as to what it would take for public policy to be *sufficient.*

Here we come to the crux of the issue of social science and social policy. We are at the point of knowing a fair amount about what we don't know. The past quarter-century has been on the whole productive in this regard. On the other hand, our social situation is vastly worse.

In 1965 we had at least slight purchase on the issue as it was then—the employment nexus. Further, the federal government, along with state and local government, was solvent. Indeed, over a fifteen-month period from early 1969 to mid-1970 I took part in a fierce debate within the Nixon White House, joined in by almost every cabinet department and, of course, the then-Bureau of the Budget, over the desirability of the President proposing to Congress that the federal government establish a guaranteed annual income. This ill-fated proposal became known as the Family Assistance Plan. The subject of cost scarcely arose. It was simply a given that if the idea was defensible on its merits, the money would be found. It will be a generation, if ever, before any such assumption will again be possible within the counsels of the presidency.

And then there are today's epidemics. We have no cure for AIDS, and no pharmacological treatment for cocaine dependency, albeit there is reasonable hope that medical science will produce some therapies. As for social science, there would seem to be less confidence than ever. This pessimism is in ways a legacy of the Great Society. In the late 1960s, the American Academy of Arts and Sciences sponsored a long and fruitful seminar on the subject of poverty. I contributed a paper, "The Professors and the Poor," which, on the well-known adage that data is the plural of anecdote, began by telling of a lady who had come to see me at the Joint Center for Urban Studies seeking support for a federal anti-poverty grant and complaining that none were being given out in her neighborhood in Boston. I demurred: Roxbury was being deluged with programs. "Exactly," came the retort from my visitor, "but do you notice they only fund programs that don't succeed." A decade later, Peter H. Rossi would distill this insight in "Rossi's Iron Law":

> If there is any empirical law that is emerging from the past decade of widespread evaluation research activities, it is that the expected value for any measured effect of a social program is zero.

A New Candor

This is not a counsel of despair. It is useful knowledge. As recently as 1960, Loren Baritz noted in *The Servants of Power:* "Intellectuals in the United States have long bemoaned the assumed fact that they are unloved and unappreciated by their society." The last three decades have seen a role reversal in this regard. Especially in foreign policy, intellectual academics assumed awesome powers. Much simpler applications come to mind, as for example a recent address by President Bush to the National League of Cities:

> The urgency is clear. We all know the statistics, perhaps you know them better than most Americans, the dreary drumbeat that tells of family breakdown. Today, one out of every four American children is born out of wedlock. In some areas, the illegitimacy rate tops 80 percent. A quarter of our children grow up in households headed by a single parent. More than two million are called latchkey kids who come home from school each afternoon to an empty house. And a large number of our children grow up without the love of parents at all, with nobody knowing their name.*

So far as I can learn, no president of the United States has ever made such a statement, ever come close to such a suggestion. And there was no objection. It was a statistic. No small achievement of social science, those numbers. But not seen as mysterious or arbitrary. If some overnight opinion poll had told the speechwriters they could or even should use such materials, well, chalk up another social-science achievement—the opinion poll. Surely, the public learned from what the President said, becoming in consequence more amenable to thoughtful action, whatever that might be. No small achievement.

This willingness was much in evidence in an extraordinary speech on "Race and the American City" delivered on the Senate floor in March by Senator Bill Bradley (D-NJ). Here is a sample:

> In politics for the last twenty-five years, silence or distortion has shaped the issue of race and urban America. Both political parties have contributed to the problem. Republicans have played the race card in a divisive way to get votes—remember Willie Horton—and Democrats have suffocated discussion of a self-destructive behavior among the minority population in a cloak of silence and denial. The result is that yet another generation has been lost. We cannot afford to wait longer. It is time for candor, time for truth, and time for action.

The speech was not only extraordinary in its explicitness, but also in its reception. It was the subject of a lead editorial in the *New York Times,* while the

---

*The President, or someone such, might usefully note that illegitimacy ratios are rising in most, if not all, industrial countries. The 1969 Canadian ratio of 9.2 percent had risen to 23.1 percent by 1989.

Washington Post reprinted part of the text. Four days later, at Yale University, Senator John Kerry of Massachusetts offered no less an explicit or extraordinary address:

> I ask you to consider a reality where more than 80 percent of babies are born to single mothers; where young men die violently at a rate exceeding that of any American war; where only one child in three finishes high school and even then, too often, can barely read; where the spread of AIDS and homelessness rips so visibly at the fabric of community; where far too many families are on welfare for far too long; and where far too many children carry guns instead of lunch boxes to school.

Riots Past and Present

On April 29, within days of these speeches, a jury exonerated white officers of the Los Angeles Police Department in a case involving the beating of a black motorist. Rioting broke out in the black neighborhoods of the city and continued for some days, with great loss of life and property and an even greater loss of composure among national leaders. On the basis of what is now known, the tumult followed closely the pattern first described by Harold Orlans (then Orlansky) in his classic 1943 report, *The Harlem Riot, A Study in Mass Frustration.* The sequence began with an altercation in which a white police officer wounded a black soldier. A crowd gathered. A "drunken cop" was said to have killed a black soldier who had been protecting his mother.

The looting that followed was near total, wrote Orlans, save for establishments where "Negro store-owners placed signs reading 'Colored.' " The rioters were young males. The police were targets. "Some 60 policemen were shot, stabbed, beaten, stoned, or even bitten by rioters." Among others, two fifteen-year-old British seamen were mobbed, but Mayor LaGuardia declared, "This was not a race riot." Orlans disagreed, observing that "The Harlem riot was essentially racial, featuring attacks upon white property and the white police force in which the mass of the Negro population joined." He ascribed this to frustration in the paradigm set forth six years earlier by John Dollard in *Caste and Class in a Southern Town.* This pattern was in place for the next half-century. Los Angeles, however, appeared different. The aggression against whites seems to have moved beyond black neighborhoods. The consequent racial fears are likely to be far greater. And so the "new crisis in race relations" of which we wrote a generation ago is now with us, and in a worse form than even we fully comprehended. And yet we seem no longer quite so willing to deny it.

Of all the changes in the political climate now taking place, none seems more important to me than the readiness of welfare "advocates," as they came to be known and indeed to so describe themselves, to acknowledge the "tangle of pathology" which set off a firestorm when I borrowed Kenneth Clark's term a generation ago. Thus, in the current welfare debate, Hillary Clinton, wife of the Governor of Arkansas and former chairman of the board of the Children's Defense Fund, insists that the message her husband is trying to get out is "Quit being a victim." The one recommendation of the 1965 paper on the Negro family was this:

> The policy of the United States is to bring the Negro American to full and equal sharing in the responsibilities and rewards of citizenship. To this end, the programs of the Federal government bearing on this objective shall be designed to have the effect, directly or indirectly, of enhancing the stability and resources of the Negro American family.

For some time, talk of responsibilities was thought suspect by many. No longer. An editorial supporting Bill Clinton in a 1992 Democratic primary contest observed that "He talks more of opportunity than entitlement, of responsibilities as well as rights."

Social Science and Social Policy

What is more, something we have known for some time, demographics are at last turning our way, if I may use that term. The proportion of fifteen-to-twenty-four-year-olds as a percent of the total population has been declining since the mid-1980s and we forecast that it will continue to do so well into the next century. The size of the cohort most at risk grows smaller, after nearly overwhelming social institutions in the 1950s and 1960s.

This is surely the case in the world of the social sciences, which is in the main politically liberal, and went through an awful period of silence and denial—or rather, denial and denunciation. A striking feature of the 1960s was that just as a large consensus in favor of social-science-oriented social action took shape, a considerable body of social science appeared which, in effect, said don't expect too much. Think, for example, of the writing in the early editions of *The Public Interest*. Almost without exception, the authors were political liberals who had stumbled upon things that weren't entirely pleasing to them, but which, as the song goes, could not be denied. I have referred to this as the Reformation. Not a few of the heretics were burned at the stake, and more than a few left the true church for good and all. But their witness prevailed. I take it as no coincidence that in 1992 James Q. Wilson is president of the American Political Science Association and James S. Coleman president of the American Sociological Association. Their influence has in the end proved immensely important; and so might their example. For while each has ever sought to make social science available to social policy, each has kept his distance from government. Not from fastidiousness, but from understanding. They have known how little is known, and how readily that which can be said to be known is misunderstood or misused.

27

The Clinton Administration and African-Americans

Monte Piliawsky

> Bill Clinton has no civil rights policy. He has, in fact, failed to address concretely the issue of racism, and instead has made every effort to distance himself from civil-rights advocates.

> —Herbert Hill

At first glance, it might appear that the black electorate came out the clear winner in the 1992 presidential election. After staunchly supporting Democratic Party candidates who lost five of the previous six contests, African-American voters overwhelmingly backed the winner, Bill Clinton. The reality, however, is that the black community again was the victim, ignored in the agenda of the transformed, centrist Democratic Party and taken for granted by the Democrats in the general election campaign. Further, the Clinton administration's policy decisions do not augur well for the interests of blacks and the poor.

There were almost 200 fewer African-American delegates at the 1992 Democratic National Convention than at the Convention in 1988.[1] They witnessed Reverend Jesse Jackson, the most prominent national black figure (and de facto leader of the party's left wing) relegated to a non-prime time appearance. In the election campaign, the Clinton-Gore team unabashedly wooed white middle-class Reagan Democrats, campaigning extensively in white suburbs, while studiously disregarding the urban black population. As Harlem Congressional

From *The Black Scholar,* winter/spring 1994, pp. 2–10. Reprinted by permission of The Black Scholar.

representative Charles Rengel observed, "You take a look at where the bus is going. You don't see it stopping in black towns, you don't see them kissing black babies."[2] In attempting to remake the party's image, the Democrats ignored the concerns of persons of color, while stressing welfare reform and a tough anti-crime package, issues with strong racial overtones.

Campaign rhetoric aside, the Democratic Party's ideological swing to the right portends bleak consequences for African-Americans. Never once in his three televised debates with George Bush did candidate Bill Clinton expressly address himself to the poor, the hungry, the homeless, or blacks.[3] Instead, Clinton rejected liberalism, replacing the Democratic Party's traditional support of government assistance with the nostrum of individual responsibility. As President, Clinton apparently has concluded that in order to gain the support of Perot backers for the 1996 election, it is in his "best political interest to avoid a discussion of the institutional and individual racial discrimination which still pollutes the country."[4] In short, Clinton's victory may prove to be a Pyrrhic victory for African-Americans.

Racial Politics: From FDR to Bush

The Republican Party has skillfully used race-tinged issues and code words— from busing, states' rights, law and order, welfare queen, "affirmative-action quotas," and Willie Horton. For its part, the Democratic Party has long followed a conscious, if less blatant, type of racism, taking care not to alienate white Southerners, a vital element in their electoral coalition.

Franklin Roosevelt resolutely refused to back federal anti-lynching legislation or the abolishing of poll taxes, claiming that "his support would lead to southern opposition to his entire economic recovery program."[5] Until the 1960s, in order to perpetuate their majority status in Congress, the Democrats hypocritically maintained an implicit compact to defend white supremacy in the South. Even in the face of the civil rights movement and the violent, racist reaction it engendered, the Kennedy Administration still took a long three years to endorse an effective civil rights bill.

Jimmy Carter was elected president in 1976 with massive black support (94 percent) overcoming Gerald Ford's majority backing from whites. Although he appointed more African-Americans to federal judgeships than all other previous presidents combined, "Carter provided very conservative leadership . . . cutting or reducing social programs that were vitally important to blacks."[6] Consequently, William Clay, a leader of the Congressional Black Caucus, noted, "We fought publicly with Jimmy Carter almost every day of his Administration,"[7] over budget policy, a full employment bill, and a Martin Luther King, Jr. holiday.

More recently, the Democratic Party expressed its racial politics in its reaction to Reverend Jesse Jackson's two presidential bids of the 1980s. Party leaders treated Jackson's 1984 campaign with contempt, assuming that being identified with the symbol of race-oriented progressivism risked losing white votes.[8] Although Jackson was the undisputed runner-up for the 1988 Democratic nomination, Democratic candidate Michael Dukakis treated Jackson "as an embarrassment, something he had to cope with, placate, keep a healthy distance from."[9] Launching his campaign in Neshoba County, Mississippi, Dukakis appealed to white voters by conspicuously refusing to mention the three civil rights workers who had been murdered there only twenty-five years ago.

In winning five out of six presidential elections between 1968 and 1988, Republican Party candidates exploited white racial fears by using racial code words. Thomas and Mary Edsall demonstrated in their recent book, *Chain Reaction*, that the Republicans had gained a seeming lock on the presidency through the unscrupulous manipulation of racial issues.[10] By 1992, many moderate Democrats endorsed the Edsalls' premise that close identification with blacks and inner cities was the party's Achilles' heel.

Thus, in the 1992 presidential campaign, the Democratic standard bearer avoided making virtually any reference to civil rights and racial discrimination. According to *Time* senior editor, Walter Isaacson, Bill Clinton "maneuvered to ensure that unlike in 1988, in fact unlike in any election since 1960, race was not an issue. Partly he achieved this by shying away from being cast as the tribute for the poor and blacks."[11] Focusing on a war on welfare and tough action against crime, the same two themes formerly used by Republicans as racial code words, Clinton became only the second Democratic presidential candidate since 1948 to outpoll his Republican opponent among white voters.

Clinton as "Centrist"

The Democratic Party has been drifting to the right ideologically since 1972, when George McGovern offered a somewhat reformist agenda. In 1988, Dukakis denied the party's heritage by rejecting the label of "liberal" until late in the campaign. Symbolic of the Democrats' shift is the changing socioeconomic character of delegates to recent Democratic National conventions. Whereas in 1980, less than a quarter of convention delegates had incomes of more than $50,000, in 1992 almost 70 percent of the delegates earned that much or more.[12]

Today, the Democratic Party presents itself as centrist rather than liberal. Much of the credit for this transformation goes to Bill Clinton, who in 1985 founded the Democratic Leadership Council (DLC), which originally was all-white. Chagrined by Mondale's 1984 defeat, the DLC (referred to by Jesse Jackson as the "Democratic Leisure Class") disavowed the liberal Democratic gospel of compassion, with its politically unpopular price-tag of high government spending. With Clinton as its chair, in 1991 the DLC "braved open intra-party warfare to pass a resolution condemning the use of race and sex-based quotas in hiring,"[13] seized control of the party's national apparatus, and laid the foundation for Bill Clinton's Democratic Party presidential bid.

Clinton's "New Covenant" acceptance speech to the 1992 National Convention provides a useful guide to the Democratic Party's current political philosophy. Clinton called for a compact "between the people and their government" that makes "opportunity" contingent on "responsibility" and "restore[s] America's founding values" of "family, community" and "hard work." The Democrats claim that their approach represented an alternative to conservatives' cold-hearted policy of laissez-faire capitalism and the liberals' knee-jerk belief in government spending as the solution to every problem. In the words of the party platform: "We reject both the do-nothing government of the last 12 years, and the big government theory that says we can . . . tax and spend our way to prosperity. Instead, we offer a third way."[14]

In reality, the Democrats' "third way," the so-called post-liberal consensus, is profoundly conservative. The primary stress is on individual "responsibility," a word that appeared over twenty times in Clinton's address. What is sacrificed in this new vision is the liberal Democratic tradition of public assistance for disadvantaged people. Accordingly, the party platform proposed remarkably modest outlays of funds in the areas of housing, job training, and education to implement its "Rebuild America" theme.

The 1992 Democratic Party platform endorsed very tough anti-crime measures, including metal detectors in schools, drug sweeps in public housing, 100,000 more police on the streets, stiffer jail sentences and using abandoned military bases as boot camps for brief, tough stays by young offenders. The party's political advertisements were carefully tailored to remind voters that Governor Bill Clinton had executed people, even flying back to Arkansas to oversee the execution of a lobotomized black convict. As President, Clinton has proposed extending the death penalty, with its demonstrably racist application, to an additional 47 federal crimes, while curtailing the number of appeals that death row inmates could file in federal court.

The Democrats' so-called "workfare" plan illustrates how "responsibility" has effectively replaced "equal opportunity" in the party's new paradigm. The punitive system of up-and-out workfare limits welfare payments to two years, after which time recipients must take a job in the private sector or perform "community service" to "pay off their grant." The workfare program erroneously presumes, however, that there will be enough jobs to employ the poor. Given the meager funds that the Democrats have allotted to job creation, it is likely that under their policy welfare recipients would remain working indefinitely for substandard wages.

Taken overall, the Democratic Party 1992 platform represented a betrayal of the needs of African-Americans and the poor, the party's most loyal voting base. During the past twelve years, federal government spending for low-income subsidized housing decreased by 82 percent, job training money declined by 63 percent, while community development funds fell by 40 percent.[15] Exacerbated by long-standing Republican neglect, the condition of blacks in nearly every major U.S. city is approaching the crisis level evidenced by the 1992 Los Angeles uprisings. Yet it is highly doubtful that the Democrats' new emphasis on self-help will furnish adequate relief for the 25 percent of American children under 6 (and 51 percent of black children) who live in poverty, a figure that is four to five times the rate of most industrialized countries.[16] Nor will the Democrats' pledge to pursue "deadbeat dads" who default on child support provide the necessary jobs to enable fathers to make these maintenance payments. "What's missing in all this talk of mutual obligations and common sacrifice is the voice of the poor."[17]

The 1992 Presidential Election Campaign

A major strategy in Bill Clinton's 1992 presidential campaign was to reach out to white voters who had abandoned the Democrats over affirmative action, busing for school desegregation, and welfare. Clinton engaged in what Reverend Jesse Jackson termed "a pattern of incidents" showing white voters his independence from the black community.[18] In spring, the candidate played golf at an all-white country club. During the Southern primaries, the Clinton campaign circulated a political leaflet featuring a photograph of the candidate in the foreground chatting to a white prison warden, while a group of prisoners, who were all black, paraded in the background. "That picture, which got wide publicity, said he was going to contain Black people."[19]

   The racially coded signal that Clinton sent to white voters in the wake of the Los Angeles riots was unmistakable. His response "only me-tooed Bush's law-and-order line and never mentioned injustice."[20] According to columnist Clarence Page, "Bill Clinton's amazingly slow and tepid response to the Los Angeles riots disappointed many but it revealed his reluctance to be distracted from his suburban crusade for the 'forgotten middle class.' "[21] Historian E. Frances White explains how Clinton's approach was to shift attention away from urban America:

> He didn't want to be identified with the cities, with urban decay. It felt like he was taking for granted that Black people would understand that we had to vote for him, that there was no choice. He assumed that Black people would recognize and agree that the cities would not be as bad with him—that they would not be great, but we knew Bush was a disaster.[22]

   The defining moment for Bill Clinton was his contrived rebuke of Jesse Jackson over remarks made by the rap performer, Sister Souljah. In late spring, the Clinton campaign was in serious trouble. A graph on the front page of the May 28 issue of *USA Today* captioned, "Who would win the electoral college as of that date?" showed Bush at 190 electoral votes, Perot at 128, and Clinton at only 6 (Arkansas). By mid-June, Ross Perot had catapulted to the top of the polls, as Clinton fell into third place. Perot continued to dominate the political coverage, to the point that Clinton seemed incapable of breaking through a television news void.[23]

Facing a losing situation, Clinton concocted the Sister Souljah flap. Appearing before the national convention of Jesse Jackson's Rainbow Coalition, Clinton publicly and deliberately picked a fight to illustrate his independence from blacks in general and from Jackson in particular. Clinton's apparent target was Sister Souljah, whom Jackson had invited to participate in a panel discussion, despite her use of racially inflammatory language in a newspaper interview two months earlier in the aftermath of the Los Angeles riots. Clinton denounced Souljah's remarks, stating that they revealed "the kind of hatred we do not honor."[24] Clinton's real target, however, was Jesse Jackson, whom he chided for giving a platform to Sister Souljah.

Reverend Jackson responded by characterizing Clinton's statement as a "Machiavellian maneuver [designed] purely to appeal to conservative whites by containing Jackson and isolating Jackson."[25] In his article, "Clinton's Daring Rebuke to Jackson Sends a Message to White Voters," *Washington Post* columnist David Broder asserted: "The gamble Clinton is taking is that more white Americans will be impressed by his 'standing up' to Jackson than black Americans repelled by his 'disrespect' to the Rainbow Coalition leader."[26] Apparently, Clinton's ploy succeeded: immediately following the Souljah episode, his popularity ratings soared into first place in the presidential sweepstakes.

Clinton continued to snub Reverend Jackson throughout the general election campaign. In September, at the National Baptist Convention USA in Atlanta, Clinton resisted when Jackson, standing next to him on the dais, moved to raise the candidate's arm. With a private plane furnished by the Democratic National Committee, Jackson traveled to twenty-seven states, registering voters and generating enthusiasm for a large voter turnout.[27] Nevertheless, Clinton maintained his distance from Jackson to the very end. For example, when the Democratic standard bearer's plane landed in Cleveland during the marathon finale of the presidential campaign, Martin Luther King III, a moderate black figure, was waiting to greet him at the speaker's podium. By contrast, Jesse Jackson was only scheduled to campaign in Cleveland some hours later. Correspondent Martin Walker of *The Guardian* of London described the symbolism of Clinton's campaign:

> There is a ruthless sense of realpolitik here, uncomfortably close to the old Southern plantation distinction between the field hands and the house negro. Like a productive field hand, Jesse Jackson is tolerated to get out the black vote, but not to appear on the high-profile television news events.[28]

Indeed, much of the Clinton campaign was a subtly orchestrated exercise in Realpolitik that bordered on covert racism. According to political scientist Adolph Reed, Jr.:

From the first, the Clinton campaign has reminded me of Southern "liberals" under Jim Crow who came to black voters quietly, saying, "I'm really your friend. Of course, I have to call you 'niggers' and appeal to the segregationist vote, but I don't really mean it. I didn't like it, and I'm only doing it to get elected. Afterward I'll take care of you; trust me." (We know how that turned out.)[29]

Staffing the White House

As President, Clinton has done little to assuage fears that he will ultimately refrain from doing those things necessary to alter substantially the miserable conditions in which poor people find themselves, particularly the black poor. Clinton's initial decisions were disappointing both symbolically and substantively.

In sending his 12-year-old daughter, Chelsea, to an exclusive private school with a tuition of $10,800 a year, rather than a public school as President Jimmy Carter had done, Clinton took a stance at odds with his verbal support for public education. By passing over "an opportunity to provide symbolic support for public education, which desperately needs it,"[30] Clinton reinforced the negative image of public schools, tacitly aiding the movement toward a voucher system.

Especially disturbing for the interests of African-Americans was Clinton's reneging on two human rights-related campaign pledges. The President abandoned his commitment to ban discrimination based on sexual orientation in the military. In addition, after attacking President Bush for forcibly repatriating endangered Haitians, almost all of whom are blacks living in poverty, Clinton, once in office, implemented the same policy.

While the Clinton administration boasts of a cabinet that is the most diverse ever assembled—four African-Americans and two Hispanics among its fourteen members—it hardly suggests a powerful promise of change. As political scientist Ronald Walters points out, no blacks were placed in charge of HUD, HHS, or Education, dealing with problems "where the pain is greatest, where the greatest number of our people are suffering."[31]

Probably the biggest jolt to those voters who took at face value Clinton's commitment to economic reform, was the appointment of Lloyd Bentsen to the vital post of Treasury secretary. Bentsen, after all, as chair of the Senate Finance Committee, epitomized the insider wheeler-dealer. Moreover, he was a champion of big business who strongly favored the Reagan-Bush redistribution of wealth to the rich. In defending his selection, Clinton claimed that Bentsen would reassure the financial markets and emphasize the president's own understanding of "realities." No doubt, many persons of color muttered that Clinton was elected to change certain "realities," not to underwrite them.

The records of Mike Espy and Ron Brown, two of President Clinton's black Cabinet appointments, further demonstrate the class orientation of his choices. Espy, the Secretary of Agriculture designate, hails from a prominent black family: his grandfather built twenty-eight funeral homes and became a major landowner. Espy opposes gun control, has appeared in advertisements for the National Rifle Association, and has forged strong ties with conservative agricultural interests in the Mississippi Delta, like agribusiness and major producers, while supporting the development of wetlands.[32]

In a similar vein, the appointment of Ron Brown as Secretary of Commerce should concern those who favor genuine change. Brown is a long-time political operative and Washington lawyer-lobbyist with a reputation for working the levers of power on behalf of wealthy, entrenched special interests. His clients include the Haitian government under former dictator Jean-Claude Duvalier and a consortium of twelve large Japanese corporations. His law firm has represented the scandal-stained Bank of Credit and Commerce International, accused of helping to finance illegal sales to Iraq.[33] Though canceled at the last moment because of highly publicized protests, Brown had planned a pre-inaugural tribute to him sponsored by some of the largest Japanese and U.S. corporations who will have issues coming before the Brown-led Commerce Department. The appointments of Espy and Brown give credence to the observation of Mary Frances Berry, the new head of the U.S. Civil Rights Commission:

> Clinton's approach to race is reminiscent of Malcolm X's statement that all that happened when African Americans elected some politicians was that some Negroes who already had jobs got good jobs in the government.[34]

Clinton's appointment of centrists Espy and Brown to Cabinet posts contrasted sharply with the rejections of Johnnetta Cole and Lani Guinier. As head of a Clinton transition team on education, labor, the arts and humanities, Cole, the highly respected president of Spelman College, had often been mentioned as a candidate for Secretary of Education. However, in December 1992, the far-right newspaper, *Human Events,* published an "expose" of Cole as a "leftist extremist," citing her writing for the World Peace Council, a pro-Palestinian group. *The Atlanta Journal & Constitution* wrote a spirited defense of Cole who is a pillar of the Atlanta establishment: member of the Atlanta Chamber of Commerce and on the board of Coca-Cola, and a founding director of President Bush's Points of Light foundation.[35] Nevertheless, succumbing to the Right's vitriolic red baiting campaign, Clinton did not offer Cole a position in his administration.

Similarly, Clinton withdrew the nomination of Lani Guinier to head the civil rights division of the Justice Department when right-wing activists characterized her writings as "radical." Guinier, a University of Pennsylvania law professor, possesses an unquestioned record of performance as a veteran litigator with the NAACP Legal Defense and Education Fund. She stands for the view that because institutional racism still exists in the U.S., the conventional remedies used in voting rights enforcement may sometimes be insufficient. Guinier's perspective of using race to fashion appropriate affirmative policies measures reflects the widely accepted dictum of former Justice Harry Blackmun: "[I]n order to get beyond racism, we must first take account of race. There is no other way."[36] Nevertheless, "for thus studiously speaking truth to power,"[37] Guinier was "demonized in a fashion unequaled by an attack on a public figure since the pillorying of Anita Hill."[38]

President Clinton's abandoning of Lani Guinier continues his pattern of "calculated rejection of the civil rights cause."[39] In distancing himself from people who claim that institutional racism endures in America, Clinton again shows his deep concern for not making conservative white voters feel uncomfortable. However, in attempting to avoid a public dialogue of the pernicious effects of institutional racism, Clinton contributes to its legitimization. Mary Frances Berry explains the devastating impact on African-Americans of Clinton's policy of sweeping under the rug the reality of racism in American life:

> While African Americans are still exulting over Maya Angelou's poem at the inaugural, and four black Cabinet officers, bank practices and mortgage lenders keep discriminating against African Americans, police brutality and hate crimes increase, Shoney's and Denny's and other restaurants and public accommodations that care to exclude or decline to serve African Americans; . . . the absence of drug treatment facilities, bad housing, unemployment, glass ceilings in employment, racial intolerance on campus, all continue to thrive. The slap at Lani Guinier was just another reminder of the racial problems that demand our attention.[40]

Clinton's Economic Policies

Following his inauguration, civil rights organizations urged President Clinton to address the concerns of the inner cities, beleaguered by twelve years of Republican neglect. The Citizens' Commission on Civil Rights emphasized that generalized economic recovery without specifically targeting the needs of African-Americans was not enough: "While economic stimulus is important, it will not lift the boats of those who are mired in poverty and racial discrimination."[41] The Milton Eisenhower Foundation called for the national government to spend $30 billion a year for the next ten years to finance inner city programs in education, housing, and drug prevention.[42] Similarly, the Urban League recommended a "Marshall Plan" for cities in which the federal government would invest $50 billion a year over ten years for education, job training, and the infrastructure.[43]

To revitalize ravaged inner cities, the White House proposed only a $16.3 billion "stimulus package," a grab bag of unemployment benefits, summer job programs and one-time public works outlays. The primary employment component, summer jobs for youth, was funded by adding the remarkably modest amount of $2.5 billion to the $4 billion already in the pipeline for Community Development Block Grants. Senate Republicans labeled the economic program "pork" and mobilized a filibuster against it. Clinton responded by trimming the package to $12 billion and then to $9 billion, before pulling it off the Senate floor. Instead of seeking out the support of the two moderate Republicans needed to break the filibuster or mounting a public relations campaign to promote his economic stimulus program, the President simply conceded defeat.

Clinton then proceeded to distance himself from urban aid. In his revised budget package, the President drastically scaled back funds for transportation, public health, Medicare, the environment and poverty programs, slashing by half the money requested for food stamps and child immunization. The White House even withdrew its request for $161 million in subsidies to help poor people pay for their home heating bills.[44] In addition, the President asked Congress to delay for two more years implementation of the 1988 Family Support Act that requires states to provide at least sixteen hours a week of on-the-job training to unemployed persons who receive AFDC.[45]

The one progressive element left intact in the Clinton economic program was a five year, approximately $21 billion increase, in the earned income tax credit (EITC), supplementing the pay of workers whose earnings fall below the poverty line. In fact, the survival of this valuable anti-poverty program was pure serendipity. The EITC expansion was included in the budget to offset the high costs to the working poor of a broad-based energy tax meant to produce $71 billion in revenue over five years. When the energy tax was scrapped in favor of a tiny 4.3 cent rise in gasoline tax, the EITC accidentally slipped through.[46]

Clinton's half-measures for inner cities were a calculated political choice aimed at holding onto his shaky, white middle-class base of support. Concluding that the needed Perot supporters preferred spending cuts and deficit reduction to economic stimulus, the President conveniently converted to apostle of austerity. As Reverend Jesse Jackson declared, while Clinton was elected with a promise to "rebuild America," the Administration was now pleading the primacy of the deficit; what Martin Luther King, Jr., had referred to as a "promissory note" was bouncing once again.[47]

Significantly, Clinton backed away from the $2.5 billion in block grants exactly when the program became associated in voters' minds with inner cities. According to Clarence Page, "the very word 'cities' like 'welfare,' 'crime,' 'drugs,' and 'poverty,' has sadly become a code word for blacks and other minorities many suburbanites moved to the suburbs to escape."[48]

Conclusion: A Progressive Agenda

Being part of the winning coalition is the name of the game in American politics. Disillusioned with the Democrats' rightward ideological shift, the black turnout in 1992 was low in both the presidential primaries and in the general election. Still, African-Americans again voted more decisively for Bill Clinton (82 percent) than did any other segment of the U.S. population. Further, the unanimous support of the thirty-eight black Democratic members of the House of Representatives furnished Clinton with the razor-thin margin of victory (218–216) for his budget package.

Nevertheless, the Clinton administration has offered little in the form of substantive policies to advance the fortunes of the black community. Indeed, the President attempts to mute the race issue, publicly avoiding any reference to poverty and racial discrimination. The message of the Guinier fiasco is that Clinton is unlikely to support strong enforcement action for civil rights. In short, the Clinton administration's stance of benign neglect toward African-Americans represents the price that "new Democrats" are willing to pay for electoral victory. With 36.9 million Americans (including one-third of blacks) living in poverty in 1992, the highest number in three decades,[49] Clinton's current silence on economic justice and civil rights is unprincipled.

Unless the Democratic Party acts as the conscience of America, no national political organization will play this critical role. If citizens are not reminded of the appalling and widening discrepancies between blacks and whites—in terms of life expectancy, infant mortality, median income, unemployment and poverty—pleas for fundamental reform will continue to fall on uncomprehending ears, as whites eagerly embrace the myth that pervasive racial discrimination has ended.

Americans can only hope that the Clinton administration will pursue "a Third Reconstruction . . . to address directly the economic inequalities that are the accumulated consequences of 250 years of slavery and a century of discrimination."[50] The Republicans' demagoguery of the past twelve years can be countered with a populism of the left, in which people of color form alliances with whites who are also feeling the economic pinch. Since many middle-class whites resent the Republicans' preferential treatment of the wealthy, Democratic leaders can win over whites not only on the basis of compassion for the concerns of blacks, but also, by demonstrating the mutuality of interests between the needs of African-Americans and those of most whites.

The key to eradicating black poverty is for the national government to provide meaningful jobs for African-Americans. Roger Wilkins cogently argues that the problems of the black community, such as the destruction of the family, crime and teen-age pregnancy, will continue as long as black people are unemployed. According to Wilkins:

> Families are the conduit of values, discipline and the belief in ourselves. You cannot build the family on poverty. We need to find jobs. We have to achieve the reconstruction of the black community.[51]

One worthwhile component in a federal jobs program would be public works structured to rebuild the decaying sections of our cities. Public works could be supplemented with a long-term system of employment vouchers in which unemployed and low-skilled workers receive federal vouchers that they could cash in for on-the-job subsidized training.

These valuable programs could be financed by a genuine "peace dividend," resulting from a significant reduction in the nation's bloated and anachronistic military budget. In fact, Clinton's 1994 defense budget of $263.3 billion is actually four percent *higher* than the $252.3 billion defense budget in 1980, at the height of the Cold War.[52] In addition, revenue for programs to reduce poverty could come from restoring progressivity in the federal tax structure, achieved by returning the corporate tax rate from its present level of 35 percent (raised one percent by the Clinton budget) closer to the 1986 rate of 46 percent.

Finally, it is imperative that the Democratic Party end the practice of racial politics, whether in the form of overt racism or Realpolitik. Instead, the White House should educate the public about the corrosive effects of institutional racism by following the prudent advice of Lani Guinier:

> We're looking for moral leadership. We're looking for a president who's not afraid to talk about race in a public forum. The entire country is running from this problem.[53]

Notes

1. Clarence Page, "News Aplenty at Convention for Blacks," *Kansas City Star*, July 17, 1992, p. C-7.

2. "Black Votes: Missing the Bus," *The Economist* 324 (September 26, 1992): 55.

3. Alexander Cockburn, "Like Carter, but Worse?" *New Statesman & Society* 5 (October 30, 1992): 16.

4. Mary Frances Berry, "Blacks Let Clinton Slide on Civil Rights Issues," *Emerge* 4 (September 1993): 39.

5. Edward S. Carmines and James A. Simpson, *Issue Evolution: Race and the Transformation of American Politics* (Princeton: Princeton University Press, 1989), p. 131.

6. Mfana D. Tryman, "Was Jesse Jackson a Third Party Candidate in 1988?" *The Black Scholar* 20 (January/February 1989): 27.

7. Kenneth J. Cooper, "Black Caucus Flexes Muscle, Independence," *Emerge* 5 (October 1993): 25.

8. Lucius J. Barker and Ronald W. Walters, eds., *Jesse Jackson's 1984 Presidential Campaign and Change in American Politics* (Urbana: University of Illinois Press, 1989).

9. Gary Willis, "The Power Populist," *Time* 132 (November 21, 1988): 63.

10. Thomas B. Edsall with Mary D. Edsall, *Chain Reaction: The Impact of Race, Rights, and Taxes on American Politics* (New York: Norton, 1992): 29.

11. Walter Isaacson, "Time for Change," *Time* 140 (November 16, 1992): 29.

12. Alexander Cockburn, "The Almost Men," *New Statesman & Society* 5 (July 24, 1992): 21.

13. Michael Kelly, "A Left Turn by Clinton? Centrists Feel Left Out," *New York Times*, May 25, 1993, p. 14.

14. "Redefined Democrats," *International Herald Tribune*, July 15, 1992, p. 8.

15. "Los Angeles Could Be Clinton's Big Break," *In These Times*, May 27–June 9, 1992, p. 14.

16. "Child Poverty in the U.S. Exceeds European Levels," *Kansas City Star,* September 23, 1993, p. A-5.

17. Sarah Ferguson, "The Communitarian Manifesto," *Village Voice,* August 18, 1992, p. 17.

18. R. W. Apple, Jr., "Jackson Sees a 'Character Flaw' in Clinton's Remarks on Racism," *New York Times,* June 19, 1992, p. A24.

19. E. Frances White, "Dis(miss)ing Clinton: Reflections on African Americans and the Elections," *Radical America* 24 (July–September 1990): 22.

20. Adolph Reed, Jr., "The Confederate Twins," *The Progressive,* 56 (November 1992): 28.

21. Clarence Page, "Three-Way Race Gives New Clout to Black Voters," *Kansas City Star,* June 11, 1992, p. C-19.

22. White, "Diss(miss)ing Clinton: Reflections on African Americans and the Elections," 23.

23. Stephen Labaton, "Lagging in the Polls: Clinton Also Faces A Cash Shortage," *New York Times,* June 19, 1992, p. A24.

24. "Sister Souljah Is No Willie Horton," *New York Times,* June 17, 1992, p. A24.

25. Apple, "Jackson Sees a 'Character Flaw' in Clinton's Remarks on Racism," p. 1.

26. David S. Broder, "Clinton's Daring Rebuke to Jackson Sends a Message to White Voters," *Columbus Dispatch,* June 17, 1992, p. 9A.

27. Timothy Egan, "At Edge of Campaign, Jackson Labors On for Democratic Victory," *New York Times,* October 20, 1992, p. A16.

28. Martin Walker, "Clinton Heads for Big Victory," *The Guardian,* November 3, 1992, p. 22.

29. Reed, "The Confederate Twins," p. 28.

30. Cynthia Tucker, "Public Schools Take Another Hit," *Kansas City Star,* January 8, 1993, p. C-7.

31. Garland L. Thompson, "Four Black Cabinet Secretaries—Will It Make a Difference?" *The Crisis* 100 (March 1993): 16.

32. James Worsham, "Bumper Crop of Problems at the USDA," *Kansas City Star,* January 3, 1993, p. J-1.

33. Charles Lamb, "Outing the Insiders: The Rainmakers in Bill's Parade," *The Nation* 255 (December 7, 1992): 693–694.

34. Berry, "Blacks Let Clinton Slide on Civil Rights Issues," pp. 41–42.

35. Susan Chira, "A Scholar's Conviction Keep Her Pushing the Power of Words," *New York Times,* January 10, 1993, p. E-7; Bruce Shapiro, "and Who's Out," *The Nation* 256 (January 18, 1993): 40.

36. *University of California Regents v. Bakke,* 438 U.S. 265 (1978).

37. Frank Michelman, "Democracy and Lani Guinier," *Reconstruction* 2 (No. 2): 33.

38. "Sinking Guinier," *The Nation* 256 (June 21, 1993): 856.

39. Berry, "Blacks Let Clinton Slide on Civil Rights Issues," p. 39.

40. *Ibid.,* p. 38.

41. Andrew C. Miller, "Clinton Must Prove Himself on Civil Rights," *Kansas City Star,* January 24, 1993, p. K-5.

42. David S. Broder, "Big Money, Local Effort," *Kansas City Star,* March 3, 1993, p. C-2.

43. "Clinton Urged to Spend Billions to Address Needs of Black People," *Kansas City Star,* January 27, 1993, A-2.

44. "Clinton Adjusting His Economic Plan," *Kansas City Star,* May 12, 1993, p. A-3.

45. "Clinton Seeks Delay in Welfare Law," *Kansas City Star,* May 12, 1993, p. A-10.

46. "Without Sacrifice," *The Economist* 328 (August 7, 1993): 25.

47. Robin Toner, "King's Speech Commemorated by Thousands," *New York Times,* August 29, 1993, p. 12.

48. Clarence Page, "Clinton's Budget Battle and the City-Suburb Rift," *Kansas City Star,* April 16, 1993, p. C-7.

49. Cheryl W. Thompson, "Poverty Hits Three-Decade High," *Kansas City Star,* October 5, 1993, p. 1.

50. Eric Foner, "Time for a Third Reconstruction," *The Nation* 256 (February 1, 1993): 118.

51. Karen Dillon, "Jobs a Priority for Black Families," *Kansas City Star,* October 17, 1993, p. B-2.

52. Mark Thompson, "Defense Cuts: Fact or Fiction?" *Kansas City Star,* August 16, 1993, p. A-1.

53. "Black Caucus Says Clinton Lacks Civil Rights Policy," *Kansas City Star,* September 16, 1993, p. A-4.

About the Editor

Theodore Rueter has taught political science at Middlebury College, Georgetown University, and Smith College. He earned his Ph.D. in political science from the University of Wisconsin–Madison.

His books include *Carter vs. Ford: The Counterfeit Debates of 1976* (1980), *Teaching Assistant Strategies: An Introduction to College Teaching* (1989), *The United States in the World Political Economy* (1993), *The Minnesota House of Representatives and the Professionalization of Politics* (1994), *The Rush Limbaugh Quiz Book* (1995), and *The Newt Gingrich Quiz Book* (1995). His articles have appeared in the *New York Times,* the *Boston Globe, PS: Political Science and Politics, World Politics, The Journal of Post-Keynesian Economics, Perspectives on Political Science, Computerworld,* and *The Journal of Politics.*

Mr. Rueter lives in San Luis Obispo, California.